MW00805074

GENDERED MORALITY

Gendered Morality

*Classical Islamic Ethics of the Self,
Family, and Society*

Zahra Ayubi

Columbia University Press   New York

Columbia University Press
Publishers Since 1893
New York   Chichester, West Sussex
cup.columbia.edu
Copyright © 2019 Columbia University Press
All rights reserved

Library of Congress Cataloging-in-Publication Data
Names: Ayubi, Zahra, author.
Title: Gendered morality : classical Islamic ethics of the self, family, and society / Zahra Ayubi.
Description: New York : Columbia University Press, [2019] | Includes bibliographical
    references and index.
Identifiers: LCCN 2018048958| ISBN 9780231191326 (cloth : alk. paper) | ISBN 9780231191333
    (pbk. : alk. paper) | ISBN 9780231549349 (e-book)
Subjects: LCSH: Sex role—Religious aspects—Islam. | Femininity—Religious aspects—Islam. |
    Masculinity—Religious aspects—Islam. | Marriage—Religious aspects—Islam. | Social
    ethics—Religious aspects—Islam. | Islam—Social aspects. | Islamic philosophy. | Religion
    and social status.
Classification: LCC BP134.S49 A98 2019 | DDC 297.5081—dc23
LC record available at https://lccn.loc.gov/2018048958

Columbia University Press books are printed on permanent and durable acid-free paper.
Printed in the United States of America

Cover image: © Zahra Ayubi. *Objection*, color pencil drawing.

To my husband and our children,
with a prayer that we find our sa'adat

Contents

Figures and Tables

Acknowledgments

Bism Allah ar-Rahman ar-Rahim.

My deepest gratitude goes to those who took on my share of family responsibilities, took care of me, and thus enabled me to write this book: my husband, my mother, my mother-in-law, my niece, my father, and the director and teachers at DCCCC. My gratitude then goes to my late father in law, who was fond of the *Kimiya-i Sa'adat* and the *Akhlaq-i Nasiri*. He introduced me to the classical world of *akhlaq* in the brief time that I spent with him before his passing.

While researching and writing that earliest version of this project at the University of North Carolina at Chapel Hill, I greatly benefited from the mentorship of Kecia Ali, Carl Ernst, Juliane Hammer, Omid Safi, Randall Styers, Bruce Lawrence, and Ebrahim Moosa. Since then, I was able to strengthen this project's contribution thanks to many fruitful conversations with generous colleagues and peer and senior mentors. In particular, Kecia Ali modeled scholarly mentorship for me when she generously commented on multiple drafts and pushed my thinking each time. Several scholars helped me crystalize this book's argument through their feedback on parts or all of it at conferences, writing workshops, or lunch meetings: Jamie Schillinger, Travis Zadeh, Kathryn Kueny, Mary-Jane Rubenstein, Dhananjay Jagannathan, Laura McTighe, Holly Shaffer, Laury Silvers, Zayn Kassam, Etin Anwar, and Danielle Widmann Abraham. Thanks also to Aysha Hidayatullah, Amanullah De Sondy,

Fatima Seedat, Ilyse Morgenstein Fuerst, and Saadia Yacub for our discussions at conferences about our respective projects. Thanks also to friends who served as writing partners at various points: Lilu Jessica Chen, Rose Aslan, Nisha Komattam, and Farah Zeb.

At Dartmouth, thanks to my religion department colleagues Susannah Heschel, Devin Singh, and Kevin Reinhart, who read drafts of some of the chapters, and the rest of the religion department colleagues for their feedback at a faculty research colloquium. And thanks to religion department administrators Meredyth Morley and Marcia Welsh. I appreciate my students, in particular Iman AbdoulKarim, who read versions of chapters from this book and always engaged me in thoughtful conversation about them. I am grateful to my research assistant, Jessica Kocan, who swooped in to help with library sources and citations. I would also like to acknowledge the support of Imam Khalil Abdullah and Rabbi Davin Litwin at the Tucker Center, Cristen Brooks at the Women's, Gender, and Sexuality Studies Program, and the Ethics Institute at Dartmouth College.

Thanks to Olga Davidson for introducing me to the richness of the Persian context of feminist inquiry. Thanks to Eric Goodson for teaching me to reexamine conventional historical narrative and Alexandra Siemon for introducing me to the academic study of Islam. Special thanks to Islamic art history professor Glaire Anderson and tezhip artist Zuhal Karamanli, who taught me how to appreciate the fine elements of miniature paintings. Thanks to my various studio art teachers, especially Jim Misner, Suzette Jones, and Gene Scattergood, who helped me develop the skills that ultimately enabled me to create the cover art for this book.

Sincere gratitude goes to my beloved mentor in memoriam, the late Tayyibah Taylor, who celebrated my scholarly pursuits, reminded me to remain humble in sharing my knowledge, and demonstrated to me how to be a strong yet spiritual Muslim woman. Although she was not a scholar, she was among the most learned and wise women I have ever known. Another tribute goes to my late uncle, Dr. Zobair Ayubi, who expressed great understanding and encouragement for my scholarly pursuits. I wish they had both lived to see this book's publication.

Finally, I dedicate this book to my husband and children. We have many privileges, but we are simultaneously oppressed along many planes of our individual and collective identities. We have a claim on flourishing, and I pray that we can achieve it.

GENDERED MORALITY

Introduction

In the climactic scene of the dramatized documentary *al-Ghazali: The Alchemist of Happiness* (2004), the eponymous twelfth-century jurist, theologian, mystic, and ethicist stands with his family in the street outside their Baghdad home, a few simple possessions strapped to his donkey's back. He is preparing to take leave of his wife and two children, perhaps permanently. Up to this point in the film, director Ovidio Abdul Latif Salazar presents a dramatic recounting of Ghazali's illustrious career in Baghdad, tracing his increasing disillusionment with the city's corrupt political climate. Ghazali's departure marks the culmination of his crisis of faith and conscience. Throughout the film, he is depicted as a troubled genius, contemplative about the nature of true happiness, living out his public life against a backdrop of domesticity. His beautiful wife and his young son and daughter appear in the film intermittently, though always silent. In this climatic farewell scene, partly based on a passage in Ghazali's autobiography, he has resolved to embark on a long journey to Damascus, Jerusalem, and Makkah. He embraces each of his children and pauses briefly to glance at his wife. Without speaking a word to her, he then turns toward his brother and says, "You understand that I have to leave."[1] As Ghazali walks off with his donkey, the voice of the actor playing him narrates in language from Ghazali's autobiography: "I gave to the poor what wealth I had, keeping only as much as would suffice and provide sustenance for my family, and I expected never to return to Baghdad."[2] A voice-over from the film's narrator, sufism scholar Seyyed Hossein Nasr, then declares this journey to be "the act which makes Ghazali, Ghazali." The narrator describes Ghazali's journey as the reason why "we are speaking about him now, nine hundred years later. That is, he left his position, his wealth, his family, the world, and disappeared in order to rediscover certitude, in order to be honest with himself in understanding the nature of the Divine reality."[3] The third item in Nasr's list of Ghazali's lofty sacrifices—his family—remains curiously submerged from our attention throughout the film.

Ghazali's wife, played by famous Iranian actress Mitra Hajjar, appears several times over the course of the film. She is shown praying at home, receiving visits from Ghazali's doctors, and delivering and picking up trays of food for Ghazali. Yet the filmmakers do not give her a single line of dialogue, as though such an omission were necessary in order to stay true to Ghazali's biographies, which do indeed omit mentions of his wife. Whatever the reason for such a flattened depiction of Ghazali's wife, her near-erasure from the film's climactic departure scene is striking. But what, precisely, is being erased? What might Ghazali's wife have said to him when he left? Did he ever have a private conversation with her about his planned journey? Did she ask when she could expect him back at home in Tus, or how she should rear the children and run the home in his absence, or what she should do in case of his death? What, more broadly, was her role in Ghazali's intellectual and spiritual pursuits? What were her own spiritual goals? The film does not raise these questions, much less answer them.

The curiousness of these omissions is heightened by the film's enactment of the director's Western Muslim quest for Eastern, Islamic (authentic) knowledge when he travels to Iran to ask local scholars and sufis about the greatness of Ghazali's message. Salazar's quest demonstrates his interest in Ghazali as an enduring figure who dealt with perennial issues, and it also demonstrates the filmmaker's own fascination with knowledge from the so-called Muslim world.[4] This outsider's fascination gives the self-reflective filmmakers' dramatization of Ghazali's domestic life a fetishized quality. Why would the filmmakers not attempt to imagine what Ghazali's wife might have thought or said, even if just to add to the drama? When imagining an Islamic role model's spiritual journey for modern audiences, why re-create the gender roles that he had prescribed in his ethics texts? Why exclude women from access to the spiritual journey?

The film is an example of contemporary reverence for Ghazali's life and legacy, a welcome depiction to those for whom he serves as a scholarly role model. For many Muslims and scholars of Islam, Ghazali remains the ultimate ethicist, a moral paragon who transformed himself by identifying his place in the cosmos at the expense of worldly comforts, including his own family—even if he too was constrained by gendered expectations to this destiny. And yet, this contemporary reverence ought not to obscure the troubling questions raised by Ghazali's life and work. In the Islamic tradition, are opportunities for lofty pursuits and self-reflection equally open to women? And to what extent, and in what ways, is the path to ultimate happiness—enacting God's will through ethical refinement of the self—an undertaking that is gendered male? What does male-centered ethics imply for the making of masculinity, and for all of society? Such questions are the central concerns of this book.

Historically, religious authority in the Islamic tradition has been predominantly the domain of men. It is men who have long written and interpreted religious texts on human existence and ethical behavior, and men who have arguably possessed ethical normativity. Such intellectual traditions leave little room for women or their concerns. Foundational scholars of gender and Islam, such as Leila Ahmed and Fatima Mernissi, argue that the lack of female participation in creating knowledge has led to the scholarly understanding that the Islamic tradition itself is male-centered.[5] Subsequently, most scholars who seek to understand how gender has been constructed in classical Islamic sources focus on close readings of the Qur'anic exegesis, Islamic jurisprudence, and, to a lesser extent, mystical discourses. In the past four decades, scholars of gender in Islam have developed multiple strategies for understanding gender roles in the Islamic tradition, primarily through study of Qur'anic exegesis and hermeneutics, or close readings of the legal tradition.[6] In addition, a substantial body of literature has developed to examine gender in the mystical tradition.[7] Several scholars, such as amina wadud, Kecia Ali, Zayn Kassam, Amyn Sajoo, Ayesha Chaudhry, and Reza Shah-Kazemi, have also used the terminology of "ethics" or "Islamic ethics" to advocate for particular moral standards that they read as implicit in the genres they study.

Islam scholars have tended to read gender in the Islamic intellectual tradition in one of two ways: either by distinguishing between the onto-logical equality of genders in the "eyes of God" and the earthly inequal-ity of gender roles, or by focusing on the various ways male authorities have described women as inferior. Amina wadud divides her commen-tary on the Qur'an into two sections, one on verses that demonstrate ontological equality and one on verses that are on earthly gender rela-tions, and argues that the latter category of verses has been problemati-cally understood by male scholars as the basis for earthly inequality of women and men, even if these scholars did concede the point of gender egalitarianism in creation.[8] Shaheen Ali argues that Muslim legal thought is specifically responsible for undoing the gender egalitarian essence of the Qur'an, advancing this point in the very subtitle of her book, which asks, "Equal before Allah, unequal before man?"[9] Elaborating on how the egalitarian message of the Qur'an and Prophet Muhammad was cor-rupted, Leila Ahmed holds that when Muslim philosophers chose the Aristotelian account of women's inferior biology over the egalitarian Qur'anic one, they introduced a tension between sexual hierarchy and spiritual and ethical equality.[10] Ahmed argues that the legal and politi-cal rulers expanded on the sexual hierarchy and not on the spiritual and ethical equality. This sequence resulted in the development of two par-allel understandings of Islam: a male-centered, hierarchical legal dis-course and a women's Islam that latched on to the "ethical egalitarian-ism" of the Qur'an.[11]

These scholars' approaches to framing gender in Islam have been useful in providing a historical explanation for patriarchal interpreta-tions of the Qur'an and for the establishment of patriarchal norms in the subsequent legal tradition, while simultaneously upholding the com-mitment to egalitarian understandings of the Qur'anic tradition. How-ever, both approaches—theorizing gender inequality in the Islamic tra-dition as an "earthly problem" and focusing exclusively on how men are constructed as superior in Islamic, particularly legal, texts—cannot, in themselves, fully illuminate gender asymmetry in the Islamic tradi-tion. Many premodern Muslim male interpreters and jurists themselves imagined a continuation or conflation between the Divine and earthly realms, except in eschatological concepts of accountability on the Day of Judgment. Further, close readings of male superiority largely ignore the ways in which human hierarchy is justified through constructions of gendered ontology. It is not sufficient to theorize that upon being confronted with egalitarianism in the Qur'an, male scholars chose to interpret that women are equal to men only in the eyes of God, but unequal to them on Earth; indeed, philosophical ethicists believed that women were naturally *and* ontologically inferior as created by God. For this reason, to understand gender asymmetry in Muslim traditions, we must revisit the philosophical underpinnings of gendered ontology in Muslim thought.

To date, scholars of Islamic philosophy have not yet paid serious attention to the category of gender—a symptom of how male-dominated the field of Islamic philosophy has been. As Kathryn Kueny remarks, the field of medieval Islamic history is

> more often than not, written, defined, and studied by male scholars and theologians. Contemporary or medieval studies about law, war, leadership, politics, theology, and economics may all attempt to reconstruct or record what "really" happened in order to buttress prescriptive views about the Muslim tradition, but they only reveal just part of the story. Unfortunately, the topics of what legitimately comprises "history" . . . are often limited to what men—in the past and present—privilege as significant and worthy of recording.[12]

Likewise, with a few notable exceptions of female scholars who have, to varying extents, interrogated issues of hierarchy or women's roles—such as Ann Lambton, Annemarie Schimmel, Louise Marlowe, Sophia Vasalou, Irene Oh, and Etin Anwar—scholars of the Islamic philosophical corpus have been male. The topics that male scholars have chosen to comprise the history and content of Islamic philosophical ethics have been mostly limited to the concept of rationality, the role of Divine authority, the field of political ethics, and the Greek epistemology of the corpus versus its Islamic nature. My own focus on the category of gender is to demonstrate the interrelatedness of Islamic ethicists' understanding of ontology, hierarchy, justice, and moral responsibilities of the self and of living with others. Their writings are not merely records of Islamic *political* ethics, as many scholars have explored; rather, they serve as a comprehensive cosmology of human existence that is gendered and hierarchical.

By attending to the genre of Islamic philosophical ethics, this book focuses on the deeper questions of gender hierarchy in human existence that permeate all genres of the Islamic intellectual tradition. More specifically, I look at classical ethics treatises that are still widely regarded as the high moral tradition of Islam and that contain discussions about metaphysics and practical virtue ethics on three levels: the self, home, and society. This work shows how the virtue ethics of each of these levels creates a male-centered imaginary of how Muslims live moral lives. Much of the gender roles embedded in these texts have been re-created across numerous Muslim cultural and intellectual productions. I argue that the Muslim ethicists' gendered understandings of existence and metaphysics compelled them to produce virtue ethics that are rooted in inequality and, as such, are unsustainable by the standards of their own ethics.

My sources in this study are three influential *akhlaq* texts, or philosophical ethics treatises, written in Persian between the twelfth and fifteenth centuries: *Kimiya-i Sa'adat* or *The Alchemy of Happiness* by Abu Hamid Muhammad al-Ghazali (d. 1111); *Akhlaq-i Nasiri* or *The Nasirean Ethics* by Nasir-ad Din Tusi (d. 1274); and *Akhlaq-i Jalali* or *The Jalalean Ethics* by Jalal ad-Din Davani (d. 1502). What all these ethics texts have in common is that they were written for male audiences; they construct their entire ethical framework around a normative elite male of high intelligence; they instruct men on how to discipline their metaphysical souls and inform them about their place in the cosmos; and they explicitly prescribe ethical behavior to men as a response to real or imagined moral threats posed by women and less intelligent men. From the individual to the home to society and the cosmos, ethics unfolds as a process of creating ethical men.

Through my close reading, I show that despite the ethicists' marginalization of women and nonelite men, the texts nonetheless speak to complex gendered and human relations that at times defy their own hierarchical cosmology. Because the texts assume equal status of all physical matter and recognize that women have the same kind of souls as men, their metaphysical premises potentially pose a radical framework of equality. And yet, the ethicists themselves, in failing to recognize the radical equality in the metaphysics they have constructed, write as if serving only elite men and further construct an edifice of hierarchical virtue ethics. I argue in this book that the classical ethicists fail to harmonize the potentially just metaphysics with hierarchical values, giving rise to exclusionary hierarchies that often do not conform to their own goals or ideal vision of societal flourishing in the Islamic philosophical ethics texts themselves. What emerges is a tension between male normativity, on one hand, and equality in human metaphysics, on the other. This tension reveals the historically entrenched nature of hierarchy in the texts and exposes the elite male focus of the texts' virtue ethics, which is based on medieval gender assumptions. Because of their exclusivist, elite, male-centric notions of ethics—and their implicit and sometimes explicit misogyny—these classical Muslim *akhlaq* texts shed light on important philosophical questions that are relevant to establishing a feminist philosophy of Islam.

THEMES IN *AKHLAQ*: METAPHYSICS, FEMININITY, AND MASCULINITY

Throughout this book, I trace the tensions between the texts' construction of masculinity and femininity and their overall goals of describing the moral path for men to live in a trilevel progression as individuals, in families, and in society. Across these three levels of moral instruction in the *akhlaq* texts I have selected, I trace three central themes: the tension between hierarchical power and justice, the construction of instrumental femininity in relation to rational masculinity, and the construction of elite masculinity in the context of homosocial relationships among men.

The first theme I explore in classical Islamic ethics is the tension between egalitarian and hierarchical metaphysics—in other words, the tension between justice and power. While the ethicists viewed all matter as created equal by God and all human metaphysical souls as identical in substance and nature, not all individuals held the power to perfect their own souls—and this was particularly the case for women and inferior men. Human hierarchy was considered part of God's justice. This tension between egalitarianism and hierarchy plays out in power relationships between individuals and on the systemic level of a hierarchical society. In Louise Marlowe's work exploring the tension among various divine notions of moral equality in Muslim philosophical and literary texts, she explains that early philosophers, such as the *ikhwan as-safa* from the tenth century, held that some people are "incapable of mastering an occupation at all: . . . the offspring of rulers, whose pride prevents them from learning a profession; prophets and their followers, who are satisfied with little and inclined towards the other world; beggars, who are lazy and slothful; and women and effeminate men, who are base and lacking in understanding."[13] Parallel to this exclusion, Aisha Geissinger has found that early exegetes of the Qur'an "present the free Muslim male in the abstract as embodying human intellectual, physical and spiritual potential in its most complete form . . . against the deficiencies and weaknesses in intellect, linguistic expression and body as well as religious practices that supposedly typify femaleness."[14] Similarly, the three ethicists in this study, Ghazali, Tusi, and Davani, all upheld a gendered and profession-based hierarchy as the optimal way to maximize each individual's function in contributing to the organization of life. The ethicists considered it only just for the strong-minded to rule over the weak-minded. Power and superiority in the texts are based on both gender and class, since only elite men possess full ethical potential, namely, the power to subjugate the other faculties of the soul to submit to the will of the rational faculty, which, in turn, translates into power over others.

Some scholars have argued that influences of sources outside of the Islamic tradition are to blame for the central role of hierarchy in Muslim thought. Marlowe finds that in all Islamic philosophical, legal, and literary texts, "some form of ranking was widely regarded not only as a legitimate, but also as a necessary, characteristic of social organization," and that this feature was a result of the extra-Islamic influences of the Sassanians.[15] Further, Marlowe argues that the profession- and class-based social structure supported by scholars such as Tusi, Davani, and to a lesser extent Ghazali is a result of prior centuries of scholarly suppression of egalitarian attitudes found in the Qur'an and in the teachings of Prophet Muhammad and his cousin 'Ali, the fourth caliph or first imam. The construction of hierarchy was an effort to shift the social structure from the Arab tribal system toward a Muslim empire that subsumed a diversity of peoples and required the adoption of cultures from acquired regions, which brought along the philosophical idea that natural association of persons forms hierarchical societies.[16] Marlowe explains the ordering principle as follows: "for the Muslim philosophers, like their Greek predecessors, the primary determinant of rank in the hierarchical order of being is knowledge; and an individual's degree of knowledge is inseparable from his occupation."[17] She and Ann Lambton have argued that the function of kingship in the hierarchical system is also modeled after Sassanian ideas.[18] Specifically on the origins of ideas about the gendered body and soul, Etin Anwar has argued that Muslim philosophers' understanding of the soul was "primarily developed using Greek science and philosophy, hoping to demonstrate that human knowledge does not conflict with God's revelation."[19] However, regardless of undoubted influence of prior traditions of learning, one of the key findings of my study indicates that Muslim philosophers truly believed that God created women with naturally inferior bodies, intellects, and souls. As I discuss in chapter 1, the seemingly foreign influences on Islamic ethics texts do not take away from their unmistakable Islamic nature. For the ethicists, hierarchy was both Islamic and just.

Also resting in tension with hierarchy is the ethicists' conception of justice, which they consider to be a foundational principle in Islamic ethics, but it is based on a circular definition: to act ethically is to act according to justice, and to enact justice is to perform ethics.[20] For all three ethicists, 'adl or justice comes forth naturally from the faculty of rationality, and it is an essential means for attaining the ultimate goals of the texts, namely, realizing true happiness for the self and facilitating happiness for others, in appropriate measure, as a vicegerent of God and as a microcosm of the world. While the ethicists define justice as balance and moderation in all actions, particularly referring to the balance of the metaphysical self, they additionally consider justice as a broad social condition referring to everyone receiving their dues in correct measure or according to their station in life as determined by their gender, class, level of intellect, and so on. Sophia Vasalou's finding that the ethicists also believed that moral desert, or one's fate, was causally determined by the choices of free agents (which were always reasoned for Mu'tazilite thinkers) seems to apply only to the normative elite male subject of ethical thought.[21] In the akhlaq texts, the former definition of justice simply as balance is implicitly hierarchical in that only men of superior intellect can achieve it. The latter understanding of justice is based on hierarchical distribution of justice. In this formulation, people do not all deserve the same kind of treatment or resources, for example; rather, their deserts are determined according to their lot in life. Thus, the ethicists' definition of justice based on relative moral deserts exemplifies the tension between egalitarianism and hierarchy in the texts. We also see this tension extended to the ethicists' views on women as equal in humanity but inferior in life.

The second theme I explore in the *akhlaq* texts, also related to hierarchy and unequal power relations, is the texts' construction of femininity as inferior, instrumental, and irrational, and the construction of masculinity as powerful, authoritative, and rational. As I discuss in greater detail in the next chapter, feminist critiques of philosophy have in the past mostly shed light on the ontological inferiority and subhuman status that the texts attribute to women's bodies. I depart from these readings, instead considering how the ethicists do recognize women's humanity and their souls,[22] but nevertheless construct women's roles based on the assumption of women's intellectual deficiency and overemotionality, in contrast to men's intellectual superiority and potential for leadership. I show how the ethicists actively sidestep egalitarian possibilities of their metaphysics in favor of hierarchical interpretations as they construct virtue ethics that assume male dominance in all realms of life.

The moral status of women—along with the complexity of men's ethical relations with them—surfaces in the *akhlaq* treatises only in sections on the domestic economy. In these sections, which focus on marriage, rearing children, divorce, and the business of running a home, Ghazali, Tusi, and Davani all detail the qualities a man should look for in a wife and the ethical responsibilities he has toward her and the children she bears him. This confined location in the texts is in itself a signal of the ethicists' ideals of gender segregation in public and the confinement of women to the domestic realm. The texts are designed to warn men against trusting women or including them in affairs that are the province of men, such as financial or political dealings. The ethicists also make occasional mention of hypothetical women meddling in men's affairs, and some of their vignettes include female characters displaying foolishness or duplicity. The ethicists' generally dismissive attitude toward women suggests a disconnect between their exclu-sionary prescriptions and the historical reality in which they lived, one where women were active in both domestic and public life.

Indeed, as Huda Lutfi and Leila Ahmed have pointed out, legal texts have often been stricter on women in historical moments when females have had more prominent public roles, and thus were more troubling to the male religious establishment.[23] For example, Omid Safi and Hamid Dabashi have shown that in the work of the Saljuq vizier Nizam al-Mulk (a contemporary of Ghazali), the vizier's lamentation against women's meddling in political affairs was a direct response to one of his female political foes, Tarkan Khatun, wife of the sultan.[24] Medieval Muslim scholars often used prescriptive texts to resist women's real-life activi-ties. Aisha Geissinger has likewise shown, in a study on early Qur'an commentaries written by men in which women interpreters survive men-tion, that male exegetes actively marginalized women commentators or hadith transmitters through elaborating on their classification as "moth-ers of the believers" or similar in order to distance these women and make them more palatable.[25] In ethics, the difference from these other genres is that *akhlaq* texts provided ethical schemas and rational argu-ments for their stances on women's seclusion and prescribed roles. These roles create a tension between the egalitarianism in creation and the hier-archal nature of society, notwithstanding the ethicists' a priori recogni-tion of women's humanity.

The third theme I investigate throughout this work, in addition to the power–justice tension and the instrumentality of femininity, is the *akhlaq* texts' construction of masculinity in the context of homosocial hierarchy. The texts describe the science of ethics (*tahzib-i akhlaq*) as the process of creating an ethical male, and they characterize the creation of the ethical world as revolving around this male and his relationships with family members and other males of various social ranks. Through-out Islamic history, texts have characterized the ideal Muslim in ways that refer only to men and their concerns. And yet, scholars of Islam have only recently begun to engage in critical study of the category of mascu-linity. Thus, in order to examine how normative masculinity is con-structed in the texts, I focus on how men are prescribed to act in the private institutions of marriage and the household, as well as in the pub-lic, homosocial institutions of court, the bazaar, the mosque, and other

locations where one interacts with friends, enemies, superiors, and inferiors. The ethicists' prescriptions for how to behave amount to an ideal
vision of masculinity. In their characterizations of same-sex social interactions, we see how they imagined social interactions to work in general: they viewed male homosocial relations as universal and male–female
heterosocial relations as exceptional and requiring different guidelines.
Homosociality was the ultimate expression of a patriarchically structured society, in which men interacted with one another in a world that
belonged to elite men, excluding all others.

In this book, I analyze the tripartite cosmology of virtue ethics of
the self, marriage, and society by attending to notions of gendered metaphysics and concepts of the feminine and masculine. I find that these
themes in widely celebrated ethics texts are so essential to Muslim gender discourses that their role in creating an ethics of excluding women
and nonelite others has become invisible.

SOURCES

My research on gender in Islamic philosophical ethics is based on a close
reading of three Persian texts that are connected to one another genea-
logically and historically. The reading reveals the texts' shared notions
of the ethical individual as gendered male, and of gender and social relations based on a hierarchy of intellect. The texts are Abu Hamid Muhammad al-Ghazali's *Kimiya-i Sa'adat* (*The Alchemy of Happiness*), Nasir-ad
Din Tusi's *Akhlaq-i Nasiri* (*Nasirean Ethics*), and Jalal ad-Din Davani's
Lawami' al-Ishraq fi Makarim al-Akhlaq (*Lusters of Illumination on the
Noble Ethics*), better known as the *Akhlaq-i Jalali* (*Jalalean Ethics*).[26] The
treatises by Ghazali, Tusi, and Davani are from the twelfth, thirteenth,
and fifteenth centuries, respectively—the classical period of Islamic ethics.[27] These works are arguably the most foundational texts of Islamic
philosophical ethics, celebrated in many countries today as Muslims' primary cultural discourse on the subject of personal discipline, as well as
being the record of Islamic moral heritage.

In this book, I analyze and synthesize these "seminal"[28] sources' complex constructions of masculinity, femininity, gender relations, and gendered ethics in classical *akhlaq*. Rather than presenting an exhaustive
summary of the *akhlaq* genre, this book analyzes the normative gender

constructions and dynamics at play in construction of the *nafs* (metaphysical soul) and moral responsibilities (virtue ethics) in the metadiscourses of ethical Muslim life. Where applicable to the gender analytic of the *akhlaq* texts, which I develop in the next chapter, I also tease apart the differences among the texts' conceptions of the *nafs*, notions of love, and gender roles in marriage and homosocial contexts.

Although each of the three treatises is separated from the others by at least a century, Ghazali, Tusi, and Davani all draw on shared experiences and traditions in constructing their ethics, and all three are responding to the patterns of life, culture, and customs that made up the premodern Islamicate and Persianate milieu.[29] There is a continuity in the development of metaphysical thought and virtue ethics that indicates the three texts' shared lineage within a single ethical tradition. The texts share several common themes, including premodern Islamicate patterns of social structures, criticism of corrupt government, and critiques of a society that complicate man's endeavors to be ethical and provide an ethical life for his wards (wife, children, enslaved[30] and free servants, apprentices, underlings) within and outside the home. The three ethicists also shared common experiences of the political culture of court; despite their own religious affiliations and political allegiances, Ghazali, Tusi, and Davani were all able to transcend or transition across sectarian and political boundaries. Ghazali and Tusi were employed by the Saljuqs and Nizari Isma'ills, respectively, and produced works meant to lend legitimacy to the regimes' brand of sectarian rule. Davani wrote from both Shi'i and Sunni perspectives and was employed for brief periods by the Aqquyonlu. All three belonged to a premodern intellectual tradition that endured historical upsets yet still contributed to a cohesive Islamicate culture.[31]

The goal of Ghazali's, Tusi's, and Davani's texts is to uplift the individual through mediation of his *nafs*, or soul, so that he may act ethically in personal, domestic, social, and political spheres, according to the best, most rightly guided standards, and become a *khalifah*, or vicegerent, of God on earth. The texts only address men, instructing them on how to act ethically with other men and with women. With citations to the Qur'an, sayings by the Prophet Muhammad, the Muslim philosophical and legal traditions, and (in the case of Tusi and Davani) Plato and Aristotle, these texts explain how to sharpen one's spiritual acumen and deal ethically in politics, distribution of wealth, household management, friendship, and marriage. In all three texts, the ethical subject strives to control the faculties of the soul and perfect the ethical virtues conducive to bringing about maximum happiness, defined as knowledge of the Divine, physical health, material wealth and influence, virtue and reputation, and prosperity, or simply as success in both this world and in the hereafter. In addition to lessons on metaphysics, the texts provide a detailed code of ethics, ranging from the lofty goals of achieving spiritual discipline, to consequential decisions like finding a wife, to the ethics of daily minutiae, including how to walk and sit, eat and drink, and comport oneself in social situations. The texts also explain the intricacies of parenting, such as how to give career guidance to one's children. Overall, the various behaviors that the texts prescribe both demonstrate and constitute spiritual discipline. At times, the texts read like psychological–spiritual self-diagnosis manuals, especially when the ethicists enumerate the vices that arise from individual faculties of the soul and explain the logic involved when the *nafs* fools individuals into believing they are acting virtuously.

The contexts of Ghazali's, Tusi's, and Davani's works are not just the normative discourses of ethics, but also their real-life observations of men and women's behaviors at home, in the city, and at court. Several side remarks within each text suggest that they attempt to solve the ethical dilemmas of their times and correct problematic behaviors they observe. Nonetheless, all three ethicists create an imagined ethical world by constructing personal and social mores. In the ethical world, men and women are meant to behave in certain ways, giving us a sense of the inescapable ways in which all ethical subjects, as well as their social interactions, are gendered.

Previous English translations of the *akhlaq* works miss the gendered nuances of terms that are important for my analysis. For this reason, all of the quotations from the three treatises I use throughout this book are my own translations from the original Persian, unless otherwise noted. I translate the Persian critical editions of the *Kimiya-i Sa'adat*, *Akhlaq-i Nasiri*, and *Akhlaq-i Jalali* edited by Hossein Khadivjam, Mojtaba Minvi and Alireza Haydari, and Abdullah Masoudi Arani, respectively. The translations of Qur'anic verses and hadiths quoted in Arabic in the texts are also mine. The extant English translations of the three texts are

Orientalist ones that assume that these texts are copies of the Nicomachean Ethics, and thus borrow terms from Aristotle that may not be appropriate or, in the case of the *Kimiya-i Sa'adat*, that are translated into English from a third language.[32] A contemporary translation of the *Kimiya* done from the perspective of a pious Muslim, Jay Crook, is sensitive to references to other Islamic texts, but in a seemingly gender-inclusive move, Crook assumes that Ghazali meant to address both men and women in the text, ignoring the fact that all of the examples within the texts and the structure of the texts pertain to men.[33] Thus, in undertaking my own translation, I pay particular attention to intertextual references to the Qur'an, hadith, *kalam*, and *fiqh*, as well as to terms used to describe gender roles that were overlooked in prior translations. I also provide transliterations following the guide of the *International Journal of Middle Eastern Studies*, but with simplified diacritics, for terms that are important to my arguments. Several of these terms appear in the glossary.

KIMIYA-I SA'ADAT

Abu Hamid Muhammad al-Ghazali was born in 1058 in Tus, which is now a small suburb of Mashhad in Iran's province of Khorasan. Scholars have been captivated by Ghazali's intellectual biography for many years.[34] As one of his final works, the *Kimiya-i Sa'adat* serves as a culmination of lifelong reflections on the state of the world and the personal ethics one needs in order to attain true happiness. As I alluded to at the beginning of this introduction, at the height of his career at the Saljuq court and as *mudarris* (head scholar) of Baghdad's Nizamiyyah, Ghazali renounced his life in Baghdad and went away on a distant journey. In his autobiography, Ghazali confesses that he explained away his resignation to the caliph and his friends by saying he desired to go on an extended pilgrimage, when in fact he had resigned on account of becoming aware of his own greed for the material trappings of success. Numerous scholars have theorized that Ghazali had still other motives for leaving, including fear of being assassinated at the hands of the Isma'ilis, discomfort over tensions with the Saljuqs, and a craving to lead a reclusive, ascetic life.[35] Omid Safi proposes that because Nizam al-Mulk established the madrasa system as a network of reconnaissance and surveillance of scholars, students, and their ideas, "Al-Ghazali's escape is not simply that of one yearning for a spiritual life; it is also the desire to escape the gaze he was under at the madrasa."[36] In the *Kimiya*, which Ghazali wrote after his spiritual journey and semiretirement to Tus in 1099, he reflects on both his newfound focus on spirituality and his reassessment of public and political expressions of Islam. Unable to completely recuse himself from government-sponsored institutions, by 1106 Ghazali joined the Nizamiyya in Nishapur, far away from the watchful eye of the caliphate in Baghdad but still close to his home in Khorasan, where his wife and children resided.

Ghazali's hiatus from public life, during which he traveled in Damascus, Jerusalem, Makkah, and Medina, included a prolific period from 1096 to 1102 in which he wrote his magnum opus, the Arabic-language *Ihya' 'Ulum ad-Din*, an encyclopedic ethico-legal compendium. Scholars estimate that he wrote the much shorter, Persian-language ethics treatise *Kimiya-i Sa'adat* near the end of that period, but certainly after the *Ihya'*. Whereas the *Ihya'* is in large part legalistic, the *Kimiya* is more philosophical. Ghazali omits technical legal explanations and *fiqh*-oriented details, instead basing the *Kimiya's* presentation of topics on how to live ethically largely on metaphysical notions of moral being. Ghazali even states that those seeking "complicated explanations and fine and difficult points" should seek out his other works.[37]

By the time Ghazali writes the *Kimiya*, he has blended together principles of reason and revelation. Although some scholars construe Ghazali's early rejection of Mu'tazilite ideas, which emphasized reason-derived ethics, as his outright rejection of philosophy as a method of thinking, more compelling is Ebrahim Moosa's description of his work as a *dihliz*, or "the intermediate space or the threshold space that Ghazali identified—one with intersecting boundaries and heterogeneous notions of practices and time."[38] In the *Kimiya-i Sa'adat*, we see the convergence of reason and revelation as the way of ethics, which even uses the methodologies of the philosophers. The merger of reason and divine authority is apparent in *Kimiya-i Sa'adat*, and closely connects the text to Tusi and Davani's *falsafa*-oriented treatises. Although in his other texts he explicitly disavows the philosophical tradition—and therefore does not have specific references to Aristotle or Plato as Tusi and Davani do—I show that much of the *Kimiya* conforms to the Greek-inspired Muslim philosophical tradition in relation to understandings of the *nafs* and its training, as Frank Griffel has shown is characteristic of other Ghazalian works.[39]

The structure of the *Kimiya* is simple. After a prologue about the nature of the self or *nafs*, followed by a discussion of the nature of God, the world, and the hereafter, the *Kimiya* proceeds in two main parts. The first part concerns issues that are apparent (*zahir*), including acts of worship and social transactions (*'ibadat* and *mu'amalat*, respectively), and the second part concerns issues that are *batin*, or hidden, including *pak kardan-i dil* (purification of the heart) and *arastan-i dil* (adornment of the heart). Following the tripartite cosmology of virtue ethics of the self, marriage, and society, in the first part of the text, Ghazali speaks as a philosopher imparting wisdom about the nature of the *nafs* and the behavioral pitfalls of the *nafs*. Then, in speaking on ethical behavior, Ghazali takes on the voice of an ethicist on matters ranging from what to do in case of marital discord to how to comport oneself socially in public and at royal court.

While the *Kimiya* may at first appear to be just Ghazali's move toward asserting the spirit of the law over its details, what it in fact turns out to be is his more philosophical exposition of individuals' spirituality and their role in the cosmos in relation to that spirituality. Not unlike its philosophical ethics counterparts, the *Akhlaq-i Nasiri* and *Akhlaq-i Davani*, the *Kimiya*'s goal is to help individuals find happiness/flourishing (*sa'adat*) through correcting their *nafs* with methods prescribed by the science of *akhlaq*. Ghazali states that his purpose in the *Kimiya* is to familiarize readers with the figurative "alchemy, which brings the virtues of the human from lowliness of brutishness toward purity and excellence of the state of angels until he/she obtains everlasting happiness."[40] Following its composition in the twelfth century, the text became one of the most important, accessible compendiums of Islamic ethics for centuries to come, both in Persian and in translation.

AKHLAQ-I NASIRI

As his name suggests, Nasir ad-Din Tusi was born in Tus (also Ghazali's hometown) on February 17, 1201. His true sectarian identity has been much debated. In his autobiography-cum-doctrinal treatise, *Sayr wa*

Suluk, Tusi defends his Isma'ili beliefs by explaining that his family followed the exoteric aspects of the shari'a, which prompted him to search for more mystical and esoteric understandings of Islam.[41] Some scholars believe he was Isma'ili to begin with because in this biography, he discusses coming out as Isma'ili and declaring his true feelings about his faith, as if emerging from *taqiyya*—which is concealing one's sectarian identity for the sake of one's safety.[42] However, according to Tusi scholar S. J. Badakhchani, such an explanation does not account for his discussion of his transformation in deliberately choosing Isma'ili ideas.[43] Wilfred Madelung suggests that Tusi converted to Isma'ilism on philosophical grounds.[44] Meanwhile, some Imami Shi'i historians have dismissed his association with Isma'ilis, and others claim that his conversion to Isma'ilism was only temporary.[45]

Early in Tusi's career, after reading a compilation of sermons and essays by a Nizari Isma'ili imam named Hasan 'Ala Dhikrihi al-Salam (d. 1166), the young polymath became convinced of the need to learn the inner meanings of the Shari'a through a teacher and, more specifically, a living imam. Tusi pleaded with the Isma'ili governor of Quhistan to join the Isma'ili community, but he was unsuccessful. Finally, after 1224, during the rule of the next leader (*muhtashim*) of the Quhistani Nizaris, a man named Nasir ad-Din 'Abd al-Rahim, young Tusi was admitted as a novice (*mustajib*).[46] He entered into service at the *muhtashim*'s court and wrote several treatises on a wide range of subjects, including astronomy, mathematics, medicine, physics, jurisprudence, philosophy, and theology. As a vizier and *hakim* (polymath–philosopher–physician), Tusi oversaw surgeries, provided astrological calculations of the auspiciousness of various dates, and advised on matters of patronage.[47] He was surrounded by the politics and happenings of the court, which formed the backdrop of social reality to which his ethical treatise *Akhlaq-i Nasiri* responds.

Tusi is notorious for the opportunism he displayed in his participation in sectarian polemics and in his conversions from Imami to Isma'ili Shi'ism and back, and ultimately for his role as advisor to Chingiz Khan's brutal grandson, Hulegu, after the Mongol invasion in 1256. Hulegu rewarded Tusi with great trust, patronage, and employment in his service, following his role in convincing the Isma'ili leadership in Alamut to surrender to the Mongols. Tusi then accompanied Hulegu in an advisory capacity as the latter sacked Baghdad. Some versions of the story allege that the Mongols' famous method of executing the caliph—namely, rolling him up in a carpet and beating him to death—was Tusi's idea.[48] Eventually, Tusi continued his intellectual activities as the head of the Maraghah observatory library, Hulegu's commission.

Tusi wrote the *Akhlaq-i Nasiri* while at the court of the Nizari Isma'ili governor of Quhistan around 1235. His first notable treatise on ethics, titled *Akhlaq-i Muhtashimi,* had been an Isma'ili-oriented approach to the question of how to live a virtuous life and was based on the *muhtashim*'s own outline of ethical topics, Tusi's favorite subject. In addition to Qur'anic verses and hadiths, the text is based on sayings of the early Shi'i imams and of later Isma'ili imams and thinkers.[49] The *Akhlaq-i Nasiri,* named after Tusi's benefactor, was a much more philosophical approach to ethics, said to be partly modeled after Ibn Miskawayh's eleventh-century Buyid-period philosophical ethics treatise *Tahdhib al-Akhlaq,*[50] though the original version contained several passages in the introduction and conclusion in praise of the Isma'ilism and the Isma'ili political regime, which Tusi later removed at Maraghah under Hulegu's patronage and replaced with a disclaimer stating that the ideas in his book are nonsectarian.[51] Ultimately, the content of Tusi's writings and his ability to transfer allegiances with changing political tides indicate that, in addition to his evident concern for his own safety, Tusi was mostly concerned with the substance of ideas, rather than with what sect they came from. Even during the Mongol invasion, his advocacy of safeguarding the libraries, observatories, and the like shows that regardless of the political regime of the day, he regarded knowledge itself as something worth preserving.

As Tusi himself asserts, the goal of his treatise is to build on the "practical philosophy" of Ibn Miskawayh's text *Tahdhib al-Akhlaq,* with the significant addition of chapters on the management of the domestic economy and the craft of running households, for the purpose of "complete revival of goodness" among "people of today, who are mostly bereft of the adornment of ethics, . . . [so they can] beautify themselves with the study of the bejeweled ideas of this collection [of ethics]."[52] Perhaps partly in response to the wayward politics, unethical behaviors, and troublesome observations of the status of personal affairs of people at court, this is a text that is meant to instruct elite men on matters of how to live the most virtuous, ethical life possible that is in accordance with the ways of God as apprehended through three domains of knowledge: the science of theology, rationality as derived through the methods of logic and reasoning, and wisdom as developed through the science of philosophy.

Tusi's ethics treatise is divided into three discourses, couched between an introduction that classifies fields of knowledge and sciences and a conclusion that contains relevant references and sayings attributed to Plato and Aristotle. The ultimate goal of the *Akhlaq-i Nasiri* is to guide the (male) reader to realize true happiness by becoming a vicegerent of God, a goal that is achieved by balancing one's *nafs* and acting ethically in both the domestic and public realms. The first discourse, "On the Refinement of Character" (*Dar Tahdhib al-Akhlaq*), is a theoretical explanation of principles of human existence and happiness, together with a subsection on objectives and methods for individuals to refine their virtues and tame their vices. The second discourse, "Domestic Economy" (*Tadbir-i Manazil*), pans out from individual ethics to the family and immediate community and focuses on the ethics of domestic life and household affairs. The third discourse, "Urban Politics" (*Siyasat-i Mudun*), takes an even wider lens, elaborating on the ethics of managing, governing, and living in a city, province, or other larger region. Central to all three of Tusi's discourses is his guidance on ethical ways to manage the self in relationships with the people one encounters in both the domestic and the public realms. The *Akhlaq-i Nasiri* is a well-studied text in the Western academy, and it remains a classic text of ethics in Persianate lands.

AKHLAQ-I JALALI

Jalal ad-Din Muhammad bin Asad Davani was born in 1426 in the village of Davan, near Kazerun, which is located in the Fars Province of modern-day Iran, west of the city of Shiraz. As a young man, Davani moved to Shiraz, where he studied the Islamic sciences of theology, philosophy, logic, jurisprudence, and mysticism. During his lifetime, he witnessed the westward expansion of the Ottoman Empire, living through Sultan Mehmet II's conquest of Constantinople and the founding of Istanbul, and in the last year of his life even witnessing the official establishment of the Safavids in Isfahan. Patronized by local courts in Shiraz, Davani first held the post of *sadr*, or religious supervisor, for the

Qaraquyunlu but quickly resigned out of dislike for court-sponsored scholarship. His subsequent patrons were the rulers from the Sunni dynasty of the Aqquyunlus, under whose patronage he wrote the *Akhlaq-i Jalali*. Later he served as the main judge (*qadi*) of Fars until his death in 1502, before the Safavid encroachment on Shiraz.[53]

Unlike Ghazali and Tusi, Davani remained something of a free agent throughout his career, in that he was not always employed in direct service to a royal court. The Aqquyunlu sultans actively sought his support because he was a respected scholar, but he sometimes chose not to lend them that support.[54] His Arabic and Persian writings were varied, including poetry as well as commentaries on works by his favorite philosopher, Suhrawardi (d. 1191), and treatises on politics and law commissioned by various courts, such as the Timurids, Ottomans, and sultans in India. His works speak to the ubiquity of the Persianate Muslim intellectual tradition in premodern times. It is unclear whether Davani was Shi'i or Sunni himself, since he wrote works from both perspectives, but sectarian polemics are even less prominent in the *Akhlaq-i Jalali* than in the *Kimiya* or *Akhlaq-i Nasiri*. Instead of professing any sectarian allegiance, Davani melds ideas from peripatetic and Ishraqi Sufi illuminationist schools, providing further evidence that commitments to patriarchal hierarchy transcended ideological divisions.

His most famous work is the Persian-language ethics treatise *Akhlaq-i Jalali*, written around 1475 while he was in Aqquyunlu Sultan, Uzun Hasan's employ. It was Hasan's son who requested that Davani write the treatise. Although the *Akhlaq-i Jalali* is from a later period and a different context than the *Kimiya-i Sa'adat* and the *Akhlaq-i Nasiri*, we see among the three texts a continuity in ideas about metaphysics and virtue ethics. In particular, Davani retains much of the peripatetic concerns of Ibn Miskawayh and Tusi in ethics of the individual, family, and society, and retains citations to Plato and Aristotle and the Ibn Sinan science of the *nafs*. But Davani also includes "native" idioms and folklore of his time and place to convey his ethics. Like Ghazali, Davani quotes Persian sages and mystics, and he also makes textual references to both the *Kimiya* and *Akhlaq-i Nasiri*.

The *Akhlaq-i Jalali* has similar chapter divisions to the *Akhlaq-i Nasiri*, with sections on the individual, domestic, and political realms, followed by an appendix of quotations by Plato and Aristotle on ethics and politics. However, the topics covered within each section differ from Tusi's work. In his first discourse, Davani sets forth the divine impetus for ethical action, for cultivating a virtuous soul, and for mitigating its vices. He also presents full outlines of the notion of divine proportion, an argument that equity is the epitome of all virtues, and a discussion of human beings' mental capacity and illness. In the second discourse, which focuses on the domestic state, Davani adds nuances to Tusi's discussion on the religious and philosophical purposes of marriage. Like Ghazali, he includes a detailed list of preparations one must make before marrying, such as accumulating food and putting the home in order. Finally, in the third discourse, which focuses on the political state, Davani adds to Tusi's discussion by including anecdotes such as parables on friendship, love, governance, sovereignty, and social interaction with inferior classes.

Scholars such as G. M. Wickens and John Cooper have dismissed *Akhlaq-i Jalali* as an intellectually inferior copy of the *Akhlaq-i Nasiri*, denigrating its author as the perpetrator of a fashionably verbose and circuitous writing style.[55] However, Davani's long-lasting influence on Persian scholarly curricula speaks to the significance of his work in the corpus of Islamic ethics. The importance of Davani's work is that we see in it the formation of continuous ideas about the sources of Islamic ethics and variations in codes of social conduct with respect to historical changes. As I discuss in the next chapter, the three texts represent a unified ethics tradition, one that seeks to answer questions about how to live as an individual, in a family, and in society. This tripartite division serves as the organizing principle for the subsequent chapters.

STRUCTURE OF THE BOOK

This book elucidates the elite male-centered nature of Islamic virtue ethics. As I show, the ethicists themselves grappled with questions about gender on some level, and there were inconsistencies in their male-dominated philosophies that open a space for deeper philosophical reflection on gender in Islamic thought. My approach departs from contemporary scholarship on the various genres of Islamic ethics, which tends to ignore questions of gender and instead focuses on searching for the higher moral standards within Islam, such as notions of justice, egalitarianism, and political ethics. Several feminist scholars have taken up ethics as a guiding concept in their scholarship on Islamic texts, but there remains a need for a more unified, philosophically oriented discussion of how gender is constructed in Islamic ethics and of what can be made of an ethical tradition we know to be problematically male-centered. The chapters of this book pursue the arc of personal, familial, and social ethics through the lens of gender to build the argument that even though the *akhlaq* genre philosophizes the nature of humanity as a whole and how to bring about cosmic justice, its elite male-centrism contradicts these goals of *akhlaq* by relying on exclusionary definitions of humanity itself.

To situate my feminist close reading of these texts, in chapter 1, "Epistemology and Gender Analytics of Islamic Ethics," I discuss the definition, genealogy, and reception history of the *akhlaq* genre, to which these texts belong, as well as the analytical tools I employ to understand the texts. I position the texts within a unified tradition that addresses questions of how to live, explains how the ethicists see their own ethical projects, and traces the nature of the texts' impact on the Islamic ethical tradition. The payoffs in reading the three texts together, and in the context of their epistemological predecessors and successors, are both historical and analytical. The historical payoff is that we see the continuity of a cohesive ethical tradition, and the analytical payoff is that we are able to understand *akhlaq* as a tradition from which gendered concepts emerge in the transition from metaphysics to virtue ethics. Although other scholars have looked at these texts as having a limited or niche contribution to Islamic ethics discourses, I demonstrate that the texts reflect a rich understanding of Islamic philosophical ideas about the nature of the Divine, humanity, and moral responsibility, and that these ideas can be more fully accessed by attending to the texts' concepts of gender.

Over the next three chapters, I analyze each component of the *akhlaq*'s tripartite cosmology of ethical behavior. The *akhalq* tradition organizes ethics on three levels—the individual *nafs* (metaphysical soul), the domestic realm, and the sovereign state—each one a scaled metaphor of the others. Chapter 2 focuses on the individual soul, or *nafs*, whose metaphysics provides the foundation for the virtue ethics of domestic and public life. Titled "Gendered Metaphysics, Perfection, and Power of the (Hu)man's Soul," the chapter demonstrates that Ghazali's, Tusi's, and Davani's conception of the human metaphysical soul is gendered male. I argue that despite their texts' potential for radical equality, their discourses of ethical perfection and of the powers of the soul are normative male. The ethicists' discussions of the soul establish the individual man's power over himself to perfect himself, as well as his power over lesser others. For the ethicists, the concept of ethics is only legible in the context of men's interactions with other humans. Thus, the soul's constituent parts and its virtues are the building blocks not only of an ethically refined male soul, but also of man's ethically endorsed power over others. This hierarchical construction of masculinity is in direct opposition to the overall goals of the *akhlaq* genre, which aims to guide all humans toward justice, happiness, and vicegerency of God.

In chapter 3, "Ethics of Marriage and the Domestic Economy," I move from gendered metaphysics to gendered virtue ethics. To explore the ethicists' understandings of masculinity and femininity in relation to each other, I examine the three texts' prescriptions for ethical behavior in the domestic arena, including marriage, divorce, running a household, and rearing children. Although ostensibly addressing only male readers, Ghazali, Tusi, and Davani outline both men's and women's roles and responsibilities within marriage. The differences in men's and women's roles as prescribed in *akhlaq* are indicative of the ethicists' biological and ontological assumptions about the nature of masculinity and femininity. In extending the claim from chapter 2 that the soul the ethicists are interested in ordering is normative male, I show that within the household, ethicists treat men as the primary ethical subject and women as ethical objects. Men partially dispense their ethical duties by heading the domestic economy and being in charge of disciplining the souls of their wives and children as much as possible. As the ethicists construct it, the woman's role is to be amenable to her husband's instruction and instrumental to running his household. Man's role as primary and woman's role as instrumental stemmed from the ethicists' understanding of men as rational and spiritual souls and women as embodied and limited by biological function. Thus, I argue that the texts demonstrate an ethics of exclusion and a metaphysical tension: the ethicists recognize women's humanity, i.e., their possession of human souls, yet are encumbered with assumptions about the metaphysical inferiority of women and their essential natures.

Chapter 4, "Homosocial Masculinity and Societal Ethics," examines the ethicists' understanding of masculinity in the context of homosocial relationships of friendship, love, and interactions with other men in government and public activities. I argue that just as the normative male conception of metaphysics leads to the assumption of male superiority over women, it also leads to homosocial male hierarchies, which are likewise codified in the virtue ethics of the social realm. The inequalities found in the male homosocial hierarchy are gendered, meaning that the elite metaphysics are about what qualities constitute ultimate masculinity and elite status. All nonelite men are less manly than elite men and are excluded from ethical refinement by virtue of their souls' imperfections. The intellectual, class, and power hierarchies in exclusively male homosocial contexts are also gendered because of the ways in which male superiority over other males is defined by contrast to women's inferiority in these areas. By looking at ethical prescriptions for how men are supposed to act in social relationships outside the home, I find that man is thought to complete his moral responsibilities by being a member of the broader society outside his home, in which ultimate masculinity is defined in terms of power, hierarchy of intellect, and ethical comportment in homosocial structures of court, civic, and community life.

In the conclusion, I summarize my findings and offer a prolegomenon to a feminist philosophy of Islam. One of my most important findings is that the textual contradiction between normative male metaphysics and the overarching goals of the discipline of ethics shows that inequalities in Islamic virtue ethics are historically concomitant to assumptions about inequalities in human existence and prevailing gender assumptions. The ethicists ignore the potential for radical equality that is present in the metaphysical cosmology itself because the stronger, normative male soul is meant to dominate over the souls of women as well as men of weaker intellects. Having explicated this textual contradiction and reflected on the category of gender in the genre of philosophical ethics, I then argue for a philosophical turn in the field of gender in Islam. My argument hinges on a discussion of several foundational, philosophical problems that my close reading of gender and hierarchy in *akhlaq* texts reveals. I take up four major issues in particular:

the problem of privileging rationality above other virtues, which results in the exclusion of women, low-class men, and enslaved people from definitions of humanity; the problem of the inherent contradiction of male-centered definitions of vicegerency (*khilafah*) and authority to the goals of *akhlaq*; the problem of inscribing hierarchies via the essentialization of women; and the problem that ethical refinement entails the utilization of others. Finally, looking toward the future of feminist scholarship on Islamic texts, I consider the importance of studying *akhlaq* texts, alongside other Islamic ethics genres, as a continued philosophical endeavor.

CHAPTER ONE

Epistemology and Gender Analytics of Islamic Ethics

The *akhlaq* treatises of Ghazali, Tusi, and Davani have been mischaracterized as not truly Islamic and assumed to have made only limited, niche contributions to the Islamic ethical tradition. This misunderstanding is largely due to the texts' Greek philosophical influences, which have been offered as evidence that the texts are derivative in nature. Further mischaracterizations of these texts include the assumption that the texts share little in common with one another because their authors hail from different sectarian backgrounds and the assumption that their scope is limited to that of etiquette manuals or political ethics treatises. This chapter counters these prevailing views, situating *akhlaq* texts as an Islamic ethics tradition of distinct contributions and continued relevance. I argue, contrary to widely held views, that these texts are in fact implicitly Islamic; that they share important historical and analytical commonalities, which warrant their being read together; that they occupy the philosophical space in Islamic thought that deals with metaphysics and virtues; and that they have long held great power in Muslim discourses about how to live. Not only do the authors consider perennial humanistic questions about how to live as an individual, in a family, and in a society; they do so by building on earlier philosophical traditions, and in the centuries after their composition, they would go on to have widespread, continued influence throughout Muslim lands.

This chapter traces the historical and analytical consequences of reading the three texts as a cohesive group. First, such a reading reveals their historical continuity. All three texts engage in the same perennial questions of how to live that had animated the Greek philosophers who preceded them and that went on to influence the ethical tradition that their own work would inspire. This historical continuity is the focus of the first part of this chapter, where I define *akhlaq* and show how its epistemological and methodological origins in Greek and Mediterranean sources imply the genre's importance to broader philosophical discourses. Based on this continuity among the three texts, I argue in the second part of the chapter that the texts ought to be understood as a unified tradition, one whose central commonality is their use of a metaphysics of the *nafs* as a basis for a trilevel virtue ethics of self, family, and society. This model has had a lasting impact on Muslim thought. In addition to this historical payoff, reading the three texts together also provides an analytic one: specifically, this reading reveals the shared notions of gender that emerge from these texts' central ethical claims, enabling us to explore how the ethicists justify their concepts of femininity, masculinity, gender hierarchy, and social patriarchy using gendered metaphysics and virtue ethics. The third part of this chapter constructs a gender analytic from two sources: feminist approaches to analogous Greek/Mediterranean texts and theories of masculinity from masculinity studies. The gender analytic set forth in this chapter provides a lens for my feminist close readings in the chapters to follow. Overall, I argue that these texts are vital to a holistic understanding of Islamic ethics and gender in Muslim thought.

DEFINITIONS, EPISTEMOLOGY, AND GENRE OF THE GHAZALI-TUSI-DAVANI *AKHLAQ* TRADITION

Ghazali's, Davani's, and Tusi's *akhlaq* texts are more than "just" niche Islamic texts or derivatives of Greek and Ancient Mediterranean sources. Indeed, understanding these texts' methodological origins in Greek/Mediterranean sources is precisely what enables us to build a picture of their larger significance and the importance of studying them together. In this endeavor, it is important to study the authors' own reflexive discussions of their intended ethical projects in the context of other ethics genres, as well as the discourses to which these texts have contributed. What did the ethicists themselves think was the nature and purpose of their works?

Definition of Akhlaq

As a central genre of Islamic ethics, *akhlaq* focuses on inculcating virtue ethics within individuals, with the larger goal of creating ethical conditions in the household and broader society. The genre of *akhlaq* is usually located within the disciplinary boundaries of *falsafa* (after the Greek discipline of *philosophia*), in a branch of knowledge called practical philosophy/wisdom (*hikmat-i 'amali*).[1] The term *akhlaq* in Arabic connotes measurement and making. It derives from the triletter root kh-l-q, which means "to measure, to determine proportion, or to create based on measure," and is also the verb that the Qur'an uses to describe God's act of creating the heavens, the earth, all the animals, and human beings. The derivative term, *khulq*, refers to a human's actual nature or temperament, which is deeply embedded in creation by virtue of the human's having been created by God. Thus, the term *tahdhib-i akhlaq* (the discipline of ethics) carries notions of creation as well as nature, and of proportion in one's behavior. The discipline of *akhlaq* is based on the premise that one should behave commensurate with one's nature. As part of his definition of *akhlaq*, Ghazali uses a proximate term, *khu*, to refer to the disposition of the heart. For the three ethicists in this study, as I discuss in chapter 2, men are obligated to be ethical by virtue of being God's most rational creation. All three ethicists discuss the *nafs*'s (soul's) disposition as having been created (*khalaqah*) by God, and all three assert its potential to be(come) ethical through employment of the science of *akhlaq*. Notably, the term for individual nature or temperament, *khulq*, has a sense of neutrality; it is neither natural nor opposed to nature, suggesting that human beings are born with neutral souls (*nafses*).[2] The plural form of *khulq* is *akhlaq*, resembling the plural form of the analogous Greek word, *ethics*. The usage of a plural form in both the Islamic and the Greek traditions suggests there are multiple behaviors or mores that compose ethical behavior and the discipline of the self (*nafs*), and that lead to the ultimate goal of becoming a vicegerent of God (*khalifah*).

The measurement, discipline, and creation that are inherent in the term *akhlaq*, and in the genre to which it refers, are transscalar in nature. *Akhlaq* is concerned with God's creation at the microcosmic and the macrocosmic levels, and it attends to the ways in which these scales of being mirror each other and build on each other as God's creation is disciplined into an ethical being. The scales (or realms) of ethics are represented in the three-part structure of each of the treatises. Tusi, for example, conceptually links personal disposition to the sovereign state by defining *khulq* using the term *malakah*, which means "habit" but shares roots with terms for "angel" and "kingship." This usage foreshadows another explanation of how the individual is considered to be a microcosm, a major part of an individual's ethical goal, which I will discuss in chapter 2. Within the very definition of *akhlaq*, we see the historical transformation of Greek ideas into the final, transscalar moral state of vicegerency (*khilafah*) through discipline of the metaphysical soul or self (*nafs*). These three concepts, *akhlaq*, *khilafah*, and the *nafs*, are the central concepts from the *akhlaq* tradition that I draw on for the gender analysis I do in this book.

Epistemology and Genealogy: Methodological Origins in Greek Philosophy and Ancient Mediterranean Patriarchy

Many twentieth-century scholars of Islamic ethics were preoccupied merely with what does or does not make *akhlaq* texts Islamic, an investigation that was pursued simply by comparing the texts' structural elements to ethics texts of Plato and Aristotle. However, this question of the texts' Islamic nature is not, in my view, the most interesting question to ask of Islamic philosophical ethics. In fact, it is a reactionist attempt to counteract the ubiquitous, obstinately Orientalist framing of Islamic philosophy as an imitation of Greek philosophy. My own concerns are more substantive and philosophical, as I seek to examine how *akhlaq* texts answer questions about how to live the good life and the patriarchal norms at play within those answers. By framing the Greek philosophy's contribution to *akhlaq* as one of shared epistemology of virtue and patriarchy, we can see that the *akhlaq* texts resonate far beyond the Islamic context and are part of a long-standing, cohesive ethical tradition that seeks answers to the questions of how to live as individuals, in families, and in society. Throughout this book, I show that even though Muslim philosophical ethics is implicitly Islamic, it is also relevant to the broader field of philosophy and makes important contributions to the construction and understandings of gender in general.

Prior to the mid-twentieth century, the main Orientalist thesis on *akhlaq* was that these texts, especially the works of Tusi and Davani, were reproductions of canonical ancient Greek texts.[3] Oliver Leaman has shown that the motivation of Orientalists was to discredit the intellectual heritage of colonized Muslim peoples in order to claim a monopoly over high philosophical ideas.[4] By the mid-twentieth century, scholars such as George Hourani and Majid Fakhry began to study the texts not as copies, but as comparisons and Islamic adaptations of their "originals."[5] Later, scholars such as Seyyed Hossein Nasr and Leaman treated Islamic ethics as centered on an Islamic worldview that both critiqued from decidedly Islamic perspectives[6] and creatively expanded upon the intellectually irresistible philosophy of prior philosophical traditions of the Greeks, as well as those of the Persians and Indians.[7] More recently, Mohammad Azadpur has asked, "Is Islamic philosophy Islamic?"[8] Azadpur's answer to this question is affirmative because philosophy is "the practice of spiritual exercises aimed at the transformation of the self and the acquisition of wisdom"; and thus, "Islamic philosophy is the Islamic practice of philosophical spiritual exercises."[9] Elizabeth Bucar argues that *akhlaq* is an imperfect "adoption of Platonic or Aristotelian theory" precisely because it is concerned with God and "is framed as a process of perfecting the soul for God, who is the perfection."[10] Throughout these successive characterizations of *akhlaq*, scholars continued to focus on questions of definition, such as how Islamic the *akhlaq* genre is, how it relates to Greek thought, and how it differs from other Muslim sources that are supposedly more Islamic.

Instead of framing the epistemology of *akhlaq* (and the discipline of *falsafa* under which *akhlaq* is most commonly classified) in terms of how closely it adheres to Islam or its Greek origins, I would like to frame it in terms of the methods the ethicists use, their context, and the varying answers they yield to the question of how to live. This way of framing the epistemology of *akhlaq* enables us to confirm two things: first, it reveals that irrespective of the question of what is Islamic about *akhlaq*, it fits within a larger history of philosophers seeking wisdom on universal questions of how to live as individuals, in families, and in communities; and second, it opens up the possibility of bringing in feminist critiques of the inherited Greek tradition and ancient Mediterranean patriarchy to offer insights into the ways philosophical traditions prior to *akhlaq* formulate male-centered philosophy and what can be done about these traditions—a concern I take up further in the gender analytics section later. This reframing of *akhlaq*'s epistemology enables us to better see how Islamic philosophical ethics, particularly matters of gender, informs the field of philosophy more broadly.

Framing the epistemology of *akhlaq* in terms of a shared history of methods, contexts, and variations on concepts of virtue ethics might entail the following narrative. The initial knowledge transfer between Greek and Muslim thinkers began around the mid-eighth century in Baghdad. In these early interactions, Muslim thinkers found themselves in encounters with irresistible knowledge that they made their own over the next couple of centuries. In what began as a translation project, the cultural and intellectual transfer from Greek science and philosophy led to the incorporation of philosophical terms and concepts into the methodologies of Islamic philosophical ethics, in particular concepts such as the metaphysical soul as *nafs* and the theorization of the individual's role in family and society.

This Muslim engagement with Greek sources was highly generative. Muslim philosophers building on Stoic and Socratic ideas, such as al-Kindi (d. 873) and Fakhr ad-Din Ar-Razi (d. 1209), were still sympathetic to rationalist Muslim theologians (Mu'tazilites) because they too held that values are reason-derived; however, the Muslim peripatetics also relied on the writings of the Greeks to debate the state of the human condition and the impetus for partaking in moral behavior. For example, Farabi's (d. 950) and Ibn Sina's (d. 1037) engagements with Plato and Aristotle led to discussions about the role of the moral and ascetic intellectual in the moral underpinnings of a polity.[11] Ibn Sina was more specifically concerned than Farabi with the perfection of the human soul in its quest to find happiness and knowledge of the Ultimate.[12] Ibn Sina's Neoplatonic ideas about the *nafs*, about virtues and vices, and about the role of the prophet-king-philosopher all became standard models that pervaded multiple genres of Muslim thought, including theology (*kalam*) and mysticism (*tasawwuf*).[13] In the *akhlaq* texts of Ghazali, Tusi, and

Davani, we see the same basic three-part framework of the faculties of the *nafs*, as well as consistent attitudes on women and hierarchy and the shared concept of the philosopher-king as the potential ultimate ethical man. These three elements correspond to the three levels of ethics in Ghazali's, Tusi's, and Davani's *akhlaq* texts. Thus, we see how the Greek–Muslim connection contributed to the development of a genre of ethics that related metaphysics to virtue ethics, and related both of these to the cosmic Islamic goal of becoming a *khalifah*, or vicegerent of God.

Throughout Tusi's and Davani's treatises in particular, we see explicit examples of the Greek influence, especially in their references to Plato and Aristotle. Tusi's text includes an appendix on maxims by Plato as told to Aristotle, known to him as Aflatoon and Arastatalis, respectively, for the express purpose of "benefiting the generality of men."[14] Tusi's chosen quotations encapsulate the highlights of the master's teachings, Plato himself pronouncing on the discipline of the *nafs*, loving wisdom above all else, and one's responsibility to know God.[15] Davani includes a shorter Plato appendix, and also adds a second appendix with a more politically engaged set of quotations comprising Aristotle's teachings to Alexander the Great. The teachings are from a letter addressed to the conqueror about how to be an ethical ruler and what kinds of ethics he should demand his subjects cultivate: love for knowledge, being wary of women, and bringing about justice in society. The teachings mirror the trilevel progression of his *akhlaq* treatise, from the individual to the household to society.[16]

For Mohammad Azadpur, the key way in which Greek philosophy influenced Muslim philosophy is in the emphasis on virtue ethics. He explains that the common thread between Greek and Muslim philosophy emerges when we reflect more on the connections between virtue and ethics in the Greek tradition through Pierre Hadot's thesis that ancient philosophy was "a way of life."[17] Azadpur argues that Muslim philosophers understood the Greek tradition, which they inherited in the particularly Islamic light of transformation of the soul, ethics "qua life, a practice," which made the Islamic philosophical corpus a distinct tradition worthy of its own study.[18] While Azadpur is still focused on clarifying the Islamic nature of Islamic philosophy as an enterprise, his focus on the practice of virtue ethics as the common thread between Greek and Muslim philosophy begins to move the conversation away from the "reception history" framework of Greek thought toward shared beliefs and practices that morph into distinctively Muslim beliefs and practices over time. This focus, he argues, and I agree, makes Muslim philosophical ethics relevant to the broader field of philosophy. In this book, I move further away from thinking about what is Islamic and what is not Islamic in the texts by looking at how the ethicists' questions fit into a lasting tradition of self-discipline that leads to gendered and other social hierarchies.

Notwithstanding the *akhlaq* texts' parallels with Greek philosophy and ancient Mediterranean patriarchy, these texts are, in my reading, implicitly Islamic: that is, to use Fatima Seedat's phrase, they take Islam for granted,[19] for both their contexts and their environments are unquestionably Islamic. The ethicists assume that their readers are Muslim, that their readers' wives and children are Muslim, and that all those they encounter in society are Muslims in a Muslim society. For example, all three ethicists instruct their readers to beat their sons if they neglect to complete their prayers on time past the age of nine.[20] Another example is that the ethicists recommend loving even a sinful man because he is a Muslim.[21] Although the ethicists do not say outright that wives should be Muslim, this expectation is implied by their statements that wives should be "pious" and have religious knowledge.[22] The texts contain few to no references to non-Muslims, suggesting that the normative subjects are Muslim and the exceptions are non-Muslim—likely also indicating that these texts are aspirational ones, depicting an ideal Muslim society with some reflections on observed reality.

In this context of implicit Islam, the ethicists' frequent quotations of Qur'anic verses and hadiths are more than just window dressing: they serve as lenses through which the ethicists philosophize about the world and men's roles within it. In some instances, ethical precepts come directly from scriptural quotations; in others, the quotations merely support discussion of ethical principles. In others still, Qur'anic and hadith references are placed in the text without the intent of presenting an argument about gender roles or anything else, but rather as a form of textual remembrance of God (*zikr*). The *akhlaq* texts are unmistakably Islamic, even while drawing on epistemology of metaphysics, virtue ethics, as well as gender norms shared with Greek philosophy. Other genres of Islamic thought also contextualize *akhlaq*'s epistemology, as I discuss later.

Epistemology and Genre: Comparison of Akhlaq to Other Islamic Ethics Traditions

How the *akhlaq* texts fit epistemologically among other genres of Islamic thought demonstrates the centrality of the genre as a distinct, yet vital, tradition of Islamic learning and practice for Ghazali, Tusi, and Davani. Comparison with other genres shows scholarly discomfort with classifying *akhlaq* as Islamic ethics in the face of other seemingly "more Islamic" genres of Muslim thought; and yet, as I argue later, the *akhlaq* authors themselves provided self-descriptions of the genre that contrast it to related prescriptive genres of Islamic thought, namely, law and mysticism, and offer insight into the ways the texts are in fact Islamic.

Within Islamic studies, there is a significant debate on what constitutes Islamic ethics as a distinctive tradition. Scholars today mainly describe theories of Islamic ethics in terms of four genres of the Muslim intellectual tradition: *kalam* (theology), *fiqh* (jurisprudence), *tasawwuf* (mysticism or sufism),[23] and *akhlaq* (philosophical ethics).[24] Scholars of *kalam* (theology) focus on the debates over sources of moral knowledge, human reason, and scriptural authority.[25] The language and methods used in *fiqh* (jurisprudence) and its *usul* (principles) are deployed in Islamic ethical discourse; in particular, its five-point scale for valuing all human acts can be used to weigh in on new matters affecting Muslims.[26] Of these four genres of the Muslim tradition, mystical discourses (*tasawwuf*) have arguably held the most influence in individual spiritual practice. The *akhlaq* genre (philosophical ethics) is considered to be a prominent genre of Islamic ethics, although often misunderstood as being limited only to personal etiquette or political ethics. Scholars have also classified a fifth genre, *adab*, or poetry and literary prose, as high-culture documentation of Muslim morality.[27] Amid this diversity of genres, no single genre is seen as prevailing for all time or for all Muslims as the primary medium of Islamic ethics.

Scholars' diverse applications of the English term *Islamic ethics* to denote various genres of Islamic thought serve to illustrate the fact that what the term really refers to is an academic construct. That is, *Islamic ethics* is a flexible term used by scholars to mean Muslim morals and values, and it may refer to any number of different sources and methods for deriving those morals and values. While each genre of Islamic ethics contributes important methodologies and approaches to ethical questions that Muslims have asked over centuries, *akhlaq* is an essential component of a holistic view of the multigenre discourse that is Islamic ethics, its genealogies, and its themes. The contributions of *akhlaq* to the constellation of Islamic ethics discourses are *methodological* in that the texts in this genre derive ethical principles for how to live, as well as *substantive* in that the texts prescribe ethical notions of masculinity and femininity and gender relations. Simply put, while no one genre is sufficient in itself for building an understanding of Islamic ethics, the *akhlaq* genre is necessary to a complete understanding of Islamic ethics and particularly to how gender figures within it. Furthermore, no Islamic ethics text is entirely isolated within the genre to which it belongs, since many ideas the texts may convey have echoes of the other genres. When the ethicists constructed the *akhlaq* tradition, they did so very much in conversation with other genres. Sometimes *akhlaq* provided a corrective against excessive applications of *fiqh, kalam, tasawwuf,* or the scriptural sources of the Qur'an and hadith, while other times, these genres provided detailed explications of ideas that are derived through methods of reasoning in *akhlaq*.

The ethicists themselves all wrote in multiple genres, including *fiqh, akhlaq,* and *tasawwuf,* and they weighed in on major debates in *kalam* of their day. Davani even served as an appointed judge for a time under the Aqquyonlus.[28] The ethicists also remarked on what they viewed as the centrality of *akhlaq* as an essential genre of learning for their audience. Like many scholars who wrote *akhlaq* treatises, Ghazali, Tusi, and Davani also served as jurists or taught *fiqh* as part of their extensive curriculum of the Islamic sciences. They viewed *akhlaq* as disciplinarily distinct from the legal rules found in the *fiqh* genre and the spiritual relationship with the Divine found in sufism. The ethicists' discussions of how *akhlaq* differs from other genres of the intellectual tradition, namely, law and mysticism, speak to the particular role they viewed philosophical ethics taking in individuals' lives. Even as they provide their readers with a guide to the bodies of knowledge in Islamic learning, they also problematize the relationship between the two genres. Although *akhlaq* contains abstract discussions on metaphysics, the ethicists viewed knowledge of it as essential to the creation of the moral impetus for following virtue ethics. In the ethicists' self-descriptions of their own ethical endeavors and the methods of *akhlaq*, they distinguish *akhlaq* from both jurisprudence (*fiqh*) and mysticism (*tasawwuf*).

SELF-REFLEXIVE DEFINITIONS OF AKHLAQ COMPARED TO JURISPRUDENCE

In the *Kimiya-i Sa'adat* and *Akhlaq-i Nasiri*, Ghazali and Tusi view *fiqh* and *akhlaq* as emerging from entirely distinct epistemologies with different purposes and mechanisms for enforcement (Davani avoids such prefatory remarks).[29] In discussions on social relations, *akhlaq* by and large fits into the contours of *fiqh*, but it also contains ethical responsibilities incumbent upon Muslim men entirely apart from the legal advantages they enjoy. When it comes to exploring the relationship between *fiqh* and *akhlaq*, there are two issues at stake. The first is distinguishing the two discursive traditions, in terms of what sources and methodologies they rely on and the kinds of questions each addresses. The second issue is identifying the impetus for people to actually learn and follow either or both traditions. For both Ghazali and Tusi, *akhlaq*'s distinct philosophical epistemology, namely, the metaphysics of the *nafs*, is key to understanding how premodern Islamic ethics of all genres position the individual and his ethical responsibilities in relation to the ethical future of the home, community, and society at large. Later I discuss Ghazali and Tusi's description of *akhlaq* in comparison to that of *fiqh* as a way to demonstrate that both ethicists saw *akhlaq* as the spiritual and practical basis of moral behavior and *fiqh* as details or laws for those lacking depth of understanding on profound matters. Following this, I compare *akhlaq* with sufi discourses as both are centered around cultivating ethical behaviors.

Ghazali's conception of *akhlaq*, which he devoted the final years of his life to writing, entailed moving beyond polemics and the outward expression of religious piety. Ghazali describes jurisprudence as "connected with religion, not directly but indirectly through the affairs of this world."[30] He continues that "as government by magistrates does not belong primarily to the science of religion but is an adjunct to that without which there is no religion, so is the knowledge of the manner of government."[31] In other words, in Ghazali's mind, *fiqh*, or, as he calls it, the rule of law, is not the rule of God, but rather is the rule of administration based upon God's intent for society, and it cannot be implemented without administrative machinery. Individuals themselves need additional rules to guide them in the path of faith (*rah-i din*). I interpret this as Ghazali saying that *fiqh* is the religious law of the land, enforced through government, while *akhlaq* is the religious ethics of individuals in society. So while *akhlaq* is meant for everyone in that its language is not technical, it is really meant only for those who have the capacity to learn.

Ghazali also acknowledges, in his expansive encyclopedia, the *Ihya' 'Ulum ad-Din* (*The Revival of Religious Sciences*), that scholars "disagreed as to what branch of knowledge man is obliged to acquire."[32] He felt that everyone did not need to learn *fiqh*. Ghazali held that because people's circumstances differ, not all are required to learn the details of *fiqh*: "the obligation is conditioned by the rise of new developments and changed circumstances relevant to it, and varies with the conditions of the individual. Thus, the mute are not obliged to know what is unlawful in speech or the blind to know what things are unlawful to see."[33] As feminist philosophers of religion would note, Ghazali holds that what constitutes knowledge is relative to the learner.[34] In other words, what is worth knowing depends on the natural disposition of the knower, which has great implications for future reflections on the gender inclusivity in *akhlaq*. Ghazali draws a distinction between elite knowledge for specialists and everyday ethics for the layman, while all the keepers of knowledge, specialist or lay, are normally men, as I show in the next chapters. By contrast, ethics as found in the *Ihya'*, as well as the *Kimiya*, is required for everyone. In comparing discussions about marriage in *fiqh* and the *Ihya'*, Lev Weitz explains that the *fiqh* genre is "more concerned with specifically legal issues such as the contracting of a valid marriage and the obligations it effects, [and thus] *fiqh* works tend to deal less with the kind of ethical ideal of the good wife that concerns al-Ghazali."[35]

In both the *Ihya'* and the *Kimiya*, Ghazali emphasizes the need to develop good character traits or virtues and curb one's vices, which amounts to *akhlaq*, while he polemicizes against *'ilm al-mu'amalat*, which amounts to the laws of human relations in *fiqh*. In the *Kimiya*, he explains the path of faith (*rah-i din*), which begins with learning about one's *nafs* and perfecting it. A non-specialist in Islamic sciences, representative of the audience of his treatise, cannot or should not have to learn all the details of *fiqh*, and should instead cultivate virtues deep in himself so that he can assuredly act in all challenging situations in accordance with revelation, which for Ghazali as an Ash'ari (determinist theologian) defined right and wrong. Just as in other prescriptive Islamic genres of learning, the proof texts Ghazali relies upon in the *Kimiya* range from the Qur'an and hadith to sayings of sufis and anonymous sages. Ultimately, Ghazali sees training of the *nafs* as the appropriate vehicle for a man to come to an intuitive understanding of the laws of God as he refines his ethical disposition (*khulq*). Ghazali's emphasis on *nafs*-training is evidenced by the fact that the text begins with a discussion on knowledge of the self or *nafs* and the process of perfecting it, rather than beginning with an exposition about knowledge of God or an explanation of specific rules for conducting oneself.

As with Ghazali, Tusi's comparison of *akhlaq* to *fiqh* rests on the difference between the target audiences for the two genres. Tusi's understanding of *akhlaq* is that it provides knowledge for people with the capacity for deep, cosmic thinking. He distinguishes *fiqh* readers and *akhlaq* readers on the basis of their capacity to learn and their depth of understanding. Tusi himself belonged to an Isma'ili-cum-philosophical genealogy more sympathetic to the Mu'tazilite (rationalist theology) position that reason determines right and wrong. Thus, his philosophical position was that the science of *akhlaq* was the path meant for people who could develop virtues through reasoning and through the study of philosophy, while *fiqh* was meant for everyone else, who lacked those capacities. Tusi places ethics of the self, domestic relations, and civic life under the broad rubric of practical philosophy (*hikmat-i 'amali*), as discussed in his introduction to *Akhlaq-i Nasiri* (see figure 1.1).

The other branch of knowledge, complementing practical philosophy (*hikmat-i 'amali*), is speculative philosophy (*hikmat-i naqli*), which includes metaphysics (encompassing theology and prophecy), mathematics, and natural sciences. Tusi finds an overlap between practical philosophy and jurisprudence on the level of broad questions of how human beings are meant to act.[36] Therefore, he includes *fiqh* in his classification of the sciences of practical philosophy, albeit as a tangential field (see figure 1.2).

The two main branches of *fiqh*, known as *'ibadat* (matters of worship) and *mu'amalat* (human transactions), contain rulings on matters that also appear in *akhlaq*. However, because of what Tusi calls the "details of *fiqh*," the methodologies, questions, and sources used to derive

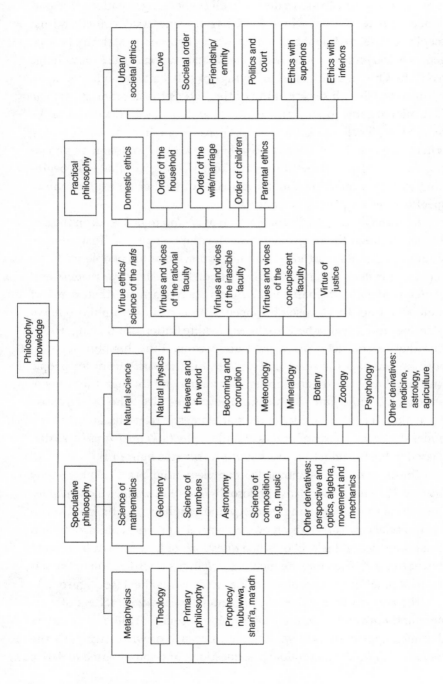

FIGURE 1.1 Nasir ad-Din Tusi's classification of philosophy/all knowledge and wisdom. *Source:* Nasir-ad Din Muhammad ibn Muhammad Tusi, *Akhlaq-i Nasiri*, ed. Mojtaba Minvi and Alireza Haydari (Tehran: Zar, 1977) 37–43.

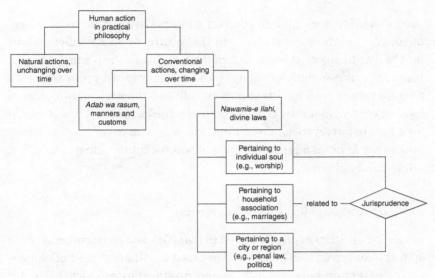

FIGURE 1.2 Nasir ad-Din Tusi's classification of human actions and their laws. *Source*: Nasir-ad Din Muhammad ibn Muhammad Tusi, *Akhlaq-i Nasiri*, ed. Mojtaba Minvi and Alireza Haydari (Tehran: Zar, 1977), 40–41.

rules on these issues are different from the ways in which the philosophical tradition has handled questions of human conduct. *Fiqh* stands outside of *'ilm-i hikmat* (wisdom) altogether; it merely appears as a general subject classified under practical philosophy because of its resemblance to matters in practical philosophy.[37]

In contrast to *fiqh*, *akhlaq* approaches moral conduct and human relations through the science of taming an individual's soul. It provides guidance on creating ethical behavior by cultivating virtues of rationality, intellect, and faith, and by curtailing vices such as anger or hedonism. Based on general rules of the *nafs*, Ghazali, Tusi, and Davani discuss both circumstance- and person-specific ethics. Examples of these include behavior with one's wife, children, friends, parents, employers, teachers, or strangers. The overall emphasis in *akhlaq* centers on understanding the human soul, its psychology, how it acts and reacts to personal and social situations, and, ultimately, what kind of tamed soul or mentality is required to act ethically. This focus on the *nafs* is predominantly what sets *akhlaq* apart from *fiqh*, although the two genres may share similar concerns regarding what constitutes appropriate behavior with certain people. *Akhlaq* does contain abstract concepts in addition to its "rules" of conduct, as the ethicists thought that abstract concepts dictate how best to live. In any case, regardless of the fact that Ghazali and Tusi came from opposing schools of thought and were wrapped up in sectarian polemics, they both held that *fiqh* established the basic parameters of legal or contractual relationships between agents and that it was meant for jurists to purvey to nondiscerning believers, whereas *akhlaq* explained how to act in human relationships and was meant for nonspecialist but intelligent believers.

AKHLAQ IN COMPARISON TO MYSTICISM

While the ethicists explicitly stated that *akhlaq* and jurisprudence (*fiqh*) appeal to different audiences and are based on different methodologies, their distinction between *akhlaq* and mysticism (*tasawwuf*) is more implicit. The ethicists themselves saw parallels between *akhlaq* and mysticism in the act of self-discipline. But they differentiated *akhlaq* as encompassing knowledge of metaphysics and the trilevel virtue ethics program leading to vicegerency, while they viewed mysticism as ascetic practices bringing one closer to the Divine. Although the act of disciplining the *nafs* is a common feature of the two genres, they are distinct in how they describe the process of that discipline and the definition of the *nafs* itself. For example, *akhlaq* contains some references to ascetic preferences that are distinct from or beyond the ethical duty of the individual.[38] Ascetic practice does not necessarily speak to man's ethical and cosmic responsibility for ordering the household and society, hence the need for *akhlaq*'s discussion of such responsibilities according to its own methodologies.

The main overlap that Ghazali, Tusi, and Davani were aware of between sufi thought and *akhlaq* is the central concept of disciplined masculinity, which some scholars have distilled as two separate features of sufism, namely, discipline of the body and soul and chivalrous masculinity. Sa'diyya Shaikh has argued that through sufi discourses' focus on self-transformation, mysticism poses "gender-emancipatory possibilities"; this is because "the primary value of a human being seems to lie in the state of the soul [in relation to God] and not in biology or any other external marker."[39] However, in the course of Shaikh's argument that the teachings of the thirteenth-century sufi master Ibn 'Arabi can support "the goals of Islamic feminism,"[40] she "endeavor[s] to delicately hold together the subtlety and potential carried by a mixed tradition that embodies both androcentric and egalitarian gender narratives."[41] Thus, while texts by Ibn 'Arabi and other sufis can be read for gender neutrality or egalitarianism, their normalization of male bodies and experiences they depict within the spiritual quest of sufism serves as a parallel to those found in *akhlaq* texts.

More specifically, the concept of young manliness (*javanmardi*) in sufi discourses sheds light on not just the ways in which sufi discourses are like *akhlaq* on the level of self-training (albeit with different foci and methods), but also how they are similar to *akhlaq* in their male normativity. Lloyd Ridgeon argues that the concept of *javanmardi* is the cornerstone of sufi spiritual training according to several sufi texts, including one by Suhrawardi (d. 1191), the founder of the Illuminationist School of philosophical sufi thought, of which Davani was an adherent. The genealogy of the term *javanmardi* provides insights into how maleness becomes inextricably linked to what is considered to be spiritual behavior.

Gordon Newby's definition of *muruwwah* as a "manly virtue"—as "a fundamental value of early Arab society [that] was taken over by Islamic peoples in emulation of the Arab model"[42]—explains the concept's persistence as a value for premodern Muslims. Unlike Ignaz Goldzihir, who argues *muruwwah* was "the Arab's" value system that Prophet Muhammad unsuccessfully attempted to replace with *din*, or the new ethical value system brought by religion,[43] Newby explains, through reading the medieval historiographer-sociologist Ibn Khaldun (d. 1406), that *muruwwah* is a natural disposition consistent with religious law, and it relates to concepts of manliness that were incorporated into Muslim ideas.[44]

Parallel to the reappropriated term *muruwwah* as spiritual masculinity are the terms *futuwwat* in Arabic and *javanmardi* (young manliness) in Persian, which Lloyd Ridgeon has shown were similarly reappropriated. *Futuwwat* first appeared in early Arabic literature as a descriptor of groups "who enjoyed a hedonistic lifestyle, whose parties included singing and wine-drinking."[45] In urban centers "ayyari-futuwwat groups had . . . engaged in extortion, violence, and political intrigue."[46] In those examples, manliness was synonymous with corruption and base behaviors, which can be best understood as equating maleness with hegemonic masculinity. Ridgeon explains that despite its indulgent history, the Persian term *javanmardi* (young manliness) reemerged as a direct synonym of *muruwwah*, the appropriated concept of moral masculinity, and completely transformed the notion of *javanmardi* to ideal masculinity that epitomized chivalry and ethics. In the *Qabus Nama*, the concept of *javanmardi* was attributed to "soldiers, merchants and Sufis."[47] Sufis appropriated the term to describe the kind of manliness that was celebrated in mystical or ascetic lifestyles, which signals a tacit debate in the premodern period over what definitively characterized masculinity. For the sufis, *javanmardi* meant "selflessness, loyalty to family and friends, and the observance of the rights owed to God," along with a diversity of opinions as to its details and practices.[48] Ridgeon examines sufi-*futuwwat* texts from the twelfth, fourteenth, and fifteenth centuries to reveal a deeply Qur'anic and Muhammad-oriented discussion of masculinity in which the Prophet's cousin, Ali, is held as the highest standard of chivalrous masculinity.[49] This masculinity was then perfected in sufi-*futuwwat/javanmardi* organizations. These male-only sufi orders excluded women on the basis of their lack of intelligence and spirituality, a parallel rationale for the male-normative framework of *akhlaq*.[50] One sufi treatise declares, "And there is no *futuwwat* for women because the Prophet said, 'They are incomplete in intelligence and in religion.'"[51] Elsewhere in some sufi discourses, the great spiritual accomplishments by women were recorded with a deemphasis on their femaleness and a reinscription of male normativity into their spiritual practices. For example, an Indian sufi Chishti saint named Shaykh Farid-ad din Ganj-i Shakar said of Bibi Fatima Saam, a codisciple of their teacher Shaykh Nizam ad-Din Awliya, that "Fatima Saam is a man that They sent in the shape of a woman."[52]

The ethicists would have been aware of the women's intellectual deficiency hadith because it had a cross-genre presence to justify the diminution of women. For example, Karen Bauer has shown this hadith has been used to interpret a Qur'anic verse that devalues a woman's testimony to half of the worth of a man's testimony and "taken for granted by authors of works in other genres, but [it was] not cited."[53] Although the *akhlaq* texts never explicitly say that ethics are not for women, and they do not quote this hadith that states women are incomplete in intelligence and religion—and, indeed, the texts do recognize women's *nafses*[54] and discuss women's roles—the texts nevertheless share with sufi-*javanmardi* (and other genres) the notion that women are deficient in rationality. This assumption, in effect, excludes women from ethical refinement altogether.

In a similar vein of male training—but retaining the term *muruwwah* instead of *javanmardi* and centering the *akhlaq* genre commitments to the science of perfecting the *nafs*—the ethicists describe how to preserve *muruwwah* (manliness) in two ways. The first is in relation to women's activities, which shows how the ethicists at times defined masculinity through a contrast with femininity. The second, more complex way to preserve *muruwwah* is by having a balanced *nafs*, which in itself is a masculine state of being. Thus, the *akhlaq* concept of *muruwwah* retains the notion of disciplining the male body found in contemporaneous sufi discourses. The ethicists' use of *muruwwah* is concomitant to their understanding of training of the *nafs* and responsibility in virtue ethics to be the masculine embodiment of the broader goal of *akhlaq* itself, namely, achieving happiness and vicegerency of God. *Muruwwah*'s equivalence with the ability to be virtuous, then, becomes a lens through which we can evaluate not just the contrast between men and women, as I discuss in chapter 3, but also concepts of ultimate masculinity—that is, the contrast among men who are thought to possess varying degrees of masculinity in homosocial contexts, as I discuss in chapter 4.

Sufism and *akhlaq* differ in their definitions of the *nafs* and in their worldly and spiritual goals. In *akhlaq,* the *nafs* is the metaphysical self, which must be trained so that its rational faculty rules over other faculties. In sufism, the *nafs* stands for the primal ego and worldly attachments and must be altogether subdued to the angelic spirit (*ruh*) and the heart (*qalb*), which receive spiritual guidance.[55] Although the boundaries around theory and praxis are imperfect, in general, sufism is centered on withdrawing from the worldly as a means of self-transformation and annihilation in God, while *akhlaq* is centered on managing the worldly as a means of enacting God's will.

Because the ethicists were very much part of the broader Muslim intellectual tradition, in which valid forms of knowledge spanned multiple genres that informed personal practice, *akhlaq* serves as an important genre in the constellation of Muslim texts classified as Islamic ethics. In the minds of Ghazali, Tusi, and Davani, *akhlaq* serves as the genre that is most concerned with the metaphysical science of the *nafs* and contains the methodologies for training the *nafs* for the purposes of living the virtuous life as an individual, in family, and in society. Based on the distinctions the ethicists drew between *akhlaq* and other genres, particularly jurisprudence and mysticism, it is clear that the categories over which the ethicists claim knowledge when writing in the *akhlaq* genre are human nature, the metaphysical soul, moral responsibility, and moral action, as well as how each of these translates into household and societal ethics.

Given this epistemological context, what is to be gained by doing a close study of the concepts of gender that emerge from metaphysics and virtue ethics in the *akhlaq* texts? I argue that such a study provides a crucial understanding of the ways in which metaphysics, ontology, the very nature of creation, and moral responsibility in this Islamic discourse are hierarchical, exclusionary, and rooted in male normativity. Specifically, tracing the ethics of the individual, household, and society in these discourses helps us understand a major epistemological thread of moral thought, illuminating how Muslim ethicists justified forms of patriarchy and hierarchy from the metaphysical human subject. Ironically, given that the virtuous life is couched in terms of moral responsibility toward others (the responsibility of *khilafah*, or vicegerency, is discharged within the microcosm–macrocosm plane), as I show in the next chapters, the ethics that emerges from these discourses is one that is built on the utilization of, and at the expense of, others. By reading these texts with close attention to their concepts of gender, we are able to glimpse the epistemological underpinnings of the ethicists' concepts of justice and see how those concepts of justice are reconciled with the ethicists' hierarchal construction of society and their assumption that "nonrational" others, such as women and weak-minded men, exist for the utilization of elite men. Reading these texts through the lens of gender reveals how prescribed gender roles are embedded in the very language and precepts of ethics and in humans' natural state. We look at both male–female relationships in marriage and also male–male relationships in public in order to more fully understand how the Islamic ethics tradition imagines masculinity as a contrast to femininity, and as a heterogeneous property that different men may embody in varying degrees.

THE UNIFIED GHAZALI-TUSI-DAVANI TRADITION

For both historical and substantive reasons, we ought to consider Ghazali's *Kimiya-i Sa'adat*, Tusi's *Akhlaq-i Nasiri*, and Davani's *Akhlaq-i Jalali* as a unified tradition of Islamic ethics. First, historically, the three authors shared common experiences of the political culture of court. At various points in their lives, Ghazali, Tusi, and Davani all served as state-sponsored scholars or court advisors on special matters, such as producing the language of legitimacy of their regimes for popular consumption, enlisting political support from members of the scholarly class (the *'ulama'*), and managing institutions of learning under the state's patronage. Notwithstanding their own religious affiliations and political allegiances, the ethicists Ghazali, Tusi, and Davani were all able to transcend or transition across sectarian or political bounds.[56] All three ethicists belonged to a premodern intellectual tradition that endured historical-political upsets yet still contributed to a cohesive Islamicate culture. In addition to their implicit assumption that philosophical knowledge amounts to practical guidelines for how to live, their texts share a continuity in the development of thought on metaphysics and virtue ethics that composes the ethical tradition. Indeed, this continuity points to the main substantive reason for considering these three ethics texts together: all three firmly employ the trilevel ethical progression from the individual, to family, to society as a unified ethical charge upon men to become microcosms of ethics and vicegerents of God (*khalifahs*). Tracing this trilevel framework reveals how ethical manhood transforms into the patriarchal order of the household and the hierarchical system of society.

Scholars who are concerned with tracing the influence of the Greek tradition on *akhlaq* focus on Tusi and Davani, ignoring Ghazali. They classify Tusi's and Davani's texts with other texts that draw on the Greek ethics tradition, such as Ibn Miskawayh's Arabic text *Tahdhib al-Akhlaq*, and overlook the substantive reasons for including Ghazali's *akhlaq* treatise in that tradition as well.[57] However, Ibn Miskawayh's text does not contain the trilevel ethical progression from the individual to family to society[58] that, I argue, is the hallmark of the Ghazali-Tusi-Davani ethics tradition. The reasons to assimilate Ghazali's *Kimiya-i Sa'adat* with *Akhlaq-i Nasiri* and *Akhlaq-i Jalali* are that, in addition to sharing the same Greek epistemology of deriving virtues from the disciplined soul and the shared definition of *akhlaq* as the most important knowledge a layperson should know, all three texts are structured around the trilevel progression from the individual to family to society from which gendered and hierarchical ideas for the cosmos emerge. One can also argue that Ghazali's text actually more easily dovetails with the Greek tradition because contained in its very title is the term *sa'adat*, or happiness/flourishing. This goal of *akhlaq* closely resembles the Greek philosophical goal of *eudemonia*, also translated as true happiness.

Another pitfall in classification that wrongly separates the Ghazali-Tusi-Davani tradition of ethics is the scholarly commitment to classifying the texts according to the sectarian identities of the ethicists,[59] which undermines the commonalities and analytical unity of their works. While Davani's work represents a synthesis of multiple schools of thought drawn from Sunni, Shi'i, Isma'ili, and Sufi Illuminationist thinkers, the works of Ghazali and Tusi originate in politically opposed camps of Ash'ari-Sunni and Mu'tazili-Isma'ili, respectively. Yet on a number of subjects, the two ethicists rely on similar concepts of the human being's soul and place in the world, and most importantly for my analysis, they produce similar ideas about hierarchy and ethical gender relations. This is not to say that the ethicists' works are all the same, but rather to acknowledge the substantive patterns of Muslim thought that run through each of their works. When it comes to gender norms specifically, whether or not we pay attention to sectarian arguments and rhetorics, what prevails in the texts are assumptions about patriarchy and male dominance in God's cosmos.

In short, Ghazali, Tusi, and Davani all draw on shared experiences and traditions in constructing their ethics, and all three respond to the patterns of life, culture, and customs that made up the premodern Islamicate and Persianate milieu.[60] As concrete evidence that they form a tradition of virtue ethics, we can look to passages of the *Akhlaq-i Jalali* in which Davani quotes both Ghazali's *Kimiya* and Tusi's *Akhlaq-i Nasiri*, sometimes side by side, to compare them or offer his own thesis on a topic.[61] The texts also have a shared legacy as a unified Persian tradition, which I describe later. Moreover, as I explore throughout this book, even though the ethicists hail from different sectarian backgrounds, as discussed in the introduction, and even though Ghazali's text does not fit within the same *falsafa* (peripatetic Muslim philosophy) category as

Tusi's or Davani's texts do, all three have shared epistemological concepts of the self, of the discipline of the male body, and of gender.

Legacy of the Ghazali-Tusi-Davani Tradition of Islamic Ethics

As I outlined in the introduction, the *Kimiya-i Sa'adat*, *Akhlaq-i Nasiri*, and *Akhlaq-i Jalali* were all famously important texts within the lifetimes of their authors. As I show here, the texts have also enjoyed a lively legacy in the centuries since. All three works have come to be celebrated as classical sources of ethics across Persianate lands, including modern-day Turkey, Iran, and India. From these three texts, we can trace a unified historical thread of a metaphysics and virtue ethics tradition, all the way from the eleventh century to contemporary works on ethics. Tracing this lineage not only reveals how these texts function as an ethical tradition unto themselves; it also helps us understand how they have widely influenced Islamic cultures more broadly.

The texts were important sources of political ethics in South Asia throughout the Mughal period. Muzaffar Alam shows that the *Akhlaq-i Jalali*, and possibly the *Akhlaq-i Nasiri* as well, entered South Asia through Davani's disciples, who migrated in the late fifteenth century to Gujarat or the Deccan, where the texts were widely read.[62] Alam postulates that the Mughals appropriated *Akhlaq-i Nasiri* as part of the origin story and legacy of Babur, their founder, who came from the Timurids of Herat. Several recensions of the *Akhlaq-i Nasiri* were prepared for him, such as *Akhlaq-i Muhsini* by Husain Wa'iz al-Kashifi (d. 1504) and *Akhlaq-i Humayuni* by Qazi Ikhtiyar al-Din Hasan al-Husaini (d. circa 1505).[63] These texts pay homage to Tusi and contain the same trilevel progression from individual ethics/metaphysics, to ethics of the household, to ethics of rulership, court, and society. In this way, multiple recensions and reproductions of the *Akhlaq-i Nasiri* and *Akhlaq-i Jalali* appeared throughout South Asian Mughal history and beyond. Alam argues that Mughals read these texts as exemplars of Muslim normativity, in conjunction with sufi thought and in place of shari'a-oriented texts.[64]

The Persian editions of Ghazali, Tusi, and Davani's *akhlaq* texts that I used in this project are modern edited and published versions. In addition to these scholarly edited versions, I also obtained several copies of the treatises from various publishers and locations. One copy of the

Akhlaq-i Jalali from Lucknow, India, is a tattered lithograph publication on acid paper with stapled binding from 1891. This edition, whose cover and frontispiece are pictured in figures 1.3 and 1.4, was the tenth print run by the publisher Neval Kishore (d. 1895), who was a trained *munshi*, or secretary, and native Indian-language teacher employed by the British Empire. Kishore was a celebrated, preeminent bibliographer and publisher who printed, among other works, lithograph versions of Persian texts important to Indian heritage, particularly those important in the Mughal period immediately preceding British colonial occupation. Lithography allowed for widespread dissemination of texts that had previously been available only in manuscript form. Because lithographs were hybrids of typeset and hand-scribing, this format enabled publishers to cheaply reproduce some of the embellishments that had been present in manuscript versions, thus preserving aspects of the earlier manuscript tradition from which they had derived.[65] The lithograph technique conveys both the importance and the ubiquity of these texts among scholars.

An Indian lithograph edition of the *Akhlaq-i Nasiri* has a similar story. The cover and frontispiece, pictured in figures 1.5 and 1.6, features more embellishment than the *Akhlaq-i Jalali*. This edition from 1957 was published by the publishing house of Neval Kishore's son, Tej Kumar, who continued his father's publishing-cum-cultural revitalization project. Both ethics texts merited membership in Neval Kishore's publishing program[66] precisely because, as Alam recounts, they were considered as having great significance to the Indian heritage of Persianate learning and to the Muslim ethical tradition that continued in India.[67]

After the onset of British colonization in India in the eighteenth century temporarily interrupted the development of South Asia's *akhlaq* tradition, the late nineteenth and early twentieth centuries saw the reemergence of this tradition. Partly in response to being colonized, South Asian ethicists sought to promote ideas about how personal conduct is tied to societal flourishing. Some scholarship from this period continued to focus on the Ghazali-Tusi-Davani tradition of tripartite virtue ethics, while others incorporated more hadith and Qur'an, following the lead of scripture-only revivalist movements of the late nineteenth and early twentieth centuries under the rubric of *akhlaq*. Sir Syed Ahmed Khan founded a journal titled *Tahzib-i Akhlaq* (Discipline of

FIGURE 1.3 Cover of the tenth printing of the lithograph of *Akhlaq-i Jalali* by Neval Kishore, Lucknow, 1891.

FIGURE 1.4 Image of the first page of Neval Kishore's lithograph printing of *Akhlaq-i Jalali*, 1891. Lithograph printing allowed for the retention of embellishment art and marginal framing of the text's commentary from the manuscript tradition.

Ethics), which promoted the Muslim tradition of ethical discipline and attempted to create social unity among Indian Muslims leading up to independence from the British. Several books bearing the title *Akhlaq-i Muhammadi* appeared in the early twentieth century, explicitly associating the *akhlaq* tradition with Prophet Muhammad himself.[68]

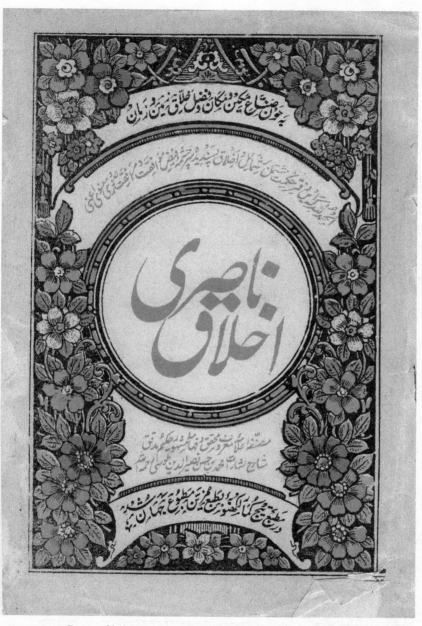

FIGURE 1.5 Cover of lithograph publication of the *Akhlaq-i Nasiri* on acid paper with staple binding. This 1957 printing by Tej Kumar Press, which continued Neval Kishore's mission, evinces the ubiquity and importance of this Persian text in Indian learning.

FIGURE 1.6 The frontispiece of my Indian lithograph edition of the *Akhlaq-i Nasiri*, published by Tej Kumar Press in 1957, attempts to preserve the manuscript embellishment tradition and conveys the importance of the text to twentieth-century Indian Muslims.

In the past thirty-five years alone, these texts have been republished many times over in Iran, India, and Pakistan, all in the original Persian. Since 1977, the edited manuscript of *Kimiya-i Sa'adat* by Hossein Khadivjam has been printed at least fourteen times and has sold more than forty-two thousand copies in Iran. Mojtaba Minvi and Alireza Haydari's edition of *Akhlaq-i Nasiri* from 1975 is less popular than the *Kimiya* among lay people in Iran, but it has been reprinted six times and has sold twenty thousand copies in Iran, an impressive number for a premodern work. In India and Pakistan, several thousand reprinted copies of the hundred-year-old lithograph versions of the *Akhlaq-i Nasiri* and *Akhlaq-i Jalali* still exist.[69] A Persian and Urdu edition by Hafiz Shabir Ahmad Haidery was completed in 2007; the translator states that there is sustained interest in the work in India, which prompted him to retranslate the work from late-nineteenth-century editions into Urdu and publish it as a modern edition.[70] The critical edition I use here, edited by Abdullah Masoudi Arani, was published in 2013 in Tehran, further evidence of renewed Iranian interest in the work.

Center and Periphery: Audience and Language

By some measures, these texts may be seen as esoteric philosophical ethics of elites, hovering on the periphery of Muslim thought. The texts belong to the philosophical corpus rather than the legal or mystical discourses, and they are written in Persian rather than the Arabic language of scholars—two features that would seem to limit the texts' larger cultural relevance to Muslims. And yet, as I argued earlier, their presence in the philosophical corpus is actually one reason they are central to understanding gender in Islamic ethics. Further, as I argue here, the fact that they are written in Persian is itself a reason for their broad historical and sociological significance: Persian-language treatises long enjoyed wider historical influence than Arabic texts did. Brian Spooner and William Hannaway explain that within a century and a half of the Arabo-Islamic expansion into Persian lands in 651, the Persian language was reintroduced to court and administration using Arabic script, "supplant[ing] Arabic into a niche."[71] Starting in the eighth and ninth centuries and continuing until the British occupation of South Asia in the nineteenth century, Persian was a language of administration and literature from the Balkans to China.[72] As Spooner and Hannaway argue, "No other language has ever maintained such a monopoly of the medium of writing over so large a territory for so long a period." They noted, "Persian provided the vocabulary that served as the medium not only for the continuation of protocols of administration, diplomacy, and public life . . . but also for important cultural features relating to administration and social norms for the whole society."[73] The ethics texts of Ghazali, Tusi, and Davani are part of that expansive cultural literature in the Persian language that established norms for both government administration and society as a whole.

For Ghazali, Tusi, and Davani, Persian represented the language of the masses. The *Kimiya*, *Akhlaq-i Nasiri*, and *Akhlaq-i Jalali* are all written for elite men, yet they also represent the ethicists' deliberate attempts to shift their audience from the Arabic-medium *'ulama'* to court elites and other upper-class members of society who would not necessarily know Arabic. In Ghazali's introduction to the *Kimiya*, he comments, "In this book, we explain these topics . . . for Persian speakers . . . if someone wishes for more methodical and fine [information] above this, he should seek out Arabic[74] books . . . for the scope of this book is the general population who have begged for such a work in Persian, and the language has been produced for the boundaries of their understanding."[75]

This comment reveals that even Ghazali sensed the importance of catering to the more expansive Persian demographic despite Arabic being the scholars' language. Travis Zadeh has shown that an important debate in the early medieval period, one that demonstrated the Persian vernacularization of the Qur'an itself, was whether ritual use of Persian translations was permissible in prayer and recitation.[76] This was a widespread question given the volume of Persian translations of the Qur'an, which indicates its normative use in recitation and sometimes prayer.[77] Even though Ghazali viewed such bilingual ritual use of the Qur'an as problematic, he held that Persian was the language in which to teach about ethics to the masses.[78] Ghazali intended his work to be not just for a Persian-speaking audience, but also for a nonscholarly one. Within the text itself, in the instances he needs to use lengthy quotations from hadiths or nonprophetic sayings, Ghazali provides only his Persian translations of them, not the Arabic originals. He does not assume that the Persian-language reader knows Arabic, even though all intellectuals of his age would have been expected to.

Like Ghazali, Tusi wrote his first treatise on ethics, the *Akhlaq-i Muhtashimi*, in Arabic; however, surviving manuscripts include a Persian translation with the original Arabic.[79] His second ethics work, the more famous *Akhlaq-i Nasiri*, was composed in Persian. Indeed, Hamid Dabashi and Farhad Daftary credit Tusi with a major expansion of technical prose in the Persian language because of the unprecedented Nizari Isma'ili move to make Persian their religious language. Tusi's writings also encouraged others to write on philosophical and theological topics in Persian.[80]

Davani, too, chose Persian over Arabic to write about ethics. Most of Davani's other works were written in Arabic, but *Akhlaq-i Jalali* was an important exception, and incidentally, it became his most famous work. The text contains many references to Persian stories and anecdotes that were circulating at the time, suggesting an even more expansive audience than that of the *Kimiya* and *Akhlaq-i Nasiri*. The work continued to be popular in its original Persian in Mughal India for centuries to come.

In the case of all three texts, making the genre of *akhlaq* accessible to Persian speakers was imperative because Persian was becoming an important Islamicate language of learning, and Arabic no longer dominated the Islamic milieu. Writing in Persian made these ethics texts available to a wider readership, extending their accessibility beyond the Arabic-speaking intellectuals to the predominantly Persian-speaking population of central Muslim lands, or at least the elite among them who may have been interested in scholarship, such as the court patricians or administrators. Although the three ethicists were not seeking to popularize *akhlaq* widely, they certainly did have a broad audience of educated nonscholars in mind. This expansiveness of purpose is in line with their stated goal of cultivating *akhlaq* in those who had the ability to flourish (achieve *sa'adat*) or reach God's vicegerency (*khilafah*). As I show in the next chapter, such an audience comprised only elite men for these three ethicists.

GENDER ANALYTICS FOR *AKHLAQ*

If these three *akhlaq* treatises are important to study, and particularly important to study together in the context of their vast legacy, how then should we go about this work? What questions ought we ask of these texts, beyond simply what makes them Islamic or not? My stance in this book is that the texts warrant investigation into how they construct gender: that we ought to examine what ideas about masculinity, femininity, and gender relations emerge from the texts. These gender constructions are important to understand because they are broadly illuminating for the larger philosophical and Islamic traditions on how to live. In the subsequent chapters of this book, the project of analyzing and uncovering gender constructions is taken up through feminist close readings of classical Islamic ethical texts. In the remainder of this chapter, I set forth the analytical lens that I will apply in these close readings. I derive this lens from two distinct areas of gender theory: from feminist studies, I draw on three theses about concepts of gender normativity, and from masculinity studies, I draw on historical and textual constructions of masculinity. Throughout the book's other chapters, I also draw heavily on feminist history of the Islamic intellectual tradition, particularly where comparisons with feminist reflections on *tafsir* (Qur'anic exegesis), *fiqh* (jurisprudence), or *tasawwuf* (sufism) shed light on ethical imperatives in the *akhlaq* texts. I weave this scholarship together into an analytic that I use to understand classical Islamic texts' notions of gender.

Femininity

One set of tools for understanding and evaluating *akhlaq* are the concepts put forth by feminist historians, philosophers, and theorists to deal with the male-centrism of analogous texts from the Greek canon, ancient Mediterranean patriarchy, and beyond. Three theses have particular salience for understanding aspects of the *akhlaq* texts that resonate with their Hellenic precursors: (1) males are presented as the default universal, with females as derivative and subordinate; (2) masculinity is associated with reason, objectivity, and transcendence, while femininity is associated with irrationality, matter, and immanence; and (3) the male-centered nature of foundational and theoretical concepts in philosophical texts can and should be exposed through gendered interpretations of those texts. An additional fourth concern, to which I will return in the concluding chapter, is the question of whether male normativity is intrinsic or extrinsic to the ethical tradition.[81]

The first thesis I draw from feminist philosophers is their explanation of the male normativity of the Greek canon, in which males are presented as the default and universal while females are construed as derivative and subordinate through the materialization of their bodies. Luce Irigaray argued provocatively that this is the foundational flaw in Greek philosophical texts: they are male-oriented and omit the female entirely, treating them as nonhuman objects.[82] Her main critique of Hellenic philosophy in *This Sex Which Is Not One* is that because philosophers do not recognize sexual differences, they present the male body as the universal human.[83] When philosophers do recognize women, it is only in the latter's capacity as vessels, as the maternal-feminine. Irigaray states:

> If traditionally, and as a mother, woman represents place for man, such a limit means that she becomes a thing. . . . Moreover, the maternal-feminine also serves as an envelope, a container, the starting point from which man limits his things. The relationship between envelope and things constitutes one of the aporias, or the aporia, of Aristotelianism and of the philosophical systems derived from it.[84]

For Irigaray, the maternal creative power in reproduction is at odds with men's relegation of women's bodies to inanimate things. She argues that men deny women's biological capability of motherhood as a subjective, rather than objective, power because "the woman-mother is '*castrating*.' Which means that, since her status as envelope and as thing(s) has not been interpreted, she remains inseparable from the work or act of man, notably insofar as he defines her and creates *his* identity with her as his starting point."[85] Here, Irigaray is pointing to how women's creative power is threatening to masculinity, so men use their power over women to define women and extract benefits from them.

This conversion of female subjects into objects happens in the *akhlaq* texts as well. Regarding medieval Muslim thinkers, Kathryn Kueny has argued that physicians and jurists would attempt to control women and reproduction by medicalizing the childbirth process and prioritizing the paternal rights.[86] Evidence of the Muslim ethicists' participation in this attempt to reinscribe the male role in reproduction is obvious in their replication of Aristotle's concept of hylomorphism in their account of biological reproduction in the *akhlaq* texts.[87] Hylomorphism, the idea that form and matter are combined in order to create new physicality, has been associated with gendered notions of metaphysics that privilege male life-forms over female ones. Charlotte Witt has argued that Aristotle's hylomorphism (and that of Maimonides, as Susan Shapiro has shown)[88] represents a gendered metaphysics in which form (male) is primary and better than matter (female), while she further argues that these gendered ideas are extrinsic to Aristotle's ethics.[89]

Irigaray's account of Greek philosophy, that it ignores sexual differences in the objectification of women's bodies and thus sees them as non-persons, is a powerful critique that applies to *akhlaq* to a certain extent. However, the *akhlaq* genre recognizes women's creative powers based on their ability to bear children, rather than their possession of intellect. Women's ability to bear children is actually the secondary reason for male primacy, as the primary reason is their belief that women's *nafses* possess weaker resolve, less intellectual potential, and overemotionality. More central is Irigaray's point, mentioned earlier, about the way male identity itself is often defined in philosophy by using women as a contrast. The Muslim philosophical ethicists likewise need women to make an appearance in their cosmology, as well as less intellectual men, in order to make ideal ethical manhood more robust.

The second salient thesis I derive from feminist philosophy, namely, from Simone de Beauvoir, is masculinity's association with rationality and transcendence by contrast to femininity's association with matter and immanence. This dichotomy helps to illuminate what I call the metaphysical tension in *akhlaq*. As I will show in the chapters that follow, the inextricable relationship between maleness and reason creates a metaphysical tension in the assigned moral value of women because of their recognizable humanity but perceived weak rationality. In *The Second Sex*, Beauvoir argues that a "woman is not born, but, rather becomes one" through sociocultural experiences. Even though a woman's role cannot be essentialized as a characteristic of her body, those experiences that define woman also define her as secondary and instrumental: "She is defined and differentiated with reference to man and not he with reference to her; she is the incidental, the inessential as opposed to the essential. He is the Subject, he is the Absolute and she is the Other."[90] Beauvoir refers to this trait as women's immanence, or their existence and actions within a system. She then contrasts this trait with male transcendence, which exists beyond the physical realm. Although transcendence is explicitly attributed to men, women implicitly possess it as well, by virtue of being self-conscious human beings. However, sociocultural forces constrain women to immanence, thereby creating a tension between transcendence and immanence. Beauvoir explains how this tension arises: "[Men] propose to stabilize her as object and to doom her to immanence since her transcendence is to be overshadowed and forever transcended by another ego (conscience) which is essential and sovereign."[91] This immanence–transcendence dichotomy is a key lens through which I read the ethicists' concept of the *nafs*, which is normalized male and is sometimes translated as the ego, and through which I understand how men are in charge of women and utilize them through marriage for their own process of transcendence.

The third thesis that I draw from the feminist engagement with philosophy addresses how to expose the male-centered nature of foundational and theoretical concepts in philosophical texts through gendered interpretations of those texts. Such textual interpretations give rise to a methodology for reading concepts of the feminine in works that are, like all the *akhlaq* texts, produced solely for a male audience and are mostly about male homosocial relationships. In texts addressed to men about men, how does one look for women and their roles? Carolyn Krosmeyer defines such a method of reading as looking for "gendered concepts [that], lacking any obvious references to males or females, or to masculinity and femininity, nevertheless are formulated in such a way that their neutral quality and universal applicability are questionable."[92] In her work on gender in rhetoricity and textuality in works by Maimonides, which also draws on shared Greek epistemologies, Susan Shapiro proposes that references, stories, and metaphors in the texts say more about the texts' gender assumptions than about the actual meaning and logic discerned from the texts. In particular, she argues that metaphors of women and the body in Maimonides's *The Guide of the Perplexed* and other philosophical texts, even those that are not explicitly about gender relations, have real-life consequences in creating a culture of gender hierarchy. The philosophical text does not remain esoteric and theoretical; rather, it plays an important part in creating culture.[93] Thus, it is not really possible to ignore the male-centered nature of philosophical ethics texts such as *akhlaq*. Even when a text does not speak on gender directly, it formulates a tradition of male primacy upon which all later ethics are built. The result is an erasure of women by abstraction.

To fully articulate the principle of the third thesis, that a gender-based critique of foundational and theoretical concepts in philosophy uncovers their phallocentrism, we can turn to Judith Butler's discussion of how the gender constructions found in the texts operate in creating gendered ethical norms.[94] Butler holds that the embodiment of sex and gender takes place through scripted expressions of "corporeal style."[95] She explains: "gender is an act which has been rehearsed, much as a script survives the particular actors who make use of it, but which requires individual actors in order to be actualized and reproduced as reality once again."[96] The scripts from which an individual performs gender can change over time and space, depending on personal maturation, historical and cultural shifts within one's lifetime, and movement from place to place. As I show, the ethicists are offering particular scripts to their male readers that depict ethical masculinity as well as what they should expect ethical women to perform. Referring back to Beauvoir's concept of male transcendence and female immanence, the scripts in *akhlaq* are ones in which men are expected to be concerned with the lofty goals of life, putting rational faculties above corporeal ones and thus becoming disembodied, while women are expected to content themselves with performing motherhood and the virtue of self-restraint.

Although these feminist characterizations of the feminine in the Greek/Western philosophical canon can help illuminate the *akhlaq* treatises, there is one major caveat that prevents the wholesale adoption of feminist critiques that are not intended for the Islamic context: namely, Ghazali, Tusi, and Davani explicitly admit that women have *nafses*, which is a tacit admission of women's humanity. For example, Ghazali states that women, like men, are humans prone to the behavioral pitfalls of the *nafs*.[97] I characterize this recognition of women's *nafses* as a metaphysical tension in *akhlaq* with respect to women's beings, as discussed in chapter 3. And this tension, I argue, suggests a possible opening for *akhlaq*'s feminist recovery in the style of Martha Nussbaum, Marcia Homiak, Sarah Pessin, and Idit Dobbs-Weinstein, who argue that phallocentrism is not intrinsic to ancient Greek or medieval Jewish philosophy. Still, despite their implicit acknowledgment of women's humanity, the ethicists do make some outright misogynistic comments about women in relation to their *nafses*. For example, the ethicists categorically state that women are deficient in rationality and are overly emotional, and thus must be ruled by their husbands. Moreover, they depict deficiencies of the *nafs* that belong to all humans as essentially feminine characteristics, thus solidifying the male-centrism of the science of *akhlaq* (ethical ordering of the self, household, and society). As I elaborate later, in the ethicists' process of defining ethical men, they create the same metaphysical tension between the elite men who constitute their intended audience and the lower-class or intellectually deficient men who are assumed to be incapable of embodying the perfect masculinity that the texts seek to inculcate.

Masculinity and Homosociality

Like femininity, masculinity is constructed; and the construction of masculinity that the ethicists present is synonymous with the process of becoming ethical. My gender analytic requires not only a feminist critique of the texts' conception of women, but also a framework for understanding how normative masculinity is constructed in the texts. The texts present ethics as the process of creating an ethical male: the male-as-process is the code of ethics itself, and the creation of an ethical world revolves around this male. Although there is a long history of texts outlining the portrait of the ideal Muslim, referring only to men and their concerns, the actual category of Muslim or Islamic masculinity is relatively new. As Oystein Holter explains, "research on gender does not just challenge the division between masculine and feminine, it challenges the division between neutral and gendered."[98] One consequence of the universalization of men is that institutions that are perceived as neutral are actually male or male-dominated structures. In *akhlaq*, the political and civic institutions are imagined as part of the male-only public sphere, even though they are presented as universal. This feature of the texts moves our understanding of gender in them beyond their prescribed structures for women's oppression (due to their relegation to the private realm), toward considering how gender, inclusive of masculinity, is construed in both public and private forms of patriarchy.

Given the universalized masculinity of the texts, I also draw on masculinity studies more broadly to theorize how the texts construct ideal manhood. Amanullah De Sondy argues that the Qur'an constructs multiple forms of being male and thus theorizes that Islamic masculinities exist in the plural.[99] Recalling Beauvoir's assertion that "one is not born, but rather becomes, a woman," so too Lahoucine Ouzgane theorizes that the study of Islamic masculinities from "a social constructionist perspective [is] premised on the belief that men are not born; they are made; they construct their masculinities within particular social and historical contexts. Masculinities in Muslim contexts emerge as a set of distinctive practices defined by men's positioning within a variety of religious and social structures."[100] Raewyn Connell explains that the social structures "includ[e] large-scale institutions and economic relations as well as face-to-face relationships and sexuality. Masculinity is institutionalized in this structure, as well as being an aspect of individual character or personality."[101] Thus, in order to examine how the texts present masculinity as a process that is enacted in stages, I follow the ethical arc of the treatises themselves, considering the ethics of the individual (chapter 2), the ethics of how men are prescribed to act in the private institutions of marriage and the household (chapter 3), and the ethics of public, homosocial institutions such as court, the bazaar, the mosque, and other locations where men interact with friends, enemies, superiors, and inferiors (chapter 4).

The *akhlaq* texts define ethical masculinity in contrast to what I refer to, using Connell's term, as hegemonic masculinity. She defines hegemonic masculinity as "vehement and violent . . . [with] severe cost, in terms of injury, ill health, and other constraints on life," while still being the most "honored or desired" form of masculinity.[102] Hegemonic masculinity is the lowliest and basest of the masculinities, yet it is held up as the most exemplary or essential way to be male and contrasted with femininity.[103] Connell speaks of hegemonic masculinity as it emerges in contemporary Western cultures with respect to violence done in a variety of contexts to men, women, and individuals who are transgender or homosexual, in the name of preserving or imposing an ideal masculinity. A parallel concept to hegemonic masculinity in the Islamic tradition is the Qur'anic concept of *an-nafs al-ammara bi'-su*, which translates to "the soul is prone to evil," a concept that is used to explain how certain people condone or partake in immoral acts.[104] In this book, the concept of hegemonic masculinity serves as a framework to examine the ways in which *akhlaq* texts provide a corrective discourse against unethical activities that were perceived as manly in premodern Muslim societies but that were out of sync with morality and ethical masculinity as delineated in the texts. The ethicists use the term *muruwwah* to describe essential manhood in the context of ethical codes that are meant to uplift the individual to realize his potential as an ethical microcosm of the world. The very goal of *akhlaq* is to take the lowly man naturally prone to behavior of hegemonic masculinity and discipline his body and soul into a virtuous vicegerent of God.

Ethical masculinity is constructed through social relations, specifically homosociality. The construct of male homosociality is essential for understanding the portrait of ideal masculinity in the *akhlaq* texts since the enterprise of ethics itself is knowledge transferred from men to other men, which in turn inculcates the moral prerequisites not just to rule over women, but also to rule over other men in the public, ideally homosocial male world. Apart from their chapters on marriage, the ethicists frame all guidelines for social interactions, including love and friendship, in terms of male homosocial relationships. The ethics of same-sex social interactions reveal how the ethicists imagined social interactions to work in general; they viewed male homosocial relations as universal and heterosocial relations as exceptional situations that required different guidelines. Homosociality was the ultimate expression of a patriarchally structured society in which men interacted with one another in a world that theoretically belonged to men, whether or not reality reflected this ideal.

Homosocial relationships between men occur in public institutions, which become the sites for enacting ethical behavior as well as male behavior. Masculinities are constructed in social institutions and interact with one another (homosocially) within those institutions. This phenomenon can be considered what Sylvia Walby theorized as the *public* phase of patriarchy, which is distinct from the *private* phase.[105]

Although Walby describes patriarchy that unfolds in sequence and in a world in which women occupy public spaces as well, the distinction between the public and private phases of patriarchy is useful in that it provides a dichotomy that describes the ideal gender-segregated world of the ethicists. In private patriarchy, men subordinate women to fulfill their own personal needs, while in public patriarchy, men compete with and subordinate one another to fulfill their social needs.

This framework requires close reading of men's roles within institutional structures in which they hold power, which includes both marriage and civil society. Within structural institutions, Connell describes how masculinities operate in relation to one another: "Different masculinities do not sit side-by-side like dishes on a smorgasbord. . . . There are relations of hierarchy, for some masculinities are dominant while others are subordinated or marginalized."[106] This hierarchism also applies to men occupying various rungs of the intellect-/profession-based social hierarchy that exists in the *akhlaq* texts, which I discuss in chapter 4.

The presence or absence of women from institutions and public life profoundly shapes constructions of masculinity. Nancy Partner argues that even in gender segregation, medieval men and women in premodern Europe thought of one another and were imagined by scholars as always together.[107] This is true in Muslim texts as well, to the extent that men and women serve as behavioral foils for one another through idealized gender segregation. Carole Hillenbrand has argued that in Persianate regions in the Saljuq period, Islamic texts convey an ideal gender segregation that was distinct from the historical reality of prevailing heterosocial interactions.[108] While several other scholars have also shown that the ideals of gender segregation did not reflect social reality,[109] as I discuss in greater detail in chapters 3 and 4, these *akhlaq* texts on the construction of ethical masculinity have everything to do with women since the ethicists use their stereotypes of women's behavior and femininity as foils for masculinity. My point here is an extension of Susan Shapiro's observation that texts that are meant to be universal tell us about gendered norms. The *akhlaq* texts only discuss heterosocial interactions in the narrow scope of ethical behaviors in marriage and kin relations, but they discuss homosocial relationships in terms of a full range of interactions in both public and private spheres. To understand the nature of ethics is to understand how ethics is synonymous with maleness—sometimes as defined through the absence or presence of women—since ethics is the male-as-process, the male unfolding through the process of discipline, that describes how one can be ethical as an individual, in a family, and as a member of society.

The marginalization of women from ethics, and specifically from the process of creating the ideal male homosocial institution, is not done simply because women are meant to be secluded. Rather, the marginalization of women is an important mechanism by which men compete with one another for power. Holter explains that the traditional view of gender hierarchy is that it emanates from and is created by men in positions of power, but researchers have recently explored the idea that gender hierarchy actually emerges when men have a lack of power in relation to other men. Though this insight comes from studies on violence against women or prostitution in modern contexts, it points to how men can always seek to have power over some women even when they may not have power over other men.[110] In other words, women are marginalized at the expense of men's struggle to rise in social rank among themselves. This framework is a compelling one for examining not only how male power is maintained in the domestic realm over women, but also how male power is maintained over men in hierarchical male homosocial institutions.

As I set forth earlier, my gender analytic in this book consists of feminist critiques of metaphysics and virtue ethics as male normative systems that treat women as instrumental/immanent and men as foundational/transcendent. Throughout this book, I pay attention to the ways that ethical masculinity is constructed in contrast to base, hegemonic masculinity, as well as in contrast to, and power over, women and weak men. Much of this practice of developing ethical masculinity and power takes place within male homosocial institutions, in which men are supposed to be practicing ethical disciplines together, even if they compete with one another.

The *akhlaq* texts' methodological origins in Greek philosophy call for more than just a discussion of what makes these texts Islamic. Indeed, reading the three texts together, as a unified tradition, yields both historical and analytical payoffs. The historical payoff is the understanding of how the *akhlaq* genre demonstrates a continuity in ethical thought on how to live, and the analytical payoff is the revelation of the concepts of gender that emerge from the *akhlaq* ethics of how to live. The feminist critiques of Greek philosophy and feminist engagements with Jewish philosophy help demonstrate how the *akhlaq* texts are not unique in their patriarchy, and when taken together with theories of masculinity, these concepts serve as a heuristic for understanding the gendered nature of *akhlaq*.

Embedded within the Ghazali-Tusi-Davani tradition are the complex origins of ethics itself. Those origins are at once spiritual (Islamic in particular) and intellectual: they combine Platonic and Aristotelian virtue ethics, deontological recommendations for moral duties set by the Qur'an, sayings by the Prophet Muhammad, the general contours of Islamic jurisprudence, the philosophical science of reason and logic, a teleological philosophy for the maximization of social good, and a mystical understanding of the individual as a mirror of the cosmos and the Creator. The three authors' *akhlaq* texts are implicitly Islamic, but also unapologetically rooted in the Greek and ancient Mediterranean traditions. The Ghazali-Tusi-Davani tradition is grounded in the broader historical and epistemological discourses of Greco-Islamic knowledge that contested the nature of ethics itself and debated the best way to live. The tradition defines ethics in terms of the happiness/flourishing (*sa'adat*), in the Aristotelian sense of *eudemonia*, that could be achieved through an Islamic conception of the world. Through these texts, the ethicists generated a gendered cosmology deeply rooted in philosophical ideas that permeated all genres of Muslim thought and praxis about how to live as an individual, in a family, and in society. In particular, the concept of *khilafah*, or human vicegerency of the Divine, is a Qur'anic concept through which the ethicists move from the human place in the macrocosm of the universe to becoming a microcosm. For the ethicists, a man's responsibility to be a vicegerent of the Divine is enacted by ascending the trilevel scale of ethics.

The purpose of this chapter was to reconfigure the *akhlaq* tradition in terms of its epistemology and context in order to construct an analytic for reading gender in the texts. First, I traced the texts' Greek methodologies and their self-reflexive descriptions of their own ethical endeavors in the context of other Islamic ethics genres in order to understand the historical continuity and cohesive nature of the texts' ethical ideas on how to live as an individual, in a family, and in society. Then, in order to lay the foundation for the feminist close readings in the chapters to follow, I developed a lens for analyzing and understanding the texts' notions of gender. This gender analytic draws on concepts of gender f̶ ̶feminist critiques of the Greek and Greek-inspired philosophical ̶s as well as from theories of masculinity. These concepts serve ̶uristic for understanding the ethical endeavors of the *akhlaq* ̶s. Although the three texts exist in particular medieval historical moments and draw on specific epistemologies, they would also go on to provide the foundational model for Muslim ethical gender discourses over centuries to follow. In the remaining chapters, I deploy this gender analytic to explore the question of how the ethicists constructed a male-centered metaphysics and virtue ethics, and to tease out the contradictions and consequences that arise as a result of these gendered ethics.

CHAPTER TWO

Gendered Metaphysics, Perfection, and Power of the (Hu)man's Soul

All animals are equal, but some animals are more equal than others.

—GEORGE ORWELL

George Orwell's quip from *Animal Farm* highlights the possibility of an ostensibly egalitarian system actually reinforcing hierarchy. We see this tension within the Ghazali-Tusi-Davani ethics tradition: on the one hand, these ethicists believed in metaphysical equality and advocated for men to treat others fairly on that basis, but on the other hand, they deployed the tools of their metaphysics to create a hierarchy of being. In this chapter, I demonstrate the ways in which the *akhlaq* texts of the Ghazali-Tusi-Davani tradition construct the normative ethical *nafs* (or self) as male, and as metaphysically and morally superior to the rest of creation, despite the texts' principle of metaphysical equality of all matter. Passages within the three *akhlaq* texts articulate the science of the individual *nafs*, the component faculties that compose the *nafs*, and the kinds of virtues and vices that emerge when certain faculties are expressed with varying intensity. I argue that these passages on virtue ethics concern more than just the refinement of individual character; indeed, the ethicists lay out a hierarchical cosmology in which elite male-centered individual virtue ethics are the building blocks of ethical society itself. Yet, crucially, this hierarchical cosmology is also disrupted by inconsistencies in the texts' gendered notions of metaphysics and their reliance on rationality.

To gender the primary ethical subject as male is problematic, as this move tends to gender the path of ethics itself as male. This critique is one that French feminist philosopher Luce Irigaray leveled against the philosophy of Plato and Aristotle. She pointed out that throughout history, "Everything concerning the relations between the subject and discourse, the subject and the world, the subject and the cosmic, the microcosmic and the macrocosmic . . . has always been written in the masculine form, as man, even when it claimed to be universal or neutral."[1] It is upon the Greek tradition of Plato and Aristotle that the *akhlaq* texts build their notions of the ethical man as a microcosm of the greater macrocosm. Like the Greek philosophers, the Muslim ethicists hold that human beings are created equal among all other physical matter created by God, but that not all human *nafses* or souls are equal. Instead, all *nafses* are arranged in a hierarchy based on intellect, along gendered and class-based lines. The ethicists describe the perfected individual self in particularly masculine terms, characterizing this ideal individual as the ethical head of his family and community, even using the Persian equivalent (*'alam-i saghir*) for the Greek term *microcosm* to evoke his role as a building block of the just, ethical larger world that he mirrors as a *khalifah*, or vicegerent of God.[2]

Building on my close readings of the ethical texts of Ghazali, Tusi, and Davani, I further argue in this chapter that the Muslim ethicists' male-centered cosmology is not perfectly maintained or substantiated in their texts. Rather, their arguments contain fissures, particularly with regard to their notions of metaphysical equality and their ideas about women possessing human intelligence. The few exceptions to their own rules about feminine inferiority reveal how the feminine disrupts their idealistic notions of society as exclusively male-centered and -controlled, even on the existential and metaphysical levels. As I return to in the conclusion of this book, these contradictions within *akhlaq* warrant greater feminist philosophical reflection.

In this chapter, which explicates the gendered/hierarchical nature of metaphysics in the *akhlaq* tradition, I first raise linguistic questions about the term *nafs*, arguing that real gender concerns arise from this term even though it is grammatically feminine in Arabic, and even though Persian-language pronouns are gender-neutral. Second, I closely analyze passages on the science of the *nafs*, including each of its faculties and respective virtues and vices, to demonstrate that the entire science of the *nafs* and path to ethical refinement are constructed in male terms. Even the virtue of justice, which is an individual's achievement of vicegerency of God and creating conditions of happiness for all, is both male-gendered and hierarchical, and therefore, I argue, promotes an unjust notion of justice. Finally, I situate the ideal ethical male self in hierarchical relation to the texts' constructions of animals, plant life, women, and other men to show how this hierarchy in fact disrupts the ethicists' imagined enterprise of male ethical perfection. My analysis of the metaphysics suggests that the ethicists' ideal hierarchy based on gradations in intellect and spirituality is at odds with their own male-centered cosmology. The possibility of women or lower-class men possessing great rationality and the texts' evident commitment to the metaphysics of equality both work to disrupt the male-oriented nature of the science of the *nafs*, and therefore the very tools of *akhlaq* itself.

GENDERED GRAMMAR AND THE *NAFS*

The grammatical nature of the term *nafs* has long masked discussions of its male-centeredness. Specifically, the texts have an unintentionally gender-egalitarian tone because the Persian language uses gender-neutral pronouns, and because the term *nafs* in Arabic is itself grammatically feminine. In this section, I show that a grammatical analysis of pronouns and the term *nafs* is insufficient to assume the gender inclusivity in *akhlaq* texts.

The first grammatically based reason why the texts appear upon first glance to be inclusive of both[3] genders, and to address the whole of humanity, is that in the Persian language, the third-person, gender-neutral pronoun, *u*,[4] is used for both "he" and "she." For this reason, passages from the Persian ethics texts can be perceived as gender-ambiguous or gender-inclusive when taken out of context. One translator of the *Kimiya*, Jay R. Crook, comments that "the female reader should not feel slighted or ignored when the translator uses the general masculine" because "Persian does not have gender-specific pronouns.... Ghazali certainly did not intend to restrict salvation and spiritual happiness to males."[5] Here, Crook inadvertently concedes that the gender-neutral pronouns really refer only to men, but nonetheless he imposes gender inclusivity onto Ghazali's intent. And he does so without questioning how gender inclusivity can be read in a text that is substantively addressed only to men.

It is true that the gender-neutral pronouns in Persian create greater accessibility to the texts for modern female readers, and that the translation of Persian texts into English imposes an artificial loss of grammatical gender neutrality. However, we cannot conclude from this that the ethicists intended their texts to be read by both men and women. On the contrary, Ghazali, Tusi, and Davani explicitly state that women do not have the requisite sophisticated intellects or reasoning ability, or even control over their own *nafses*.[6] To be sure, contemporary readers who seek to apply *akhlaq* to their lives today are not obliged to read the texts in the male-centered way their authors intended. Nevertheless, it is crucial to record the gendered nature of the *akhlaq* ethics in order to discern the deeply engrained, systematic gender biases that render this system unethical by today's standards.

As amina wadud points out in *Qur'an and Woman*, context and authorial intent are key to understanding whether the gender ambiguity is created from the use of plural male pronouns (which may include females) in Arabic texts. Women must be written into the text explicitly unless there is reason to believe that any use of plural male pronouns includes women. These grammatical issues raise a problem of method in Muslim feminist hermeneutics: how to distinguish general prescriptions in religious texts from exclusively male ones. With respect to the Qur'an, wadud interprets that

> every usage of the masculine plural form is intended to include males and females, equally, unless it includes specific indication for its exclusive application to males. . . . As there is no form exclusively for males, the only way to determine if the masculine plural form . . . ([for example] *al-tullab fi al-ghurfah*) is exclusively for male . . . would be through some specific indication in the text. Thus: [the example] *Al-tullab wa al-talibat fi al-ghurfah* indicates that the use of the masculine plural (*al-tullab*) refers exclusively to males since the inclusion of the female plural form distinguishes the female students present.[7]

Here wadud's point is that there is no way to know whether a text excludes women in its usage of masculine plural form unless there are specific contexts or applications in which it is clear that the pronouns apply only to men. In the case of the Qur'an, assuming that its authorial intent is to extend the text's audience to all of humanity, it makes sense to assume that plural masculine pronouns include women, except if they appear with feminine plural pronouns or seem to be only referring to men by context or application of a verse.

In the case of the *akhlaq* texts, the context and applications of ethical precepts show that the usage of the Persian gender-neutral pronouns in the entirety of the texts, with few exceptions, is in fact intended to refer only to men. The seeming inclusiveness of the gender-neutral pronoun is merely a mask for the male exclusiveness of the texts' content and their specific ethical precepts. The substance of the treatises makes undeniable what the authors intend. As I show throughout the rest of this book, the authorial intent is to address men about their ethics in a variety of situations: when alone, when with one's wife, as head of a domestic economy, in society, with friends, at court, and so on. The ethical precepts presented in the texts are meant to apply exclusively to men.

In the important exceptions where pronouns should be read as inclusive of women, the ethicists are clearly discussing some aspect of the whole of humanity. For example, when they discuss the reasons for division of labor in society, they include occupations that may have been carried out by women of some social classes, such as sewing, washing, cooking, and so on.[8] There are also sizable passages on "the ethics of living with a woman from the beginning of marriage to the end" and on "household management" in which there is obvious use of the gender-neutral pronouns to refer to women.[9] In both of these kinds of passages, however, the authorial intent is to address men regarding the science of civic association and the proper maintenance of a wife. Apart from these examples, if women are present in the third person in the text, the authors specifically say so. For instance, in Tusi's chapter on ethics at court, it is safe to assume that he addresses the ethics of political wheeling and dealing exclusively among men, regardless of historical reality, since the ethicists specifically state that women's opinions on politics should be ignored and disregarded.[10] In short, women are explicitly referred to in the text only when needed; in all other cases, it is logical to assume that the gender-neutral Persian pronouns refer only to men and that the authorial intent is to speak only to men.

The second grammatical feature of the texts that seems to bely my claim that Ghazali, Tusi, and Davani thought of the *nafs* as normatively male—and that therefore seems to undermine the male focus of the science of the *nafs* in *akhlaq*—is that the Arabic term *nafs* is itself grammatically feminine. In Islamic philosophy, or *falsafa*, of which *akhlaq* is a part, the word *nafs* translates to "soul" in English and "anima" in Latin.[11] The term is also used in Arabic and Persian for breath. Both definitions suggest that the *nafs* is the animating component of a living organism.[12] The term appears in the Qur'an as a noun 295 times, to refer to a self, soul, person, or mind as possessed by both males and females.[13] Moreover, all the ethicists mention that women possess *nafses*.[14]

As Tanvir Anjum has shown, in some sufi works, the fact that the *nafs* is grammatically feminine plays out as "the image of the soul as a longing female" receiving God's masculinized love.[15] Annemarie Schimmel explains that more common in sufi works is viewing the *nafs* as a wild aspect of human metaphysics, which construes the *nafs* as the feminine carnal self that tempts the male spiritual, intellectual self:

> Wasn't the grammatical gender of the very word *nafs* feminine? Couldn't [the *nafs*] serve as a symbol for the woman whose sensuality always thwarts the religious inclinations, the high-minded strivings of the rationally oriented man? Since she possesses more animalistic traits than does the man, she constantly tries to seduce him through her sexual wiles. . . . One of [the *nafs*'s] most important manifestations, however, is in the form of woman. This feminine element, then, is subordinate to the *'aql*, the intellect or reason, which has as its task to tame and train it.[16]

The *akhlaq* genre shares with sufism the notion that masculinity is synonymous with rationality, and that femininity marks an absence of rationality (and a surfeit of the other faculties). Another commonality between *akhlaq* ethics and sufism is the idea that the *nafs* requires taming of the more feminized carnal traits. However, in *akhlaq*, the *nafs* itself is not seen as a female to tame, per se, or entirely base since some good can come of its desires if balanced properly (and because the trait of anger is seen as masculine). By contrast, in these *akhlaq* texts, the grammatical terms and discussions that accompany explanation of *nafs* are either gender-neutral on the surface (as in discussion of the *nafs-i insani*, or human soul) or even explicitly gendered male (as in *nafs-i adami*, or man's soul).[17] One of the faculties of the *nafs* is rationality, which, the ethicists hold, all human beings possess by virtue of their humanity—even women, though they may be deficient in this faculty compared to men.[18] With masculinity being distinguished on the grounds of superior rationality, which is a faculty of the *nafs*, the *nafs* itself is not seen as an exclusively feminine concept as it is in some sufi discourses. This, however, does not mean that *akhlaq* texts address the female *nafs*.

In *akhlaq*, both women and men have *nafses*, but only men have the potential and divine responsibility to perfect their *nafses* through the science of the *nafs*, and thereby become vicegerents of God. Further, although Ghazali, Tusi, and Davani use the gender-neutral terms *insan* for human and *nafar* for an individual person, they also use the term *muruwwah*, or manhood (also a shared concept with sufism), in discussions about the measures one should take in marriage or social settings in order to preserve manhood. Therefore, the texts' grammatical features— namely, the gender-neutral pronouns in Persian and the fact that the term *nafs* is grammatically feminine—cannot be used to negate the claim that the authors intended to instruct only men about their *nafses* and their ethics. I take up this claim as to the male-centric intent of the *akhlaq* ethicists in the next section.

THE *NAFS* AND MALE NORMATIVITY: EMBODIMENT AND METAPHORS

In this section, I discuss the features of the *nafs* that normatively function to gender it male: anatomy, embodiment, and the metaphors used to elucidate it to readers. I analyze the first part of the science of the *nafs*, which is for men to understand that the *nafs* is itself not physical, nor eternally preexistent: it comes into being with the creation of the human body and is subject to the male body's tendencies and whims. The ethicists hold that the *nafs* is not part of the physical body; it is not an organ, nor can the body sense it.[19] Yet, it operates using the organs and senses. The faculties of the *nafs* allow for "corporeal perception" that enables the body to experience pleasure and pain and carry out the cerebral functions of evaluation, analysis, and judgment of things perceived by the physical senses of touch, taste, smell, vision, and sound.[20] As such, even though the *nafs* is not physical, it is still embodied (by gendered persons), and the ethicists' focus on the rational faculty is what normatively genders the *nafs* male for them. In the very process of describing the *nafs*, all three ethicists rely on gendered metaphors of male power or on male arenas of knowledge production and transmission as models for the *nafs*.

Ghazali and Tusi describe the *nafs* as having three equal faculties that originate in three distinct organs, which also comprise three parts of the soul, each with its own traits essential to human life (its embodiment). These faculties of the soul are the rational, irascible, and concupiscent faculties (see table 2.1).[21]

The ethicists employ gendered metaphors to explain these faculties of the *nafs*. Using an analogy of male sovereign power, Ghazali describes the status and authority of the *nafs* by presenting it as the metaphorical king of the body. In keeping with the idea that the self and body are a microcosm of the world, Ghazali conceived of the soul and body as being

TABLE 2.1

Ghazali's and Tusi's Conception of the *Nafs*

Faculty	Part of Soul	Traits	Organ
Rational faculty/ *quwwat-i 'ilm* **or** *'aql*	Angelic soul/ *nafs-i malaki*	Seeks reason	Brain, responsible for human reflection and reason
Irascible faculty/ *quwwat-i ghazb*	Savage soul/ *nafs-i sabu'i*	Repels injuries and perils, yearns for authority	Heart, innate heat and source of life
Concupiscible **faculty/***quwwat-i* *shahwat*	Bestial soul/ *nafs-i bahimi*	Seeks pleasure, food, drink, and women	Liver, nutrition and replacement of distributed solubles

Source: Abu Hamid al-Ghazali, *Kimiya-i Sa'adat*, ed. Hossein Khadivjam (Tehran: Ketabhaaye Jibi, 1975), 1:18–28; Nasir-ad Din Muhammad ibn Muhammad Tusi, *Akhlaq-i Nasiri*, ed. Mojtaba Minvi and Alireza Haydari (Tehran: Zar, 1977), 58–72.

a world unto itself: "the metaphor of the body is a nation, and its limbs and organs are its workers."[22] This soul as monarch also has armies, viziers, tax collectors, and more, which are metaphors for its faculties, which lead humans to succumb to their baser instincts and unethical behaviors. These behaviors ultimately lead to unhappiness because the main objective of the *nafs* is only to achieve happiness for the body: for example, physical pleasures or relief that comes from consuming food or engaging in sexual activity with women.[23] In seeking to achieve that bodily happiness, one can immoderately exceed bounds of acceptable behavior.

Ghazali resolves the *nafs*'s conflict of interest between momentary physical pleasure and eternal spiritual happiness—both of which are acquired by actions of the *nafs*—by explaining that God created the *nafs* for the hereafter, and its true happiness lies in learning about God and the spiritual path. Thus, one tames the appetites of the *nafs* for one's own good. So the individual's *nafs* is more than merely a microcosm of the world; it is "like a mirror; whoever looks in it sees the Truth, most high."[24] Ghazali's use of "Truth, most high" (*haq-i ta'ala*), one of the names of God, implies that the act of knowing one's own *nafs* is a way to know the ultimate Truth as part of the *rah-i din* and find ultimate happiness. More profoundly, as a mirror a man can reflect God/*Haq*, who in turn can be seen in the reflection of a man, or indeed as a man.

The *nafs* is the king of the body, which itself is akin to a sovereign state. The carnal appetite (*shahwat*), as the tax collector of the state (i.e., the human body), lies and deceives the body to find more pleasure. Anger (*ghazb*) is the state police; it has a hot temper and is fueled by rage. Intellection ('*aql*) is the king's vizier, which is meant to keep the former two under control by holding them accountable and punishing them when they have transgressed. The *nafs*/king must "consult" with each of these "armies" to keep the body fully functioning.[25]

This metaphor of the *nafs* as king of the sovereign body, which also appears as the "human's internal kingdom" in Davani,[26] is no "mere metaphor," to borrow a term from Susan Shapiro, who argues that the use of gendered metaphors to explain nongendered concepts contributes to a real culture of gender hierarchy.[27] Likewise, Ghazali's metaphor of the state and its armies is gendered in the sense that power, rulership, and force reside with male bodies. Ghazali's reference to state officials in the metaphor is not just his attempt to provide a comprehensible analogy for the *nafs*. Rather, it is a way to equate the individual with powerful actors of the state who demonstrate strength, discipline, and the power of correcting wrongs.

Since the rational faculty is akin to male sovereign power, the seemingly gender-neutral faculty of rationality is then only imagined in male terms, as possessed by males, open to perfection in men, and akin to male power itself. Ghazali contrasts rationality with the baseness of animals as well as the "weakness and vulnerability of women."[28] Thus, the rational, intellectual faculty (*'aql*) to reign over the bestial and savage facilities (*shahwat* and *ghazb*) is a male expression of power that enables man to gather spiritual knowledge, wisdom, and the virtue of leadership. As I show through the rest of this book, the privilege of correcting the ethics of others and showing leadership is not just a virtue associated with the faculty of rationality: it is also a prerogative that elite males have over women and men of lower classes.

Tusi, like Ghazali, also uses an enterprise only accessible to men, the production and transmission of knowledge, to describe the very structure of the *nafs*. He defines the *nafs* itself as the rational soul (*nafs-i natiqah*) because for him the very essence of the human *nafs*, what distinguishes it from that of animals, is its rational ability.[29] He also calls it the angelic soul (*nafs-i malaki*) because it is all good. He explains that *nafs*'s faculties "act and practice in collaboration with opinion, judgment, discernment, and intent."[30] He attributes the abilities of the rational faculty to the ways it acquires different kinds of knowledge. The faculty allows for the "perception of intelligibles and differentiating between right and wrong acts."[31] The rational faculty is physically represented by the brain, which is the "location of thought and contemplation."[32] The faculty has two subdivisions of its own, the theoretical faculty (*quwwat-i 'ilmi*) and the practical faculty (*quwwat-i 'amali*), which correspond, respectively, to two branches of all knowledge: speculative philosophy (*hikmat-i nazari*) and practical philosophy (*hikmat-i 'amali*).[33] Speculative philosophy comprises mathematics, theology, and natural sciences, while practical philosophy houses all the branches of *tazhib-i akhlaq*, which are virtue ethics, domestic ethics, and political ethics. In his classifications of the subspecialties of each branch of philosophy/knowledge, we see how all knowledge that

Tusi deemed worthy of learning and teaching corresponds to the professions that men held.

As I indicate in figure 1.1 in the last chapter, it is through the *male* professions or roles that the very structure of all human knowledge is embodied and transferred between humans. As I show in the next chapter, even the ordering of the household is a task of male leadership.

Davani likewise structures his model of the *nafs* based on the kinds of roles men play and the types of knowledge men acquire. He describes the whole of the human soul as the rational soul (*nafs-i natiqah*) in order to show his emphasis on humans' presence of mind. By way of critiquing Ghazali and Tusi's models, Davani explains that the rational faculty of the soul cannot simply be "equal" in value to the concupiscible faculty (*quwwat-i shahwi*) or the irascible faculty (*quwwati-i ghazabi*); this is because the rational faculty is meant to rule over the other two in order to produce an ethical human being. For Davani, equity and justice cannot be embodied without thinking of the mental powers as already above the others. The physical powers must be subdued to the mental ones in order for "the state of the human's internal kingdom" to be put in order.[34] Thus, Davani's model of the *nafs* divides mental and physical faculties.

As I show in table 2.2, Davani understands the *nafs* as having two major faculties, each of which has two branches.[35] The first faculty is the power of perception (*quwwat-i idrak*), which is equivalent to Tusi's and Ghazali's rational faculty (compare tables 2.1 and 2.2). The power of perception's first branch is the speculative intellect (*'aql-i nazari*), which perceives the natural and celestial worlds through observation and imagination. From this speculative intellect stems the virtue of wisdom. The second branch of the power of perception is the practical intellect (*'aql-i 'amali*), which Davani describes as follows: "the use of thought and reflection, which is the remote origin of partial movement of the body, . . . produces partial arts and production from its position relative to the speculative intelligence, and the marriage between them is the basis of obtaining the complete arts relating to practices such as the beauty of truth and the ugliness of lies."[36]

This second power, the practical intellect (*quwwat-i idrak*), is the power of thoughts and imagination, and is responsible for the expression of emotions such as shame, crying, and laughter. The "marriage" (*azdavaj*) between the speculative intellect (*'aql-i nazari*) and the practical intellect

TABLE 2.2

Davani's Conception of the *Nafs-i Natiqah*

Faculty	Branch of Faculty	Traits
Power of perception/ *quwwati-i idrak*	Theoretical intellect/ *'aql nazari*	Receives ideas and knowledge from celestial sources
	Practical intellect/ *'aql amali*	Reflection, thought, imagination cause action in the body
Power of incitement/ *quwwat-i tahrik*	Power of desire/ *quwwat-i shahwat*	Power of desire, attracts beneficial things
	Power of anger/ *quwwat-i gazb*	Power of avoidance and repulsion of bad things

Source: Jalal ad-Din Davani, *Akhlaq-i Jalali*, ed. Abdullah Masoudi Arani (Tehran: Intesharat-i Italat, 2013), 73–79.

('*aql-i 'amali*), which together make up the power of perception (*quwwat-i idrak*), creates the full range of thoughts and emotions within a person. The two branches of Davani's intellectual faculty also correspond to the two branches of philosophy/knowledge (the speculative and practical), which makes all knowledge and the *nafs* male.

It is possible that Davani sees the speculative intellect as a masculine trait and the practical intellect as a feminine trait, since he uses the term *marriage* to refer to the relationship between the two; however, he does not say as much explicitly here. Evidence supporting this interpretation, which I discuss in more detail later, is that he, as well as Ghazali and Tusi, sees the resulting virtues that stem from the faculty of rationality as masculine qualities, while they see the virtue of self-restraint (*'iffat*), stemming from the concupiscent faculty, as comprising some feminine qualities. However, in this passage, because Davani (unlike Ghazali and Tusi) accounts for differences between rational and emotional qualities of the power of perception (*quwwat-i idrak*) and describes the relationship between them as a marriage, we see evidence that Davani thinks of rationality as a masculine quality and emotionality as feminine. In drawing a parallel between Islamic and Chinese thought, Sachiko Murata argues that the perfected human soul, particularly in sufi discourses, contains both complementary yin (generally feminine) and yang (generally masculine), and is able to be a microcosm of the world and carry out God's plan.[37]

MASCULINE NATURE OF THE VIRTUES AND VICES

Even as the embodiment and metaphors within the *akhlaq* texts suggest a normative male *nafs*, a close reading of the second part of the science of the *nafs* in the Ghazali-Tusi-Davani tradition—knowledge of each faculty's potential to express virtues and vices and recognition of one's power over the *nafs* and that of others—intensifies the male normativity of the *nafs*. Amina wadud reminds us that the context and illustrative examples provided within a given religious text tell us about its gendered intent. As I show later, the ethicists outline the respective virtues of the rational, irascible, and concupiscent faculties, namely, wisdom (*hikmat*), courage (*shuja'at*), and self-restraint (*'iffat*), as particularly masculine qualities. For the ethicists, the three virtues function as a roadmap to men's ultimate goals of embodying happiness/flourishing (*sa'adat*), or in the case of Tusi and Davani, vicegerency (*khilafah*) through achieving the culminating fourth virtue of justice. These male-only virtues demonstrate how the science of *akhlaq* is an exclusively male endeavor as a whole, as well as how power, namely, the power to place rationality above the other faculties and the power to rule over others, is a male provenance.

The ethicists mention examples involving women's *nafses* (albeit briefly, and alongside male examples) only for the third faculty, the concupiscent faculty (*quwwat-i shahwat*). Because the ethicists viewed women as servile to their bodily functions, it makes sense that the only faculty they could imagine women possessing was the one that involves the body and carnality. They also viewed sexual appetite (*shahwat*) as being amplified in women, which, as Kecia Ali notes, is the basis for Ghazali's "fram[ing of] his discussion of the sexual act in terms of a husband's responsibility for keeping his wife satisfied" because of the "discord-producing effects of female dissatisfaction."[38] As a corollary, the ethicists also viewed the virtue that stems from the concupiscent faculty, self-restraint (*'iffat*), in a milder and more feminine light (which I discuss in chapter 3); however, its most virtuous applications and forms of expression of self-restraint (*'iffat*) remain masculine, like all the other virtues discussed in the ethics texts.

The virtues emerge when a person follows the golden mean, the principle of moderation in expressing each faculty, and when the irascible and concupiscent faculties are subordinate to the rational. For Tusi, as well as Ghazali and Davani, moderation can be understood by imagining the faculties of the *nafs* on a continuum of behavior, a straight line.[39] One must not stray too far in either direction, or he will fall off the straight line. This is Tusi's way of claiming *akhlaq* as the straight path of faith (*sirat al-mustaqim*) that is named in Surat al-Fatiha, the opening verse of the Qur'an. Knowledge of the *nafs*—its components, its corresponding virtues and vices, and its tricksters—will help a man to perfect his *akhlaq*.

More specifically, the virtue of wisdom emerges when the rational soul (*quwwat-i 'ilm*) is expressed in correct measure and placed above the other two faculties. When the irascible faculty (*quwwat-i ghazabi*) is expressed in moderation and is subordinated to the rational faculty, the "virtue of mildness [or *hilm*] appears, and the virtue of courage [or *shuja'at*] becomes necessary by nature."[40] Finally, the virtue of self-restraint or *'iffat* emerges when the concupiscible faculty (*quwwat-i shahwi*) is expressed in equilibrium and subordinated to the faculty of rationality.[41] Each virtue has its own distinct subcharacteristics, which I refer to as ethical qualities.

Parallel to the virtues of each faculty are the vices of the human soul, which are behaviors that arise from the immoderate expression of the three faculties, as when the concupiscent and irascible faculties are insubordinate to the rational faculty. The ethicists outline correctable patterns of unethical behavior that arise in social situations when any given faculty is expressed too much or too little. The ethicists also discuss pseudovirtues, the behaviors of each faculty of the *nafs* that may fool a man into thinking he is virtuous.[42] The descriptions of pseudovirtues resemble the sufi idea of the *nafs* as a trickster that guides men to act upon their baser impulses but is unrecognizable to the untrained or undisciplined man.[43] Table 2.3 delineates the virtues and vices associated with each faculty of the *nafs*.

Overall, the three ethicists dedicate considerably more space to describing the irascible and concupiscent faculties (and their

TABLE 2.3

Virtues and Vices of the Faculties of the *Nafs*

Faculty	Virtue and Qualities	Vices	Pseudovirtues
Rational/ Quwwat-i aqli	Wisdom: quick thinking, speediness of understanding, lucidity of mind, ease of learning, elegance of thinking, excellence of memory, recollection	Too little expression: stupidity, foolishness, other faculties amplify Too much expression: craftiness, deception, paranoia, evil (rational faculty has no vices for Ghazali)	Acquiring knowledge produces pretension, applying knowledge to produce conjecture
Irascible/ Quwwati-ghazabi	Courage: honor, high-mindedness, valor, mildness, endurance, calmness, beauty, control of anger, greatness of soul, determination, boldness of soul, humility, compassion	Too little expression: cowardice, dispassion, self-deprecation, powerlessness, impatience, sedateness, abjectness Too much expression: impetuousness, heedlessness, boasting, conceit, pride, recklessness, self-exaltation, attracting danger	False courage, overconfidence, suicidal thoughts attract harm
Concupiscent/ Quwwati-shahwi	Self-Restraint: modesty, contentment, patience, coolness, elegance, agreeability, shame, congeniality, beautiful guidance, peacefulness, tranquility, patience, dignity, moderation, regulation, freedom, generosity	Too little expression: unmanliness/impotence, lethargy, madness Too much expression: greediness, gluttony, impudence, unmanliness, uncleanliness, jealousy, despicable to the powerful, contemptuous to the poor	Self-deprivation from the lawful, self-deprivation in false hope of receiving double rewards or protection from disease

Sources: Abu Hamid al-Ghazali, *Kimiya-i Sa'adat*, ed. Hossein Khadivjam (Tehran: Ketabhaaye Jibi, 1975), 1:25–27, 2:7; Nasir-ad Din Muhammad ibn Muhammad Tusi, *Akhlaq-i Nasiri*, ed. Mojtaba Minvi and Alireza Haydari (Tehran: Zar, 1977), 112–13; Jalal ad-Din Davani, *Akhlaq-i Jalali*, ed. Abdullah Masoudi Arani (Tehran: Intesharat-i Italat, 2013), 83–85.

corresponding virtues and vices) than to the rational faculty and its corresponding wisdom. They likely make this choice because their interest in the treatises is in teaching the science of regulation (*tahzib*), i.e., regulating the less desirable faculties, rather than simply extolling the end goal of becoming rational. In this sense, the texts function as manuals of psychological-spiritual guidance and self-diagnosis: men should school themselves in the science of the *nafs* and then move through the sections of the virtues and vices, attempting to correct the levels of how they express the faculties. The ethicists' discussion of the pseudovirtues helps the reader to test whether his true intentions for acting virtuously are in fact pure. The description of the virtues and vices reads like a study in ideal masculinity because of the examples given, but also because of the rhetoric of superiority that is articulated in patriarchal terms of responsibility and God's vicegerency (*khilafah*). As a result, the science of *akhlaq* excludes all nonelite men, whom the ethicists do not understand as having the ability to subdue their animalistic faculties and vices and embody justice.

The Rational Faculty and Male Wisdom

The ethicists equate the rational faculty with male power and describe it as the most important of the *nafs*'s three faculties for creating ethical behaviors. The natural possession of rationality gives men the power to subdue the nonrational faculties and, by extension, irrational, less ethical people. The virtue that stems from the faculty of rationality is wisdom (*hikmat*). Ghazali identifies the rational faculty's distinguishing quality as the ability to know the difference between the truth and lies in speech and in acts of faith. Other qualities of the rational faculty include "good regulation, correct opinion and thinking, just action and discernment."[44] For Ghazali, virtuous applications of the rational faculty are related to leadership skills involved in being master of a trade, household, or polity. For Tusi and Davani, wisdom (*hikmat*) is both knowable and doable, speculative and practical. All three construe rationality as male nature that establishes men's birthright to rule over others.

They define wisdom (*hikmat*) as "quick thinking, speediness of understanding, lucidity of mind, ease of learning, elegance in thinking, excellence of memory, and recollection."[45] Quick-thinking (*zaka'*) is the speedy production of hypotheses and conclusions.[46] Speed of understanding (sur'at-i fahm) refers to habitual understanding of the relationship between causes and consequences.[47] Lucidity of mind (safay-i zahn) is the freedom of the soul from being confused or agitated by irrelevant things.[48] Ease of learning (sahulat-i ta'allum) refers to sharpness of vision and a sense of focus on goals and desired objects.[49] Elegance in thinking (hasan-i ta'qul) is the proper examination of reality in its proper limits and quantities.[50] Excellence of memory (tahaffuz) is the ability to hold and grasp something over time that has been examined or elucidated by the rational faculties.[51] Finally, recollection (tazakkar) refers to a man's ability to habitually contemplate mentally conserved forms any time his soul desires.[52] The exercise of all these qualities occurs in men's activities of teaching and learning a trade, as well as in expressing critical thinking in men's leadership over others.

While Ghazali does not believe that any vices can arise from the rational faculty, Tusi and Davani caution that if the rational faculty (quwwat-i natiqah) becomes excessive, the mind becomes occupied with evil works and deception.[53] The nafs can cause one to overthink every situation, become paranoid, and craft plots. By contrast, deficiency in rationality gives rise to stupidity and foolishness, and the potential for the vices of the two other faculties amplifies. It is also easy to fool oneself into thinking that one is training the rational faculty (quwwat-i natiqah), while in fact avoiding the hard work of doing so.[54] The worst counterfeiters of knowledge are those who are pretentious because of having obtained certain knowledge, or people who use knowledge for conceit or conjecture about observations and facts. Davani classifies these antics as common among those pretending to be philosophers.[55] These are also the descriptions of various types of unvirtuous men whom one will encounter in society, which I discuss in chapter 4.

The Irascible Faculty and the Masculine Virtue of Courage

For the ethicists, the irascible faculty (quwwat-i ghazabi) is a power of anger and repulsion, which is necessary for avoiding harm to one's person. As with rationality and wisdom, the ethicists view the irascible power itself, as well as the virtue that stems from its expression, courage (*shuja'at*), in a masculine light. Not only do the ethicists imagine the qualities that make up courage to be essential in male leadership over a general polity; but they also appeal to male notions of bravery and honor when they advocate for balanced expression of the irascible faculty (*quwwat-i ghazabi*).

For Tusi and Ghazali, the irascible faculty (*quwwat-i ghazabi*) is one of the three faculties of the *nafs*. Davani accounts for this power as a sub-faculty of the power of incitement (*quwwat-i tahrik*). But for all three ethicists, the powers of incitement are the powers of anger (*ghazb*) and (*shahwat*) desire, which work in similar ways, as Ghazali and Tusi describe.[56] Tusi explains that the irascible faculty (*quwwat-i ghazabi*) is the bestial aspect of the soul (*nafs-i sabu'i*) and is located in the heart, the "quarry of innate heat and the fountain of life."[57] In animals, this faculty is roused by the repulsion of harm; it is the instinct of self-protection that allows animals to identify danger. However, in humans, the instinct of self-preservation and repelling injury can lead one to "crave for authority" as a natural order of his soul, and to treat others badly out of real or imagined fear of others.[58] In a sense, these passages in the *akhlaq* texts present authorization for men to exercise authority, within ethical bounds, over women in the domestic economy and over other men in the public sphere.

The virtue that comes from perfecting the irascible faculty (*quwwat-i ghazabi*) is courage (*shuja'at*). Ghazali explains that courage comes about when this power of anger is expressed moderately, giving rise to "honor, high-mindedness, valor, mildness, endurance, calmness, beauty, and control of anger."[59] Tusi and Davani elaborate on similar qualities of courage: "greatness of soul, valor, high-mindedness, determination, mildness, calmness, boldness of soul, endurance, humility, honor, and compassion."[60]

Several of these qualities involve a man's interaction with others or his place in God's cosmic plan. Greatness of soul (*kibr-i nafs*) characterizes the soul that is resilient in the face of good and bad things, prosperity or lack thereof, pleasant and unpleasant circumstances.[61] Valor (*najaddat*) is self-confidence.[62] High-mindedness (*buland himmati*) is a fearlessness of death in the pursuit of the greater goals of life, namely, to become a microcosm of the universe unto oneself.[63] Davani emphasizes that "the *nafs* in seeking real beauty and psychic perfection does not see as important the benefits and disasters of this world, so it does not become sad or happy at obtaining or losing them."[64] Instead, the courageous have a yearning for death from striving for perfection.[65]

Determination (*sabat*) is defined as persistence in the face of failure.[66] Mildness (*hilm*) is defined as keeping one's anger at bay when a repugnant event occurs.[67] Calmness (*sakun*) refers to the soul's ability to maintain honor specifically in the face of hostility or war, also a gendered male endeavor.[68] Boldness (*shahamat*) is the courageous soul's eagerness to win, while garnering a reputation for fairness.[69] Endurance (*tahammul*) is wearing out one's body and organs by what is required by mind and soul, or in other words, putting the body entirely at the disposal of the mind.[70] Humility (*tavaz'a*) is the abstention from assigning greater merit to the accomplishments of one's own soul over those of people in lower stations.[71] Humility refers to man's position in the hierarchy of intellect, which is correlated with a man's profession and with the clime he is from. Despite the existence of social hierarchy, it is a virtue not to feel proud of one's own station or achievements. Nonetheless, a sense of honor (*hamiyyat*) is interestingly included as a component of courage; it involves "protecting the dignity of the faith and honor . . . to its furthest limits."[72] The term Davani uses for faith here is *millat*, which evokes a sense of a community of believers in the faith and limits the irascible faculty to this male application of responsibility over others.[73]

The quality of honor (*hamiyyat*) is also characterized as particularly masculine by the ethicists. This shows that they think of the faculty of the *nafs* from which honor originates, namely, the irascible faculty (*quwwat-i ghazabi*), as itself masculine. Davani expands on honor (*hamiyyat*) by quoting a hadith about *ghayrat*, commonly thought of as manly pride: " 'God has *ghayrat* and, for His *ghayrat*, has outlawed immoral deeds [or *haram al-fawahish*. . . .] Sa'd has *ghayrat*. I have more *ghayrat* than Sa'd, and God has more *ghayrat* than I do.' "[74] The original context of the hadith is that a man named Sa'd ibn 'Ubayda had said, "If I saw a man with my wife, I would strike him with the blade of my sword."[75] The Prophet heard this and said this comment about *ghayrat* which Davani quotes. According to Bukhari, the Prophet then stated that the immoral deeds (*haram al-fawahish*) are outlawed whether "done in open or in secret."[76]

The term *ghayrat* itself comes from the triletter root *gh-y-r*, which is generally used to mean the "other" or something outside of a category.

The noun *ghayrat* is defined as jealousy, almost always of a wife or some "other" person approaching one's wife. In the context of Sa'd's initial envious comment about his wife committing adultery, it makes sense to define *ghayrat* as jealousy; and yet the Prophet's response about himself having more *ghayrat* (or God as having the most *ghayrat*) suggests that the word cannot merely mean sexual jealousy. The Prophet's statement— "God has *ghayrat* and, for His *ghayrat*, has outlawed immoral deeds done in open or in secret"—implies that having *ghayrat* means defending what is right and wrong and morality in general, and not just in the case of defending one's honor in the case of a wife's adultery or a man's advance upon one's wife. Yet, the term *ghayrat* has become synonymous with a type of male honor that is rooted in the wife's sexual behavior.[77]

The *ghayrat* hadith is typically interpreted as disallowing sexual jealousy, prohibiting the individual from taking retribution into one's own hands, and emphasizing God's omniscience.[78] Davani deemphasizes sexual jealousy as an element of *ghayrat* by omitting the end of the hadith, thus decontextualizing the term *ghayrat* from the notion of defending one's manly pride over his wife or over another man's sexual enjoyment of one's wife. However, just by using the *ghayrat* hadith in the first place, he casts it as a positive virtue. To have *ghayrat* is to emulate the Prophet and to internalize a divine virtue. We can therefore conclude that Davani is quoting the *ghayrat* hadith in order to say that zeal is essential for displaying the quality of courage (*hamiyyat*). The partial use of the hadith allows him to bring up language that evokes male pride. A man is supposed to uphold his own honor and that of others, and to protect the faith to the "furthest limits" as a display of possessing courage, a component of the broader masculine virtue of courage.[79]

The last quality in the virtue of courage that Tusi and Davani discuss is compassion (*riqqat*), which is the soul's ability to be affected by the distress of others without its own functions being affected.[80] A man should be compassionate while maintaining his own integrity, in order to feel for others. To summarize, then, the virtue of courage is defined by the strength and bravery required to better oneself and improve the lives of others. The ethicists thought of courage as masculine because it comes from the soul's aggressive faculty of irascibility, which prompts men to subdue others. Courage is also paternalistic in that men are instructed to "protect" the faith, and embody honor, dignity, and endurance.[81]

Finally, the ethicists discuss the vices that arise from too much or too little expression of the irascible faculty (*quwwat-i ghazabi*). Ghazali explains that if a man uses the irascible faculty excessively, he becomes impetuous and heedless.[82] He undertakes unnecessary actions and exhibits the common vices of "boasting, conceit, pride, recklessness, self-exaltation, [and] throwing [him]self into dangerous situations."[83] Conversely, if a man exercises too little of the irascible faculty, then he becomes cowardly and dispassionate, which leads to "self-depreciation, powerlessness, impatience, and sedateness, and abjectness."[84] He does not take action when it is necessary.[85] Impostors who feign courage, the irascible faculty's virtue, attract unnecessary harm to themselves, bodily or otherwise. This includes both people who are prone to suicide and people who appear overconfident because of coincidental triumphs they have had over their peers.[86]

The Concupiscible Faculty: Its Masculine and Feminine Power, Virtues, and Vices

The third faculty of the *nafs* is the concupiscible faculty (*quwwat-i shahwi*), which is also known as the bestial aspect of the soul (*nafs-i bahimi*). Like the irascible faculty (*quwwati-i ghazabi*), the concupiscible faculty (*quwwat-i shahwi*) is associated with bodily functions and animal-like powers. This faculty is roused by the soul's attraction to beneficial things such as food, sexual mates, and pleasure-giving activities. Tusi locates the concupiscible faculty in the liver, known to him as the organ of "nutrition and distribution of solubles exchanged with other bodily members."[87] In humans, the drive toward beneficial things can be so strong that it leads to ills or evils such as gluttony or sexual depravity.

The ethicists consider the concupiscible faculty to rule the *nafses* of women in particular, through the virtue of *'iffat*, which translates to self-restraint, chastity, continence, or virtuousness. They discuss the concupiscible faculty's corresponding virtue, self-restraint (*'iffat*), in their sections on the domestic economy to describe qualities of an ideal wife, as part of their recognition both that women have *nafses* and that they can posses (at least some) virtues.[88] In fact, the Persian lexicographer Francis Joseph Steingass defines the term *'iffat* itself as a modest woman.[89]

However, in Tusi's and Davani's description of the science of the *nafs*, they cast self-restraint (*'iffat*) and the faculty of concupiscible faculty (*quwwat-i shahwi*) in an entirely masculine light. This masculine characterization seems incongruous with their admission later in their texts that women can display the virtue of self-restraint (*'iffat*). This apparent inconsistency within the texts represents a gendered disruption in the science of *akhlaq*. The ethicists describe the concupiscible faculty's training (acquisition of *'iffat*) as a crucial part of establishing masculinity, and they assert that women are not able to train their *nafses* (even though they can display the virtue of self-restraint).

Tusi explains that the concupiscible faculty "seeks pleasure from food, drink, and marriageables."[90] The latter term, *manakih* (marriageables), can be taken as a gender-neutral term, since both men and women can be marriageable. Thus, the statement can be interpreted to mean that the concupiscible faculty (*quwwat-i shahwi*) seeks pleasure from food, drink, and one's marriage partners. However, as Steingass defines *manakih* as "marriages; women," the term *manakih* in Persian texts refers only to women who are marriageable.[91] Further, the grammatical construction of the term, *mufa'al* or passive form of the word *nikah* (marriage), implies a passive marriage partner, as opposed to an active one. Instead of using the terms *hamsar* (spouse), *zan* (woman/wife), or *ahl* (usually female family members)—which the ethicists use elsewhere to refer to women in relation to men—here they use a term that is a variation of *nikah* (marriage), implying a legalistic definition of marriage in which a man actively offers marriage, which is called *ijab* (offer), and a woman's male guardian passively accepts it, which is called *qabul* (acceptance). In addition, the term *manakih* is plural, so it can refer to a man's legal right to marry (or have sexual intercourse with) multiple women, although this would exceed what is ethically permissible when the concupiscible faculty (*quwwat-i shahwi*) is properly subdued to the rational faculty (*quwwat-i natiqah*).[92] The normative ethical practice is for all students of ethics to be monogamous, except for kings, who may have multiple wives in order to secure multiple heirs; thus, this subtle but telling mention of marriageables is a way that the concupiscible faculty is normalized as being possessed by men. Thus, the whole *nafs* in question, even if women possess *nafs*, and even if men might be passively married to women in less legally conventional circumstances, is thought of only in regard to how men embody it.

Ghazali briefly explains how this virtue of self-restraint (*'iffat*) as men embody it comprises such qualities as "modesty, contentment, patience, coolness, elegance, and agreeability."[93] Tusi and Davani identify twelve constituent qualities that demonstrate freedom from bondage to the soul's pleasures: "shame, congeniality, beautiful guidance, peaceful-ness, tranquility, patience, contentment, dignity, moderation, regula-tion, freedom, and generosity."[94] Shame (*haya*) is the soul's inhibition from committing foul things.[95] Congeniality (*rifq*) is a kind of gentle mildness or submission to whatever may happen.[96] Beautiful guidance (*husn-i huda*) is the soul's internal willingness to improve itself using the methods of perfection, likely referring to the discipline of *akhlaq* itself.[97] Peacefulness (*musalamat*) is the soul's ability to resolve situa-tions where there is a conflict between rising to reach its potential and relying on old habits.[98]

Particularly gendered male is tranquility (*da'at*), the soul's stillness or quietness amid the vigorous satiating of its concupiscible faculty's demands.[99] When a man with tranquility (*da'at*) is indulging in food, sex, or other bodily pleasures, his soul is not swayed by these acts. Men are thought to be able to control their concupiscent appetites, while women are thought not to be able to do so. As Kecia Ali has noted, the "classical Muslim tradition . . . [views] women as sexually insatiable and thus prone to create social chaos."[100] This gendered assumption has historically led jurists to prescribe more stringent restrictions on women's appearance and mobility than on those of men, who are thought to possess the abil-ity to control themselves.

The next qualities of self-restraint have to do with cultivating prophet-like resistance to temptations. Contentment (*qana'at*) is being at peace with whatever one is given in regard to food, drink, and cloth-ing, and restricting oneself to indulge only in necessary quantities of these things.[101] Davani states that the Prophet held that "contentment is a cache that never vanishes," as opposed to the temporary pleasures one derives from indulging the concupiscible faculty (*quwwat-i shahwat*).[102] The quality of patience (*sabr*) is the ability to resist foul pleasures; for Davani, it means having patience in trying times.[103] He likewise declares it to be the virtue of God's prophets and the Persian sages.[104] Davani's reference to prophets and sages as the perfect exemplars of patience is gendered in that prophets and sages are paragons of male perfection; only men are prophets, and to aspire to perfection of patience is to be a man. Women lack this level of self-control. By contrast, Tusi's and Davani's domestic ethics chapters refer to women's version of self-restraint in terms of the patience they need to support husbands.[105]

The next qualities cultivate male comportment and prerogative under the virtue of self-restraint. Dignity (*vaqar*) is the soul's tempered pace when tested by desirable objects.[106] Beyond Tusi's and Davani's shared definition of dignity, Davani elaborates that one should always avoid haste and hurried movements, even if one is about to miss Friday congregational prayers. One should never deviate from steadiness of movement.[107] As with the quality of honor within the virtue of courage (*hamiyyat*), which Davani explains through the concept of manly pride (*ghayrat*), there is a gendered element to dignity (*vaqar*), because there is an expectation that the man who possesses this quality under the broader rubric of the virtue of self-restraint (*'iffat*) and the balanced concupiscible faculty (*quwwat-i shahwat*) attends Friday prayers. In the laws of worship (*'ibadat*) in *fiqh*, only men are required to attend Friday prayers. Historically, even if women may have attended prayers, Davani's mention of it refers exclusively to men's attendance. This is both because men are the only ones required to attend, and because elsewhere he advises men to seclude women as much as possible.[108] Accordingly, the next quality comprising self-restraint (*'iffat*) is *war'a*, which often means conscientious piety and meticulous attention to the details of ritual, or also ability to follow moderation.[109] The quality of regulation (*intizam*) is the soul's habit of estimating and judging affairs and ordering them according to what is best.[110]

Next is *hurriyat*, which translates to integrity.[111] Although integrity can have numerous meanings, Tusi and Davani explain that in this case it refers to the soul's ability to acquire wealth in legal ways, perhaps because wealth is a quantifiable standard for integrity, which tends to be the executable form of justice in legal literature.[112] Also, since this definition of integrity is about earning wages, it assumes a man is performing the virtue of self-restraint (*'iffat*). The guideline to acquire wealth in legal ways refers to men's endeavors to earn because, as I show in the next chapter, the ethicists assume that men are the financial supporters of women—even though, during the ethicists' lifetimes, as Rapoport has shown, it was possible for elite women to own property or businesses, and some less elite women were even compensated for work done at home, such as spinning textiles or producing handicrafts.[113] Men are told in chapters on marriage to marry once they secure a lawful source of income to support a wife and family.

The last quality of self-restraint (*'iffat*), generosity (*sakha*), requires a man to disburse money to those who deserve it. Generosity is essential for a man's leadership to be effective, namely, for maintaining the loyalty and productivity of individuals outside the home in the city or sovereignty. This quality corresponds to the third level of ethics that I discuss in chapter 4. Because generosity is so important to male leadership, Tusi describes this quality as having the subqualities of "munificence, preference, forgiveness, manliness, greatness, good doing, beneficence, and lenience."[114] These subqualities assume elite social status and male power of the virtuous subject.

Generosity is particularly male-gendered through its subquality of manliness (*muruwwah*), which Tusi defines as "the soul's true desire to be adorned with the ornament of benefits and munificence for necessity or greater good."[115] In this circular definition, in which manliness is the desire to display the virtue of generosity and the virtue of generosity is defined by manliness, Tusi equates generosity with manhood. Conceptually, this sense of the word is very similar to the Latin word for virtue, or *virtus*, which stems from the word for male, *vir*. By denotative definition, men are the virtuous. The role that ethical males play in the household and in the city is intimately tied to finances and distribution of resources. In Davani's commentary on several hadiths that extol liberality, he identifies this virtue as being among those that God likes best. Liberality can save someone from punishment on the Day of Judgment, making it a crucial ethic connecting divine favor with financial power and male power.[116]

A similar circular definition of ethical manliness is seen in texts by the eleventh-century Hanbali sufi from Herat Abdullah Ansari. Minlib Dallh explains that Ansari's texts present four cornerstones of spiritual maturity: "morality (*akhlaq*) and good conduct (*adab*) as well as chivalry (*futuwwa*) and magnanimity (*muruwwa*)."[117] Dallh argues that while *muruwwah* "literally means 'manliness' [it] may also be rendered as 'being just and fair, having compassion, being benevolent.' For Ansari, *muruwa* [means] living with and upholding one's convictions."[118] This too is a circular definition: what it means to be a man is to be good and just, and what it means to be good and just is, in fact, the very definition of a man. In other words, if one is just and good, then one must be a man.[119] Similarly, as Gordon Newby has shown, Ibn Khaldun also defined *muruwwah* as manhood that consisted of the natural disposition consistent with religious law.[120] Similarly, since Tusi states that *muruwwah* is "the soul's true desire to be adorned with the ornament of benefits and munificence," he likewise equates masculinity with particular ethical principles.[121]

Conversely, according to Ghazali, when the concupiscent faculty (*quwwat-i shahwi*) is expressed excessively, a man becomes greedy. He becomes a glutton, which gives rise to "impudence, foulness, unmanliness [*bimuruwatti*], uncleanliness, jealousy, [and] being despicable to the powerful, and contemptuous to the poor."[122] Ghazali's use of *bimuruwatti*, the Persianzed Arabic term for "unmanliness," assumes that being more animal, or less human, is the same as being an overly sexual male; in this way, he confirms that he sees the concupiscent faculty as normatively male, and exclusionary to females. The association of too much expression of bodily desire (*shahwat*) with inhumanness and unmanliness underscores both the association of women with animals and the corporeal limitations of women's bodies, as well as the permanent association of bodily discipline with men. To use Beauvoir's terms, women's permanent corporeality is their immanence, and men's discipline is their transcendence. Unmanliness (*bimuruwatti*) as the result of expressing too much of the concupiscent faculty (*quwwat-i shahwi*) shows that Ghazali's definition of manhood is partly the control of virility and sexual prowess—not its deployment. To Ghazali, carnal appetite (*shahwat*) is an animalistic characteristic that takes away from one's humanity. In contrast, later in the same passage, Ghazali explains that if a man limits his carnal appetite too much, this also brings about unmanliness (*namardi*), lethargy, and madness.[123] This usage of a second concept of unmanliness, using the Persian term *namardi*, can refer to impotence, since here Ghazali implies a lack of male sexual function. According to the ethicists, a man should procreate in order to do his part to continue the human race and create opportunities for himself to earn blessings.[124] Taken together, Ghazali is prescribing moderation: one must display manliness by procreating but also display manliness by disciplining one's sexual appetite so as not to become animalistic.

Tusi and Davani define deficiency in exercise of the concupiscent faculty (*quwwat-i shahwi*) as "being at rest from movement in search of necessary pleasures in which the law and the intellect have given him leave to partake."[125] Like Ghazali, they prescribe moderation, but they are more interested in highlighting the lawfulness and necessity of food, clothing, and sex, the things that concupiscent faculty (*quwwat-i shahwi*) seeks in order to warn against a false show of self-restraint. Tusi and Davani state that the counterfeiters control the concupiscent faculty (*quwwat-i shahwi*) for the wrong reasons. They deprive themselves of comfort in the hopes that they will receive it in double measure, in either this life or the hereafter, or in the hopes of preventing diseases that arise from overindulgence.[126] Tusi and Davani stress that one should strive for consuming enough to fulfill one's needs and not more. It is a disciplined perfection that only elite men can achieve. The same male exclusivity is true of the culminating virtue of justice.

Justice: The Ultimate Virtue and Male Responsibility

The ethicists conceive of justice (*'adalat*) as the crowning, ultimate male virtue that encompasses both the principle of moderation and the social responsibility of fairness and equitability for the purpose of cultivating vicegerency of God (*khilafah*). It is the virtuous behavior that allows for the patriarchal ordering of women and other intellectually deficient non-elites in God's name. For Tusi, justice is the composite result of the three faculties of the *nafs* producing their respective virtues; an ethical man emerges who exudes the quality of justice (*'adalat*) in his dealings.[127] Further, he states that, "among virtues, none is more perfect than the virtue of justice, as is obvious from the discipline of ethics."[128] By this he means that the discipline itself is ultimately about achieving justice (*'adalat*), which in this case means moderation. For Ghazali and Davani, justice comes forth naturally from the exercise of the faculty of rationality. All three ethicists agree that justice is an essential means for attaining the ultimate goals of *akhlaq*, that is, realizing true happiness for the self and facilitating happiness for others as a vicegerent (*khalifah*) of God and microcosm of the world. The masculine nature of the virtues leads up to this ultimate male responsibility of creating the circumstances of justice ('adl) in the world. As such, men's unique ability to moderate the faculties of the *nafs* in order to yield justice ('adalat), the association of rationality, and therefore justice, with the male *nafs*, and the moral responsibility of becoming a vicegerent (*khalifah*) all make justice a quintessentially male virtue, and a prerogative of males to dole out.

Although Ghazali's sectarian commitments preclude him from discussing 'adalat, or justice, as a cornerstone of his science of the *nafs*,[129] he does state that equilibrium, justice, and moderation are important in an individual's achievement of ethical behavior.[130] In the *Kimiya-i Sa'adat*, Ghazali discusses the kindness required of an ethical man in terms of his treatment of relatives, children, friends, neighbors, enslaved people, and strangers.[131] He uses terms such as "kindness," "responsibility," "love," and "mercy" to describe behavior required of a man who is the leader of his household and a leader in his community.[132] These closely resemble the qualities that make up the virtue of justice ('adalat) in Tusi's and Davani's texts. The students of *akhlaq* from either the Ghazali or the Tusi-Davani perspective would have a similar definition of *khilafah* and goal of orienting themselves as a mirror of the cosmos.

In Tusi's and Davani's works, the major indication that justice is a gendered male virtue is the male-oriented responsibility of becoming a vicegerent (*khalifah*).[133] Quite contrary to wadud's application of *khilafah*,[134] the ethicists saw *khilafah* (vicegerency) in a male light, particularly since they enumerated women's role in life as subservience to their husbands, and since they furnished the concept of *khilafah* using the male dominance of the public sphere. They enumerate twelve qualities of the virtue of justice ('adalat): "friendship, affinity, loyalty, compassion, care of kin, requital, good companionship, good judgment, affection, submission, trust, and devotion."[135] These qualities can be divided into two categories—a man's worldly ethical responsibilities and a man's cosmic role in this universe—although they all are interconnected with a person's unified practice of *akhlaq*.

The ethicists articulate the worldly ethical responsibilities either in male homosocial terms or in terms of patriarchal care for friends, family, and society at large. Friendship (*sadaqat*) is the true love a man has for a friend, enough to drive a man to put everything he has toward providing relief for his friend in distress.[136] Davani elaborates that in accordance with a hadith, a man should dislike for his friend what he dislikes for himself and desire for his friend what he desires for himself.[137] Here Tusi and Davani are speaking of friends who are equals. The element of affinity (*ulfat*) is defined as cooperation between two distinct groups who share opinions and beliefs on the regulation of daily life.[138] Achieving affinity (*ulfat*) involves an element of leadership and male authority. The third quality of loyalty (*wafa'*) is staying committed to the charity and aid of others.[139] The fourth quality of compassion (*shafaqat*) is the awareness that bad luck can befall anyone and the willingness to do what one can for an unlucky person.[140] Davani elaborates on compassion using gendered metaphors: "to the masters of clarity and people of perception, it is evident and true that all the atoms of the universe are construed with existence from the true Living Unity, and all the possible creations sucking milk of discipline from breasts of divine guidance are equal in spirit and close in station and destination, especially human beings who according to clear commands of the book have a strengthened unifying spiritual affinity."[141]

Divine guidance and discipline are metaphors of the nourishing maternal body. The powers of giving life and sustenance are clearly seen as feminine, and as I discuss in the next chapter, they are also the essential aspects of motherhood that afford it respect from the ethicists. The feminine powers of God sustain and give wisdom to all creation, of which every atom is equal. It is by virtue of their ontological equality that human beings treat one another justly. Further, the kinship established by spiritual equality ensures ontological equality.

Despite this supposed ontological equality, compassion (*shafaqat*) is not a natural reflex; rather, it is dependent upon a man's ability to empathize with others. Davani cites a ninth-/tenth-century sufi, Shaykh Shibli, to explain that empathy is like the line between imagination and reality: "The marks of the stick with which he hit an animal appeared on his [own] body parts."[142] Then he uses the metaphor of the fear of heights when walking across a high wall as opposed to an equally narrow stretch of land to explain the way the "imagination acts upon natural affairs" as being similar.[143] In the context of compassion (*shafaqat*), these examples mean that one's feeling of compassion for others is situational and dependent upon one's own perception; one can feel compassion if one uses one's mind to perceive another's hardship.[144] Empathy is key for displaying the virtue of justice, even if, as I show later, it might be contradictory to the limited scope of how the ethicists suggest to apply justice.

Another quality of the virtue of justice is "care of kin" (*sila-i rahim*), defined as allowing one's family and associates to share in one's worldly possessions.[145] Additionally, Davani defines moral and spiritual kin relations as people with whom one has spiritual affinity.[146] This aspect of justice extends a man's doling out of resources as a head of household or of society. Requital (*mukafat*) is the habit of paying back kindness done to oneself with what was given to one, and retaliating against an evil with a lesser evil than was done to one.[147] Good companionship (*husn-i shirkat*) is being considerate of others' natural inclinations during transactions and avoiding offending one's partners. Because Tusi and Davani use the term "transaction" here, good companionship refers to one's work or business relationships, not domestic ones, although one can argue that because the *nikah* (marriage contract) is a transaction in the legal genre, good companionship with partners also includes one's wife.[148] Good judgment (*husn-i qada*) is repaying someone without regret or grudge and keeping oneself free from favoritism or blame.[149] Affection (*tawaddud*) is seeking love of virtuous men and peers, those with continence and fair speech (which excludes women).[150] Davani adds that one may bestow kind words, favors, or gifts upon such men.

The remaining three elements of justice (*'adalat*) account for a man's cosmic role in deploying his power to subvert or maintain society's status quo as part of God's will. The first is submission (*taslim*), the happy acceptance of actions that are solely taken for the Creator's pleasure and abiding by the commands of God.[151] In Tusi's definition of submission, he includes submitting to those against whom opposition is not possible, even if it goes against one's natural inclination.[152] This definition implies that one's search for justice is limited by the amount of power one has against an oppressor. The ethicists teach selflessness but only insofar as one can maintain the ability to be good and do good for others. For instance, taking an action, however right, that would result in danger or one's incarceration would be ill advised according to this code of ethics.[153] Accordingly, Tusi and Davani define the required element of trust in God (*tawakkul*) in justice as follows: "In acts that are not entrusted to the power or capacity of the humans and that the opinions and knowledge of creation have no ability to control, do not seek to create benefits or harm or hastening or delay, and do not incline against the way things are."[154] Men should surrender to the reality of extant power structures as the will of God.[155] This instruction not only speaks to the practicality of the ethics genre, but also shows that ethical men must always think of their attitude with respect to the Divine, not just their behavior.

The last element of justice, devotion or worship (*'ibadat*), reinforces awareness of God as essential for reaching the ultimate goal of vicegerency. To be just, one should be devoted to one's Creator, as well as "those close to His presence, such as angels, prophets, imams, and saints (peace be upon them) and following and obeying them, and submitting to the commands and prohibitions of the people of the law. One should cover and clothe oneself in the things that complete and perfect in meaning the concept of *taqwa* [consciousness of God]."[156]

Davani adds that one should be devoted to the Creator regardless of any prior benefits one has received from God's blessings. This remark shows that a continuous awareness of God is necessary in order to maintain justice.

The two aspects of justice, the worldly and the cosmic, are brought together by the overarching goal of becoming a patriarchal vicegerent (*khalifah*). Tusi explains the importance of justice as a virtue being displayed when a man reaches the ultimate station of having a perfected *nafs*.[157] He states that "wisdom comes from justice and justice comes from wisdom, or (one may say) that what is meant by 'wisdom' here is the use of the Practical Intelligence in the proper manner, which is also called 'practical philosophy.'"[158] This declaration shows not only that the virtue justice's relationship to the virtue of wisdom (*hikmat*) is circular, but also that the two virtues support each other in practice and emerge with the practice of *akhlaq*. A man's wise acts are identical to his just and ethical acts, and these are closely tied to a man's ultimate goal of achieving happiness and vicegerency of God (*khilafah*).

Becoming a source of justice is to become a mirror of God's justice in a cosmic sense. Tusi explains the relationship between a man's microcosmic and macrocosmic ethics as follows:

When the human reaches to this level [of perfection], that he becomes fully aware of the ranks of the universe, the infinite particular rules are recorded under the general rules . . . and when his practice becomes familiar [to him], such that his sayings and doings are achieved on account of strength and preferred habits, that person becomes a world unto himself, comparable to the *'alam-i kabir* [macrocosm], and he deserves the right to be called *'alam-i saghir* [microcosm].[159]

Tusi explicitly explains how the individual is the first level for ethical knowledge and practice. Becoming a microcosm (*'alam saghir*) is akin to internalizing the balance and beauty with which God has endowed the world, to the point that one's actions are a balanced and ethical world unto themselves. Put another way, it is only when a man has internalized the knowledge of the order of the world that he is able to mirror that world order. This means that he not only accepts the hierarchy of the prevailing cosmology of the world, but actively partakes in maintaining it as a *khalifah*, or vicegerent of God. It is in becoming a microcosm of the world unto himself and a *khalifah* that he is able to fulfill God's intent for his role in the cosmos: "Thus he becomes the vicegerent of God most high among God's creations, among God's pure saints, a complete and absolute human. Complete and absolute is one who has permanence and persistence, is blessed with the benefits of eternal happiness and sustained mercy, and is fit to receive God's abundance."[160]

According to Tusi, the ultimate goal of ethical training of the *nafs* is for the human to better himself and his world, as part of God's vicegerency.

Davani supports his simpler model of the *nafs* by quoting Ghazali's definition of *al-'adl* (justice) from the *Ihya' 'Ulum ad-Din*, arguing that this *nafs* achieves justice more readily: "Equity is a state of the *nafs*; its power overtakes anger (*ghazb*) and carnal appetite (*shahwat*) and guides them according to wisdom, and orders them when necessary during their exertion and contraction."[161] By adding Ghazali's definition of justice to his own, Davani holds that the virtue of justice comes from within the balanced intellectual mind, rather than being a composite or resultant virtue.

Synthesizing Ghazali's notion of justice (*'adalat*) as moderation and Tusi's notion of justice as equity for the sake of achieving *khilafah*, Davani describes a human being's responsibility to train his *nafs* in order to fulfill the purpose for which God created him. In the introduction, which he titles "Sunrise" ("Matla'"), as well as in the final "flash" of the treatise (*lam'ah*)—before the conclusion of the treatise titled "Sunset" ("Maghrib")—Davani discusses humanity's ultimate goal: "The end of the human, which is the essence of the worlds and the eye of eyes, the selected one of the world, is the vicegerency of God. . . . Mankind's right to the title of vicegerent is because of the perfection of his potential."[162]

The human's vicegerency of God is completed through the administration of just governance, as I discuss in chapter 4,[163] but is also carried out by "the common men" through the equitable distribution of money and resources, which are in the hands of men in their capacity as "citizens" and "men of reason and discernment [who] realize that wisdom and justice make up the conditions of aptitude for such rank."[164] Tusi explains that money has this effect because it "is the equalizer of diversities," though it is in the hands of men to dole out.[165] Thus, when discussing justice or fairness in real-life situations on the domestic and societal levels, they at times speak of men enacting justice in monetary or economic terms.[166] The association of monetized notions of justice with vicegerency (*khilafah*) emerges from romantic Sunni narratives about the four righteous caliphs' use of the treasury (*Bait al Mal*) to enact distributive justice among the early Muslim community.[167] Justice through money is specifically associated with male leadership.

In the final component of their discussion about justice, Tusi and Davani outline the vices related to the false or poor expression of justice. Tusi defines the opposite of justice as tyranny. Again in financial terms, tyranny is the "obtaining of the instruments of livelihood in reprehensible ways" and it creates suffering by "enabling the seeker of a livelihood by means of violence and plunder, complying with seizing it without just claim."[168] The impostors of justice "favor people who are not marked by the path of merit" or who squander wealth accumulated through the hard work of predecessors.[169]

Ghazali, Tusi, and Davani articulate the science of the *nafs* as a means for a man to achieve the ultimate goals of happiness for himself, happiness for the world around him, and adherence to God's plan for humanity. For Ghazali, man achieves the ultimate happiness by follow-ing the ethical path of faith and moderation. Likewise, in Tusi, man's bal-ance of the *nafses* makes him a microcosm, and thus a vicegerent of God (*khalifah*)—the ultimate goal. For both Tusi and Davani, the hard work that preserves the intellectual over the bodily powers enables him to ful-fill his purpose as the vicegerent of God.

The three ethicists differ in the specific terms they use to describe man's goal of carrying out God's plan, in the specifics of their models of the human *nafs*, and in their sectarian or philosophical allegiances. Nev-ertheless, a comparison of their treatises demonstrates that all three conceived of the human *nafs* in normative male terms. The examples they use in describing the *nafs*'s faculties, virtues, and vices all revolve around male contexts and male powers of self-discipline. The ethicists imagine the science of the *nafs* as being only applicable to men. This science is further gendered male by the fact that it assigns the male student of *akhlaq* the responsibility to be a steward of ethics in his world. The ethi-cists assert that possessing virtues is praiseworthy, but only if a person uses them in interacting with others, or passes those virtues on to oth-ers by example.[170] As such, the science of the *nafs* lays the foundation for men to take their place in the hierarchy of beings, a hierarchy that is built upon the assumption that no other individuals, including men of lower status and women, have access to this cosmic science. As such, *akhlaq* is an ethics of exclusion.

IMPERFECT HIERARCHY OF THE *NAFSES*: ANIMAL, VEGETABLE, MAN, AND WOMAN

Even though the *nafs*, with all its virtues and vices, is normatively male in *akhlaq* texts, the ethics of exclusion is imperfect; the texts contain at least three significant textual contradictions to the ethicists' cosmology, which disrupt their elite male-centrism. First, the primary standard for achieving the goals of *akhlaq* is use of the intellect, and yet the ethicists imagine that not everyone has the requisite intellectual capacity to do so. Despite the cosmic equality of all matter, existence is hierarchical, and so is humanity. The second textual contradiction is that, even though the texts explicitly state that the females in any species are infe-rior to the males, they also internally break this rule when describing other criteria of superiority, such as the ability to search for nourishment. Third, the very principle that makes humans superior as a class—their possession of rationality—does not apply to women or to inferior classes of men, who are considered to be deficient in rationality, just as animals are. I demonstrate how the Muslim ethicists hold that humans, as a class, stand above animals but exclude women from rationality such that they deny their full humanity. There is only then an a priori metaphysical equality in creation; the ethicists did not believe that God created women and nonelites equal to elite men. The three contradictions lead us to understand the very tools of *akhlaq*—namely, reliance on rationality and understanding of the nature of men's souls (compared to that of women and nonelites)—as well as the resulting hierarchical cosmology as contradictory. Although I focus this section on Tusi's work, since it is he who most extensively discusses the natural world, I also refer to Ghazali's and Davani's animal metaphors of human behavior.

In Tusi's attempt to contextualize the human *nafs* in all of creation, he states that man's goal is to become a microcosm of the universe by establishing his *nafs*'s superiority and *khilafah* or vicegerency. He then provides a detailed classification of all living creatures' *nafses*. Tusi's foray into the natural world shows how the dimensions of gender, social class, and even race complicate the living world's intellect-based hierarchy. As Tusi explains the hierarchy of creation based on the intellect, it becomes apparent that many traits of the *nafs* appear on a spectrum across plants, animals, and human animals. In the process of explaining why some vegetables turn out to be superior to some animals, or why some females are superior to males—on the grounds that intelligence is the paramount criterion for establishing rank, and indeed ethical potential—he breaks his own principle of unconditional male superiority in all species.

Tusi explains that all living things are created of equally valued substances and particles but are ranked hierarchically according to the abilities of their *nafses* to perform higher-order acts of intelligence. According to Tusi, "natural bodies, from the perspective of being bodies, are equal to each other in rank; one is not above another in virtue or nobility, for one definition includes all of them and one form of principal matter values them, as a whole."[171] This explanation implies not only that all human beings are equal, but also that human beings are equal with animals and vegetation. Yet, differences exist in rank among natural bodies, based on the potential of their faculties to commit intelligent acts. The human *nafs*'s faculty of rationality is the highest order of intelligence and is the distinguishing characteristic that defines human beings' exceptionalism as a species. Humans are superior to species of animal and vegetable because they possess rationality and the ability to perceive and discriminate among things.[172] Men who have the capacity for ethical perfection are placed at the top of the hierarchy of existence in the living world because, in the male-centered science of the *nafs*, rationality is equated with male power. According to Tusi, not all human beings possess these gifts equally, and women and men of lower classes are particularly deficient in them.[173]

Tusi's hierarchical spectrum of the traits of the *nafs*, as well as by extension his classification of all living creatures, re-creates the Greek philosophical concept of hierarchy. According to Arthur Lovejoy, who described this hierarchy as the "great chain of being," it was central to Western philosophy from the medieval period to the eighteenth century.[174] Lovejoy identifies three principles, systematized by Plotinus, that Plato and Aristotle held to describe all the beings in the universe: plenitude, continuity, and gradation. Plenitude meant that the world contains all the beings that could possibly exist and that they rank from highest to lowest. Continuity is the idea that beings of various grades possess traits on a continuum, and that traits possessed by one grade of beings are also possessed by the next class on a chain. The third concept, gradation, dictates that the chain of traits from one class to the next is organized in "*scala naturae* according to degree of 'perfection,'" which was the "degree of development reached by [an] offspring at birth."[175] The traits were "powers of the soul," such as nutritive and rational powers.[176] For Aristotle in particular, these general rules did not mean that all beings could be placed consecutively on the chain of being; instead, because some potentialities existed in beings that may or may not be realized, individuals could exist above or below their own rightful intellectual or natural class.[177]

As a general rule, for Tusi, plants, animals, and humans all exist on a spectrum of intelligence and active principles. Grass and trees that exist merely as a result of the mingling of the elements of wind, sun, and water do not possess a desire for reproduction—they lack a concupiscent faculty—and thus are lowly forms of vegetation. Seed-bearing grasses and fruit-bearing trees are superior to those that exist without these, since they exhibit a will to live, an instinct to reproduce and continue their own species.

Tusi also draws gendered distinctions within classes, albeit still based on the principle of the being's potential for intelligent acts. For example, among the seed- and fruit-bearing vegetables, "the nobler of some of these are the male individuals, which are the original form of progeny, and are distinguished from the female individuals, which are the origins of the matter."[178] So, even though the females are from the same matter, or are even the source of the matter, the males are the "original form of progeny," meaning they are the prototypical, and thus primary, embodiment of the fruit-bearing organism.[179] The males provide the form; therefore, they are the more active, intelligent members of the species. In Tusi's classification of nafses, as seen in the example of elemental vegetation versus seed-bearing plants, gender is important in determining the relative value of beings and ascertaining the superiority of certain beings over others. This point coheres with how Tusi compares the human reproductive systems of men and women, with the former being ascribed greater importance in conception and in the offspring's expression of traits.[180]

One curious example in Tusi's classification of a fruit-bearing tree, the date palm, departs from Tusi's general principle of male superiority, illustrating again how Tusi's hierarchy of nafses is driven by notions of intelligence and active principles. He says that the Prophet "called the date tree the paternal aunt of the human species and has said, 'Honor your paternal aunt, the date palm, for she was created from the remainder of Adam's clay.'"[181] Tusi explains that even as this tree possesses the vegetative soul (nafs-i nabati), it also possesses reproductive characteristics similar to animals, such as the odor of its fluids and its ability to die when submerged underwater, taken over by pests, or cut off at the head. The date palm also cannot pollinate with any species other than itself, which signals to Tusi that it is capable of love and affection. In short, the date palm possesses everything an animal's soul does, except for the will to uproot itself "from the ground and move away in search of nourishment."[182] In this example, Tusi extols all of the qualities of the date palm's soul but does not say that it is considered a female in the Prophet's hadith, even though the tree is both fruit-bearing and obviously a superior vegetable (superior even to some animals) in the hadith. The date palm is a superior female that does not fit neatly into his gender cosmology. The tree's adherence to active principles and its superior intellect are his main standards for measuring the potential of its *nafs*. In other words, in this example, intelligence can supersede gender in establishing criteria for hierarchy. This contradiction in rules for gender and standards for intellect-based hierarchy actually contradicts *akhlaq* cosmology itself.

Like Tusi, Ghazali uses the natural world, particularly animal metaphors, to explain that humans' possession of the rational faculty is what distinguishes them from animals. He groups the soul's appetites into four categories. First, the bestial disposition (*akhlaq-i bahayim*), which is another term for the concupiscible faculty, has a predilection for excessive eating, copulation, and anger, all behaviors associated with animalia. Second, the predatory disposition (*akhlaq-i saba'a*), which corresponds to the irascible faulty, drives human beings to behave like "dogs, wolves, and lions, beating, killing, and falling upon people by the hand and tongue."[183] The third appetite, which Ghazali omits in the earlier discussion of metaphysics of the *nafs*, is the devilish disposition (*akhlaq-i shayatin*), which is responsible for foul behavior toward others, such as "deceit, fraud, misrepresentation, instigating disagreement and discord between people, and doing devilish deeds."[184] The final appetite discussed by Ghazali is the angelic disposition (*akhlaq-i malakah*, pl. *akhlaq-i mala'ika*), which enables a human being to "do angelic acts, love knowledge and propriety, refrain from ugly acts, seek goodness among people, keep himself above lowly acts, be happy in the knowledge of works, and find fault with ignorance and foolishness."[185]

According to Ghazali, people can act like angry dogs, greedy pigs, evil demons, or cerebral angels (see table 2.1 for names of parts of the *nafs* and their corresponding traits, virtues, and vices). Ghazali explains, "If you succumb to the carnality of the pig, in you the attributes of filth, shamelessness, greed, sycophancy, lowliness, being happy in others' sorrow, and envy manifest."[186] The way to control piggish carnality is through disciplined thinking, reflection, and control,[187] and the opposite of piggishness is "contentment, self-restraint, shame, peace, ingenuity, piety, noncovetousness, and moderation."[188] Next, Ghazali notes that "if you submit to the dog of anger, in you manifest rashness, impurity, arrogance, scheming, pomposity, ridicule of others, demeaning others, contempt, and oppression of others."[189] Once the dog is treated with discipline, the opposing attributes that will come through are "patience, forbearance, forgiveness, stability, courage, peacefulness, boldness, and generosity."[190]

According to Ghazali, the key wonder of the human soul is its ability to "subdue to itself powerful animals such as the elephant, lion, or horse. Everything in the world, its skills and wonders are [man's] calling and that knowledge is acquired by way of the five senses."[191] The soul is also a mirror reflecting the celestial realm, which can be known to human beings through dreams and through the inner voice that guides the sages, who have perfected *nafses*. The final goal for Ghazali is to train the *nafs* in order to perfect one's practice of the path of faith (*rah-i din*), which leads to ultimate happiness/flourishing (*sa'adat*). This involves becoming the least animallike as possible.

Like Ghazali, who focuses on distinguishing human from animal, Tusi focuses on the ways in which the metaphysical soul is housed in the physical body and how rationality distinguishes man from animallike behavior. Also like Ghazali, Tusi compares the behaviors of pigs and dogs to people who do not control their pleasure and hunger impulses.[192] The human soul is distinguished from the animal's by its rationality, although the rest of their faculties are shared in common.

In animals, Tusi valorizes the qualities of self-sufficiency, the ability to guard oneself, and, above all, the ability to adapt and change. Animals that possess their own tools for protection, such as antlers, horns, or claws, are of higher station than animals that are defenseless. Although vegetative souls are generally inferior to animal souls, there are some exceptions in the case of very simple animals, such as seasonal insects.[193] The most noble (*sharif*) of any "animal species," according to Tusi, "is the one whose sagacity and understanding reaches the extent that it accepts discipline and education until it attains perfection that was not originally created in it. Such are the disciplined horse and trained falcon."[194] For Tusi, the horse and the falcon are noble precisely because they have the wisdom to accept discipline in order to attain perfection. He notes, though, that the distinction between the highest animal and the lowliest of human beings is that the latter has the ability to perform a task merely by observing it, "without training or wearisome toil spent for them."[195] In Davani's comparison of animal and human *nafses*, he points out that humans who simply memorize or copy knowledge, as parrots or monkeys do, are not really thinking deeply. The acts of copying or memorizing cause humans (or, at least, just men) to fall below their potential for full rationality.[196] Applying the ethicists' main standards for ethical perfection—intelligence and the acceptance of discipline—disrupts the ethicists' own hierarchical ideas about who possesses rationality.

The idea that each human can individually rise above or fall below peers of their own class on a hierarchy of noble qualities has serious implications for where to place women or nonelite men. Sarra Tlili explains that premodern Muslim exegetes, including those with and without training in Hellenistic *falsafa*, recognized that in the Qur'an, animals are capable of crossing over the line between animals and humans by possessing intelligence, problem-solving skills, and even morality and spirituality.[197] Tlili's ecocentric reading of the Qur'an problematizes the way premodern Muslim thinkers understood the status of human as *khalifah* over animals vis-à-vis internalizing the notion of the great chain of being. If some vegetables, like the date palm, can possess animallike faculties while others do not, and some animals can possess humanistic elements of rationality while others do not, then the humans who possess less rationality, such as women, are more animallike in this cosmology. Returning to the example of the falcon and the horse, Tusi praises these animals in particular because they are used by men for transportation, hunting, and recreation. This praise reinforces the idea that within the hierarchical cosmology, beings of low classification are in service to the higher.

All three ethicists assert that the primary difference between the human animal and other animals is the endowment of the rational *nafs*. Tusi explains that humans are ranked according to three major stations of virtue:

The first rank of persons is those who by means of intelligence and speculative faculty bring about noble productions and order precise skills and graceful instruments. Above them is a group who by reason, thought, and much contemplation plunges into the sciences, knowledge, and acquisition of virtues. Beyond them are persons who receive revelation and divine inspiration of knowledge of the truths and laws from those close to the Divine presence without intermediary bodies. These [people] are for the perfection of the disposition, the ordering of affairs of life and hereafter, and the basis of comfort and happiness of people from all climes and ages.[198]

Beyond these ranks come the angels and abstract intelligences, whose station is closest to the Divine. This scheme of humanity's virtue, which is similar to that laid out by Ibn Sina and the peripatetics, is based on individuals' material or intellectual contributions to society and largely corresponds to trades. The hierarchy of human beings corresponds to the classification of knowledge, sciences, and philosophy, with the more exalted persons practicing the more exalted sciences (see figure 1.1 in the previous chapter).

These ranks have a gendered dimension, even if Tusi does not speak of specific roles for men and women. With only men participating in the advancement of human skills, knowledge, philosophy, and ideas, the very classification of human beings based on professions existing in the public, urban sphere is limited to the male-gendered realm. Men's ranks are primary and determine the relative value of all beings. As I show in the next chapter, women are conceptualized in terms of their utility for men, particularly child-bearing and the lower-order work they do to free up men for higher-order tasks.[199] The passage just given shows that the imagined ethical world itself is this intellectual and occupational hierarchy of the premodern Muslim, Persianate society. Even though women possess *nafs* by virtue of being human, they are weak and lack superior rationality. Likewise, the *nafs* as it is thought about in the science of ethics (*tahzib-i akhlaq*) is normatively male, and it has the power to control other *nafses* that are dominated by their bestial and savage components.[200]

The hierarchy of the three major stations of virtues also shows how people of various "climes and ages" exist in various classifications, including enslaved labor. In the premodern Persian world, interactions between people of different climes usually occurred in the context of enslaved labor. Tusi suggests how lower-ranked individuals sustain the lives of the virtuous ones who are ranked at the top: "Nourishment is not created without organization of sowing, harvesting, milling, kneading, baking, and compounding. Neither is clothing attained without application of spinning, weaving, tailoring, and tanning leather. Neither do weapons come into being without art, purifying, and measuring."[201]

Although these activities are necessary for the sustenance of humanity, they are considered lowly. Ann Lambton finds that, in medieval Persia, enslaved men and women composed a significant contingent of agricultural labor. This included both local and foreign individuals from Abyssinia and Greece, as well as "Turks, Qazvinis, Anatolians, Gregorians, Indians, Rus, [and] negroes (*zanji*)."[202] In Tusi's two passages or social classes, he creates a labor-based hierarchy of manliness in which the highest classes are intellectual and the lowest classes are instrumental. This hierarchy corresponds to women's roles in the domestic economy in relation to their husbands-cum-masters, as well as to assumptions about race. Regarding "the people who live on the sidelines of the inhabited world like Sudan and the Maghrib and others," Tusi states, "the movements and actions of the likes of these types correspond to the actions of animals."[203] For Tusi, people from sideline regions were racialized to some extent, and their darker complexion roughly mapped onto lower rank in the intellectual hierarchy of humanity, as well as heightened concupiscent faculties.

Race itself is relevant to human hierarchies, though not necessarily associated with slavery. The ethicists lived in a world in which men and women from various races could be enslaved. Premodern sociologist Ibn Khaldun held that certain negative behavioral characteristics, such as stupidity and animal impulses, were associated with being of darker race (or from hot climates),[204] but this is quite separate from the *akhlaq* rationale for the reduced rational condition thought to have been associated with enslaved persons of all races. In *akhlaq* texts, enslaved persons are not specifically racialized, which does not mean that the ethicists did not pay attention to racial characteristics of the enslaved; rather, it means that they relied primarily on their circular reasoning that slave status was the primary explanation for these individuals' substandard rationality and life of enslavement, and that slave status degraded their human capability of rationality, as opposed to relying on specific racial explanations for their inferiority. In this way, elite men justified their rule as the most rational class of persons. However, the ethicists' reliance on rationality as the ethical justification for hierarchy unravels when we consider the variations in both males and females' animalistic needs and rational potentials.

Irigaray has argued that, in Greek philosophy, men are understood as disembodied because they are concerned with lofty intellectual goals, while women are embodied—and implicitly limited by their bodies—because of their biological function of reproduction. By conceiving, birthing, and nurturing children, a woman "aids and abets the phallic order."[205] In accordance with women's supporting role, they are concerned with "the minor arts: cooking, knitting, embroidery, and sewing. . . . Whatever their importance, these arts do not currently make the rules."[206]

Irigaray's critique of philosophy's disembodied intellectual man highlights how the training of the *nafs* is a mental discipline, by which man can perfect himself and fulfill the cosmic role he was meant to play on Earth. But her critique also helps us to see a fissure in the *akhlaq* texts that gives an opening to women. Even though the *akhlaq* discipline is intellectual, and therefore male, the male student of ethics still remains embodied to some extent since the ethicists claim it is by virtue of a man being a human animal that his *nafs* is so sophisticated. The *akhlaq* texts prescribe rationality over the body's functions, but still not only respect the body's needs, but also view the virtues that can come of the more corporeal irascible and concupiscent faculties. Man remains corporeal even in his transcendence and achievement of *khilafah*.

It is precisely the ethicists' recognition of the man's need for the corporeal faculties, as well as recognition of women's *nafses*, that disrupts their own gendered cosmology. Women are limited by their baser instincts, but so are men—hence the need for ethical refinement. Extant medical ideas that were inspired by Galenic and Hippocratic medicine, for example, that of Abu Bakr ar-Razi (d. 925), demonstrate how metaphysics was embodied, inextricably linked to the body's potentiality.[207] For ar-Razi, the soul is material and must be refined in order to return to God.[208] The exclusivity principle in *akhlaq* emerges when only elite men are presumed to have the ability for refinement, and indeed, as I show in the preceding section, the entire path of *akhlaq* is designed for them.

Ultimately, characterization of the *nafs* as human, distinguished from animals, disrupts the gender hierarchy in *akhlaq*. It is in this characterization that the ethicists recognize women's humanity. But paradoxically, the ethicists' gendered assumption that women have weaker rational faculties and stronger concupiscent faculties than men is at odds with recognition of their humanity since this assumption nearly dehumanizes women to the level of irrational animals.

In *akhlaq*, the *nafs* has an androgynous, egalitarian potentiality, but the ethicists' reliance on rationality as both a potential and a prerequisite for ethical refinement genders the language and concepts of *akhlaq* male. The ethicists describe the training of the *nafs* as it pertains only to elite men's lives. Man's training of his rational faculty allows him to express the virtue of wisdom, which comprises leadership qualities that he will enact in his role as the head of a domestic economy and as a leader or ruler in his city. For example, taming the irascible faculty curbs anger and cultivates courage, which is marked by masculine zeal. The ethicists imagine the concupiscible faculty as possessed by women as well as men, because it is the faculty of corporeal functions. Because the ethicists think of women as distinguished from men on the basis of their biological functions, they thought of women almost exclusively in terms of their bodies, and not their minds. Thus, the virtue coming from the concupiscible faculty, self-restraint, does not just contain feminine attributes; it is also the main virtue that women can express. For men, balancing the concupiscible faculty involves expressing the right amount of desire for comforts such as food, clothing, and sexual intercourse. Too much expression of the concupiscible faculty results in animalistic, and therefore unmanly, acts, and too little leads to lethargy, which is also unmanly.

Through the work of balancing the *nafs*, a man becomes a microcosm of the world. For all three ethicists, this leads to acting ethically in the world. For Tusi and Davani, acting ethically specifically means enacting justice either as a composite of the virtues or as a function of the faculty of wisdom. A man's ethical acts with members of his household, his community, and his city are a key means of achieving the goal of ultimate happiness/flourishing (*sa'adat*) and vicegerency (*khilafah*) of God on Earth. The identity of an ethical man, as tied to his broad social role, is defined in terms of two dimensions: the power, hierarchy of intellect, and ethical comportment he exercises in the home, which I discuss in the next chapter; and the homosocial structures within which he exists in court, civic, and community life, which I discuss in chapter 4.

Not only do the ethicists imagine the science of the *nafs* in male terms, but in their cosmology, they also imagine that not all human souls are created equal. Even though all of God's creation is equal, rationality supposedly distinguishes the human species as a whole from animals and vegetables. Human beings themselves are part of a gendered and intellectual hierarchy, in which some men stand above others. As the ethicists create a cosmology in which there are exceptions to the hierarchy of intellect—and the standards of ethical behavior are based solely on the intellect—they unwittingly create a space in which at least some women can be superior to men. This fact disrupts the science of the *nafs* they are constructing, calling into question the very criteria—rational capacity, gender, and class—that the ethicists use for deriving the supposedly ethical hierarchy. Indeed, how ethical is a system of ethics that assumes only men have the capacity to be ethical? In the next two chapters, I discuss how the assumption that only elite men have the capacity for ethical refinement creates gendered and class-based hierarchies that are codified as ethical, even as they create exclusivity.

CHAPTER THREE

Ethics of Marriage and the Domestic Economy

The female of the species is more deadly than the male.
—RUDYARD KIPLING

The ethics of marriage have very little to do with love. While all three ethicists, especially Davani, expand at great length on what love for a (male) friend signifies, their sections on marriage conspicuously omit a full explanation of what love for a wife means. Instead, in their passages regarding marriage, the ethics treatises of Ghazali, Tusi, and Davani each imagine the household as a macrocosm of the ethically ordered *nafs*, rather than a shared home built on a male–female love partnership: a husband applies discipline and principles from *tadhib-i akhlaq* to rule over his wife and the rest of the household for the purpose of his greater good. In the texts, women function as moral foils to men in the construction of masculine ethics; men are the subjects, women are the objects, and the relationship between men and women is merely a site of the man's ethical refinement. As such, the Muslim ethicists imagine the domestic economy as a utilitarian hierarchy, much like a sovereign state, that comprises a husband who acts as governor, a wife who plays his deputy and subject, their children, their enslaved or free servants, and perhaps elderly parents. In all three ethical treatises, the sections on domestic economy read like how-to guides for the men in charge, offering pragmatic advice on maintaining effective domestic rule and dominance. The treatises offer guidelines on four key areas of domestic economy: how to determine whether one is financially, emotionally, and spiritually ready to marry;

how to identify a wife who will be appropriately instrumental in running one's estate; how to live in an orderly way with one's wife and children while managing their *nafses*; and finally, how to develop a contingency plan in the event that the marriage does not work—that is, if one's wife subverts the proper male-headed hierarchy and makes divorce necessary. The ethicists' scrupulous effort to describe for men how they ought to control their wives is rooted in their anxiety that men could be manipulated by the sentiment of love into losing their power to women. They ameliorate this concern by emphasizing all the discipline men should exercise over members of their household and the ways they could adhere to and enforce what they regard as the natural order, even when they carry a tone of fear of women's fierceness—as Rudyard Kipling's poem conveys.

In considering how the ethicists construct gender roles within marriage, Judith Butler's conception of gender as scripted performance is useful.[1] Specifically, the ethicists' behavioral advice for courtship, marriage, rearing children, and divorce serves as performative scripts for men to enact with their wives. The *akhlaq* texts make men aware of such scripts so they can embody ideal masculinity, ensure their wives conform to their ideals, and best execute their roles as leaders of the domestic economy. The ethicists do prescribe ideal feminine roles, but not for the benefit of women: these prescriptions, which appear within descriptions of virtuous and wayward women, are directed only at men in order to illustrate what behaviors they should expect from women.

On one hand, the ethicists recognize women's *nafses*, their basic intelligence and potential virtues, and the need to be generous with them owing to their husbands' power over them.[2] The ethicists believe that women and men are the same species on a humanistic level, and that women, like men, have *nafses* and humanistic impulses. But on the other hand, the ethicists also consistently imply that women are overly emotional, intellectually deficient, and lacking in self-control and self-awareness. In the ethicists' view, women need men to rule over them and keep them in their instrumental roles. And just as the metaphysical conceptions of the human *nafs* are gendered (as I showed in chapter 2), so too is the virtue ethics practice of *akhlaq* in the domestic context, which in effect excludes women from *akhlaq* training and relegates them to the path of instrumentality because ethical refinement is for elite men's *nafses* alone.

Because of this double standard in the ethicists' understanding of men's and women's potential, I argue that in the Ghazali-Tusi-Davani tradition's guidelines on marriage, we can detect a serious metaphysical tension in attitudes toward women: on one hand, the guidelines are designed to preserve and justify a man's power over his wife and to preserve and justify his wife's instrumentality, and yet on the other hand, the guidelines are also premised on her status as fully human, in possession of a *nafs* just as her husband is. As I argue in this chapter, we see this metaphysical tension within the ethicists' occasionally ambivalent teachings on how to treat a wife with regard to sex, money, parenthood, and the potentiality of divorce. Notwithstanding the metaphysical tension, the ethics that results is one of exclusion, domination, and utilization of women, premised upon the primary understanding of women as flawed creatures with flawed *nafses*.

One reason why the ethics texts describe women as having flawed *nafses* is because their driving idea is that men's ethical perfection occurs at the expense of women. In his careful analysis of how the *Ethicon* of the Syrian Orthodox bishop Bar Hebraeus (d. 1286) adapts Ghazali's discussion of the ideal wife from the *Ihya' 'Ulum ad-Din*, Lev Weitz argues that the image of the ideal wife in the *Ihya'* is compelling for bolstering male piety because it "has more to do with facilitating men's pious obligations than with women's own devotional practices."[3] Each of the ideal wifely characteristics Ghazali outlines ensures her instrumentality to her husband's endeavor to live a pious life and to the "proper ordering of household life."[4] The same is true in Ghazali's *Kimiya* and in Tusi's and Davani's ethics. Weitz applies Karen King's analysis of Philo's texts, which were intended for men but feature women in order to think "with women," as a textual device.[5] Elizabeth Clark has likewise discussed how Christian propaganda literature from the first three centuries of Christianity featured women in order to "think with" women, or use them as examples of mentally deficient people to whom "the Christian message is both easily comprehended and reforming of morals."[6] In *akhlaq* texts as well, women act as moral foils to men in order to create masculine ethics. Their moral weaknesses serve as the call for men's dominance over women's *nafses* and justify the patriarchal order of the household. However, as Weitz points out, even though such texts are ultimately for and about men, and even though they are really "cultural fantasies," they also shape men's and women's cultural expectations about the normative behavior of women.[7]

Teasing out the texts' assumptions about gender reveals a striking contrast between, on one hand, the fantasy of absolute gender segregation and women's imagined roles and, on the other hand, the actual gender relations that the ethicists themselves or their male audience likely encountered in real life. Carole Hillenbrand has shown that urban, rural, Persian, and nomadic Turkish women all primarily played roles of wife and mother and kept house, while rural women had additional responsibilities of working the land. Urban women of lower classes held employment as craftswomen, servants, nurses, midwives, singers, dancers, or prostitutes.[8] Marion Katz has shown that like men, women used the mosque for a full range of social, leisure, and legal purposes, much to the chagrin of 'ulama' at various periods in history.[9] The akhlaq texts tell us about the ethicists' assumptions about gender. Such assumptions are conveyed by premodern prescriptive texts addressed to men, whether examples of real or imagined women actually appear in them.[10] The normativity of the texts indicates that men's control of women's behavior was construed as essential to women's identity formation as well as the establishment of men's own moral character.

Along these lines, texts of other genres and historical records show that men's moral identities were reliant on that of women—or more precisely, that (male-centric) civilizations depended for their sense of worth on the characteristics of their women. Nadia El Cheikh has argued of women in Abbasid texts that women's piety, sexuality, and behavior all become markers of the worth of a civilization.[11] Even in men's travel narratives, comments about women are specifically oriented toward evaluation of women's morality. In a close reading of commentary about women in Ibn Battuta's journal of his thirty-year journey around the world, Roxanne Euben explains that Ibn Battuta describes women in terms of binaries, including "veiled and naked, visible and secluded, aristocrats and slaves, learned and illiterate, rich and poor, autonomous and obedient, . . . that overlap and intertwine."[12] She argues that his comments on different types of women "function as a kind of legend, as on a map, by which his male audience can decode the Rihla's taxonomy of peoples and cultures."[13] Unsurprisingly, Ibn Battuta praises pious women, properly veiled women, and certain aristocratic women who show him generosity and favors as a sign of their piety. Euben explains, "Ibn Battuta's focus on what he regards as proper religious observance also fuels a consistent preoccupation with women's sexual behavior and appearance, and a concomitant tendency to transform women into an index of the virtuous or value of an entire people, as when he deems the citizens of Shiraz particularly pious because of the modesty and purity of their women."[14] Yet Ibn Battuta also "frequently represents women as objects of sexual pleasure, indices of piety, or both at once," as indicated by his praise of Meccan women (who are "strikingly beautiful, pious, and chaste"), or the women of Marhata (Bangladesh), who have "in sexual intercourse a deliciousness and a knowledge of erotic movements that other women do not have."[15] It is in this context of gendered morality as civilizational worth that the *akhlaq* texts, concerned with ethical conduct, construct women in their ideal servile state or else as threatening to male power.

In this vein, Huda Lutfi has argued that prescriptive texts' presentation of strict guidelines for women express a form of wishful thinking and an attempt to curb or condemn scholars' real-life observations of morally loose women. In her examination of a Mamluk-era Cairene ethico-legal treatise by Ibn al-Hajj (d. 1336), Lutfi finds a significant "discrepancy between the theoretical and actual restrictions on women," particularly because the texts attempted to "correct" women's behaviors.[16] He deplores Mamluk women's active participation in public life, with frequent visits to sufi shrines, mosques, bazaars, and public baths to be "unislamic practices and extravagances" in the male domain.[17] He further holds that a "Muslim man should be responsible for the proper legal-Islamic behavior of his females, and he complains that in actuality women were left unguided and unrestricted, inviting and following their own ways."[18] In other words, scholarly literature indicates that, beyond the ethics tradition, there are other instances where premodern Muslim scholars conveyed ideals about women to men, ignoring social reality, in order to shape men's attitudes about and behaviors toward women, thereby shaping ideals, and possibly realities, of masculinity itself.

Men's responsibility for their wives is a central theme in the ethics treatises. The three ethicists advocate that men should ensure proper seclusion and control of their wives in order to maintain household order and discipline their own *nafses*.[19] The ethicists' injunctions appear to be motivated not only by having observed objectionable morals in real women, but also by a desire to control women's *nafses*. In the ethicists' focus on ordering the individual *nafs*, a key assumption they make is that women's rationality is inferior to that of men. Even though the ethicists all recognize women's humanity—as indicated by their belief that women are in possession of *nafses*[20]—they also regard women as deficient in rationality. Within this metaphysical tension—humanity versus deficiency—the ethicists believe that women are not able to discipline their own *nafses*, and that they need their husbands to do it for them. It is only in this hierarchical dynamic that the wife can fulfill her rightful, instrumental role and the husband can discharge the domestic component of his cosmic role.[21] Even though there is a metaphysical tension in the ethicists' understanding of women's existence, marriages only stay intact as long as these roles are maintained.

MARRIAGE: ITS UTILITARIAN HIERARCHY, RATIONALE, AND PREREQUISITES

Several scholars, including Karen Bauer and Kecia Ali, have described marriage as a gender hierarchy in Muslim thought, particularly genres of early/medieval Qur'anic exegesis and jurisprudence.[22] In *akhlaq*, the hierarchical marriage is more particularly an arrangement that provides men with the opportunity to execute ethical behavior toward their wives and wards, for the purpose of men's own ethical refinement. In this sense, marriage plays a crucial role in a man's ethical perfection and the ultimate goal of being a vicegerent of God (*khalifah*). In his capacity as the primary ethical subject, a man partially dispenses his ethical duties by heading the domestic economy and directing the ethical object, his wife, who herself does not have such ethical obligations. The hierarchy in marriage is rooted in the principles of governance that apply to running a state. In the ethical scheme of the domestic order, men and women play their respective roles to maintain the overall happiness of the members of their household. In *akhlaq*, this means that the marital relationship is based on a wife's instrumentality and a man's function of managing the wife, keeping her occupied, happy, and therefore productive. For Tusi and Davani, the man can accomplish his function by following a system of economic administration in the management of the wife and household.

Ghazali suggests that a man can achieve his purpose by displaying good behavior and comportment to his wife and by establishing moderation in all aspects of life, including household expenditures and time spent in worship or entertainment. This stance is reflected in Ghazali's title for all household-related ethics, "Comportment in marriage" (*Adab-i nikah*).

The basis of the marital bond in a hierarchal political model is evident in the title of Tusi's chapter on marriage, "Siyasat wa tadbir-i ahl" (The governance and management of the wife/family).[23] In Davani's treatise, his equivalent section is simply titled "Siyasat-i ahl" (Governing the wife/family).[24] The word *governance* (*siyasat*) connects the husband's marital rule to the model of sovereign rule by a governor or prince, and also refers back to the sovereignty metaphors used in discussions about ordering the *nafs*. Christian Lange has pointed out that the term *siyasa* meant not only governance and order in premodern Muslim courts, but also political expediency that formed the justification of penal authority and discretionary harsh punishments.[25] The premodern readers of the Ghazali-Tusi-Davani ethics tradition would have been aware of that coercive connotation of the term *siyasat*. The term *tadbir*, which appears in chapter headings in works of *falsafa* and *akhlaq*, has been translated by scholars of Persian philosophical texts as economics, reflecting the similarity of content between these texts and concepts of *oikonomia* and household governance in Greek philosophical treatises. For example, G. M. Wickens translates Tusi's *tadbir-i manzil* simply as "economics."[26] A more accurate translation would be "household management." Finally, the Persian word *ahl* means people, family, or kin. The ethicists also use the term with singular pronouns when referring to women, which means that the word can also mean "wife."

In what read like incentivizing expositions, Tusi, Davani, and Ghazali outline for their readers the purposes and benefits of marriage. According to Tusi and Davani, the main reason that one should marry is to procreate and sustain humanity. For Davani, a significant benefit of marriage is that it can protect the soul from the sin of adultery,[27] while for Tusi, marriage is advantageous because a wife can assist in the "protection of property" by serving as a deputy to her husband's estate.[28] Because Tusi is focused on the utilitarian use of the wife, he insists that control of the carnal appetite is not a good reason to marry.[29] Ghazali agrees with Tusi and Davani that one should marry in order to procreate and sustain humanity. More specifically than the other two ethicists, Ghazali points out five benefits of marriage for men. First, regarding the immense spiritual reward (*savab*) that comes from procreation,[30] Ghazali mentions that there are blessings in increasing God's favorite creation and increasing the number of followers of the Prophet. Providing for a wife and children is counted as a great act of charity, even nobler than committing oneself to a struggle for the sake of Islam. Further, children pray for their parents long after the latter's death.[31] The second benefit of marriage for a man is that it strengthens his faith by providing a legal avenue for sexual intercourse. In other words, marital sex is the means through which the concupiscent faculty (*quwwat-i shahwat*) is controlled. Thus, marriage is a crucial component to balancing a man's *nafs*. The third benefit is the affection and comfort one feels in a woman.[32] Although the main framework for marriage is management of the domestic economy, Ghazali (like Tusi and Davani) recognizes that a man's emotions are bound up in the marital relationship. The fourth benefit of marriage for a husband is the instrumentality of the wife, who "gives leave" to the husband to pursue loftier goals such as the improvement of his *nafs*.[33] The final incentive for a man to marry, according to Ghazali, is that his faith is fortified in marriage, and there is a lot of spiritual reward, for dealing with the antics of a wife.[34] In short, managing a wife strengthens one's faith.

Having delineated these benefits, Ghazali then states that before one can marry, three prerequisites should be met. The first is that unless a man is on the verge of having illicit sex, he must have a lawful means of earning a living before getting married.[35] Ghazali decries what he sees as a corruption of his age, that people turn to unlawful or unethical ways to earn money or provide for their families. The second prerequisite for marriage is that a man must have a balanced *nafs*. He needs to have a good nature, kindness, and patience to tolerate the amount of distress his wife's/family's inanities will inevitably cause.[36] Ghazali asserts that because a man is not ever allowed to leave or abandon his wife/family, "whoever cannot control his own *nafs*, it is better that he does not take charge of someone else's *nafs*."[37] Finally, Ghazali's third prerequisite of marriage is that a man needs to have the strength to resist his wife's power to distract him from the remembrance of God.[38] This prerequisite, like the others, also requires him to have a balanced *nafs*.

In Ghazali's statement of the purposes and prerequisites of marriage, as in the ethical treatises more broadly, we see metaphysical tension at work regarding attitudes toward women. On one hand, Ghazali recognizes women's *nafses*, and therefore recognizes their humanity and the potential of their *nafs* to develop. But on the other hand, he also sets up a marital paradigm in which her *nafs* cannot or should not actualize its potential. Ghazali believes a woman cannot be trusted to fulfill her own marital role or religious duties, possibly because of her *nafs*'s deficiencies, or because her *nafs* might have its own agenda that contradicts that of her husband. Ghazali even states that as part of his husbandly duties, a man should ensure that his wife stays ethical, prays routinely, keeps the fast, and remains free from sin.[39] In any case, women's moral weaknesses serve as the call for men's dominance over their *nafses* and justify the patriarchal order of the household. As Weitz noted, "wifely piety in al-Ghazali's text has more to do with facilitating men's pious obligations than with women's own devotional practices."[40]

As I noted earlier, Ghazali states that "whoever cannot control his own *nafs*, it is better that he does not take charge of someone else's *nafs*."[41] Similarly, Tusi (along with Davani) advises that "whoever is incapable of fulfilling the conditions for the treatment of wives should rather remain a bachelor, for the mischief of associating with women, quite apart from its disorder, can only result in an infinite number of calamities."[42] Their caution to their male-only audience stems from the view that womankind are an ordeal that must be dealt with properly, or else not at all. The texts attempt to demystify life with women, who have a predilection for wayward activities or going astray because they do not have the capacity for the science of *akhlaq*. Their incapacity to control their own *nafses* forever infantilizes them and is indicative of the metaphysical tension in the texts. Women are fully human with agency to make choices that affect a marriage, but remain defective in their rational capacity, thereby giving up decision-making power to their husbands.

For the three ethicists, the ethical relationship between husband and wife is fraught with challenges and paradoxes. The husband must honor his wife's humanity while keeping her safely under his control. In order to do so, he must keep two principles in mind. First is the notion of moderation, which corresponds to the principle of balance that is so essential to actualizing the virtues of the *nafs*. The second principle he must remember is the idea that marriage is a microcosm of state governance, and the husband executes administrative power in maintaining the wife's instrumentality. As the ethicists make clear, marriage is an integral part of ethical refinement,[43] and it requires a precise explanation of guidelines.

THE IDEAL WIFE

The ethicists are highly concerned with urging men to marry the right woman, rather than just any woman. This is crucial because a wife is meant to play arguably one of the most instrumental roles in her husband's life, and the wife's willingness to surrender her body and soul to her husband is essential in determining the nature of the marital relationship and how the household will run. An ideal wife will bear a man his children, take care of his home and property, and serve as his deputy so as to "give leave" for him to pursue his own lofty goals.[44] But even as the ethicists take care to define the ideal wife, their discussions on this subject demonstrate their conflicted views on the nature of women and how best to deal with them. Even though the ethicists did not have concepts of gender as an identity marker, they communicate understandings of appropriate gender roles as well as concepts of *muruwwah* (manhood) and natural character traits of women. Their detailed inventories imply that there is such a thing as an ideal wife, but they consistently present this ideal as a flawed being, depending on her husband's rule and serving as his moral foil. Paradoxically, only such a dependent wife, one with this ambiguous moral status, can support his *akhlaq*, that is, his *nafs*'s ethical refinement into a vicegerent of God. The ethicists' descriptions of the wife are all oriented toward the pragmatic purpose of the husband's refinement. One significant difference between Ghazali's language for describing the ideal woman and the language used by Tusi and Davani is that the latter two, surprisingly, employ virtues and qualities men would be familiar with from their own training in their descriptions of ideal women, suggesting women might possess these qualities/virtues even if in limited capacities. This feature of the texts illustrates the metaphysical tension that permeates their work—women have *nafses* but a limited ability for refinement.

Ghazali's Ideal Wife

Ghazali is utilitarian in his concept of the ideal wife. The eight qualities he identifies are devoutness, good disposition, beauty, affordability, fertility, virginity, respectable family, and distance in blood relation. Her foremost quality, he asserts, is the virtue of being devout (*parsa*). Marion Katz has shown the contradiction that exists within medieval scholars' views about women's religiosity in that they sometimes "explicitly expressed their awareness that women suffered from a religious ignorance (that is, of the forms of Islam favored by the scholars themselves) that arose directly from their relative seclusion. However, the same authors often discouraged women from frequenting mosques even when this limited their exposure to the religious norms that the scholars themselves sought to instill."[45] Ghazali provides a rubric for religiosity in women that confirms this contradiction: an "undevout woman will be treacherous with property, disturb the lordship of her husband, and perhaps betray him with her body."[46] The preservation of property—which Tusi lists as an incentive to marry that is equivalent to the importance of procreation[47]—is for Ghazali just as important as her surrendering her physical body. In other words, even if women are ignorant about religion, they perform devoutness by seclusion or fidelity, not with greater education. Accordingly, after devoutness, the next significant quality in a wife is good disposition (*khulq-i niku*), which ensures she will be obedient, grateful, and kind.[48]

The third quality of an ideal wife is beauty (*jamal*), "for it is the foundation of the husband's affection" for the wife, although it is fraught with caveats since it can impinge upon a man's focus on his ethical refinement.[49] Ghazali explains that it is the Prophet's Sunnah to see the bride before the *nikah* to confirm her attractiveness,[50] but pairs it with the following hadith and explanation: "'You should want a woman for her faith, not her beauty.' This means that you should not want her only for her beauty without faith; this does not mean that you should not look at her beauty."[51] Earlier in the treatise, Ghazali states that "it is known that if one marries a woman for wealth and beauty he will be deprived of both, but if he marries for her devoutness, the goal of wealth and beauty will be obtained by itself."[52] Here he does not negate wealth and beauty as reasons to marry, but rather emphasizes that a woman of faith is beautiful and wealthy in a different way. In these statements, he reveals a "well-known" tension between beauty (*jamal*) and faith (*diyanat*) in a woman, which serves as his personal commentary on societal superficiality and complexities of matchmaking. Ghazali further states that marrying a woman just for the sake of having children, without regard to her beauty, is a matter of ascetic preference. He recounts an anecdote of the ninth-century scholar Ahmad ibn Hanbal, who "chose a one-eyed sister over a beautiful one because she was more intelligent."[53] Ghazali does not extol this example because, as a practical ethicist, he states the importance of beauty in sexually attracting the husband; however, he does suggest it as an alternative arrangement for his ascetically inclined readers who may be in danger of entirely dismissing marriage for its worldly trappings, and thus missing its many blessings.[54] The anecdote of the one-eyed woman with greater intelligence is the *Kimiya*'s only mention of the term *'aqil* (intelligent) in relation to women. Ghazali does not list intelligence as a quality one must look for in a wife, as Tusi and Davani do. The example shows that although it was possible for Ghazali to imagine a woman with intelligence, he did not see it as a common enough characteristic that it was worth advising men to take intelligent wives. As we saw with the date palm tree example in the last chapter, the notion of females being higher than males was not an explicit possibility to the ethicists. Even Ibn Hanbal's one-eyed wife is more intelligent compared to another woman, not another man.

After devoutness, good disposition, and beauty, the fourth quality of an ideal wife, according to Ghazali, is affordability. He rather pragmatically recommends a woman who "makes the marriage dower (*kabin*) lighter," meaning one who comes more cheaply in marriage.[55] This is possibly a commentary on women's greed, or that of their families.

The fifth quality of the ideal wife is fertility. On this point, Ghazali quotes a hadith: "A straw mat in the corner of the house is better than a wife who does not give birth."[56] For Ghazali, a woman's main utility comes from her child-bearing function; he compares a barren woman to a plain household item of little use that one keeps in the house. Kathryn Kueny argues that the many rituals in premodern Muslim communities surrounding birth celebrated women's maternity, but also served to "marginalize others whose anatomies are blamed for failing to produce offspring that are the ultimate adhesive to a communal life structured around paternal relations."[57] Women who did not participate in perpetuating patriarchy by giving birth were considered a liability to their families.

In his sixth point regarding the ideal wife, Ghazali states that one should marry a virgin, "for she is closer in affection. She who has had a husband, it happens more often that her heart remains occupied with him."[58] As the reasoning goes, a prior husband would have already left an impression on the woman, so that she would not be open to her new husband's concerns. Kecia Ali and Carolyn Baugh have shown that virginity is a concern in *fiqh* with respect to consent to marriage and its validity.[59] Jurists generally ruled that "those who were neither virgins nor minors could not be compelled [into marriage] but had to give their spoken assent to any proposed marriage."[60] Although not universally, which posed conceptual challenges to the legal concept of consensus, virgins and minors could be married off without their consent.[61] Also not universally, many jurists held that virgins who reached their majority must give consent. Ali argues that the jurists were concerned with virginity and age (to a lesser extent) because they were concerned about the exercise (and limit) of paternal control specifically.[62] Here in his *akhlaq* mode of writing, in recommending men to marry virgins, Ghazali only cares about preserving the hierarchical dynamic between a husband and a wife. He does not raise the hadith in which the Prophet recommends men to marry virgins because they are more playful, indicating that men's sexual pleasure from marrying virgins is not his concern.[63] This is consistent with his deemphasized, utilitarian view of satisfying desire by subduing the concupiscible faculty (*quwwat-i shahwi*). Instead, his focus is on how a wife's virginity indicates that she will play an instrumental role in a man's home by conforming to his needs.

The seventh quality of an ideal wife is being from a respectable family. Although this quality is ranked lower on Ghazali's list of desirable wifely qualities, it is still important because good breeding means being schooled "in faith and righteousness, for without this origin, she will not have *adab* [etiquette] and have an *akhlaq-i napasandidah* [unlikeable ethic], and she will pass that ethic on to the children."[64] Here again we see the metaphysical tension within descriptions of the ideal wife. This statement acknowledges the possibility of a woman having righteous *akhlaq*, but only in the context of her motherhood. Her *akhlaq* needs to be good enough to be passed on to the children, while also accommodating her husband's goal of being vicegerent. These responsibilities to her family, not her own goals, represent the limits to a woman's practice of *akhlaq*. The statement also presumes some base-level *akhlaq* or education in women, which Asma Sayeed and Richard Bulliet have shown would have been the case for women from elite or *'ulama'* families since education was considered hereditary at the time.[65]

Finally, the eighth quality of the ideal wife is that she should not be too closely related by blood to her husband, both because a husband's sexual desire (*shahwat*) for such a wife will be less and because children from such a marriage are considered "weaker."[66] For Ghazali, the ideal wife is less of a blessing than a vehicle for a man's spiritual and ethical refinement. He selects ideal qualities specifically for this purpose: her ability to deliver children, comfort him, and be affectionate and relatively painless to deal with, despite her natural flaws due to the limitations of her sex.

Tusi and Davani's Ideal Wife

Tusi and Davani's list of criteria is similarly utilitarian. They prioritize intelligence, piety, and general ethical comportment, insofar as these qualities can be found in women:

> The best wife is a woman who has *'aql* [intelligence], *diyanat* [piety], *'iffat* [self-restraint], *fatnat* [understanding], *haya* [modesty], *riqqat-i dil* [kindness of heart], *tavaddud* [is affectionate], *kutah-zaban* [is short in speech], is obedient to her husband, grants her husband liberal use of her *nafs* in his service, has preference for his happiness, *vaqar* [dignity], and *haybat* [gravity]; she should be beautiful to her own family, should not be barren, and with respect to the management of the household and budgeting, she should be knowledgeable and capable in watching expenditure. . . . And if other than these virtues she is adorned with a beautiful face, has [fine] lineage and wealth, it would be a combination of all kinds of qualities and there would be no better picture imagined than this.[67]

In essence, this list of attributes identifies the conduct and abilities that are desirable in a wife—namely, those that contribute to her instrumentality, and that incline her to the obedient posture that is necessary in that instrumental role.

The ideal wife's conduct is, first of all, pleasant to those around her: she is kindhearted, short in speech, and obedient, and prefers her husband's happiness over her own. But in addition to these "feminine" qualities, Tusi and Davani also list other types of conduct using terms that they elsewhere use to refer to male behavior, with small but important variation in meanings: self-restraint, dignity, and gravity. The virtue of self-restraint (*'iffat*) is the same virtue of the concupiscent faculty I discuss in chapter 2. Both genders possess this faculty, although they define self-restraint in the context of women as their "likability." A woman who exercises self-restraint (as opposed to any other virtue) is likeable. Her conduct should also be marked by dignity (*vaqar*), which I discuss in chapter 2 as a masculine quality of having a tempered pace, as part of his virtue of self-restraint (*'iffat*), which comes from the tamed concupiscent faculty. Third, a woman should have gravity (*haybat*), which is the same term that Tusi and Davani use to describe how a husband and a king should conduct themselves in relation to wives and subjects, respectively. Although Tusi and Davani do not explain what dignity and gravity mean for women specifically in the context of the list of wifely virtues, it is likely that the authors mean women should carry themselves with maturity since they believed that the concupiscent faculty is dominant in women. The ethicists' praise of these three qualities in women that they elsewhere prescribe for men—even using the same terms as used in the science of the *nafs*—underscores the metaphysical tension inherent in their ethics of marriage and the domestic economy. The ethicists recognize the virtues of women's *nafses* but deny their potential for fully actualizing those virtues. Or they may believe that women have partially developed *nafses*. Because the science of the *nafs* does not apply to them, I must deduce which of the faculties the ethicists believed the most refined women to be in possession of (certainly not full rationality) based on the virtues they instruct men to look for in them.

In addition to the ideal wife's conduct, Tusi and Davani are concerned, like Ghazali, with the particular abilities and skills that make her useful to her husband. One of a wife's major instrumental roles is to bear and rear a man's children; Tusi simply states that a good wife should not be barren.[68] Similarly, Davani instructs his reader to ascertain whether a woman might be fertile by checking whether her female kin have had many children.[69] Another key skill is managing a budget, as one of her wifely duties is to protect her husband's assets by watching his budget and helping him manage the home, the servants, and possibly his lands. To be her husband's deputy in running the home, she must have some measure of intelligence (*'aql*) and understanding (*fatnat*). Moreover, she must direct these faculties at household affairs, not at achieving transcendence (to use Beauvoir's term) or pursuing lofty goals like perfecting her *nafs* or becoming a microcosm of the world. However, for Tusi and Davani, as with Ghazali's reference to Ibn Hanbal, taking an *'aqil* wife does not mean that she has the virtue of wisdom (*hikmat*) that arises from the rational faculty (*quwwati-i 'ilm*); rather, she has a general intelligence and comprehension that go along with competence for the "protection of property," a major function of a wife.[70]

The conduct and skills that are valued in a wife are those that contribute to her instrumentality to her husband's home and estate, for as Ghazali notes, preservation of property is an important principle in marriage.[71] Yet the ethicists seem less preoccupied with a wife's material instrumentality than with her spiritual instrumentality. For Tusi, a good wife happily surrenders charge of her *nafs* for her husband's instrumental use; as quoted earlier, she "grants her husband liberal use of her *nafs* in his service."[72] This again demonstrates the metaphysical tension: a woman has a *nafs* to give up and she should be willing to do so without reflection on her own *nafs*'s refinement since his is the *nafs* that matters.

Ghazali describes the wife's surrender of her *nafs* as domestic labor that aids his spirituality:

[a] benefit is that the wife takes care of the house and completes the work of cooking, sweeping, and washing. For if a man becomes occupied with these, he will be kept from knowledge, work, and worship. For this reason, the wife is a friend on the path of faith. For this reason Abu Sulayman Darani has said, "A good wife is not from this world, she is of the hereafter." Meaning, she gives you leave so that you can attend to the work of the hereafter.[73]

The ever-practical ethicists recognized that marriage facilitated the exchange of a wife's domestic labor for the ability to attend to a man's loftier goals, even though, as Kecia Ali has shown, the marital arrangement in *fiqh* required furnishing the wife with financial support and household services due to the wife in exchange for her sexual availability.[74] In this passage, Ghazali even casts the wife's spiritual mission in life in instrumental terms. Thus, in surrendering her *nafs* over to her husband's rule, she is fulfilling her life's purpose. Overall, the qualities that the ethicists list as criteria for the ideal wife are evidence of their sense of the limits of the woman's *nafs*: they relegate the wife to an instrumental role in the marriage, while the husband plays the principal ethical subject.

Finally, for Tusi and Davani, the wife's pride in her family, her humility, and her virginity all converge in the single characteristic of obedience. The ethicists believed that though obedience was a natural feminine character trait, it could be more easily cultivated in a young, previously unmarried wife, who could be shaped or molded to a husband's tastes. An ideal wife has a sense of pride in her family that is complemented by a modest view of herself, such that she is humble enough to serve and obey her husband. Tusi and Davani say, "a virgin woman is preferred to a nonvirgin, for she will accept customs and assimilate with the husband in character and habits and submit more closely and be obedient to him."[75] All three ethicists held that virginity is associated with humility, obedience, and greater impressionability, such that a husband can more easily establish her instrumentality.

After identifying the attributes that characterize an ideal wife, Tusi and Davani describe the women whom men should avoid. Like Ghazali,[76] they refer to a saying by Arab sages that warns against marriage to three kinds of women: the *annanah*, a woman who laments the loss of a former husband; the *hannana*, a remarried widow who gives her current husband's money to her previous husband's children; and the *mannanah*, "a rich woman who obliges her husband with her own wealth."[77] These warnings have not just ethical but financial implications. For example, marrying a previously married woman, a *hannana*, can drain one's finances because "a grief-stricken widow is a woman who has children from another husband and shows kindness to them with the wealth of this [new] husband."[78] One would think that marrying widows with children would be considered a charitable, and therefore ethical, act that emulates the Prophet's example. However, for the ethicists, an ethical act is actually that which promotes an individual man's potential to create domestic and societal happiness and be vicegerent of God's will. Marrying a virgin meant that one could inspire change, mold a *nafs*, and create an ethical household from scratch.

In their own summary of the image of the ideal wife, Tusi and Davani state that she is like a mother, a friend, and a concubine (*kaniz*) all at once.[79] Tusi elaborates that a worthy wife is like a mother in that "she desires the husband's proximity and presence, while hating his absence; and that she will bear the burden of her own suffering in the course of attaining his desire and satisfaction."[80] The second role that a wife should play is that of a friend, in that she "should not grudge him [the use of] her own property, and she should conform to him in character."[81] This description of wife as friend shows the truly limited way in which wives could be friends with their husbands; as I discuss in the next chapter, male peers who are friends do not require one another to conform to their ideas. Finally, the wife must "play the part of a mistress [by] humbling herself in the manner of a concubine."[82] This means not only making herself sexually available, but also acknowledging that marriage is ownership—not unlike slavery, as Ali has shown—and a wife must fully succumb to her husband's wishes because she belongs to him.[83] Based on these three recommendations, we can conclude that the duty of a wife is to be submissive yet affectionate toward her husband. Taking into account all of the ethicists' guidelines on the subject, we can conclude that the conduct and abilities that characterize the ideal wife are those that contribute to her instrumentality and incline her to obedience.

MARRIED, NOW WHAT?: ETHICAL ORDER OF DAILY LIFE IN MARRIAGE

After instructing men on how to identify ideal wifely candidates—women who will willingly surrender their bodies and souls to their husbands—the ethicists attend to discussing how men ought to behave in marriage in order to maintain their own power and their wives' instrumentality. The prescriptions strike a balance between two approaches to fulfilling men's *akhlaq* goals: on one hand, defensive behaviors that enable men to maintain their personal *akhlaq* in the face of family obligation, and on the other hand, kind and self-sacrificial behaviors toward family members, at times calculated to placate wives or make them easier to manage. Both approaches are meant to establish the husband's power over his wife and promote her utility and proper conduct. Toward that end, the ethicists' main concern is with teaching men the psychology of women as a species, as evidenced by the caveats about women's nature that they pepper in among their ethical precepts on how to rule a wife.

The ethicists use two terms to describe power over one's wife, *haybat*[84] and *karamat*, or being awe-inspiring and showing benevolence. They elaborate on men's *haybat* as follows:

> *Haybat* is that he keeps himself awe-inspiring in the eyes of his wife so that she does not consider his sayings, commands, and prohibitions permissible to ignore. This is the most important condition in ruling the wife, for if there is negligence on this condition, the path will be found for the wife to follow her own desire and wishes. She will not limit herself on this. In fact, she will bring the husband into her own obedience and make him the means to her own wishes, and she will obtain her own purposes by [his] subjugation and service to her.[85]

Tusi advises husbands that the very power dynamic of the marital relationship depends on their ability to perform *haybat*. Davani adds that *haybat* is the most important condition in ruling a wife, and that it can be done by displaying the husband's merits and hiding his flaws. A man must hold power over his wife and effectively command her respect in order for there to be order in the household, and for him to be able to counteract her default nature of going beyond the limits of the acceptable. This instruction by the ethicists is understandable given that the irascible faculty (*quwwat-i ghazabi*) prompts human *nafses* to seek leadership. However, as I mentioned in the previous chapter, the ethicists can only conceive of men as being in control of the irascible faculty and as possessing leadership. Thus, even though the ethicists require a form of *haybat* in women—and an ideal woman has some level of moderation of her irascible faculty—the ethicists only accept men's superiority in marriage. Tusi and Davani assume that women lack the necessary self-awareness to control their *nafses*.

Ghazali's guidelines, like those of Tusi and Davani, are intended to preserve the husband's *haybat*. In his section on the "etiquette of life with women from the beginning of marriage to the end," he recommends that husbands

> joke with [wives], play, not be reserved, and approach them on their own mental level . . . [but] joke and play should not exceed a limit whereby husbands' *haybat* declines. One should not aid [a wife] in [pursuing] wrong desires; instead if [the husband] sees an act that is against his manhood or the lawful path, he should manage it. For if it comes to pass, then [wives] will make fun of [their husbands].[86]

Ghazali explains to men that women require careful rulership that balances lenience and firmness. He assumes that women do not possess the maturity to control themselves, and that they have the power to carry out acts that diminish their husbands' manhood. Ghazali quotes a phrase from verse 4:34 to explain that this behavior in a woman is unacceptable because "men have *qiwamah* over women" and "it should always be that the husband is dominant."[87] The concept of gender relations implied by the Qur'anic term *qiwamah* has long been understood across genres of Muslim thought as the essential summary of gender dynamics prescribed by Qur'an even though it appears only once[88] in the Qur'an.

Another way for the husband to maintain his status as the leader is by showing *karamat* (benevolence). As Tusi and Davani explain, "*karamat* means one bestows the things on the wife that call for love and compassion, so that the absence of this state makes her apprehensive and she attends to matters of the household with beauty and accepts the order of the husband; the intended organization [of affairs] results."[89] In this shrewd piece of advice, Tusi and Davani recommend that a husband strategically show or withhold benevolence in order to coerce the wife into submission. Ghazali holds that men should treat women well, with patience, but this does not mean husbands are not allowed to displease their wives because they should maintain power. While there are some prescriptions of outright kindness—for example, one should not eat delicious foods alone, but rather share them with one's wife and family—Ghazali frames it with tolerance: "be patient with their [wives'] absurd speech and ungratefulness."[90] Where the texts reference kindness and benevolence to a wife, these behaviors are merely tools, conveying love and compassion in order to preserve the ethical order of marriage, the husband's rulership over the wife. The intent of kindness is to keep the wife in line.

Tusi and Davani recommend six specific actions that a man of good ethics should take toward his wife: keep her appearance fair; veil and seclude her from strangers; consult with her in the early stages of a decision so long as she does not expect her husband to obey her; give her a "free hand" in deciding the financial budget and expenditures of the household and provisions for each member; establish close ties with her relatives and family as a gesture of mutual support and cooperation; and finally, if she has integrity and propriety, a man should not take other wives because inciting women's natural jealousy and vindictiveness against the husband or the other woman can lead to disaster.[91] These practical pieces of advice take a woman's feelings into consideration— especially the advice about consulting with her, allowing her to decide expenses, and having regard for her family—but nevertheless, these thoughtful gestures are framed as being largely for her appeasement.

Davani limits his interpretation of the Qur'anic permission to marry as many as four women to kings: he elaborates that, although kings marry multiple wives in order to ensure many heirs, other men should not take plural wives.[92] Davani justifies this ethical prohibition of polygyny based on his understanding of women's penchant for jealousy and vengeance. To explain this point, Davani interrupts his chapter on marriage to include a story of al-Hajjaj ibn Yusuf's chamberlain and the chamberlain's wife, whose jealously almost costs the chamberlain his life.[93] Hajjaj told this chamberlain never to reveal court secrets to his wife. The chamberlain responded by saying that he trusted his very wise and affectionate wife to the fullest since she had always kept his secrets when he had tested her. Hajjaj vowed to prove to his chamberlain that trusting his wife was foolish. So, one day, Hajjaj told the chamberlain to take a purse of a thousand gold coins bearing the treasury's seal to his home and tell his wife that he had stolen it for her. Later, after some time had passed, Hajjaj gifted an enslaved woman to his chamberlain. The chamberlain's wife asked him to sell the woman, but the chamberlain refused upon the orders of Hajjaj, saying that he was not allowed to sell a gift that Hajjaj had given him. Shortly thereafter, the chamberlain's wife appeared at

Hajjaj's palace with the purse of gold coins, confessing her husband's crime so that Hajjaj could punish him for theft. Hajjaj stated to his chamberlain that had he not knowingly conducted the experiment on his wife, he would have sentenced the chamberlain to be thrown from the tower.

With this story, Davani attempts to demonstrate to his readers not only that wives cannot be trusted with their husbands' secrets, but also that they suffer from jealousy and vengeance. The chamberlain's wife was so jealous of the enslaved woman who had entered her household that she exacted mortal revenge on her husband by betraying his trust.[94] This story serves to illustrate why, even though it is legal to have concubines and up to four wives, all three ethicists forbid this practice for protecting husbands' status. Polygamy can incite a wife's jealousy and destroy the order of the household, which is the very opposite of what a man's domestic duty ought to achieve.[95] Curiously, and in a backhanded way, as the ethicists dissuade their readers from taking concubines and additional wives, they also ask their readers to consider their wives' feelings.

A clear implication of the story of Hajjaj's chamberlain is that even though men might attempt to regulate wives, ultimately women are uncontrollable. Legally, a husband has the right to control the wife's mobility, particularly because a wife has to remain sexually available to her husband;[96] however, even if sexual intercourse remains the foundation of their legal contract, the ethical reason to seclude one's wife has more to do with preserving the wife's time and attention for managing the home and preventing her from running amok. Ghazali refers to the Prophet's giving women permission to appear in public and attempts to qualify this permission: he quotes Umar ibn al-Khattab, who said that the Prophet allowed women to go into public back in the days when they used to veil themselves properly, but that if he saw the ways of women today, he would rescind that permission. Ghazali then states that "there is greater harm to women at public sites and gatherings" than in the past.[97] Here, Ghazali echoes the common argument of the 'ulama' lamenting the loss of a golden era when women knew how to conduct themselves in public. He does so in order to comment about the differential between his post-Muhammad ideal of gender segregation and the ubiquitous presence of women in real life.

For Tusi, the wife's appearance in public is inextricable from the husband's masculinity:

> She will become busy with going out, and beautifying [herself] for the purpose of excursions and visiting sites and seeing strange men, until both the matters of the home will be neglected and the husband will not be respected or appear awesome in her eyes. In fact, when she sees other men, she will count him as contemptible and small and will be emboldened to take steps toward hideous acts, and will also excite admirers to desire her, until at the end there will be negligence of daily life, loss of manhood, and acquisition of perdition and misery in [the world and hereafter].[98]

Tusi uses these ethical precepts about secluding the wife in order to fortify the reader's masculinity. He warns that certain actions of a wife can result in the husband's loss of manhood: mingling with other men, losing awe and respect for her husband, destroying or neglecting the home, or causing abomination in both worlds. Here, Tusi attempts to connect ethical and spiritual responsibilities. For example, the sinfulness of neglecting the house implies that the wife's seclusion is not just an earthly duty; it has ramifications for the afterlife as well.

In addition to telling husbands how to "rule" their wives, Tusi also describes how married men should *not* act in ruling their wives. First, husbands should guard against showing excessive love, which could cause the wife to expect to dominate over her husband, a grave corruption. Second, in opposition to his earlier statement that considers her as "coparcener," a husband should never "consult the wife on affairs of universal importance, and certainly . . . not inform her of [his] secrets," including information about his property and capital. Finally, a husband should restrain his wife from foolish pastimes such as people-watching or listening to stories and gossip about men and their activities.[99] Here again, Tusi (along with Davani) is concerned with the ethics of ruling over the wife such that the husband maintains her instrumental role, preserves the organization of daily life, and reinforces his status as the head of household. Tusi elaborates on what it means to keep the wife's mind constantly occupied:

[It means] taking responsibility of the important matters of the household and overseeing its interests and attending to that which requires organization of daily life, for the human soul does not have patience for idleness, and to be at leisure from necessary matters draws attention to unnecessary matters. Thus, if the wife is free from management of the house and educating children and seeking the welfare of servants, she will concentrate her efforts on things which call for damage to the home.[100]

Here again, Tusi refers to the wife's soul as human, but not for the purposes of her *akhlaq* training; rather, he mentions it for the limited purpose of being instrumental. Tusi assumes that the husband's behavior toward his wife should be specifically geared toward preserving her role in household management.

Since these precepts are ethical ones, they may be read as suggestions on how to keep a wife happy. However, it seems clear on close reading that the intent of these recommendations—including the injunction to keep her appearance fair and befriend her relatives—is to keep the peace at home, or to provide the wife with distraction that is sufficient but not excessive, so as to keep her functioning as a useful and productive accessory to her husband's domestic needs and refinement. Like Ghazali, Tusi states that women have the same kind of human soul as men; however, the potentially idle souls of women are to be kept busy with the affairs of running the home, rather than occupied with the ethical exercises of perfecting virtues of wisdom, justice, temperance, and courage. The perfection of these virtues is the exclusive provenance of rational, male souls. As I show later, the marital ethics of sex, money, and childrearing all reflect the principle of preserving husbands' dominance and safeguarding their path to ethical refinement.

Marriage and Sexual Ethics

The purposes of sexual ethics in the *akhlaq* texts are to maintain moderation of the concupiscent faculty (*quwwat-i shahwat*) and to appease the wife's needs arising from her uncontrolled nature. The ethicists advise that one should only have sex in moderation, should have only one wife at a time and no concubines due to women's penchant for jealousy, and, according to Ghazali, should be kind during sexual intercourse. As discussed in the previous chapter, it is through the concupiscent faculty that the ethicists account for human sexual desire. The arena of sex is another place that wives serve as instruments for husbands, providing a licit mechanism for having sexual relations. This function is relatively less important, however; as an indicator of how low Ghazali ranked sexual relations in an ethical marriage, he lists guidelines about intercourse tenth in a series of twelve rules of married life. The reason for this low ranking is that even though intercourse is a natural and necessary component of life, it needs to be curbed as part of the larger discipline of balancing the *nafs*.

As Kecia Ali has shown, traditional legal sources have gendered ideas about sexual needs.[101] She points out the contradiction within the prevailing legal attitude that women have uncontrollable desire but that men have greater sexual rights in marriage. This attitude is consistent with the *akhlaq* notion that women's concupiscent faculties, which correlate with sexual desire, are stronger and more volatile than men's. In the law, the wife only has a right to intercourse on one occasion, the consummation of the marriage; after that, it is her duty to fulfill her husband's desires, whether strong or weak. The same model of "gender differentiated rights and duties" that is seen in legal sources also exists in the ethics texts.[102] However, in *akhlaq*, sexual desire is treated as merely a part of marriage, not as central to it. This deprioritization is largely attributable to the difference in genre. Legal texts are concerned with the legitimacy of sexual encounters; they are not concerned with how frequently people are having sex, or whether they are masturbating or having wet dreams. *Akhlaq* texts, on the other hand, are more concerned about the totality of men's sexual activity because they are making utilitarian arguments about meeting the needs of the concupiscent faculty (*quwwat-i shahwat*) and ensuring that it stays subdued to the rational faculty (*quwwat-i 'aql*). The two main concepts that the ethicists use to discuss sex are the husband's biological/metaphysical need for sexual enjoyment and release, and the husband's ethical duty to fulfill the wife's recognized need for enjoyable sex (to curb her more prominent concupiscent faculty). Both spouses have these needs and rights, but the role each is supposed to play in the sexual relationship is gendered, based in part on assumptions of biologically distinct feminine and masculine nature.

Ghazali's specific guidelines for sexual relations turn the husband's *right* to sex on its head by addressing a husband's *duties* during intercourse. The framing of these guidelines shows an element of compassion for the woman and a recognition of the needs of her *nafs*; according to Ghazali, the husband regulates her concupiscent faculty by being kind to her during intercourse. Quoting the Prophet, Ghazali counsels his reader not to "fall on a woman like a beast."[103] Although Ghazali's perspective shows sensitivity to women, it is also admittedly androcentric, and based on an assumption of women being "made of weakness."[104] His prescriptions on sex reify the power relationship between husband and wife, giving men control over all sexual relations, albeit somewhat tempered by compassion.

The remainder of Ghazali's guidelines on sex is supported through hadiths that reveal that sex is part of a broader cosmology of God's creation and reproduction. Foreplay is required, and one must begin and end sexual encounters with stating the formulas of the *bismillah* (In the name of God), *takbir* (God is great), and verse 25:54, which is about the creation of man from water and of his kindred by blood and marriage.[105] One should also ask for protection from satan, in case a child is conceived. Ghazali explicitly states that during sex, a man must be patient so that his wife can climax, an important recognition of women's sexual needs. He quotes a hadith in which the Prophet stated a neglect of this recognition as the third of three infirmities that may plague a man: "a man is afflicted with three infirmities: the first is that he sees someone he likes but does not remember his name, next is that a brother does a good thing for him and he rejects it, and next is that one engages in intercourse before kisses and caresses and when one has obtained his need, he does not wait until his wife also obtains her need."[106] Another injunction is that one should avoid intercourse during the first and last days of the month, during the full moon, and during the wife's menses. Finally, Ghazali also says based on a hadith that '*azl*, or coitus interruptus, is acceptable in order to avoid conception.

Sa'diyya Shaikh has interpreted Ghazali's guidelines as support for women's rights to sexual fulfillment and the right to use contraception.[107] However, Kecia Ali points out that legally speaking, the recognition of women's sexual needs and Ghazali's recommendation of allowing one's wife to climax are moot points since most jurists agree that women do not have a "right" to sexual intercourse as their husbands do. Husbands can deny wives sexual pleasure by denying them sex altogether.[108] From an *akhlaq* point of view, Ghazali's guidelines for a man to engage in foreplay and to be patient until the wife reaches climax serve as the basis for ethical sexual relations. As with all ethics discourses, Ghazali's guidelines for sexual relations, framed as duties of the husband, attempt to raise the bar for what is considered proper male behavior in the name of *akhlaq*, largely apart from the question of what is legally required. In the *akhlaq* texts as a whole, sexual ethics are framed within the broader marital hierarchy, in which a husband controls his own and his wife's *nafs*, particularly her impulses of sexual desire (*shahwat*). Sexual needs are understood to come from the soul's animalistic concupiscent faculty, which is responsible for sexual desire and other natural impulses.

All three ethicists explicitly state that it is not preferable for a man to marry for the purpose of fulfilling sexual desires unless he is on the verge of having illicit sex, the likely reason for this instruction being that an impulsive marriage could lead to a bad match. Tusi and Davani explain that sexual desire (*shahwat*), as one of the three important functions of the human soul, comes with responsibilities. In order to amplify one's predilection for virtuous behaviors, *shahwat* must be put into perfect balance. The virtues that arise with the control of *shahwat* are self-restraint (*'iffat*) and liberality (*sakha*); a man controls his sexual appetite in order to open his mind to enhancing virtuous behaviors. To do so, the ethicists propose that one keep good company and befriend people who are not corrupt or lewd. Tusi says,

> It is imperative to take caution against lending an ear to their reports, stories, listening to their news, profanity, recitation of their poetry, superficiality, attending their parties and gatherings, especially when the quest of the soul and the inclination of nature is related to this. For from attending one gathering, or from listening to one quip, or from reciting one line of poetry in an amorous way, so much filth and impurity join the soul that purifying one's self from it takes but many long days and difficult treatments.[109]

In other words, if a man allows his mind to entertain lasciviousness, his sexual appetite will increase to excess, exacerbated by his innate natural

disposition or needs. As a means to curb sexual desire, the ethicists recommend fasting, although one must never eliminate sexual desire (*shahwat*) altogether because its deficiency is accompanied by sloth, laziness,
and a lack of desire to have children. Indeed, according to the ethicists,
a wife should humble herself like a "little concubine" (Tusi uses the
diminutive form of the term, *kanizak*), an analogy that suggests that the
mind-set about sex they are advocating for is one of dominance over
women.[110] How else can a man be attracted to a woman who is metaphysically inferior and subjugated and when association with her is not
about love? The dominance is a kind of eroticism that allows men to be
attracted to their wives.

Another reason Tusi uses the language of concubinage to establish
a husband's sexual dominance over a wife is that the ethicists discourage men from taking real concubines. Although many important premodern legal texts discuss the legal guidelines for sexual relations with
enslaved women, all three *akhlaq* texts only mention good conduct with
household servants and slaves as a general principle, without distinguishing between male and female slaves or concubines.[111] The ethicists' dis-
couragement of men from marrying enslaved women—taken alongside
their omission of any discussion on sexual relations with enslaved women
from their ethics texts and their inclusion of general discussions of the
ethics of keeping slaves as domestic servants—suggests that the ethicists
frowned upon sex with enslaved women. They disliked concubinage on
the grounds that it would distract men from ethical refinement by fos-
tering household disorder through rousing a wife's jealousy and producing stigmatized children. Tusi mentions that marrying a free woman is
better than marrying an enslaved one, and Davani adds that marrying a
free woman will ward off social enemies and taint from one's children.[112]
A nonroyal man would not be able to provide the brightest future for his
sons if their mother were enslaved. Although the ethicists do not specifically mention sexual activity outside of marriage, one can assume that
they would advise against having concubines because all three ethicists
advocate for the curtailment of excessive sexual activity.

For the same reasons that they discourage concubinage—to avoid
household chaos—all three ethicists discourage taking multiple wives.[113]
As mentioned earlier, the ethicists explicitly state that only kings may
ethically have multiple wives, and even they should avoid doing so if

possible: "For [kings] also it is primarily objectionable, because the man relates to home as a heart relates to the body, and that one heart is not able to be the source of life to two bodies, so one man cannot manage two homes."[114] Here, in addition to preventing a wife's jealousy or stigmatizing children, the other reason to have one wife has to do with the husband's control of the household, as the macrocosm of his *nafs*. Just as a single household cannot have two leaders, one leader cannot run two households. The idea of the man as the heart of the household places him in a position analogous to a governor ruling a city; he is the central source for all the provisions that are distributed within the household by the deputy wife.

As I discuss in the previous chapter, women's *nafses* are characterized by a prominence of the concupiscent faculty (*quwwati-i shahwi*) and deficiency in the rational faculty (*quwwat-i 'ilmi*). As such, their main virtues stem from control of this facility. A husband facilitates this control partly by keeping his wife's mind consumed with care of the household surroundings and his own needs, but also through control of her sexuality. The ethicists state that a husband should undertake great endeavors to keep his wife in *satr va hijab* (curtain and veil) and away from *ghayr mahram* or *na mahram* (nonkinsmen) in order to shield her from people who might tempt her, and vice versa.[115] The man should prevent his wife from meeting male strangers, carrying on with strange men through window peepholes or on rooftops, attending superfluous social gatherings, and even talking to older women who no longer veil and who recount stories about the local social scene.[116] Katz has shown that the category of the *'ajuz* originated with Ibn Rushd and increasingly came to mean that a woman who "stands at death's door" was legally nonthreatening to mosque-goers because, "as a matter of custom, a woman considered too old to marry was free to appear in public in mixed company."[117] In the ethics texts, old women were still threatening because they could cross boundaries of gender segregation and upset domestic peace by inspiring young women to desire greater contact with the outside world.

However, Ghazali also warns his readers not to become too overzealous in veiling and secluding their wives, or in trying to find out about their personal secrets.[118] He cites a story of a group of men who returned early from a journey with the Prophet. He had advised the men not to return to their homes until morning, when their wives expected them. Two men disobeyed, only to find their wives engaged in illicit sexual activities. Ghazali interprets the Prophet's prohibition to mean that a man's responsibility to seclude his wife is a duty to protect her and prevent social chaos (*afat*), but not to prevent her from committing adultery or other sins that are between her and God.[119] In this context, the term *social chaos* (*afat*) refers to the upheaval caused by women's sexual desire.

In the cultural milieu of the ethicists, possessing a certain amount of *ghayrat* (often translated as male pride) was an important marker of masculinity and proper male behavior. The term *bi-ghayrat*, an adjective that literally means "without *ghayrat*," is a pejorative term and also an insult that means "shameless man without any self-respect," implying that a man's dignity is inextricably tied to his wife's conduct, physicality, and seclusion. However, as I mentioned in the previous chapter, the ethicists evoke *ghayrat* to curb the irascible faculty (*quwwati-i ghazabi*), giving rise to the virtue of courage, which is marked by *ghayrat*, in the sense of masculine zeal, not manly pride over women. Here Ghazali further curtails the cultural meaning of *ghayrat* by quoting Ali Abu Talib as saying "carry *ghayrat* for women to an extent, because men will know about it, and knowing it will become the basis of insulting them."[120] Here, Ghazali is also deemphasizing the sexual jealousy connoted by *ghayrat*, since having too much *ghayrat* is dishonorable and amplifies vices.

All three ethicists discourage excessive engagement in sexual activity. Tusi says that when the soul's natural desire (*shahwat*) is exercised to excess or deprived, one desires inappropriate sexual partners such as children or strange women.[121] Thus, the ethicists tacitly disapprove of men having too much sex, multiple sexual partners, or underage partners; such activities are too distracting from the discipline of *akhlaq*. As far as women's desires, the ethicists consider women not to have control over their concupiscent faculty (*quwwat-i shahwi*), and they believe that husbands should control this faculty for their wives by secluding them. Of the three ethicists, only Ghazali mentions consideration of wives' needs and requires men to be kind in intercourse. The ethicists comment that women's jealousy, evident in wives' desire to have exclusive sexual/marital relationships with their husbands, is a tool for husbands to use in preserving order in the household, and is in line with the main goal of the sexual ethics in *akhlaq* texts: to curb men's sexual appetite.

Marriage and Money

While sexual ethics takes into account what is good for both the husband's and the wife's *nafses*, the ethics of money in marriage is strictly about maintaining the husband's power in the relationship. Wealth is a key element of an ethical marriage, since one of the main purposes of marrying is the "protection of property."[122] The ethicists see money as a potential source of marital tension, so they discuss its management in some detail. They explain which rules men should establish for their wives with respect to money. Ghazali, Tusi, and Davani all create financial ethics that is sensitive to women's needs, as well as their legal rights, but also maintain the husband's position as the leader and financial maintainer of the household and those living in it.

According to *fiqh*, a woman has a claim on the wealth of her husband in the form of maintenance (*nafaqah*); Ali states that this is a result of the "marital bargain, due in exchange for making herself available to him (*tamkin*)."[123] Aside from the contours of this contractual relationship, the ethical treatises recognize that any number of financial arrangements may exist between husband and wife. This recognition reflects the typical division of property wealth in premodern Muslim societies. Yossef Rapoport writes that in Mamluk, Cairo, Damascus, and Jerusalem, during a period that overlaps with the authorship dates of the treatises in this study, it was common for parents to spend copiously on a daughter's dowry and wedding trousseau, with the precise amount depending on her social class.[124] Items given to her would legally belong only to her but would be for household use, such as furniture, luxury utensils, cookware, cushions, bedding, and textiles. In elite families, parents would also give their daughters jewelry, silver, and occasionally cash, land, and domestic servants. The ethicists' guidelines on money in marriage reflected the reality that women could be independently wealthy, could be wealthier than their husbands, or could have family members who were financially involved with their husbands. The three ethicists admit that a woman's independent wealth could be an attractive quality in a wife.[125] Even though a husband was still legally responsible for his wife's financial maintenance, marriages in the premodern period were certainly contracted on the basis of a wife's financial worth, and the husband could perhaps expect to benefit from her wealth. Still, Tusi, along with Davani, advises that one should not marry a *mannanah*, "a rich woman who obliges her husband with her own wealth."[126]

This noble sentiment, taken by itself, seems to extol self-control over the vice of greed; however, Tusi's reasoning for giving this advice is that the wife's money and property could cause her to desire domination and authority and to think of her husband as subservient. He writes,

> A woman's wealth should not become the reason for desiring [her], for women's wealth calls for their search for authority, despotism, search for service, and self-exaltation. So [even] when the husband controls the wife's wealth, his wife considers his station as a servant and assistant, not giving him honor and respect. Unrestrained chaos is inevitable until corruption of affairs of the household and life takes place.[127]

Although greed is a vice that stems from an excessive expression of the concupiscent faculty (*quwwat-i shahwi*), in this piece of advice, greed is not under ethical scrutiny. Rather, Tusi is interested in maintaining the ethically sanctioned hierarchy of the husband-dominated marriage, which supersedes warning against greed.

Another wealth-related potential threat to the marital hierarchy is a wife's superior lineage. Davani warns that "As lineage is the basis of pride, and since women are known to be at a deficiency of mind, for this reason, they reject following their husbands. In fact, there are times that they see their husbands in the place of servants, they break the order, reverse the status quo, and cause loss of money. Wealth and beauty are similar disasters."[128]

Along these lines, Tusi and Davani simply advise men that if they do not marry a woman particularly for her rank or her money, they will not have the problem of being made a servant by her. Proper order in the marriage depends on the husband governing the wife, which is not possible if a wife is of higher financial and social rank. A woman in such a situation, coupled with her rational deficiency, is not able to understand why she must serve her husband.

Judging from the defensive recommendations given to men in the texts about how to manage their household expenses, it seems that wives may have had significant access to their own or their husbands' money. In fact, as I mentioned earlier, Tusi and Davani recommend choosing a wife who has knowledge about budgeting, as she will be most useful to one's estate and can effectively fulfill one of her main wifely obligations, to aid in the protection of property. Tusi's very definition of a good and proper (*salih*) wife is "a man's partner in property, his co-parcener in housekeeping and management of the household, and his deputy in his absence."[129] A wife is responsible for running a husband's estate when he is away and functions as a vizier to her husband's sultanate. For Tusi and Davani, it is crucial that the husband give his wife "a free hand in controlling the provisions of the household and hiring servants for important matters."[130] This can mean delegating tasks to the wife, such as budget decisions, household expenses, and hiring and firing servants. Tusi notes that the husband should still oversee her bookkeeping, in case she is fraudulent with her husband's wealth or asks for money without need.[131] Both Tusi and Davani prescribe secrecy about the husband's total net worth, lest the wife use that information against him.[132] Ghazali, like Tusi, warns against being tightfisted with one's wife and family, but he takes a more spiritual perspective, reminding readers that the Prophet stated that spending on one's family is better than spending on defending the faith, freeing a slave, or charity.[133] All three ethicists recommend a general discretion in spending.

Wives' independent wealth posed challenges to the husband's absolute financial power. According to Rapoport, urban women in premodern Muslim societies, including some from elite and scholarly families, commonly earned wages for spinning textiles and sewing.[134] These wages, in addition to any independent wealth from a dowry, possibly allowed many women to have a modest income at their own disposal, outside of the husband's financial support. Rapoport explains that many women participated in a "women's economy" in professions servicing women, working as midwives, hairdressers, matchmakers, bath and hospital attendants, and wet nurses.[135] He argues that the existence of this shadow economy, in which women were transacting outside the home, created a dynamic between husband and wife that threatened the patriarchal ideal of the Muslim household. In the Muslim ideal, the wife, children, servants, and enslaved persons all constituted the people (*ahl*) of the home and served as "one indivisible economic unit."[136] This meant that just as servants and enslaved persons did not earn wages, wives did not "earn" money from their husbands. They were given provisions and sums by the husband, the leader of the home. Rapoport cites fourteenth-century Hanbali jurist Ibn Qayyim al-Jawziyya, who "equated the support of wives with the support of slaves" on the basis that "absence of wages [for household services] shields the supposed mutual loyalty and love between a master and his slave from the disharmonious market economy. The same should hold true, ideally, for the relations between husband and wife."[137] All three ethicists consider a husband's financial support of his wife to be either a household expenditure or an act of charity.

From Rapoport's discussion of the effect of a wife's contact with the external world on the marital relationship, we can extrapolate that a marriage could also probably be strained by financial transactions such as the wife lending money to the husband. The ethicists do not directly discuss money-lending between wives and husbands, although Tusi does mention that the exchange of money should take place on friendly terms: "A wife is like a friend in that . . . [she is] content with whatever the husband gives her and forgives whatever the husband keeps from her and does not give her and does not refuse [him] her own wealth."[138] Tusi makes it clear to his readers that it is ethical for a husband to take money from his wives, and that an ethical wife would not refuse his request. Tusi considers it ethical for wives to grant their money and give up control of their land to husbands,[139] even though women were not legally required to share their wealth, and even though he advised men to establish power by not marrying women who were richer than themselves. As with sexual ethics, men are meant to dominate the area of money too. However, we see less concern for women's desires or station, perhaps because money is directly related to a man's capacity as vicegerent (*khalifah*), which is partly being the holder and distributor of wealth.

Marriage and Children

As in their ethics of money in marriage, Ghazali's, Tusi's, and Davani's ethics of rearing children is about discharging ethical duties toward them, while maintaining patriarchal control. And because grown men are also someone's children, they owe ethical duties to their elderly parents as well. The ethical guidelines toward one's children and one's parents show that the ethicists framed children, like women, as instruments of men's ethical refinement, a framing that has the effect of nearly excluding mothers from *akhlaq* of childrearing. Irigaray has critiqued Greek philosophy for essentializing women's bodies as mere maternal envelopes that carry children. Likewise, in the Ghazali-Tusi-Davani tradition, fathers command more respect than mothers since they give life both physically and intellectually. On the other hand, the three ethicists also convey the seriousness of mothers' biological sacrifice in carrying, birthing, and initially caring for children.[140] Here, as elsewhere in the ethical treatises, the metaphysical tension in creating a patriarchal ethics is present: the ethicists recognize the Qur'anic and hadith-mandated respect accorded to mothers, yet still primarily construe women's maternal role as being mere vessels that bear children. As Kathryn Kueny has argued, this framing of maternity is how male scholars attempted to regain male control over the reproductive and nurturing process, even as "medical, literary, theological, or other legal narratives [demonstrate] alternative modes of maternal subjectivity" in place of nonexistent, nonexplicit records of maternity.[141] Thus, the ethicists create an ethics of exclusion even in an arena in which they give women credit for sacrifice, which they construe as the primary purpose of women—to have children. Although the ethicists vary in their approaches to describing ethical fatherhood, they prioritize fathers' control in three ways: Tusi[142] and Davani reference medical ideas that emphasize fathers' contributions in reproduction, while minimizing mothers' roles to that of a biological vessel that carries children; all three ethicists outline a detailed financial and nurturing role of fathers in their children's lives, particularly male children; and all three ethicists designate gendered standards for how men are to repay debts to their fathers and mothers.

INSCRIBING PATERNAL BIOLOGICAL DOMINANCE

In Tusi's and Davani's texts,[143] the father's role as the immediate cause of a child's conception and development is more prominent than the role of the mother, who is merely the vessel. In fathering a child, a man carries out an act of God's vicegerency (*khilafah*) by being a means (*sabab*) of God's act of creation. Tusi states that the father is God's instrument of creating and sustaining a child's existence (*vajud*): "First, the father is the primary cause in the contiguous causes of the child's existence. After that, he is the cause for his upbringing and perfection and until he also reaches bodily perfection due to the advantages of the father's body, such as growth, nourishment, and other causes of stability and perfection of the child's *nafs*."[144]

The father is the primary cause among contiguous causes (*avval sababi az asbab-i malasiq*), not only for the existence of the child but also for his bodily form.

Although the ethicists considered it important for the strength of the offspring to find a healthy wife who was not too close in blood relation, in general mothers were not thought to have much physical contribution to a child's physical and mental attributes. It was thought that breast milk could transmit diseases, but not all women nursed their own children. Certainly no other biological information was thought to be transmitted from the mother, either before or after birth. The period of gestation mothers endured did afford them respect and explained their unconditional love for their sons, but the ethicists did not believe that mothers contribute to the child's perfection. Sons especially were thought to "inherit" the bodies and minds of their fathers, perhaps because they are of the same sex. The ethicists do not discuss a mother's role in a daughter's physicality or upbringing.

In Kathryn Kueny's study of medieval Muslim maternal identity construction, she explains that "following Hippocratic thought, many Muslim sources assert [that] male and females both emit seed that carries traits inherited by offspring."[145] Thus, theoretically, a child could resemble one's father or mother, or even neither, as it was believed that the seeds of both parents contained information that could result in children resembling distant ancestors. However, Kueny continues:

> Despite the fact that the Qur'an and subsequent medical literature
> assert that men and women contribute equally to the generation of
> life, and that only God—not men—imparts the life-giving "breath,"
> male physicians tend to favor the seed/soil theory of procreation in
> their clinical discussions of the maternal body. Although medical

scholars confirm a woman's "sperm" must mingle with the man's to generate life, they still cast the mother as the passive partner in whom the privileged male seed is planted. . . . The majority of medieval scholars contradict . . . sound prophetic advice, along with the Qur'anic edict that God fashions in wombs what he pleases, by claiming that offspring must always resemble the fathers that sired them.[146]

Kueny explains that scholars constructed maternal identities as passive through the mechanics of reproduction, despite their Qur'anic and medical knowledge to the contrary. Tusi's and Davani's descriptions of reproduction, from Irigaray's and Beauvoir's points of view, treat the mother's role as that of a vessel that carries children and thus fulfills one of the ways in which her husband can achieve transcendence. Kueny explains,

The male impulse to assert control over the maternal body suggests a certain level of discomfort with the Qur'anic ideal that God creates in wombs whatever, and however, he pleases. Such a statement assumes an erotic intimacy between women and God that leaves men completely out of the equation. In order to privilege their own procreative power, men usurp God's omniscience and omnipotence through a variety of authoritative discourses to guarantee the entire reproductive process is directed toward their desired outcome of self-replication.[147]

Tusi's and Davani's privileging of men's biological contributions in reproduction asserts men's power over women and helps explain why men become more Godlike in the process of creation.

The ethicists acknowledge a much smaller, albeit important, role for mothers. All three ethicists consider mothers' love for their children to be more intense than fathers' because the former is understood as instinctual and based on a mother's desire for the physical protection of her child. Tusi and Davani identically write:

The mother in the beginning of the child's existence is the collaborator and partner of the father in causality, in the way that the mother is receptive to the effect led [or performed] by the father;

she is weighted with the hardship of nine months, endures the dangers of giving birth and pain and suffering of that state, and is also the proximal cause of giving strength to the child, for she is the feminine matter of life. She is occupied with direct physical nurture in drawing benefits to him and warding off harm from him for a long time. From the excess of her affection and benevolence she prefers his life to her own life.[148]

In this description, a mother's biological function is passive. Although she is the father's collaborator, her role is merely to receive and grow his seed. In this description, she gestates the child, possibly nurses him, and cares for his physical needs, protecting him out of love. The depth of her love stems from the experience of physical labor: "a mother loves her child more ardently than a father, for she had suffered greater pains and privations in its nourishment."[149] According to Judith Tucker, court records from Ottoman Syria and Palestine also show that a mother's "fullness of affection" was occasionally an important factor in courts' decisions to award the mother custody of her children in divorce cases.[150] However, the limit of that affection is related to the physical toil the mother endures in carrying and birthing a child. As I show later, this reproductive labor serves as the only possible basis for any reciprocal duties a son may owe to his mother.

FATHERS' ROLES IN CHILDREARING

The *alkhlaq* texts' elevation of the father's role over that of the mother extends beyond the initial reproduction to the extended process of rearing children to adulthood. In the Ghazali-Tusi-Davani tradition, fathers are meant to play an active role in rearing sons into ethical men. As I have shown elsewhere, the fact that the ethics treatises are addressed to men, and yet include detailed instructions on how to rear sons,[151] shows that the cultivation of a particular ethical masculinity of a son is a key part of a father's ethical duties that contribute to his being a vicegerent of God (*khalifah*). Ghazali, Tusi, and Davani all expect fathers to be very hands-on from the point at which a boy is weaned until he begins working in his chosen profession and is married. Tusi states that the father's role is integral in all of these teachings to shape the boy's personality:

"Also, from the father's management, he attains perfections such as etiquette, talent, skills, sciences, and way of living which are the basis of growth and perfection of the child's *nafs*."[152] There are four areas of nurturing that correspond to successive stages of childhood. The first is general discipline of a young *nafs*, which includes listening to one's parents, having self-control, and being timely with prayers and religious observances. Aside from the absolute rule that fathers should beat their sons after age ten if they do not pray,[153] the ethicists are cautious in how they recommend instilling discipline. Here Tusi provides readers with several gems from his study of child psychology, including the requirement that fathers chide their children privately so that they do not become prone to insolence. Explaining reverse psychology, he notes that "humans eagerly desire what is forbidden."[154] The second area is instilling moderation and avoiding extremes with regard to desiring food and drink, comfort, clothing, and money. They prescribe utilitarian rules such as presenting food as sustenance, not as indulgence, in order to train the concupiscent faculty.[155] The third area of nurturing concerns proper education and career preparation, which require careful selection and monitoring of boys' intellectual predilections.[156] This area also includes the training of the irascible faculty so that a child may conduct himself well in society.[157] The fourth area is long-term preparation for independent life as an adult, husband, and father, as well as reciprocator of care for one's parents. Assuming the mantle of these responsibilities is the culmination of the son's becoming a vicegerent of God. Assuming that only a father can provide ethical guidance to the son, the father becomes wholly responsible for the son's upbringing, body, and soul, from conception to adulthood.

When boys are small, a father's discipline of them shares several principles with the discipline of wives, because the ethicists think of women as having underdeveloped, childlike faculties of rationality compared to adult men. The father maintains his charge over the mother's body and soul by secluding her and keeping her *nafs* occupied. These acts are conceived as acts of care because she is assumed not to have the self-control to manage her own *nafs*, even if her choices affect the marital relationship.[158] The difference between the guidance for wives and sons is that while the wife's soul remains infantilized and dependent upon the husband's discipline, the son grows into his own refinement.

Perhaps because of the stasis of a mother's *nafs*, none of the texts instructs men to convey a parenting plan to the mother, and in fact, after she gives birth, she has no stated role to play in parenting. Her only explicit appearance in Tusi's text is that fathers are commanded to ensure that both male and female children respect and obey their mothers, fathers, and tutors.[159] Perhaps the mothers were responsible for overseeing the daily minutiae of life, such as ensuring that children ate their supper, did their chores, and completed their lessons. However, mothers' roles in *akhlaq* cannot be known for sure since the texts contain no notion of coparenting, nor do they discuss women's ethical behavior in any terms except as wives. One reason for not mentioning mothers' roles could be that parenting may have been gender-segregated,[160] but it also could be that the father's control over the household left him with the ultimate responsibility. Just as marriage is defined as taking charge of a wife's *nafs*, so too parenting is taking charge of nurturing a child's *nafs*. The father's great role in nurturing, as indicated in the level of detail in the parenting advice given to the male audience, is impressive in that it puts great responsibility on the shoulders of fathers to condition their sons, secure their ethical masculinity, and prepare them for the trials of adult male life.

With the absence of similar details about rearing girls or about the roles of mothers in parenting, it is also possible that Ghazali, Tusi, and Davani expected that parenting would also be gender-segregated even though husband–fathers are in charge of perfecting the *nafses* of people in the household according to the measure of their potential. Daughters can only amount to becoming wives when they grow up. Instructing fathers, Tusi and Davani simply write, "employ what is favored and befitting them. . . . Instill in them attachment to the house and seclusion, dignity and self-restraint, shame, and other qualities we have enumerated in the chapter on wives. . . . Prohibit [girls] from reading and writing, and teach them skills that are praised in women. And when they reach the bounds of maturity, attach them with one of similar status."[161]

Likewise, when Ghazali mentions hadiths with regard to the blessings of having female children, he is thinking of settling them down and marrying them off.[162]

Although these suggest that caring for and rearing children are not wholly the mother's responsibility, scholars Giladi, Tucker, and Kueny all show that mothers did play much more expansive parental roles than the normative and theoretical texts let on. Kueny argues, and I agree, that the discrepancy between real-life and textual assertions of fatherly contributions could be attributed to the texts' function as arenas in which men asserted and codified the patriarchal order against the potent Qur'anic and real-life functions of motherhood. For Kueny, premodern Muslim mothers' agency is actually located within the patriarchal system; she argues that "women, through pre- and postnatal rituals, habits, and practices, often create corresponding, inward dispositions that conform but also contribute to the 'ideal mother' within a medieval context."[163] Through the ethicists' treatises, they create and exert patriarchal power in shaping children's lives over the maternal power of giving life and nurturing.

With fathers being responsible for existence, growth, nourishment, education, and morals, at least for boys, there is very little left for mothers to do for their children. The husband–father is the source and distributor of all resources—genetic, financial, educational, and otherwise. The father is the complete guardian, primary life-giver, caretaker, and spiritual and ethical guide; and the mother, meanwhile, is a secondary life-giver and short-term early nurturer. These gendered parental roles, in turn, place gendered responsibilities upon sons, which I elaborate next.

GENDERED DEBTS TO PARENTS

A third way that the ethicists use guidelines on rearing children, particularly sons, to prioritize fathers to the exclusion of mothers is in their descriptions of the debts a son owes to his parents. Adult children owe their parents for bringing them into the world and caring for them. The ethicists assume, as a dictate of nature, that although parents' love for their children is unconditional, children's love for their parents does not come naturally; rather, children must labor to return their parents' affection.[164] Tusi says that a child's kindness and respect for his parents are even more important than worship of God because, whereas "the Creator does not need compensation of his bounty," parents do look for that in their children and even rely on it in their old age.[165] Unsurprisingly, those debts are incurred and repaid along gendered lines that reflect a double standard: mothers need and are accorded financial support and provisions of physical comfort, while fathers need and are accorded respect and prayers. Tusi and Davani justify their differing recommendations on what constitutes ethical behavior toward one's father and mother as a function of the differing physical and intellectual care each parent provides.[166]

The ethicists' discussion of reproduction reveals how they connected sex and physiology to gender roles. And yet, the ethicists' expositions of children's duties toward their parents contain the metaphysical tension that we see elsewhere in the texts: women's subordinate status is in tension with their humanity. Here the ethicists vacillate between scriptural traditions that simultaneously elevate motherhood and dictate men's dominance over women. Some passages instruct men on how to pay off debts to both parents in such a way that is inclusive of both parents, while other nearby passages stipulate differences in what children owe their mothers and fathers. These passages reveal a discomfort with mothers' potential hold over their sons, a discomfort that the ethicists ameliorate by reassigning to fathers debts that seemingly belong to a mother—underlining women's exclusion from a central parental role and the metaphysical tension I have been tracing throughout this book.

Both Tusi and Ghazali frame sons' debts to parents as being inclusive of both mothers and fathers. Tusi states that "observance of the rights of one's mother and father is being devout in the worship of the creator."[167] He quotes the first half of verse 17:23—"Your lord has decreed do not worship but the One alone and to the parents be good"—to explain that "kindness to parents belongs alongside worship of the creator in the verse because of its importance."[168] Respect for parents flows naturally from worship of the creator, giving parents a Godlike status. Likewise, Ghazali narrates scriptural references that are inclusive of mothers. He first emphasizes the importance of having family ties: "Whoever is not rebellious or cut off from kinship can smell the scent of heaven from a distance of [a journey of] five hundred years."[169] He provides a quotation from Moses to emphasize parental obligation, even over allegiance to a prophet: "God most high sent a revelation to Moses, peace be upon him, that 'Whoever obeys the command of his mother and father, I will record him as obedient; and whoever obeys Me but does not obey them, I will record as disobedient.'"[170] The next hadith likewise ranks the station of both parents very high, next to God, in terms of whom one should prioritize when doing good deeds. Performing good deeds for one's parents is better than all of the obligations one performs for God: "doing good deeds for one's mother and father is better than prayer, fasting, pilgrimage, and just struggle [*ghaza*]."[171] The third hadith that Ghazali quotes builds upon the idea that children are a source of one's own spiritual rewards: "What is wasted if someone gives charity, for reward for his deceased mother and father, for they are rewarded and nothing is lessened from his reward?"[172] Along the same lines, he narrates an exchange someone had with the Prophet that keeps both parents on equal footing: "My mother and father are deceased; what rights of theirs have remained upon me to accomplish? He said, 'Pray on their behalf, ask for forgiveness, carry out their testament, hold their friends dear, and do good deeds for their relatives.'"[173]

Although children's responsibility to respect their parents is gendered in the sense that it is based on biologically grounded assumptions of what each parent does for a child, the ethicists do present three gender-neutral ways to respect both parents. First, the child should

> have pure love for them in the heart, intent to please them in promises and action, like honoring [them], obedience, service, softness of speech, humbleness, and such things that are not against the pleasure of the Great One, most high, or anything damaging that He prohibited, and if there is a request of one of them, you need to oppose but in a polite way, not by exposing it or fighting.[174]

The second responsibility of the child to the parents is to "help them with things before asking, without putting them under obligation or expectation, in the measure of possibility."[175] Finally, the third way to honor both parents is "expressing good will to them in private and public, for the world and the hereafter, protecting their testament and works for which they have given instruction, both in their lifetimes and after their deaths."[176]

This egalitarian language referring to devotion to both mothers and fathers, and indeed perhaps a little more to mothers, is disquieting for the ethicists who have reinscribed fathers' roles in reproduction and childrearing, further reifying fathers' dominance through differentiated rights of parents over their children. Tusi states that the debt to a father arises "with many kinds of hardship, trouble, and carrying of burdens[;] he makes a worldly accumulation and savings for [his son], and after his death, puts [his son] in his place."[177] The father's continuous financial support of the child and eventual bequeathing of an inheritance are the chief actions for which the son owes his father respect.[178] Kueny sheds light on how normative Islamic texts' focus on men's power in conception, over God's omnipotence in creation, allows for "the innate, dichotomous, and hierarchical relationship between men and women based on reproduction, and the male's self-proclaimed authority within the context of that relationship to govern and suppress the maternal body so that he alone may proliferate the type of life God commands in an earthly capacity."[179] As parents, mothers and fathers do not command the same form of respect.

Tusi and Davani outline the gendered differences in what an adult son, or the reader, owes to his parents based on what each has provided:

> The difference between rights of the father and rights of the mother is evident from what we have said, for the rights of fathers are more spiritual, and for that reason awareness of this comes to children after acquiring intellectual understanding. And the rights of mothers are more physical [or bodily] and also for that reason from the beginning of sense of feeling children understand it and show more inclination toward mothers. With this reasoning, rights of the father are fulfilled by putting forth obedience, good mention, supplication, and praise, which are more spiritual. Rights of the mother are fulfilled by giving money and bestowing means for living, and by conferring various kinds of favors that are more physical.[180]

In this passage, the ethicists set up gendered modes of respecting both parents. Tusi and Davani interpret a mother's physical contribution to a son's life as repayable with money and provisions for her physical comfort. By contrast, sons are indebted to fathers in ways that cannot be repaid monetarily; fathers deserve prayers, obedience, and good mention. Although this list of what a son owes a father closely mirrors the three ways one respects both parents, the verbs that they use to explain what is due to each parent indicate differences in the attitudes reserved for each parent. For fathers, Tusi and Davani state that one's debt is "fulfilled" by "obedience, good mention, and supplication and praise."[181] For mothers, they state that the debts are fulfilled by *ithar* (bestowal) and *ihsan* (conferring an obligation). The subtle addition of the terms *ithar* and *ihsan* indicates Tusi's and Davani's discomfort with awarding a mother for what he sees as limited contributions to the existence and self-actualization of a man, even if it is her son. The addition of the terms also reemphasizes the nature of the home and family as a domestic economy headed by the man, with resources distributed to each member based on their deserts.

Ghazali emphasizes the role of fathers in the patriarchal hierarchy through two quotations. He says, "Know that the right of an elder brother approaches the right of a father; it is known that 'the right of an elder brother over a younger brother is similar to the right of a father over a son.'"[182] The saying is not attributed to anyone, but Hossein Khadivjam, editor of the text's critical edition, puts it in quotations because it is a common saying. Although this particular tradition does not necessarily diminish a mother's status, the fact that a father's power transfers to an elder brother over a mother indicates a well-developed cultural hierarchy of male power. Ghazali also quotes a hadith in which the Prophet said, "No person has fulfilled the rights of [his] father until [the son] has become his [father's] slave: he [the father] buys and frees [the son]."[183] Essentially, a son is indebted to his father, and only a father has the ability to free him, so one should do good toward one's father, and perhaps also give him money if he needs it. Implicit in Ghazali's worldview is the notion that money is a primary distinction between what a father provides and what a mother provides, even though debt to her is paid with money and debt to him is paid with multiple forms of devotion.

The ethicists even insert fathers into a parent–child debt that would seem to uniquely be owed by the child to the mother—namely, breast-feeding of the child. In the *Ihya' 'Ulum ad-Din*, we see Ghazali demonstrating that the physical act of nursing creates a material debt upon children; however, this nurturance is under the father's purview because it is he who locates the nurse. Ghazali advises fathers to find their children pious nurses who are also healthy.[184] In Tusi's addendum on the rights of parents, he mentions that mothers physically nurture and nourish the children, so in Tusi's context, wet-nursing probably existed alongside mothers' nursing of their own children. Avner Giladi explains that medieval medical and normative ethics texts do not definitively indicate whether wet-nursing or maternal nursing was more prominent, but suggest that maternal health, family planning, and social class were the factors behind individuals' choices.[185] The ethicists and others from their time period do take for granted, following ideas from Greek medicine, that maternal-nursing established a mother's unconditional love for her child, which forms the basis of a child's indebtedness to her. But even with this seemingly mother-specific debt, female parents are partially written out of this by the use of wet-nursing, and by the fact that fathers, at least in ethical theory, chose the wet nurses.

One way to think of the metaphysical tension within at least Ghazali's work—the fact that he elevates mothers, but not at the cost of the fathers' stature—is his ethical discomfort with codifying dominance to his male audience since there is a clear power differential in men's and women's status. The section on the rights of children is about three times longer than the section on parents' rights, yet Ghazali explicitly states that the latter have far more rights than the former.[186] We can draw a parallel with his sections on the rights of wives and the rights of husbands, in which he likewise states that husbands have far more rights over their wives. Ghazali, keenly aware of the power differential between the male readers, on one hand, and their wives and children, on the other, emphasizes in both sections that the male reader must observe the rights of the women and children in order to be ethical. Ghazali is thus not afraid to quote the hadith: "The rights of a mother are twice the rights of a father."[187] Elsewhere, in the section on children's rights, he also quotes the hadith in which the Prophet sends a young man who wanted to go to battle to go sit beside his mother because his "heaven lies beneath her feet."[188] These statements serve to elevate mothers but are sufficiently counterbalanced by his statements about fathers' roles. The work reads less as a celebration of men's power than a set of instructions to men on their responsibilities in maintaining an ethical household. As Lev Weitz has argued, the much greater length of the *Ihya*'s section on wives' rights in marriage, as compared to the section on husbands' rights, is a counterintuitive indication that Ghazali is keeping the central focus on men. In this reading, the section on marriage is actually about the ideal characteristics, rights, and responsibilities of *women* as they are oriented toward men and the safeguarding of men's interests. Thus, the section on what makes an ideal husband does not actually instruct men on how to be ideal husbands to their wives—which would misplace power into the hands of wives—but rather continues to focus on men by discussing what qualities a man should look for when contracting a marriage for his daughter.[189] Similarly, the discrepancy in length between Ghazali's sections on the rights of children and the rights of parents could be read as evidence that he is staying focused on the utility of rearing sons for dispensing men's responsibilities, rather than talking about safeguarding children's rights. The entire section is, after all, about rearing children correctly to dispense fathers' obligations, even though it is cloaked in children's rights–based discourse.

An extension of the husband-centered marriage, father-centric childrearing in the *akhlaq* texts has less to do with love and care of family members than with solidifying man's rule over the domestic economy. The metaphysical tension we observe in the simultaneous mentions of motherly sacrifice and minimization of their contributions to childbearing and childrearing is the result of threats the ethicists perceive a mother might pose to a father's stature. For all three ethicists, the father's rights are all encompassing and spiritual, while mothers only deserve worldly, and therefore lowly, compensation of money for their physical contributions. The specific acts of respect accorded to each parent are gendered, and they reflect the patriarchal family's status as a microcosm of the cosmos.

WHEN AND HOW TO DIVORCE

While the ethicists take great pains to detail how a man is to lead his household and the expectations he should have of his wife to play an instrumental role within the domestic economy, they also recognize that she may fail to fulfill that role—and if and when she does, it may be acceptable or even necessary for him to divorce her. In the *akhlaq* texts, a man may initiate *talaq* (husband-initiated divorce) against his wife if she subverts his power or if she becomes an obstacle to his ethical duties. However, for the sake of his own *akhlaq*, a man must take great care in deciding whether to divorce. As the ethicists repeatedly emphasize, a husband is responsible for ruling over his wife's *nafs* and providing her financial support, even through the process of separation. The ethicists offer two types of guidance for husbands facing decisions about whether and how to divorce: they describe the behaviors of divorce-worthy wives, as a sort of manual for husbands to use in assessing their wives' unworthiness; and they explain how to treat women with kindness throughout the process of divorce.

Although no statistics are available on the prevalence of divorce in premodern Muslim societies, legal records of divorce cases from the Andalusian, Mamluk, and Ottoman periods indicate that it was common and normal for both men and women to initiate divorce, and it was much less stigmatized than it became in modern periods.[190] Indeed, in the eyes of the ethicists, divorce was permissible and at times advisable, although it did raise several moral and ethical concerns for them, particularly with regard to the treatment of women. As Rapoport has shown, "The prevailing cultural assumption in Mamluk society, at least until the end of the fifteenth century, was that divorce was a disaster for women."[191] This attitude prevailed even though divorce was common and many women earned sufficient income, especially from spinning and sewing, to remain single for long periods of time between marriages.[192] The ethicists do not discuss in detail this negative view of divorce, but they do base their guidelines for divorce on this assumption that divorce caused hardship for women.

Why Divorce?

The ethicists all agree that in certain situations, divorce is a wise decision. Tusi and Davani emphasize that character deficiencies of a divorce-worthy wife offend a man's prestige, implying that wives are responsible for their husbands' reputations. Ghazali warns, "an ill-mannered wife is ungrateful, sharp-tongued, [and] will be deceitful with orders; living with her will make life miserable and destroy your faith."[193] A bad marriage, then, can even have spiritual consequences. When women refuse their immanence and attempt transcendence, to use Beauvoir's terms, they impinge on men's transcendence and thus become inimical to their husbands' overall enterprise. As I stated earlier, the ethicists saw problems with husbands being dominated by wives who were excessively beautiful or wealthy. All three ethicists warn that, for a woman, wealth and beauty are a catastrophic combination when they are not accompanied by piety or intelligence.[194] Tusi says, "For someone who is infatuated with an unworthy woman, advice for him is to seek liberation from her, for being close to a bad woman is worse than being close to wild beasts and snakes."[195] The term *liberation* is key here, since the ethicists view marriage with a bad woman as a reversal of the rightful power dynamic, a sort of slavery of the husband. In a well-ordered marriage, it is the wife who is in service to her husband.

The *akhlaq* texts' likening of the husband–wife dynamic to the master–slave relationship is not unique. Kecia Ali has shown that this connection between marriage and slavery is frequently found in early Islamic jurisprudence, with a husband's legal status being analogous to that of a slave owner and the wife's status to that of a slave.[196] Ghazali extends this relationship in the *akhlaq* genre. In the context of warning his readers to select a proper spouse for one's child, he quotes a hadith in which the Prophet says, "marriage is slavery; be careful about to whom you give your own child as a slave."[197] In citing this hadith, Ghazali briefly upsets the wife-as-slave analogy by reminding his male audience that the Prophet said marriage is like slavery even for men. For Ghazali, this means two things. First, legally contracting a marriage is akin to undertaking a commercial transaction involving humans. Second, and more relevant to Ghazali's discussion on marriage in the *Kimiya*, this meant that men should not allow themselves to feel enslaved and trapped by bad wives, even if women are meant to serve as slaves to husbands.

In the ethics of the domestic economy, the hierarchical relationship of marriage is one of master and underling. The husband is to remain dominant, and the wife is to be in his service. Ghazali states, "the rights of the man over the woman are greater, because she is really the man's *bandah*."[198] The term *bandah* literally means someone who is bound or in bondage such as a servant or slave. It is the same term used to describe a servant or slave of God. Here Ghazali is referring to the metaphorical relationship between husband and wife as dictated by the *nikah*. Like Ghazali, Tusi and Davani also affirm this analogy, in a passage where they quote an Arab saying what a woman should be: in addition to being like a mother and friend who desire a husband's welfare and unconditional love, she should also be as a *kanizak* (little concubine), and "should degrade herself in the manner of a *parastar* [slave], pledge her service, and tolerate his anger."[199] Here marriage is a woman's enslavement, consistent with jurisprudence as Ali has shown.[200] As I note elsewhere, a reversal in this dynamic constitutes grounds for divorce, especially if the husband feels enslaved by the wife's actions. The ethicists all subscribe to the idea that one must take steps to improve the situation before considering divorce, but they also do not hesitate to lay out a plan for men to follow as they go about divorcing wives who enslave them.

In order to define a standard to guide men's vigilance during marriage, the ethicists provide lists of characteristics and behaviors that unworthy wives may commit. Tusi and Davani give the following description of the traits and actions of a bad wife:

> An unworthy wife is similar to a tyrant in that she likes laziness and idleness, uses abominable speech, and has a lot of anger; she is inconsiderate of that which brings about her husband's satisfaction or anger, and gives a lot of pain to the servants. She is similar to an enemy in that she considers the husband as contemptible, holds him in low esteem, shows bad manners, disavows his favors, has rancor for him, complains, and recites his faults. She resembles a thief in that she defrauds him with respect to wealth, asks [for money] without need, and deprecates his kindness; she is incessant in doing that which he hates, she shows insincere friendship, and she prefers her own benefit over his.[201]

With a wife like this, a husband has few options. If a wife disobeys her husband's commands, then Ghazali recommends a methodical approach to disciplining her, based on his interpretation of verse 4:34. The approach has four steps: "request her obedience with kindness and friendliness; if she does not obey, separate the bedclothes and put your back to her. If she does not obey, separate the bedclothes for three nights. If there is no improvement, then hit her, not on the face and not hard such that something breaks."[202] The Qur'anic term for disobedience in 4:34 is rebellion (*nushuz*). Ali explains that jurists generally defined a wife's *nushuz* in four ways: "sexual refusal; departure from the conjugal home without permission; disobedience or disrespectfulness more generally; and, in a minority view, a wife's nonperformance of her religious duties."[203] Ghazali does not use the term *nushuz* in the *Kimiya*. Instead, he explains that one can take the aforementioned four-step approach to correcting a wife if she negates her husband's decrees by her disobedience (*nafarmani*) and does not possess the quality of obedience to her husband (*ta'at-i shuhar*); she therefore possesses a rebellious disposition inherent in her character.[204] Ghazali explains the wife's offenses using a series of Persian terms, which may be his way of defining a Qur'anic/legal concept for his audience of Persian-speaking laymen, or it may be a way to skirt around what actually constitutes outright wifely disobedience. I argue that since the genre's focus is on an individual's ethics and how a man should interact with others based on their individual dispositions, Ghazali's idea of disobedience (*nafarmani*) refers to a principle similar to the third jurisprudential definition of rebellion (*nushuz*) that Ali outlines, general disobedience, without actually using the Qur'anic/jurisprudential term of *nushuz*. For Ghazali, the prerequisite for correcting the wife is her overall disobedient nature, as opposed to isolated disobedient acts she may commit, such as sexual refusal or departure from the home. Ghazali's understanding of a wife's *nushuz* as disobedience in nature may explain his departure from jurisprudence, which is concerned with suspension of a wife's financial maintenance (*nafaqah*) as a consequence of disobedience.[205]

In the event that a wife is deficient in performing religious obligations such as prayer or fasting, Ghazali instructs his reader to separate from his wife for up to a month, following the example of the Prophet, who did so when he was angry with his wives over too many petty disputes. Why Ghazali opts for the more peaceful guidelines only in matters of religious adherence, while recommending the four-step approach in all other matters of disobedience, has to do with the Prophet as the ultimate interpreter of the Qur'an. The instruction to abandon wives for a month recalls the Prophet's own example of how he dealt with his wives' bad behavior. Also, as Ayesha Chaudhry has shown, Ghazali reads verse 4:34 as a series of incremental steps to take against a rebellious wife, with striking her as a last resort; hitting her would not be for her benefit, but rather for his own.[206] Consistent with the *Ihya'* interpretation of 4:34—that striking a disobedient wife would potentially be ineffectual in correcting her—Ghazali prescribes, in the *Kimiya-i Sa'adat*, the prophetic example of abandoning the wife for up to a month. In any case, once a man has decided to divorce, he must do so ethically.

Types of Divorce

Classical Islamic law provided for several types of juridical and nonjuridical divorce. The most common, and the most relevant in the ethics texts, is *talaq*, or repudiation pronounced by a husband. According to the jurists, after a husband pronounces *talaq*, the wife observes a three-month waiting period (*'iddah*), at the end of which the marriage is dissolved. During the waiting period, a woman continues to receive financial support (*nafaqah*), but a man can also take back his wife and indefinitely suspend the *talaq* pronouncement. He may repudiate her and take her back two times, but a third pronouncement of divorce is irrevocable. In *talaq*, the husband forfeits the marriage dower (*mahr*) that is either paid to the wife or deferred at the time the marriage is contracted. The jurists' discussion of husband-initiated divorce, *talaq*, allows for an element of moral discernment in that the husband is allowed to consider which procedure is best to follow in his situation, given the legal assumptions[207] that staying married is always preferable to divorce and that efficiency in the process is best because it shows kindness to women.

The "better *talaq*" (*talaq al-ahsan*) is defined as the husband's single pronouncement of divorce in between the wife's menstrual cycles, during which there are no sexual relations with her, so as not to interrupt the *'iddah* waiting period. During the *'iddah*, a man should not change his mind, as that would toy with the wife's emotions and make the divorce more painful.[208] According to the jurists, what makes this form of *talaq* better than others is that it allows time for the wife to attempt reconciliation, yet it is still efficient enough to be concluded within three months. A second form of divorce, also efficient, is the "good *talaq*" (*talaq al-hasan*). This is defined as the husband's repeated, monthly repudiation of the wife in between each of the three menstrual cycles of the *'iddah* waiting period. This is less desirable than the "better *talaq*" because it leads to a divorce that is irrevocable, meaning the two cannot remarry each other after the divorce is final. A third type of divorce, "divorce of fabrication" (*talaq al-bid'a*), is obtained through three pronouncements of *talaq* on a single occasion. It is also notoriously known as "triple *talaq*." This type of divorce is both swift and irrevocable. The jurists discourage this method because it precludes any chance of reconciliation during the *'iddah* waiting period.

In addition to the male-initiated divorce, another kind of legal divorce—one that jurists discuss but the ethicists do not, though it is relevant for interpreting *akhlaq* guidelines—is wife-initiated divorce, or *khul'a*. *Khul'a* is an irrevocable divorce, meaning the two cannot remarry each other once the divorce is final. It is initiated by the wife in exchange for a negotiated sum or the return of the marriage dower (*mahr*). Jurists always interpreted wife-initiated divorce, *khul'a*, as requiring a husband's consent or juridical intervention, which meant that while a man could independently and unilaterally secure a divorce for himself, a woman could not. In a *khul'a*, a woman essentially ransoms herself for a sum upon which the husband agrees, or else seeks juridical intervention by proving legitimate grounds for divorce.

The jurists' distinction between good and better divorces reveals a conflict between the principle of efficiency in the divorce process and the value of reserving the possibility of a marriage being saved. Apart from the fact that efficiency and opportunity for reconciliation are contradictory, the moral value of these procedural differences is fixed according to the jurists' unchanging assumptions that reconciliation and efficiency are always desirable in all circumstances. Of course, this assumption does not reflect real-life practices or applications of divorce law in premodern Muslim courts.

Divorcing Ethically

The ethicists sidestep the legal complexities of the divorce process as delineated in *fiqh*, instead considering how individuals can assess their own situations and marital responsibilities with respect to divorce. Since the only legal impediment for a man who desires to divorce his wife unilaterally via *talaq* (husband-initiated divorce) is insanity, legality is not a concern for the ethicists; but ethical responsibilities in the process of divorce are. In several passages in the *akhlaq* texts, the ethicists indicate that they are concerned with the weighty moral responsibility placed on men by the unilateral right to divorce. They also seem to recognize the emotional weight of severing marital ties. The ethicists affirm that it is not unethical to exercise one's unrestricted right to divorce, nor is having that power unethical, but the way in which a man exercises that right has the potential to be ethical or unethical. Tusi, Ghazali, and Davani each have a distinct approach to the question of how to divorce ethically. Tusi is the least compassionate, suggesting strategies to manipulate the wife into wanting divorce; Ghazali emphasizes observation of proper boundaries of kindness and discretion during divorce; Davani, the most compassionate of the three, urges husbands to avoid being the cause of devastation in the divorce process.

One might expect the ethicists to advise readers to pronounce *talaq* in gentle or kind ways, known in legal literature as the "better *talaq*" (*talaq al-ahsan*).[209] But Tusi suggests a different strategy: instigating in one's wife the desire for divorce. He provides the following guidelines:

> If quitting her is impossible, there are four types of plans that can be employed for this. First, [liberal] expenditure of wealth: for protection of the soul, manhood, and reputation is better than protection of wealth. If you should expend a lot of wealth to buy yourself from her, you should consider that money as very little. Second, *nushuz* [with her], [show] bad manners and temper, and move sleeping places, in a way that does not lead to chaos. Third, adopt mysterious tricks, such as inciting old women to [cause her to] fear herself and lure her toward another husband, and [while] show[ing] desire for her on the surface, and refusal to leave her, so that it happens that an eager desire to leave appears in her. In summary, use all types of connivance, obstacles, encouragement, and provocation that cause separation. Fourth, after exhausting other strategies, leave her and embark on a distant journey, on conditions that impede her from taking steps toward implementing abominations, so that her hopes are cut off and she chooses separation.[210]

In Tusi's view, these covert tactics to manipulate one's wife into desiring divorce are more ethical than an outright *talaq* because he is not explicitly recommending divorce.

At first glance, it seems that Tusi's advice for how to end a marriage might be a pragmatic accommodation to the tangible impediments a man might encounter when exercising his right to unilaterally divorce his wife. Historically, the legal parameters of payment and return of the dower (*mahr*) have affected whether or not a couple divorces as well as who initiates divorce. If the dower is set high enough, it can sometimes serve as a deterrent to the husband pronouncing *talaq*. By the same token, a high dower could also discourage a woman from seeking a wife-initiated divorce (*khul'a*), lest she has to pay back the dower. In such a situation, the breakdown of marital relations could end in a stalemate, with neither party initiating divorce. However, Tusi's first proposal is to just pay off the unsuitable (*na-shayestah*) woman for the sake of freedom, suggesting that for him the payment of *mahr* should not be a deterrent against *talaq*. Other common incentives to stay married, such as protecting one's social image, do not explain the advice in this passage because Tusi held that a bad wife is a man's downfall in all personal and social matters and should be quitted at once. How then to explain his counterintuitive advice?

Tusi's idea to manufacture situations that could cause a wife to seek divorce makes sense as a means of releasing a man from the ethical quandary of divorcing a woman. Such a move is necessary because, even where there may be no reason to stay married, *talaq* posed a moral dilemma for men. The ethicists recognized that, in addition to having financial responsibility for the wife, a man may also feel ethically responsible for her well-being; he may feel that staying married is better for the children involved; or perhaps, the man enjoys some social benefits from the marital alliance, which led him to the marriage in the first place. Whatever the reason, Tusi outlines these tactics so that the husband can be absolved by his wife of the moral burden of initiating divorce.

One key tactic that Tusi recommends for coaxing a wife to desire divorce is to make her fear desertion by committing *nushuz* against her, using the term as a verb, meaning to display repulsion. Ali explains that while the jurists had four definitions of wifely *nushuz* (as I discussed earlier), jurists viewed a husband's *nushuz* as a display of his repulsion from his wife.[211] Here, then, instead of focusing on a woman's rebellion as in Qur'anic verse 4:34 as grounds to discipline or divorce a wife, Tusi recommends that a husband display *nushuz*, as in Qur'anic verse 4:128, as a way to put the onus of divorce on the wife. Verse 4:128 refers to what women should do if their husbands commit *nushuz*: "if a woman fears from her husband *nushuz* or desertion, then there is no sin on both of them that they make terms of peace between themselves, a reconciliation, and the reconciliation is best. The souls are swayed by greed, but if you do good and fear God, then indeed God is of what you do."

The verse suggests reconciliation as the best path for such a couple. Since Tusi suggests that a woman would seek divorce if her husband commits *nushuz* against her, she would be in violation of God's command to reconcile. Any sin would be hers.

Tusi is not too concerned with the moral burden associated with a man's manufacturing a desire for divorce in his wife. Nor is he concerned with posing an ethical dilemma to the wife for staying in the marriage, because in his mind, a woman has no ethical responsibility to stay in a marriage. Tusi, like Ghazali, imagines the ethics of marriage from the husband's perspective, which in part means that women's incentives in marriage must be money, protection, and the privilege of increasing the Muslim population by bearing children. If a wife forfeits these privileges, it is of no ethical fault on the part of the husband.

Like Tusi, Ghazali is also concerned about the ethical challenge that *talaq* poses, though his approach is kinder. He affirms that divorce is to be avoided if at all possible: "As far as you can try, do not divorce, for God Most High dislikes divorce of all lawful acts."[212] The latter part of this saying is a hadith, but he does not cite it as such, likely because it was a common sentiment.[213] The specific term in the hadith is *talaq*, thus excluding any kind of wife-initiated divorce that the Prophet had approved. In the context of an ethics that gives men a unilateral right to divorce, it makes sense that the hadith is used to discourage men from divorce, even though they are thought to possess the rationality to exercise that right wisely.[214]

Although *talaq* is to be avoided, Ghazali advises that when it cannot, men ought to at least observe proper boundaries throughout the *talaq* process. First, Ghazali explains that one should be kind: "Be apologetic in divorce—in a way of kindness—do not give a divorce with anger and hostility. At the same time, give her gifts that make her heart happy, and never reveal her secrets to anyone." Kindness also calls for discretion: "Do not make known the flaw in her for which you gave her a divorce."[215] Here, Ghazali is doing more than just prohibiting backbiting; he is attempting to protect the privacy of the husband–wife relationship, in principle, even at the brink of divorce. To demonstrate this point,

Ghazali constructs a didactic exchange between two men: "One was asked, 'Why are you giving your wife a divorce?' He said, 'One is not able to reveal one's wife's secrets.' After he gave her the divorce, they said, 'Why did you do it?' He said, 'What do I have to do with another woman that I relate things about her?'"[216] The primary principle that Ghazali is illustrating in his discussion of ethical divorce is the protection of the proper boundaries between unrelated men and women. Ghazali says in other contexts that hearing is like seeing and that hearing and feeling are the same. Revealing a woman's attributes would be akin to seeing her, which was against the manly pride (*ghayrat*) of her husband. A related principle is the protection of a woman's privacy and reputation, which enable her to remarry, as was common practice.

Ghazali's final point in this exchange is to urge husbands to relinquish familiarity with their ex-wives after divorce. He emphasizes the power of divorce to break the marriage tie with finality, lest one feels the divorced woman is somehow still one's wife. In jurisprudence, the notion of a relationship with an ex-wife does not exist beyond *nafaqah*, that is, financial maintenance to be paid to an ex-wife through the *'iddah* period or until the end of a pregnancy, whichever is later. An ex-wife, Ghazali points out, is the same as any "other woman" with whom one has no ties. I read this part of the exchange as an ethical rule that is external to jurisprudential regulations, and that speaks to a man's emotions in divorce—namely, warning him to guard against intimate or husbandly thoughts of his freshly divorced ex-wife.

Davani's approach to correcting or divorcing a disobedient wife is the most compassionate of the ethicists. He does not discuss divorce in any substantive detail except to say that one may pursue "separation, provided that it does not involve devastation such as loss of children."[217] This provision shows that in Davani's context, child custody did not always belong to fathers—although, because he does not use the word *talaq*, it is not clear whether Davani is warning fathers about the potential loss of custody as a legal possibility in divorce, an extrajudicial reality in divorce, a possible outcome of informal separation, or any of those three scenarios.[218] More importantly, he is concerned about the fate of children in separation or divorce. Davani recommends that if one cannot be sure that divorce will cause no devastation, then one should either try being kind to an unsuitable (*na-shayestah*) wife in the hopes that she will reform or else leave her in the care of someone who will correct her and embark on a distant journey oneself.[219]

The sections of the *akhlaq* texts that deal with ethical divorce reveal Ghazali's, Tusi's, and Davani's discomfort with granting men the unilateral right to divorce absent any ethical regulation. In the ethicists' minds, the laws of jurisprudence govern the legal process of untying marital bonds, but *akhlaq* governs how men manage divorce and act ethically in the moment. Tusi describes a way out of having to repudiate one's wife, but Ghazali explains a much more sensitive approach to *talaq* than the law would require, including providing one's wife with gifts and protecting her privacy throughout the divorce process. In the ethics texts, the bottom line is, as Ghazali says: "Of all things, do not give someone distress unless it is necessary."[220] Both Tusi and Ghazali remind their male readers of the potential cruelty of *talaq* and of men's ethical responsibility to dispense it wisely even as they legitimately pursue divorce. Davani prefers separation, omitting the term *talaq* as well as any discussion of its details. However, despite the ethicists' apparent compassion for women, it is unlikely that they had women's perspectives in mind. Ghazali, Tusi, and Davani are ultimately advocating for men to ensure their own ethical safety by protecting their responsibilities as providers to women and children.

In the Ghazali-Tusi-Davani tradition, the relationship between husband and wife is one of interdependent, but not mutual, responsibilities and duties, rather than one of love. The ethicists understood men as rational, disembodied intellectual and spiritual souls, and women as embodied, irrational, emotional, petty beings who are limited by biological function. A husband's primary ethical responsibilities are to create a family, provide for the family by ethical means, keep his wife's mind and *nafs* occupied with his affairs, show measured affection, and be an involved father. A proper wife has an instrumental role; she preserves a man's dignity and manhood by respecting him and attending to his needs, such as running his household, bearing his children, keeping his books, managing his servants, and maintaining his public reputation, all while guarding her own purity. In the domestic economy, a husband-father is meant to dispense his divine charge to become a microcosm of God's work through vicegerency (*khilafah*) and by achieving happiness/

flourishing (*sa'adat*) through taking charge of his wife and children's *nafses*. The husband is responsible for keeping the wife instrumental as his deputy and rearing (male) children in accordance with the science of *akhlaq*.

In the ethicists' prescriptions for marital *akhlaq*, they focus on the husband's ethical role in marriage and the domestic economy. As the utility of marriage is bound up with procreation and protection of the household order, the ethics texts present a host of guidelines for choosing an appropriate time to marry, selecting a suitable marriage partner, and managing married life. These guidelines have little to do with marital love, and much to do with the power dynamic between husband and wife. Tusi refers to his rules as "the foremost condition for ruling womenfolk" as though women and men are two different species. He asserts that "the one who should command commands, the one who should obey obeys, and the regulator regulates."[221] The commanders and regulators are men, and those who should obey are women. Disruption of this order calls for *talaq*, though one must be sure of the wife's unworthiness and be kind in the process. The man's ability to unilaterally divorce his wife does pose an ethical challenge, but that challenge can be mitigated by following the guidelines of the ethical treatises.

I have shown that the ethics texts are fraught with metaphysical tension with respect to the nature and role of women. Both the Qur'an and their studies about human (versus animal) rationality demand that the ethicists think of the nature of the individual *nafs* of men and women as the same. The human *nafs* is prone to base behavior because of its animalistic or self-indulgent tendencies, but it is, for men, capable of reform and being steered in ethical directions. The hierarchy that exists between men and women, and particularly between husband and wife, is based on the assumption that women are unable to reform their *nafses*. This assumption demonstrates the metaphysical tension: the ethicists are attempting to preserve the husband's power and the wife's instrumentality at all costs, even while considering the wife's *nafs* and emotions.

In this chapter, teasing out the organization of the domestic economy—including the relationships between husband and wife and between parents and their children, as well as the obligations of children to their parents—has revealed an internal contradiction in women's metaphysics in the Islamic ethics texts. Nonetheless, the ethicists sidestep the metaphysical tension in favor of husbands' primacy and wives' instrumentality because they do not believe God created men and women as equals. *Akhlaq*, then, excludes women from refinement and places them in an instrumental position to men. The next chapter considers how this metaphysical tension emerges in the *akhlaq* texts' discussions of how ethical man dispenses his duties on the broader scale of society as he becomes a vicegerent (*khalifah*).

CHAPTER FOUR

Homosocial Masculinity and Societal Ethics

The universe is male.
—AISHA TABRIZ

There it is, then, before our eyes, the procession of the sons of educated men, ascending those pulpits, mounting those steps, passing in and out of those doors, preaching, teaching, administering justice.
—VIRGINIA WOOLF

In the Ghazali-Tusi-Davani ethics tradition, a man becomes fully ethical through association with other human beings in the public sphere. Only by interacting with and relating to a range of friends, acquaintances, colleagues, servants, and superiors—all of whom are imagined as male— can a man understand his place in society's hierarchy of power and in the cosmos. The ethicists describe male responsibility at both the microcosmic and the macrocosmic levels using a single term, *governance* (*siyasat*), which connotes coercive ordering of not only the ethics of household management and domesticity, but also the ethics of how to live among and treat a group of male individuals within a community, city, or the world at large. This third level of *siyasat*, after individual and domestic governance, deals with friendship, community, society, and sovereignty. A man must master this level of governance in order to thoroughly dispense his ethical responsibilities. Tusi explains the relationship between the individual man and society as follows: "Just as each person is a part of the household, so each household is a part of the locale, each locale is a part of the city, each city is a part of the nation, and each nation is a part of the inhabitants of the world."[1] Within this nested cosmos, each man, as a microcosm unto himself, can achieve a perfected *nafs* only once he is ethical on all the scales of human existence.

In the previous chapter, I considered how the texts present ethical masculinity in the domestic realm by analyzing their discussions of husband-father and wife-mother roles and their occasional contrasts between masculinity and femininity. In this chapter, I broaden my analysis to the public sphere, uncovering how Ghazali, Tusi, and Davani construct masculinity and men's ethical relations with one another in the context of society, specifically the urban homosocial environment. Several questions drive this inquiry: What are the ideal kinds of masculinity for men interacting with one another in society? Is there a possibility for social and intellectual mobility? What are the elements that make social behavior ethical? Which men are excluded from ethical refinement, and why? From this inquiry, the picture of the ethical man that emerges is of one who is mindful of his surroundings and elite station in society, responsible for himself and his friends and family, and careful with his words and actions. Overall, the ethics texts define ultimate masculinity in terms of elite power, intellectual hierarchy, and ethical comportment within the homosocial structures of community, civic, and court life. Occasionally, they also define this public masculinity in contrast to women's behavior.

As I explore Ghazali's, Tusi's, and Davani's ethical precepts for the all-male urban homosocial environment—where superiors, equals, subordinates, friends, and foes are all hierarchically ranked by their intellectual abilities and ethical refinement—I show that ethics is not just *gendered* in essentialized masculine ways, but also *classed*, constructed within and subject to social hierarchy. The public arena of the ethicists' conception, which is exclusively male and homosocial, is based on a kind of male power and hierarchy such that men of lower classes or intellectual stations are precluded from taking part in the enterprise of ethics. This feature of the *akhlaq* tradition is crucial because it points to how the ethicists are working to construct masculinity not only by defining it in contrast to femininity, as shown in chapter 3, but also by framing it within (male-only) hierarchies and social processes. As this chapter demonstrates, in the *akhlaq* texts, we see social processes that define ethical masculinity unfolding along the lines of class determining rational ability, and age determining what stage of involvement a man has with society. Thus, we see how men are gendered and ranked not just through their interactions with women, but also through multiple kinds of homosocial male interactions in which the exemplary ethical man is contrasted not with women, but with unrefined men.

In order for us to understand how social ethics in the public realm is gendered and constructed as normatively male in *akhlaq*, we have to look at how the ethicists construct elite masculinity itself. Specifically, this chapter examines the general principles of and guidelines for homosocial association, including a hierarchy of loves that places "spiritual" masculine love above "physical" feminine love, principles for ethical conduct within individual relationships, whether they are characterized by love and friendship or by enmity, and explanations of how individuals develop the love for society that becomes the basis of *khilafah*, or vicegerency of God, in which the individual functions as a microcosm of cosmic-scale ethics. After analyzing these general principles for the ethics of homosocial association, the chapter explores ethical masculinity within hierarchal institutions and structures in urban life, and within court life, including guidelines defining the ethics of kings toward subordinates and vice versa. I argue that the ethicists' construction of masculinity as it operates to create the ethical macrocosm is based on social hierarchies—namely, social classes based on superiority of intellect—that are untenable because they oppose the ethicists' own concept of justice as well as *akhlaq*'s stated goal of helping every individual fulfill their responsibility to become a vicegerent of God. Because the ethicists' construction of masculinity in their ideal homosocial vision excludes women and nonelite men, this construction is disruptive to their system of ethical refinement, which prioritizes rationality and vicegerency (*khilafah*).

Although the ethicists conceptualize ethical principles in terms of nested realms emanating from personal ethics to cosmic ethics, a conception that suggests a universality of perspective, their guidelines actually grew out of their specific civic contexts. Premodern Muslim lands were organized around urban centers that were ruled by dynasties and defined by hierarchal class institutions, such as the court, intellectual circles, the open bazaar, neighborhoods, and the city in its entirety. The ruling dynasties of the Saljuqs, Isma'ilis, Ilkhanids, Aqquyonlus, and others all sought to rule through superior statecraft and to build their legacies by establishing durable urban and civic institutions. It was within these urban, hierarchal social structures that each of the three ethicists lived, maneuvered, and formulated their ethical systems. At the high points of their respective careers, each ethicist was supported by court funds to engage in work meant to enhance the intellectual, religious, and ethical profile of his ruler. The ethicists' ideas about how an ethical society should function are reactions to their observations of behavior in the urban environment as a whole, both within and outside of court. As such, the ethics texts address multiple levels of the social hierarchy, from the enslaved to nonroyal and royal courtiers to rulers themselves. In the treatises, the ethicists present theories of urban and civic association, justice, love, and friendship that explain human social behavior and association. They also provide specific guidelines for interaction with superiors, equals, subordinates, friends, and foes.

In the ethicists' minds, ethical masculinity is shaped not just by social processes, such as marriage, but also by institutions, such as the social class to which a man belongs. Raewyn Connell theorizes that "the patterns of conduct our society defines as masculine may be seen in the lives of individuals, but they also have an existence beyond the individual. Masculinities are defined collectively in culture, and are sustained in institutions."[2] Where a man is located in the hierarchy of intellect and his class situation—two characteristics that are often related to each other—determine the proper situational conduct that is required of him in interactions with various other kinds of men. As men of all classes, ages, religions, and races interact in social situations with superiors, employees, and friends, they continuously perform gender.[3] The ethicists recognize that the nature of particular institutions, from neighborhoods to bazaars to courts, all call for particular kinds of male, homosocial behaviors. The prescription of such behaviors is an important function of the treatises, wherein the ethicists explain how different classifications of men in such institutions can come to embody ethical masculinity by comporting themselves ethically in their various social interactions. The actions that distinguish a man as ethical in the male public realm are the acts of a balanced *nafs*, such as treating others according to what is due to them. Still, even though society (and, by extension, ethics) is "for" men, it still has everything to do with women. In societal ethics, as in the domestic ethics described in chapter 3, the ethicists continually reference women or feminine behaviors as foils for ideal masculine behaviors.

The ethicists conceived of the public sphere as male-dominated and homosocial. As I showed in the previous chapter, their conception of a gender-segregated society left room for women to serve only as instrumental players in the ethics of the household, while the outside world was dominated by men interacting with other men. This male-centric conception persisted even though it was at odds with the historical reality, now known via historical evidence, that premodern Muslim women did participate in public activities.[4] We can contextualize Ghazali's, Tusi's, and Davani's distaste for women's presence in the public sphere with the historical presence of women at mosques and bazaars and their "meddling" in public and political affairs at court. While the texts support a relationship between male power and structures of urban space and visibility, historical evidence of women's involvement upsets this prescribed gender segregation as the ethical structure of society and men's exclusive hold on power.[5] The almost complete absence of women in the societal ethics of the Ghazali-Tusi-Davani tradition is telling of the ethicists' prescriptive view that the public realm belongs to men. The male-dominated cast of premodern Muslim ethics is consistent with Luce Irigaray's contentions that philosophy considers the masculine to be the universal form and that the entire edifice of ethics is constructed with a male-centered view.[6] Irigaray's critique of the male as universal in philosophy helps to illuminate how Ghazali, Tusi, and Davani conceived of the entire cosmos as belonging to men. The principles the ethicists articulate, which are intended to guide ethical relationships among humans on all levels of interaction, are entirely oriented by the universal male's goals in life, namely, to be a means of happiness/flourishing (sa'adat) and God's vicegerent (khalifah) for all people. Ironically, a man's ethical responsibility for others is fundamentally about his own ethical advancement.

HOMOSOCIAL ASSOCIATION: PRINCIPLES AND GUIDELINES

In the ethics texts, the fundamental principle underlying homosocial association is that of love. The ethicists understand love to be a natural feeling between fellow humans, born out of their visceral need to associate with one another. Tusi defines love as a yearning for collaboration: he states that because man "has been created with natural tendency toward perfection, he has natural desire toward collaboration. This yearning for collaboration is called love."[7] Man as the primary being needs and feels natural love (*mahabbat*) for other men, which in turn enables societal cooperation. Homosocial male associations among friends, neighbors, acquaintances, and even enemies all have a role in shaping and testing one's ethics. To illustrate the various functions of friendship, Tusi and Davani quote Aristotle:

> Men are dependent upon friends in all states: in a state of comfort because of their need for visitation and assistance, in a state of difficulty because of their need for consolation and companionship. . . .
> The search for the virtue of friendship, which is natural in the souls of men, causes them to cooperate in transactions, be sociable in fair societies, play [sports or joke] with one another, and gather for exercise, hunting, and prayers.[8]

In other words, a full range of social activities, from recreation to worship, are conducted within male homosocial contexts in which men are meant to be the full companions of one another. Tusi says emphatically, in a rare use of the first-person voice, "it is my belief that the worth of friendship and power of love are greater than all the treasures and buried resources of the world, the kings' reserves, the profits that the people of the world are known to covet, and the jewels of the land and sea."[9] The ethicists recognized the superlative value of love and affection between male friends, and affirmed the preciousness of the bond between honorable men who see eye to eye. Such affectionate relationships undoubtedly contrasted with the cutthroat nature of social interaction at court and in public life in general. In this section, I discuss the ethical principles of homosocial association, as well as general guidelines for conducting oneself within such associations. These principles reify the exclusive nature of ethical refinement and define love and social engagement on male terms to achieve vicegerency (*khilafah*). First, I explicate the ethicists' hierarchal model of love to show how this model functions as a mechanism of exclusion, ranking male love, which is spiritual and cerebral, above female love, which is physical and bodily. Then, I analyze the ethicists' guidelines for loving other men, as in homosocial friendship, and for ethically comporting oneself in relationships with enemies. Finally, I discuss all three ethicists' explanations of how and why to develop a love of society at large.

Hierarchy of Love: Spiritual Over Physical, Men Over Women

According to the *akhlaq* texts, true love is spiritual and intellectual, and it can be experienced and received only by men, not women. The ethicists devote considerable space to discussing the hierarchal nature of love, even ranking the objects of love and the motives for love. Options for how and whom to love are all ranked according to the principle that loving with the mind is better than loving with the body. This principle of love follows from the ontological idea of emanation, in which the noblest people and acts are closest to God (e.g., philosophers in the act of contemplation), and the lowliest people and acts are closer to corporeality (e.g., farmers working the land to nourish the body).[10] According to this hierarchical model of love, only men are capable of the loftier forms of love, since women are not present in the highest echelons of rational people. The form of premodern heteronormativity prescribed by the ethicists was that marital relationships with women were not much more than corporeal (sexual and physical protection and maintenance), while relationships with men were cerebral, rational, intimate, and spiritual. Indeed, the deepest love discussed by Ghazali, Tusi, and Davani is homosocial love between men, a love that is spiritual and mental. The ethicists do use the gender-neutral term *human* (*insan*) to refer to the individuals between whom love exists, but in light of the texts as a whole, it is reasonable to conclude that they refer only to men, and that they are concerned chiefly with how men need other men for enhancing their own perfection. In prior chapters, I have already discussed the ways that men need women; here, in sections on social governance, they discuss women explicitly whenever they mean to include them. Usually, they do not.

Davani clarifies the difference between bodily and mental pleasures as follows:

> As the human body consists of various temperaments, so every bodily pleasure that is concordant with one temperament is against another temperament. Thus, bodily pleasure is not unsullied from the mixture of pain. As the human *nafs* is a simple essence, which is absolved and free from contradiction, every pleasure that is particular belongs to its own essence and is an unmixed pleasure. That pleasure is wisdom, and love is the origin of this type of pleasure of perfect degree. And that is complete and Divine love.[11]

Love that comes from the body yields physical pleasure and pain, while love that stems from the perfected human *nafs* is perfect and disembodied. Thus, in the ethicists' minds, only men were capable of the perfected kind of divine love, and men could only have perfect *nafses* if they had full rational faculties. Even the examples Davani provides of what constitutes praiseworthy love, namely, human beings' ability to love constructively based on their natural propensity to associate with one another, are male-only public displays of spirituality: the community prayers held in cities during Fridays and Eid holidays are instituted in order to reinforce humanity's love and association with one another in service and worship to God.[12]

By contrast, women's lack of full rationality rendered them largely incapable of any love but the corporeal. The only form of divine love that women possess is the love for their children. That too is entirely nonintellectual and mostly physical, and relates to their maternal role of protecting their infants: "if the [natural] type of love were not innate in the mother's nature, she would not nurture the child, and survival of the species would not come about."[13] Similarly, Tusi describes maternal love as natural (*tabi'*), not intentional (*aradi*).[14] The ethicists divide all remaining subjects of love into hierarchically ranked types. They also rank the objects of love and the motives for love.

Ghazali defines two degrees of love, both of which exclude women. As I mentioned earlier, the higher degree of love is the one that emanates from excess of love of God for God's servants. It is love for friends, who in turn remind one of God. The second degree of love is affection for someone with whom one is linked for a religious purpose. This includes finding friends based on their good deeds or through collaboration on a good deed, such as feeding the poor together or giving someone "bread and clothes to free him up so that he can worship; this is friendship for God, for the purpose of freeing him up is worship."[15] There is an element of charity involved in this degree of love. Ghazali provides two examples of friends who share this love:

> A great many scholars and worshipers have friendships with the powerful and rich for this exchange. Both of them are among the friends of God, Most High. In fact, if one loves one's own wife for guarding him against depravity and on the basis of bringing forth children who make innocent prayers for him, this is love for the sake of God. And every amount of maintenance spent on her is a charity.[16]

In the first example, even though, at the time of writing the *Kimiya*, Ghazali had foresworn association with the "rich and powerful," he sees the spiritual good that comes out of such an alliance. Ghazali articulates such a relationship in similar terms as the utility of a wife in the second example, who not only "gives leave" to the husband to pursue religious activities, as I discuss in the previous chapter, but also is the vessel for providing him with children. However, the difference between a wife's act of "giving leave" to her husband for his spiritual benefit and men giving leave to one another is that women are unquestionably expected to do so while men give leave to one another as an act of voluntary love. Further, Ghazali considers men to be engaging in charitable love for their wives through the fact that their maintenance (*nafaqah*) is counted as a charity (*sadqah*), which indicates that the sentiment of love itself is not separated from the (gendered) legal arrangement in which a wife is paid maintenance in exchange for her service. Love for a woman remains corporeal and entwined with her ability to produce children, while between men, love is greater and more spiritual. Ghazali quotes a sufi, Hasan Basri, confirming this idea: "brothers for us are dearer than the wife and children, for they teach us about faith, and the wife and children teach us about the world."[17]

Like Ghazali, Tusi provides a list of those whom an ethical man should love, and his list also excludes women.[18] This list is more of a sequence of whom one should love in order of importance, rather than types of love. The first love, which is also the best love, is for the Creator; it belongs only to men of divine learning and cannot be disturbed. Because the Creator is the reason for one's existence, this love can also be considered instinctual, stemming from loving oneself. Next in importance is the love of parents, although here Tusi specifically only mentions the father, who is the proximate cause of one's existence.[19] Then there is love for one's teacher, who completes one's existence. Because spiritual existence is superior to physical existence, the love of a teacher can rank above the love of the father.

Davani approvingly quotes Tusi's ranking of love objects according to their deserts, but expands the list to include love for the Divine, love for parents, a king's love for his subjects and vice versa, and finally, love of friends and companions.[20] Davani notes that "one should observe the principle of equity between the Creator and creation by loving each one according to their rights."[21] If a man does not do so, God's love for him is lessened, meaning that equity is important for gaining God's favor. Davani reasons that a benefactor loves his supplicator far more than the reverse because of the hardship he suffers and the effort he invests in the supplicator. For example, a creditor wishes for the longevity of his debtor so that he may be paid back. Humans' well-being interests God. Davani then provides the example of a mother, who loves a child more than a father because of her physical labor in birthing him.[22] However, as I discuss in the previous chapter, Davani states that a son repays a mother's debt by financially and physically supporting her later in life.[23] Thus, a favor itself requires gratitude in return. This principle of returning God's favors equitably by loving God's creations also illustrates the idea that equity, or 'adalat, which is the same term used for the nafs's virtue of "justice" in the texts, is achieved not by loving humanity equally, but by loving each according to their deserts. Love, which is a stand-in for cosmic justice, is relative to the one receiving it, and equity does not connote equality.

As seen in the work of all three ethicists, the lowest forms of love, such as conjugal love, are those that are tainted by physical affection. One can deduce, given the relative status of wives, mothers, and sons, that love for a daughter would be next, ranked above love for a wife, since she is his biological offshoot, but the ethicists do not mention this love specifically. Although both daughters and sons are biological offshoots of a man, a daughter would not be provided, or presumed to benefit from, rigorous ethical training, as a son would be. A man's love for his son is ranked higher because it is rooted in rationality—father and son share an intellectual connection based on maleness—and because it is based upon a father's desire for his son to surpass him in accomplishments. The father's affection is akin to that of a king or patron for his subject or ward.[24] Still, this relationship is not the ultimate love because a father's love for his son still stems from his physical replication in bodily and mental traits. Love between blood brothers is lower still because, as Davani states, brothers compete with one another.[25] Ultimately, the most perfect, divine-like form of love between humans can only occur between male peers, specifically between true friends.

Although the ethicists mostly focus on love in homosocial relationships, the different motives for love can also be seen within the husband–wife relationship. Love between a husband and wife may stem, in part, from the need of their association in organizing a family and household.[26] However, the ethicists discuss love between husband and wife more in terms of the physical (and occasionally emotional) comfort this love affords to the husband's *nafs*, as a woman provides a man with refuge from the difficult world. Based on what husbands' responsibilities are, I surmise that women, in turn, need protection and financial support from them, but the ethicists do not address women's needs directly. Since love (*mahabbat*) for the sake of pleasure (*lazzat*) is the basest kind of affection, love for a woman does not rank high in terms of ethics of affection.

According to Davani, the ultimate pleasure that can come from love and affection only occurs when there is a "complete separation" between body and soul.[27] It is the love for the Divine that one experiences when one can metaphysically transcend one's body. In other words, concerns of the worldly life and the corporeal needs that are associated with the love of women encumber the heart from truly knowing the Divine; thus, love with the body is base and lowly.[28]

In summary, the ranking of different kinds of love in Ghazali, Tusi, and Davani's texts shows that love conducted with the mind and soul is superior to love with the body. This ranking means not only that sexual pleasure is lowly, but also that blood relations and kinship are not as strong as love for fellow man with whom one has no relation. Love itself is gendered, in that the lower forms of love are tainted by interaction with the female body or reproduction. As I discuss later, this gendering is consistent with the ethicists' ranking of true friendship between men as the purest kind of human love, so pure that such love can even become Godlike.

Ethics in Individual Homosocial Relationships

The ethics of individual male relationships clarifies how male homosociality functions in *akhlaq* to complete one's potential for vicegerency (*khilafah*) since friends cultivate ethical behaviors in one another, and enemies present one another with challenges to the exercise of ethical behavior. The ethicists emphasize that friendship is a sacred bond that exists between men, one that leads to their ultimate happiness/flourishing (*sa'adat*) and facilitates spiritual success. Davani explains: "the best kind of love is that which is caused by a love for good and true perfection," since it has to do with achieving true happiness and fulfilling one's purpose on earth.[29] To find true friendship is to find "true enjoyment and divine pleasure, . . . not bestial pleasure."[30] Comparing friendship to salt and seasoning, Tusi and Davani say that the truest friendships can be rare and potent, and they are to be used sparingly, just as spices are necessary in cooking but cannot take the place of food itself. Tusi underlines the importance of friendship by saying, "Failure to acquire friendship of one who loves greatly becomes failure to acquire happiness." Similarly, Ghazali quotes several hadiths about friendship and brotherhood and discusses the merits of caring for one's fellow man.[31]

In an essay on the key role of friendships in the twentieth-century renewal movement of French Catholicism, Brenna Moore argues that religion scholars must look at such relationships as a "crucial matrix for analyzing th[e] intermediary realm between individual and society," whereby interactions with individuals are just as responsible for creating "religious sensibilities" as large-scale institutions are.[32] Specifically, she calls for attention to the "practice of friendship and the power [that] relational bonds can exert on the inner lives of the subjects we study."[33] While Moore studies religious exchanges in historical letters between individuals from a very different historical context, her focus on the "affective intensity of friendship [as the] key factor in generating religious experience, deepening or losing faith, and converting or returning to the religion of [childhood]" is a useful lens for understanding how the ethicists expected friendship and other interpersonal relationships to work in men's lives.[34] The ethicists create guidelines for friendship under the assumptions that men carry affective influence on one another, form close bonds, and are closely involved in one another's lives—and are thus intimately involved in one another's practice of ethics. Importantly, the intimacy of true friendship is never shared with women. As Fedwa Malti-Douglas notes in her book on gender in Arabic and Islamic literature, it is the rare female character, such as Shahrazad, who works against the culture of homosociality when she builds a romantic relationship with a man in "attempts to create a functioning heterosexual couple played out against a greater civilizational pull for a male homosocial couple."[35] The ethics of interpersonal relationships that the *akhlaq* texts outline is principles of friendship between men, the boundaries of intimacy within these relationships, and the nature and causes of enmity between men.

PRINCIPLES OF FRIENDSHIP

Ghazali, Tusi, and Davani all provide detailed guidelines to help men understand how to conduct themselves in close homosocial relationships. In the ethicists' guidelines for male homosocial friendship, they explain how to make friends, what to look for in a friend, how to keep friends, and what to do in sensitive situations that involve friends. From the ethicists' concrete commentary on friendship, we find specific characteristics that the ethical man displays in relation to his social circle, such as being compassionate and forgiving. Together, the three ethical treatises present a comprehensive vision of the nature of friendship and how best to manage one's friendships: Ghazali delineates the rights that are implicit in the bonds of friendship, while Tusi and Davani present readers with detailed criteria to use in selecting friends, advice for conducting oneself with friends, and warnings as to how friendships can break. As Roy Mottahedah has argued, true friendships are the ones that enable pursuit of mutual flourishing.[36] I show that in the case of the *akhlaq* ethicists, the conditions they define for friendship only allow for its perfect achievement among elite men.

According to Ghazali, male friendship can be forged for one of two reasons: for personal growth or for the sake of God. The former kind of friendship involves an element of utility and obligatory reciprocity, but the latter, Ghazali explains, is a great and selfless act of worship. He explains his use of a rights-based discourse to characterize the bond of friendship by comparing friendship to marriage: "when a brotherly contract and association is made, it is like a marriage contract in that it has rights."[37] Using legalistic language transforms friendship from a casual association to a more deliberate form of human association that falls under the governance of the ethical realm. Here Ghazali "thinks with" women, using men's marriages to women as a foil for men's friendships with other men. Unlike those of marriage, the bonds of friendship are forged between intellectual equals, and thus are much more intimate than those lowly, corporeal relations between husband and wife. Moreover, friendship is egalitarian in that friends' rights are reciprocal. Taken together, Ghazali's ten rights of friendship are about generosity, communication, intimacy, and love.

The first three rights of friendship define ways of showing consideration and generosity to friends. According to Ghazali, the first right of friendship is sharing one's property. There are degrees of this, from giving one's own share up to a friend, to considering property as jointly held, to simply giving to a friend as "one gives to one's slaves and servants."[38] One should be giving in excess if a friend requests aid. The second right of a friend is to anticipate his needs before he makes requests. This could be kind gestures, like asking friends who live nearby whether "they need any firewood or bread."[39] Third are rights of friends upon one's tongue. One should speak well of friends in their presence and absence, but not unnecessarily flatter them. Listen when they speak and do not argue with them. One should not reveal his secrets or speak about his family, children, or possessions to others. This particular right is meant to maintain the boundaries between public and private, which friends can easily traverse.[40] One should seek forgiveness from friends for violations of these rights.

Ghazali's fourth and fifth rights concern honest communication between friends. The fourth right, according to Ghazali, is to "declare affection and friendship with the tongue. The Prophet says, 'If one of you loves his brother inform him of it.' Whoever loves someone should inform him."[41] This is important so that a friend can reciprocate and love can grow between them. The fifth right is that one should counsel his friend about God's kindness and mercy and teach his friend religious knowledge, especially if he sees shortcomings in his friend. This instruction should happen in private so that the friend is not shamed. If a friend is aware of his own shortcomings, then one should be indirect in providing counsel. If a friend's shortcoming affects oneself, then it is better to forgive one's friend on the grounds that he was being momentarily thoughtless; bringing up the issue will diminish the friendship.[42] The goal in friendship should not be to change one's friends, but rather to "refine your own disposition in being patient with brothers."[43] Indeed, friends may test one's ethics. The term for disposition in this statement is *khulq*, which implies that one should always be reflexive and paying attention to one's own *nafs* and ethical behavior when confronted with someone else's shortcomings.

The sixth right that Ghazali delineates is that one should be forgiving of one's friend's errors and shortcomings. Ghazali argues against the school of thought that states one should cut off relations with a friend who has sinned. He argues instead for the way of Abu Darda, who says, "when a friendship is contracted, it is like kinship, and it is improper to cut off blood relations because of transgression."[44] To demonstrate this principle, as well as the closeness he expected between male friends, Ghazali provides an interesting story about two Jewish friends who were praying on a mountaintop. One of them had gone into the city to find something to eat, when

> his eye fell upon a bad woman. He fell in love with her and became hopeless. He stayed together with her. After a few days went by, the other came in search of him and heard of his state and went close to him. Out of embarrassment he said, "I do not know you." He replied, "Oh brother, do not worry your heart, I have never felt the affection and friendship for you that I feel now." And he put his hand on his neck and kept kissing him. When he saw his affection, he knew that he had not fallen in his eyes. He stood up and repented and they departed together.[45]

In this story, a (male) friend's steadfastness in the friendship and ability to love his friend while overlooking his sins appear as a form of compassion to the sinning friend. The latter is immediately overcome by his friend's show of love.

Paired with a seventh enumerated right of friends, that "formality between them should be taken away, one should be with his friend the same as if he were alone," this story also indicates how intimate Ghazali expected relations between men to be.[46] Although Ghazali refers to the woman in the story as "bad," his friend's staying with her for days without discussion of marriage and his later repentance indicate that she is likely a prostitute. As this example illustrates, friends can rescue each other from sexual depravity, enter each other's personal space, and make physical interventions such as embracing and kissing, in this case to help deliver the friend from sin. Here Ghazali also "thinks with" a woman who serves as an unethical contrast to the ethical male friend to support the idea that homosocial male friendship is the comprehensive human relationship, based on male spirituality and true love, while simultaneously placing men above women. Since in the ethical worldview, sexual intercourse could only take place with women, this comprehensive male homosocial friendship is, I argue, an example of the texts' version of heteronormativity.

The eighth right of friends, according to Ghazali, is for one to remember them and their families and children in supplications and prayer, both while he is living and after he dies. The ninth right is to "guard loyalty to friends."[47] This means being faithful to a friend's personal interests, such as honoring his family and children after his death and being compassionate with his students and slaves. Also, one should be faithful to preserve the friendship if one's own circumstances change, for example, if one comes into money, rank, or property. Finally, the tenth is that one should "think of oneself to be lower than all of one's friends. One should not expect things from them or hope for any consideration from them."[48] This means that even if both men are ethical and would care for each other, a man should never actually create expectations in his own heart, lest he think of himself as superior to his friend, which is a grave sin. Although this final rule is a preventative measure against arrogance, it also shows that one should pursue friendships with peers who are one's equals in many ways. They too have the ethical responsibilities of wives, children, students, and slaves and are engaged in similar activities in the public realm. Most importantly, it demonstrates that even though overall friendship and intimacy within it are necessities for the path of *akhlaq*, it is still a lonely endeavor in which elite men serve as one another's companions, while wives, slaves, servants, and subordinates serve as their instruments.

Davani and Tusi go beyond Ghazali's articulation of the rights within friendship to provide practical guidance on all phases of a friendship, from the selection of a friend to the efforts one can make in attempting to save a waning friendship. To a large extent, the course and nature of any given friendship are shaped by the motives that give rise to it. Davani and Tusi agree that men can fall in and out of love for any of three reasons: pleasure, profit, or seeking good. Tusi explains the different life cycles of each type of love:

> Love on the basis of pleasure is quick to contract and conclude, for pleasure with its all-encompassing existence is characterized by its speed of alteration and demise. . . . Profit is a basis of love that is slow to contract and quick to conclude. . . . Good is a basis of love that contracts quickly and is slow to conclude, quick to contract because of agreeability of being between good people and slow to conclude because true intimacy . . . is necessary to the qualities of good.[49]

Davani also notes that love and affection are general feelings that can extend to many people, while friendship is a special kind of affection that is reserved for very few people. Similar to Ghazali, in Tusi's and Davani's views, passion is a reprehensible form of affection because it is characterized by excess of seeking pleasure by the concupiscent faculty, which is the case for corporeal love with women. But when passion is channeled into seeking the good, by training of the virtues of the *nafs* (indicating male homosocial passion), it can be a most praiseworthy feeling. For Davani, the least praiseworthy bases for affection are pleasure and profit. Both motivations are fickle, and the "lovers are querulous and aggrieved, whereas in reality they are oppressive themselves. For they demand for the pleasure of vision and quick fulfillment of their wants and delay in compensation of profit."[50] This kind of affection is marked by one-sided giving and selfish receiving, even though both parties stand to benefit from the friendship. Examples of profit-driven relationships are the relationships between people of different classes: kings and subjects, rich and poor, and owners and the enslaved. Although Davani avoids using terms of instrumentality because these relations are between men, because the relations exist across classes they are based on some level of utilization. This, coincidently, makes them less important friendships than those between equals. Throughout their detailed passages on friendship, Tusi and Davani provide criteria to use in selecting friends, offer guidelines for conducting oneself with friends, and give advice on saving a waning friendship.

In Tusi's and Davani's criteria for selecting friends, they advise that one should try his best to identify associates who are "people of virtue." They consider it incumbent on the individual to seek benefits from such people, and to appreciate the opportunity to "help and assist them, and struggle to become one of their kind."[51] Another recommendation, particularly for the young, presumably unmarried man, is to find out how a potential friend acts with his parents, relatives, and other friends, and how he takes care of himself. Regarding more aged friends, Tusi and Davani do not discuss testing their comportment with their families, presumably because, as Ghazali explains in his discussion on divorce, matters between husband and wife are always private.[52] Another consideration about a potential friend is to find out how he has acted in response to favors and benefits previously given to him because the first and foremost quality one must look for in a friend is gratitude. A grateful person is generous, verbally expresses his thanks, and, according to Tusi and Davani, is probably pious. Next, one should test how strong the potential friend's desire is for amassing wealth or for acquiring elite status. Someone who is enamored of authority, domination, and superiority will not be an affectionate friend. Moreover, excessive indulgence in "foolishness and drivel," such as too much sport, music, or gossip, or "cavorting with singing women," signals someone who would be distracted easily and not available to a friend in his time of need.[53] This guideline speaks to Tusi's and Davani's association of women with foolishness and their emphasis on the utilitarian aspect of friendship—the notion that human association fulfills material needs, though friends should be generous without expectation of reciprocation.

Next, after discussing how to choose friends, Tusi and Davani elaborate on how to be an ethical friend, specifically by being like a brother. Friendship is a *nafs*-to-*nafs* affinity that is deeply rooted in human nature to associate with other people, especially like-minded people. One should be sincere with friends and supportive of them, as true love involves complete trust and familiarity with the friend's disposition. In addition, one should share a wide range of experiences with friends, including good news and joy, sorrow and misfortunes, and even knowledge of his trade and craft. Sharing about his accomplishments helps to prevent feelings of superiority over his friends.[54] Mottahedeh takes this instruction as evidence that Tusi endorses friendships with inferiors. However, even though Tusi (along with Davani) advocates for ethical behavior with all men, he recognizes that it is not possible to have true friendship across social ranks since inferiors do not have the same ethical responsibilities to seek flourishing or vicegerency (*khilafah*).[55] Yet, some cross-class friendships can or should be normalized: "if one achieves a rank of greatness or lordship, he should absorb his intimates and friends with himself into that nobility."[56] One should also bestow favors upon friends without their asking. Davani sums up friends' responsibilities succinctly: "One should include friends in one's own riches and ranks [and] . . . protect the act of generosity from disgrace of obligation. If a calamity befalls, one should help them with one's wealth and self and one should join them in griefs."[57] A true friend is there in times of vulnerability, when others would forsake one. As mentioned in chapter 2, a quality of the virtuous man is that he treats his friend like a brother; the ethicists' fraternal comparison has to do with treating one's true friend as one wishes to be treated. However, Davani says regarding true blood brothers that because brothers are equals in terms of existence and parentage, they are only beloved if they are true friends; or else a friend is better than a brother.[58] Again, a cerebral love out of choice for someone or a true friendship stands above a physical relationship, in this case, blood relations. The best love that the ethicists can imagine is between men who have no relation to one another because they exercise and enhance one another's virtues in being friends; thus, their friendship is for the sake of God and seeking the good.

Davani's remedy for an imbalanced relationship is to revert to the rule of justice, which is to treat each person according to his need and station. For a friendship that begins to wane, Tusi and Davani have additional advice on how to save it. They recommend that, if one's true friend becomes less interested in the friendship, one should frequent him more often and exert oneself to keep him as a friend. If one commits an offense against a friend, Tusi and Davani recommend, similar to Ghazali, that he should repent to him with an open heart. If, on the contrary, the friend is an offender, then one should be gracious even while pointing out his friend's error.[59] It is a kindness to the friend to point out his flaws or errors, but one should do it in a way that helps him. Also like Ghazali, Davani says that if one finds fault in a friend, he should first employ circuitous methods to point it out, and if he does not realize his error, then allude to it to him with hints. Then, if the friend does not correct himself, then one should tell him in private so that the "edifice of affection" is not harmed by others brandishing his faults to him in public.[60] Tusi further advises that one must be careful not to get caught up in heated debates that turn into ad hominem attacks, whether in public or private, because such acts diminish love between friends. A person who does this "is of the people who are oppressors and tyrants of the age, for tyrants, when they become insolent out of great wealth and prosperity, besmirch one another as despicable and insignificant, and they slander one another's manhood. They consider it commendable to investigate one another's faults and defects."[61] However, making a man's faults public is an attack against his manly pride (*ghayrat*). Here Tusi equates manhood (*muruwwat*) itself with one's reputation and public persona. He implies that manhood and human perfection are equivalent by stating that probing into "faults and defects" is attacking manhood. To define flawless human beings as those who embody proper *muruwwat* is to confine friendship itself to the male domain.

Tusi goes beyond advising readers on how to choose friends, conduct themselves in friendship, and rekindle a waning friendship; he also warns readers about whom not to befriend. Tusi warns that there are several supposed friends who are not "true friends" but show "artificiality and empty flattery."[62] The proper course of action to take with them is "as much as possible [to] be courteous and kind, to not waste a minute giving tidings to them; to be reconciliatory and patient with them; and to transact honestly with them." One should keep hidden one's own secrets and shortcomings, and likewise special news and circumstances, one's means of profit, and one's amount of wealth."[63] One should also not really criticize them or demand anything from them, but should lend a hand in dire circumstances. Some may eventually become true friends, while others may not, but in any case, one must always present oneself in a manner that invites true friendship, such as showing "characteristics of generosity, ethics,[64] [and] good manners."[65] The same goes for "foolish people" who are not really friends or enemies. Around these people, one should be alert: "one should not attend to or heed their foolishness so that they [will] abstain from their annoyingness. If one is overtaken by their abuse and foolishness, he should discount it. . . . [He should] with patience and calmness improve the situation, or else quit and abandon conversation with them."[66] Davani explains that the test of a true friend is that if one is in distress, he is able to rely on that friend.[67] Here we see the underlying principle of the properly balanced *nafs*: acting with restraint, caution, and being generally congenial. This middle-of-the-way approach is not just nonconfrontational; it also serves as a defense mechanism against potential transgressions of the *nafs*. This in turn protects one's dignity and masculinity, which are often synonymous terms in the texts. Another caution that Tusi and Davani provide is to beware of people who pretend to be intermediaries or counselors between friends, but who are actually working to destroy the friendship. Tusi tells a story about a lion and an ox from the *Kalila wa Dimna*, in which "a strong beast was brought to a place of annihilation by a great animal, through the deceit of a weak fox."[68] Tusi's story serves as a warning of the treacherous terrain of the social sphere, which in his historical context may have been a reflection of social or political tensions. In any case, it is clear that bonds of friendship, no matter how ideal or rooted in the "sake of God," can be broken. Preserving friendship wherever possible is not just a matter of personal ethics and being a good friend for its own sake; rather, it is a much more serious matter related to the individual man's role in human existence: "caution in the protection of love, the necessity of which is apparent in the needs of civilization, is the most important of important matters."[69] For Tusi, the preservation of love and friendship is tantamount to preserving civilization itself. Notably, though, the three ethicists' guidelines for friendship describe intimacy that is only possible among equals.

As I have shown, homosocial intimacy is central to premodern Muslim ethics. But the intensity and passion with which male friends are supposed to love one another, according to the ethics texts, raise the question of whether or when homosociality can take on an erotic or sexual nature. In the ethicists' view, an ethical man has to strike a delicate balance, practicing homosociality without verging into improper homoeroticism or homosexuality. Marriage to one woman is their only ethically sanctioned site for the expression of sexuality. To enforce this boundary, the ethicists implicitly draw a line between homosocial and sexual love. They do so by characterizing homosocial love and intimacy as entirely cerebral, and sexual relations as being a base behavior that is tainted with the corporeal. In so doing, their construct of ethical masculinity amounts to a premodern heteronormativity.

The ethicists draw boundaries around homosociality in rather indirect ways, as there were no concepts of homosexuality or normative heterosexuality at the time. Such concepts, as Jonathan Katz has shown, did not emerge until the late nineteenth century. As Katz explains, "the concept of heterosexuality is only one particular historical way of perceiving, categorizing, and imagining the social relations of the sexes. Not ancient at all, the idea of heterosexuality is a modern invention."[70] Indeed, among premodern Muslims, there may have been some inconsistency in what was considered improper, and by whom. While Katz is focused on European examples, Khaled El-Rouayheb explains that in the Arab-Islamic world between 1500 and 1800, seemingly conflicting precepts were at work:

> What unfolded in public was . . . courting and expressions of passionate love. . . . Islamic religious scholars of the period were committed to the precept that sodomy (*liwat*) was one of the most abominable sins a man could commit. However, many of them clearly did not believe that falling in love with a boy or expressing this love in verse was therefore also illicit. Indeed, many prominent religious scholars indulged openly in such activity.[71]

For all the ambiguity around what constituted acceptable homosocial behavior, premodern Muslim thought on heterosexual relations was clearer: they must be purposeful, and the list of acceptable purposes, beyond procreation, included bodily/medical necessity and ethical/religious discipline. In her study of prescriptive discourses on sexual intercourse in premodern Persian sources, Susanne Kurz considers medical, ethical, and erotological texts: a medical treatise of Sayyid Isma'il-i Jurjani (d. 1136–37); several works in the *akhlaq* genre, including the works by Ghazali, Tusi, and Davani I discuss in this book; and several Persian adaptations of the Indian erotological treatise, known in Persian as *Pleasure of Women* (*Lazzat ul-nisa*). Based on these texts, Kurz argues that across the genres she studies, we find common ways of thinking about sexual intercourse, including viewing intercourse as "an activity conducted solely by men and rather 'applied' to women."[72] Sexual activity always has a specific purpose and is "never just for fun."[73] In the medical treatises, she finds, intercourse is about expelling heat from the internal organs and preventing disease. In ethics, the purpose is to sire children and to prevent oneself (and, to a lesser extent, one's wife) from exercising the concupiscent faculty (*quwwat-i shahwi*) excessively. In erotology, the science of sexual domination over women, sex is framed as a religious duty to preserve chastity. This would also imply that same-sex sexual activity, which presumably would be merely for pleasure, would not fit into the "purposeful" modes of intercourse. In sum, Kurz observes that this mandate for purposefulness was one of the reasons that sexual activity was seen as normatively heterosexual. Scott Kugle has shown that one of the arguments against same-sex sexual acts is that "pursuing pleasure for egoistic purposes transgresses moral bounds, it becomes *fahisha* [or] 'immorality.' "[74]

One passage in the *Kimiya* discussing bathhouse etiquette suggests that Ghazali was aware of and discouraged potential sexual attraction between men in intimate homosocial settings. In this passage, he advises readers never to reveal their nakedness (*'awrah*) to other men in the bathhouse, which was the space for urban elites to retreat, gossip, and politick.[75] Premodern heteronormativity also prohibited men from seeing one another in a state of undress. Ghazali explains the limits of exposure and physical contact: "prohibited acts in the public bath are not clothing the nakedness from the navel to the knees, or presenting one's naked thigh to the bath attendant for massage or exfoliation. In fact, it is not appropriate to put the hand under the waistband, for rubbing has the same significance as seeing."[76] The navel to the knees is considered a man's nakedness ('awrah), which he should not expose, even in the all-male space of a bathhouse. Further, it is out of the question for a man to touch another in the region of his 'awrah. In general, social behavior involving men's nakedness would be considered transgressive. However, as demonstrated in the anecdote in which a man rescues his friend from the prostitute's hold, true friends did regularly reach into one another's physical, personal space. Kissing, embracing, or caressing in casual or dramatic circumstances would all be unquestionably normal forms of physical interaction between the most intimate of male friends. A level of physical familiarity would not necessarily be acceptable between superficial friends, though, since the ethicists recommend distance from such friends and acquaintances and extreme caution before establishing intimacy with someone.[77]

However, the ethicists do not explicitly discourage the publicly common forms of homoeroticism to which El-Rouayheb refers. Ghazali's discussion on public morality asserts that spying is not permissible, nor is it permissible to accuse someone of a sexual crime without the pre-requisite number of witnesses needed to attest to it.[78] Even if an imam witnesses a wrongdoing, "it cannot be assumed that the imam can act on his own knowledge of this; he is obligated to hide it."[79] Although Ghazali is referring to illicit heterosexual acts here, the same policy, which, as Kecia Ali points out, amounts to "don't ask don't tell," could be extrapolated for same-sex sexual activity.[80]

Regardless of such a policy of concealment of one's own and others' sexual transgressions, and notwithstanding the ubiquity of homoerotic love, Ghazali and Jurjani condemn pederasty. The former condemns it for being a sin of excessive shahwat, and the latter for medical reasons. Kurz explains that Jurani's position on pederasty is that it is "against nature and procreation, but also harmful from the medical point of view: Since boys do not attract semen, one has to put in much effort and motion and this is regarded [as] harmful for health" for both parties.[81] Other treatises that Kurz explores condemn sexual relations with "children as well as women not suitable for marriage or [those with] an ugly face" because their fertility is questionable.[82] The ethicists never explicitly discuss licit sex with enslaved women, although Ghazali does mention the story of Hasan Basri, who inquired how much a beautiful slave who caught his eye costs in the context of alms-giving, and Davani gives an example of how the gift of an enslaved woman to a courtier made his wife jealous.[83] In mentioning pederasty, Ghazali and Jurjani clearly are arguing against an extant practice. Marshall Hodgson comments that relationships between adult men of elite social classes and teenage boys were common and fetishized in literary sources, including the popular poetry of the half-Arab, half-Persian poet Abu Nuwas (d. 814), which Tusi dismisses as "unsubstantial poetry which are poems of love and drunken wine."[84] When Tusi discourages close interaction with young boys, this may be a reaction to the obvious, highly ubiquitous, and sometimes explicit eroticism of male youths in the court arts, poetry, and literature of premodern Muslim contexts.[85] Ultimately, the ethicists recognize *shahwat* as being implicit in human nature and independent of marriage, though ethically it should take place within the boundaries of marriage to free women.

Recognizing the need for explicit boundaries around homosociality, the ethicists provide readers of their ethical treatises with specific guidelines that amount to prescriptions for what we might call a premodern heteronormativity. In the *akhlaq* texts, men have love and intimate friendships that may even be homoerotic, but the texts also include remarks that explicitly discourage any sexual encounters between men. According to the guidelines, men must remain disciplined in the midst of intense proximity to other men. Men are supposed to be intellectually, emotionally, and even physically proximate to one another but may only be sexually involved with women. It was normal and expected for men to have emotionally intimate relationships with other men and be familiar with one another's physical person, but in doing so, they had to carefully observe the appropriate boundaries. Overall, the texts present us with a very particular kind of heteronormativity for both men and women, in which the imagined ethical social relations are both gender-segregated; they encourage homosocial love, but the only erotic love they conceive of is heterosexual. Intimacy between men could only ethically take place within homosocial bounds, and the erotic could only ethically take place in marriage to one woman. It is for this reason that the ethicists find it necessary to draw careful boundaries around the concept of appropriate homosocial love.

MANAGING ENMITY IN RELATIONSHIPS

Both Ghazali and Tusi emphasize that how a man comports with his enemies is a test of his own ethical refinement. They conceived of enmity as conflict between men with trained, balanced *nafses* and those without such *nafses* who displayed traits of hegemonic masculinity such as aggression and tyranny in the male homosocial environment. The ethicists' discussions of enmity shed light on how they thought of elite power struggles between men of the same or proximate social classes as a competition of masculinity often characterized by resentment and unfair treatment.

For Ghazali, enmity should be practiced only for the sake of God, for the purpose of detesting oppression, disbelief in God, or any other unethical act or belief. With Muslim enemies, the enmity should be for their sin and oppressive behavior, rather than for their person: "If there is a sinful Muslim, you should love him for his being Muslim and have enmity for his sin."[86] Ghazali explains that love and enmity for someone can coexist in the heart when considering that person's own good: "One must add together friendship and enmity, just as one rewards a child but also punishes or beats a child. From one perspective he loves him, and from another perspective, he is his enemy."[87] This statement is indicative of Ghazali's paternalistic sense of how ethical men should behave toward people on various social planes, including one's wife, one's children, and the various Muslims around him. All behavior, whether done in love or in enmity, should be aimed at teaching a lesson or promoting *akhlaq*.

In the same passage on enmity, Ghazali discusses how eighth-century jurist Ahmad bin Hanbal refused to speak with friend and fellow scholar Yahya Ma'in without an apology after Ma'in made a statement about being content with his wealth but willing to accept something from the king if he offered. Ma'in defended himself by saying, "'I was making light and joking.' [Ibn Hanbal] said, 'Your nourishment comes from the faith; do not play with the faith.'"[88] Although Ghazali meant for this anecdote to convey that one must punish sinful behavior just as Ibn Hanbal had done, the example also tells us about the role of the ethical man in his community. Ghazali sees the role of learned men and students of the *rah-i din* to be educating others, not only themselves, in matters of religion and faith in God.

Finally, Ghazali teaches that one should reciprocate an enemy's display of both opposition and agreement; in short, treat him exactly as he treats you. Further, in encounters with the enemy, one should "be serious, and as he transgresses limits, give him harsh language and make him unhappy."[89] The same treatment is recommended toward someone who is being unjust. However, if someone takes away one's rights, then "forgiveness and endurance are the right course."[90] This last piece of advice encourages restraint and tolerance even against those who hold enmity toward you, perhaps because a person depriving one of rights would be someone in power, in which case it may not be possible to reciprocate contempt without serious repercussions.

Tusi's teachings on conflict between men are more pragmatic than Ghazali's. First, Tusi summarizes five potential causes of enmity, all of them worldly: "dispute over property, dispute over rank, dispute over things missing, acting on lust that renders dishonor to womenfolk, and disagreement in opinions."[91] If one has such disputes with another man, then he should attempt to repel harm from himself by trying to reform the enemy's soul if possible; if not possible, then "the relationship between them must be reformed."[92] Tusi advises his readers to refrain from all interactions with such a man by going so far as to move to a different neighborhood or go away on a long journey. This is a defensive response intended to protect one's own reputation.

Tusi goes on to identify six conditions under which one may take action against an enemy: first is that the enemy is wicked by nature and there is no way to correct him; second is that one sees no escape from his oppression by any means except suppressing him; third, the enemy can be victorious if he takes more measures than one would oneself; fourth is that one has witnessed the enemy's intention and effort to destroy one's good deeds; fifth is that one cannot engage in any betrayal or perfidy in suppressing the enemy; sixth no outcome considered despicable in this world or the next should be the result of taking action against the enemy.[93]

More specifically, regarding enemies at court, Tusi says one must be very careful in acting publicly against enemies because one can easily invite worse calamities upon oneself, including notoriety or sin for exceeding ethical bounds of vengeance. One should find out about the enemy's tactics, his news, and his every fault, weakness, and source of anxiety. Also, in order to gain advantage over one's enemy, one should truthfully inform princes, masters, and other men about the enemy's ruses and unethical behaviors, but with careful circumspection, lest the enemy should become immunized by constant publication of his faults, and lest one should become untrustworthy in the eyes of his audience. As another tactic for dealing with enemies, Tusi suggests one should feign friendship with the enemy and cavort with his friends.[94]

Tusi's final guideline for dealing with enemies is that engaging with them mercifully prevents damage to one's own *nafs* and public reputation. In general, "articulating abuses and curses and attacking the bodies of enemies is extremely despised and remote from intelligence, for these acts bring no damage to their souls or property, but the *nafs* and essence of the transgressor are damaged in that moment."[95] It is merciful for a man to warn his enemy that he will publicize the enemy's actions in order to instill fear in him. If there is a conflict of interest and "the enemy comes under a man's protection, making a refuge out of his sanctum, or entrusts [him] with something that requires loyalty or trust," then a man is required to be both generous and courteous toward his enemy because his "beautiful faith and good disposition will be known to everyone."[96] Tusi reminds readers that their conduct with enemies is public knowledge and provides opportunities to demonstrate ethical conduct—and bolster one's own reputation as ethical. Overall, Tusi's and Ghazali's ethical guidelines for dealing with enemies or those posturing against one reflect how the ethicists understood the public sphere to be a competitive homosocial environment full of tests of the *nafs* and a man's honor (*muruwwah*). In this sense, it is not unlike the domestic realm, except that the opportunities it offers for refinement are through ethical associations with equals.

Love for the Whole of Society: Becoming a Khalifah

A man's love for other individuals, including his ethical relations with those with whom he has enmity, translates into a more expansive, markedly paternalistic love for society at large. It is through the addition of this larger societal love that the individual can attain vicegerency with God (*khilafah*) and become a microcosm of ethics for the macrocosm. Ghazali, Tusi, and Davani each articulate distinct visions for how human association coalesces into this macrocosmic ethical love. Ghazali emphasizes the force of naturally occurring love for one another (*mahabbat*); Tusi, more pragmatically, emphasizes the human need for division of labor for the sake of survival; and Davani, taking a cosmic perspective, emphasizes the ultimate goal of justice for all. The ethicists' focus oscillates between individual ethics and societal ethics as they create a male-only *khalifah*, and for all three, what emerges from their project is an exclusionary ethics that is available only to elite men and a definition of justice that is inherently unjust because it is premised on that exclusion. Ultimately, in the ethical system constructed in the *akhlaq* texts, only men with social influence are able to fully realize the perfection of the human *nafs*.

For Ghazali, individual love translates into macroscopic ethical love because of a naturally occurring force, the "sake of God" that binds humans.[97] Such ideal human love exists only when there is no expectation of return, and when an excess of passion for God overflows like a natural force into passion for all of God's subjects. Ghazali relates how such naturally occurring love (*mahabbat*) reaches the very bounds of passion:

> Anyone who falls in love with someone loves his town and neighborhood. He loves the walls of his home. He even loves the dog that stays in his neighborhood, and he loves that dog more than other dogs. He has no choice but to love the friend of the beloved himself, and the beloved's own beloved, and anyone who obeys his beloved, be it servants or his slaves, or his relatives. . . . Thus, whoever is overcome by the love of the Truth—most high—until he reaches the boundaries of passion loves all of His servants, especially His friends, and he loves everything that has been created, for all things in existence are an effect of His creation and power.[98]

As Ghazali explains, loving an individual is the same as loving the community around that individual, and even the same as loving God. For Ghazali, love for society is a function of faith: the more one loves his fellow man, the more faithful he is to God. Ghazali illustrates love for God's sake using the analogy of a journey. He explains that the earth is a station in a long journey to God. This is similar to tenth-century philosopher Ibn Sina's allegorical references to life as journey to God.[99] Ghazali instructs readers, "Know that the world is a station among the stations on the path of the Truth (most high); everyone in this station is a traveler; and the caravans of travelers, like the purpose of that travel, are one. . . . Between them should be friendship and union and mutual assistance. They should observe the rights of one another."[100] Each follower of *akhlaq* completes his journey by transforming his love into aid of society for the sake of God.

For Tusi, the mechanism that transforms an individual into an ethical force in the macrocosm (a *khalifah*) is a combination of human nature and utility. As a natural force, according to Tusi, love causes human beings to crave association with one another; it prompts people to identify with one another and to feel one another's triumphs and pain. The sympathy between individuals, in turn, promotes justice. Even though love is natural, humans as a species can easily lose feelings of love, giving rise to injustice.[101] As Tusi explains, love exists in varying degrees, which leaves room for differential treatment of others and, hence, corruption. Based upon this definition of love as a natural human attraction, Tusi then explains how society works by applying a Farabian approach based on utilitarian organization of labor. Tusi refers to Farabi on the natural purpose or functions of animals and their role in the ecosystem in general as a blueprint for human association.[102] Tusi explains that for the preservation of human individuals and the human species, the aid of other human beings and use of other species are necessary for performing collective and delegated tasks. This is because "every individual of humankind has limited power, but when many individuals come together, inevitably their power is many times that of the individual."[103] Specifically, human beings depend on one another for their collective skills and trades:

> If every individual should arrange his own sustenance, clothes, dwelling, and armor, first acquiring the tools of carpentry and metalsmithing, and knowing the tools and instruments of farming, harvest, milling, kneading, spinning, weaving, preparing other

skills and crafts, then with this he becomes busy with important matters, and his survival without food all this time will not last. . . . When they aid one another, each one attending to one of these important tasks sufficiently, and observing the law of justice in transactions by giving in excess in exchange for taking of the labor of others, the basis of living comes together. The succession of the individual and survival of the species become possible and arranged this way.[104]

For Tusi, the survival of humankind depends on cooperation, on giving and taking in accordance with the laws of justice. Because love and association are a matter of survival, they occur naturally between people. As I discuss later, this natural order is understood as hierarchical, based on assumptions about individuals' skill sets that rest on constructions of gender, class, and race.

Whereas Tusi believes that love between human beings is "natural" and that humans desire to associate with one another positively, Davani regards humans as fundamentally selfish, pursuing their own self-interest at the expense of others. For Davani, human association coalesces into macrocosmic ethical love in a tension between justice and love, which is only resolved by ethical discipline. Elite men need to discipline society: "If [people in society] were left to their own natures, their cooperation would not be possible, for everyone views their own profit in harming others leading to disputations and causing them to be busy with thieving and corruption against one another. Thus, there should be management in which everyone is content with their rights and cut off from aggressing his hand over others."[105]

This management of society is achieved through the law of the state, which ensures that people who have come to live together out of necessity follow the rules of civilization. This is necessary because natural desire for association is not the same thing as love for fellow man.

For Davani, justice is still a goal of civilization, but it does not flow from love. In no uncertain terms, "love is superior to justice."[106] He explains how the two are incompatible: "love is unity of nature and justice is unity of effort. It is a truth that nature is a step above effort. Because love demands the dismissal of the rule of duality, for this reason it does not necessitate justice. *Insaf* is a term that means cutting into two halves, meaning a just person divides a thing under dispute into two halves between himself and the other party. In this way it is a kind of plurality."[107]

In other words, love and justice are incompatible because love causes unity, while justice requires division into equitable parts. The notion that love is unifying while justice is divisive aligns with Davani's thinking that if human beings were left to their own devices, they would not help one another out of natural affection. Davani solves this problem, the incompatibility of love and justice, in the same way that Ghazali does: by requiring "the sake of God" to be included in notions of love, so that love does not become selfish, and therefore divisive.

Still, even though love is not natural in Davani's conception, he holds it to be the paramount force that theoretically causes human beings to act ethically toward one another, to cooperate with one another for the sake of God and for producing conditions on Earth that would fulfill human responsibility as vicegerents.[108] Davani closes his exposition on affection by saying that while there are people who naturally love wisdom and the Divine, or can be taught to do so, there are those who are good only "because of the law. And the law with respect to this group is like water with respect to someone who has food stuck in his throat."[109] In this statement, Davani is prescribing love for God as an ultimate metaphysical goal, and he proposes that love for God can be built into society and the institutions that human beings create, perhaps through mosques, centers of learning, and ishraqi-sufi practices that he discusses elsewhere. Whether or not the law inculcates love of the Divine is debatable, since Davani understands the apparent trappings of religious practice to be for the less intellectually sophisticated.

For Ghazali, love for society is the same as love of God. Tusi's love for society is constructed as naturally occurring in human beings for the utilitarian sake of success of the human race. For Davani, love for God is the ultimate metaphysical goal, which is enacted through acts of love and justice. Although each ethicist differs on how love for society is constructed, they agree on a man's responsibility to create an ethical world, which he does through refining the self, through ordering the domestic economy, and on the societal level: framing male love as spiritual and superior to ostensibly physical, female love; conducting oneself with friends and enemies in a way that contributes to one's own and their refinement; and regarding all of society as an arena for ethical work.

ETHICAL MASCULINITY ACROSS HIERARCHICAL LINES AND URBAN LIFE

As Ghazali, Tusi, and Davani construct the ethical man, they locate him as a member of an elite class within a hierarchy. Individual ethics, domestic ethics, friendship, enmity, and love of society all exist within the context of the community and city, which are dominated by the hierarchical and male-gendered institutions of urban life. It is within these social institutions—neighborhoods, mosques, bazaars, bathhouses, and courts—that the texts' sections on city planning and ethical cities construct elite masculinity. As such, the ethicists instruct readers on relationships with people who are from different class and intelligence levels than oneself within a city physically designed to mirror and concretize those hierarchical divisions.

Indeed, masculinity is inextricable from class power, as sociologist David Morgan has explained: "class is gendered, and men have assumed or have been allocated the role of class agents."[110] Men define the standards of their class, and when men are in positions of power, they hold power in gendered ways. Although the notion of patriarchy is defined as a world ruled and ordered by unified masculinity, Morgan explains that this concept of a unified masculinity breaks down when we consider class:

> On the one hand, we have the identification of men, all men, with the public sphere, the sphere of production, which contained those areas in society where the action was. Many men, whatever the amount or source of their income, could identify with the provider role [of the household] and the sense of moral responsibility that this implied. But at the same time, class experiences and practices pointed to different ways of being men, different ways of being constituted as effective social actors. These differences . . . become embodied in a range of finer distinctions, such as those between "mental" and "manual," "skilled" and "unskilled."[111]

So, while men are heads of households and privileged over women in the domestic sphere, when they are among men, they relate to one another on the basis of their class and other identity markers. As I discuss later, the ethicists make recommendations on how men should behave with intellectual/class superiors, inferiors, and equals on the basis of their own social class, even as they generally speak to the urban elite.

The Hierarchal City

Cities were a crucial site of personal identity in premodern Muslim society. In a study of travel narratives that chronicle journeys to and within Muslim lands, Roxanne Euben argues that "cities, rather than larger political units such as states, served as first source of identification and allegiance."[112] From a normative ethics perspective, the act of identifying with a city was gendered since the ethicists strongly advised readers to limit women's involvement and presence outside the home. In the *akhlaq* texts, the ethicists devote space to explaining the nature of cities in order to provide the male reader with an aerial perspective for measuring the collective ethical character of his locale. The passages provide us with a macrolevel view of how the ethicists imagined men were meant to live together and cooperate in sustaining human life through creating social structures of power and hierarchy.

The ethicists describe cities, their conditions, and virtuous and objectionable things that go on in cities based on the cosmological notion that the personal ethics of individual men and the politics of a city are one. Indeed, Davani defines a city as "an analogy of the home, a place of public congregation that is disciplined to [the] organization of affairs."[113] The connection between ethics and social order was well established in Islamic discourses by philosophers such as al-Farabi (d. 950), Ibn Sina (d. 1037), and Ibn Rushd (d. 1198). The cornerstone of Farabi's political philosophy is that man's virtue can lead to political ordering of virtuous cities in order to achieve happiness.[114] Ibn Sina departs from this philosophy in that he privileges individual ethics over domestic and societal politics, but does hold that political science enables man to fully realize divine wisdom and prophecy on a broad scale.[115] Ibn Rushd, whom Tusi and Davani quote directly, teaches that ethics are inseparable from politics because both involve people living together in civic association and people's relationships with one another.[116] Ibn Rushd expands upon the Platonic idea that justice means that each person serves the role that he is meant to play in the city according to his skills and intelligence.

The plans of historical Abbasid and post-Abbasid cities in Khorasan and beyond reflected class-based hierarchy, the notion of utilitarian association of people, and also the idea that the world is created for the ethical male. For example, Baghdad itself was built as a circular city with the caliph's palace in the middle, complete with a mosque and an open plaza for parades. Amira Bennison describes Baghdad's layout as a series of concentric circles, segregated along class lines, with gates that were oriented toward Makkah: "There was an inner ring of residences inhabited by princes and high officials and then an outer ring of less sumptuous dwellings for the caliph's Khurasani army, their families, and assorted serving staff. Four thoroughfares cut through these rings from the central plaza to four city gates located in the outer double walls."[117]

Meanwhile, the suburbs were teeming with support labor, and people of all classes lived inside and outside the city in their respective communities.[118] Concentric circles, with the ruler at the center and ancillary staff situated in the outer rings, is a critical image that emerges in the *akhlaq* to represent the macrocosm of class-based hierarchy centered on the ruler as the most ethical man. In the case of Baghdad, the quintessential modern Muslim city, the city plan quite literally translated to the cosmology of social classes and an individual's place in society. Although not all premodern Muslim cities were circular, they were all designed to reflect social hierarchy, and all retained the major physical elements of basic urban needs, such as city walls, gates, mosques, madrasas, a main bazaar, hamams, soup kitchens, and other amenities, depending on the size of the populations they served.[119] These physical locations served as the backdrop where homosocial interactions took place and, as such, required ethical regulation. For instance, Ghazali discusses ethical conduct among men at the bathhouse, the bazaar, and the mosque.[120]

Because the urban environment is an essential site for ethical behavior, Tusi describes the ideal, virtuous city and four types of unvirtuous cities. He posits that cities can have their own dispositions, and the inhabitants of a given city can be characterized as having particular qualities and temperaments.[121] Also, as a result of the cosmological connection between personal and societal ethics—which I argue are both gendered as male—the primary character of theoretical cities is largely determined by the ethics of its male inhabitants, even if in real life women's conduct determined its moral value.[122] In the *akhlaq* genre, the behavior of men of a city creates its ethical character. A city, in turn, serves as a fundamental part of a man's ethical identity.

According to Tusi, the virtuous city (*madinah-i fazilah*) is a macrocosm of the virtuous individual and the virtuously led household. Tusi explains that it is a

> combination of a peoples whose efforts are destined upon acquiring good and removing evil. . . . Their agreement in actions means that everyone recognizes acquiring perfection in the same way, and the acts that proceed from them discharge in the mold of wisdom and set in intellectual refinement and right guidance and are destined to follow the laws of justice and conditions of governance; so that even with people's disagreements and differences of their states, the end goal of their actions is one, and their ways and manners are consistent with one another.[123]

Tusi's concept accounts for differences among individuals, likely in terms of their rational abilities or skill sets; as I discuss in more detail later, such differences defined the various social classes of men according to Tusi and Davani. However, the overall character of the virtuous city comes from the fact that it comprises ethical men who are kind and aspire to do good. The inhabitants of the city act together and agree on the same values of goodness.

The unvirtuous cities, or *madinah-i ghayr fazilah*, contain a critical mass of unethical men whose *nafses* are imbalanced in some way, and who exhibit behavioral symptoms outlined in chapter 2, such as greed, anger, or laziness, depending on which faculties are deficient or overperforming. The first type of unvirtuous city is the ignorant city (*madinah-i jahilah*). In these cities, people do not use their faculties of rationality. They are materialistic, greedy, hedonistic, opportunistic, dominating, self-serving, or some combination of these.[124] Among the several subclasses of the ignorant city is one called the "city of freemen" (*madinah-i ahrar*), which Tusi argues is wrongly admired because of the individuality of its inhabitants of diverse appetites, who are all seemingly equal to one another and do not attempt to better one another or use one another. Here, because no difference is made between stranger and resident, wise men and fools, the distinction between good and evil is lost in this kind of city, and good and evil are expressed in extremes.[125] The second kind of unvirtuous city is the impious one (*madinah-i fasqah*). Men of these cities can distinguish the good from the bad, but they give in to the bad because they succumb to the desires of the concupiscent or irascible faculties over rationality.[126] The third type of unvirtuous city, the errant city (*madinah-i zaalah*), contains people who are entirely deficient in the rational faculty, so they are never able to fully achieve true and lasting happiness.[127] Finally, growth cities are those that attempt to improve their own ranks by developing nearby virtuous cities. Their inhabitants are delusional, hypocrites, impostors of virtue, rebels against the rule of law, apostates who negate the laws of ethics because they do not understand them.[128] Tusi uses these various types of unvirtuous cities as foils for the perfect city, which he and Davani both imagine as the place that preserves a perfect social hierarchy and ethical masculine leadership. The ethical city is where a wide range of men interact to coconstruct a civilization that is ethically ordered by the elite among them.

Fixed Social Classes in the Homosocial Society

In order to make interactions between men of various classes productive, the ethicists provide guidelines on how best to navigate within and across hierarchal levels. As a basis for such guidelines, Tusi and Davani (though not Ghazali)[129] provide detailed descriptions of the social classes that compose an ideal society, demonstrating how they thought of the classes as intellectual, profession-based, and fixed.

Tusi's and Davani's description of social classes that compose ideal society reveals a hierarchy of power, rationality/intellect, and masculinity.[130] Unlike the greater genre of *falsafa* texts, in which the hierarchy begins with prophets as paragons of human perfection,[131] the *akhlaq* genre begins with men who can all potentially be naturalized to perfection. As I described earlier, the classes correspond to the series of concentric circles in city plans, reinforcing the idea that power and privilege reside at the core of the city, with the ruler and those closest to him. Outside the ruler's central core reside those who practice those rules and those who enforce them, and in the outermost ring are the ancillary supporters of these primary classes. Although any ethical man is a microcosm of the city and of the world, the ethicists focus on elite men as the possessors of the full ethical potential to be microcosms of the world. The ethicists discuss social classes at length in the treatises in order to give their audience knowledge of who belongs where, how to treat others, and how to navigate society.

Tusi describes five social classes based on profession. These descriptions appear in passages on characteristics of the virtuous city and the conditions in which justice can be served. The premier social class that regulates the city and its members are called "men of virtues, the perfect philosophers, who are distinguished from peers of their own kind by their rational faculty and well-directed opinions on significant affairs. Knowledge of realities about existent things is their skill, and they are called the most virtuous."[132] Tusi holds that the intelligentsia of a virtuous city sets the moral compass and, at least in theory, influences what laws and policies are enforced in the city.

The second class of people in the city is those who practice and disseminate the ideas generated by the first class. They are called the "masters of tongues" or sometimes the "men of the pen." Their function is to "bring the public and the inferior peoples to degrees of relative perfection, and invite the general people of the city to that which the first group believes, so that whoever is fit to accept their exhortations and counsel progresses above his own rank. Their craft involves the sciences of scholarship, jurisprudence, delivering sermons, rhetoric, poetry, and calligraphy."[133]

In this passage, we see not just a snapshot of the social class hierarchy, but also an articulation of the idea that some men can uplift others by following the ethical ideals set by the wisest men of society, the philosophers. The people of the pen serve as intermediaries of ethical development even though many of them are high-class officials such as "the masters of the sciences and knowledge, the judges [fuquha], secretaries, accountants, geometricians, astronomers, physicians, and poets, upon whom the constitution of the worldly and faith affairs depends." Many men of this class worked in mosques, which Marion Katz has shown were heavily used by women historically, though the ethicists thought of them as male-only spaces.[134]

The third class of people Tusi describes is those who are in charge of measures and justice. They "oversee the laws of justice among the people of the city, observe necessary measurement in taking and giving, and advocate for equality. Their crafts are sciences of accounting and demanding and receiving, geometry, medicine, and astronomy; they are called the measurers."[135] Some professions overlap between the second and third classes, but ultimately one's function in society, establishing and practicing rules for society or measurement, determined which group one belongs to. Also included in this class are "the men of the sword," who are members of the state's defense forces. Tusi explains that "the order of the world is kept by their interventions."[136] As I discuss in chapter 2, the ethicists thought of justice as a virtue that could be acquired and perfected by individuals. They also thought of it as a societal virtue insofar as individuals in the community were practicing and enforcing it. Thus, professions of measurement and law enforcement are conceptually linked to justice because, on the societal level, justice is a tangible, measurable, and equitable division of resources.

In Tusi's section on creating just conditions in society, he deviates slightly from his earlier description of the ontological/moral value of individuals from various social classes that I discuss in chapter 2, in that he adds warriors as constituting their own separate fourth class. These men "are marked with having to protect women's quarters and defend the dignity of the people of the city, preventing the lords of the unvirtuous cities from coming to them. They possess the conditions of bravery and zeal in fighting and defense."[137] The term Tusi uses for women's quarters is *harim*, which generally means private quarters where women lived. Because male relatives, particularly husbands, are responsible for women's safety, the people designated to protect women's quarters might be akin to police forces specifically dedicated to watching women to keep them in their place, thus enforcing gender segregation in public. Nowhere else in the text do Tusi and Davani mention protection of the *harim*, nor do they elaborate on what the tasks of this protector group would be. Thus, the ethicists reify the notion that women are a class of people that, structurally, stands altogether outside of the hierarchy of social classes. The passage brings to mind Heidi Hartman's definition of patriarchy as "relations between men, which have a material base, and which, though hierarchical, establish or create interdependence and solidarity among men that enable them to dominate women."[138] Just as Hartman's definition of patriarchy frames male classes as a hierarchy that stands entirely above women, so too the ethicists confine women to a peripheral place outside the societal order.

Tusi's fourth class (or fifth, if the warriors are considered a class of their own) is the community that "puts in order the sustenance and provisions, whether by way of transaction or production or by way of tax collection or other means, and they are called the men of property."[139] These men are also called the "the men of negotiation, such as merchants who bring goods from region to region, artisans, masters of crafts, tradesmen, and tax collectors, without whose assistance life for the species would be impossible."[140] Essentially, this class of people is the middlemen and merchants at the bazaars who deal the goods and services to the people above them in rank. Bennison describes the marketplace, which for men of these classes served as "a second public space [after mosques] for people—primarily men—to gather."[141] These merchants and middlemen share their social class with the producers of the goods sold in the marketplace, including "the men of husbandry, such as ploughmen, farmers, tillers, and agriculturalists, who organize provisions for every community. Perpetuity of individuals would cease without their help."[142] All four (or five) social classes are construed as essential in sustaining life for the human species, in which its members live in association with one another, even though women are imagined as a separate class of beings outside of society's structure, and enslaved persons are not mentioned in these passages at all.

In addition to this civic description of social classes, Tusi, along with Davani, employs an analogy of earthly elements that must be in balance according to God's natural law for the virtuous city's existence. The analogy uses the term *mathabat*, which implies the scheme in which people will be rewarded by God for playing their part. In order for there to be justice, or, for Davani, in order for cities to remain virtuous, there needs to be a balance of the natural elements of water (men of the pen), fire (men of measures and justice), wind (men of negotiation), and earth (men of husbandry),[143] and each needs to do their part to create equilibrium, thereby harmoniously reflecting God's laws of nature on Earth as a society.

Notably, the ruler of the city is not included in the scheme of social classes, not because he cannot be compared to common men (as women cannot be), but rather because the ruler has the most ethical potential of all. He is responsible for the acts of all men and for maintaining order among them. Tusi describes the head of the city as the one who "brings every class in its place and district and arranges leadership and service, such that each group is inferior relative to another group but leads relative to another group, until one reaches the people who do not have aptitude for leadership, and these are the absolute servants."[144] In this passage, the hierarchy of society is based on fitness for authority, which for the upper classes comes from knowledge and for lower classes comes from skill sets. Thus, one's intellectual ability is an essential criterion for locating one within the class structure. The ruler can set the ethical tone for the entire city, and can set the course of the city's fate and character, by orchestrating its structure and by dividing goods, services, and resources fairly. The institutions of the city, such as the learning centers, mechanisms of producing and distributing goods and services, and the military or royal order, all contribute to a city's ethical character.

Compared to Tusi, Davani retains the idea that the classes represent elements of God's natural law, but he has a slightly different organization for the social classes that constitute the righteous city, as well as for the specific occupations that comprise the classes. Davani's framework combines the philosophers and the various types of scholars into the first class (water), "upon whom organization of the city depends. These first-class men have the ultimate practical wisdom and perfect philosophy by whose power they achieve excellence."[145] They include all men of the pen: "religious scholars, jurists, judges, scribes, accountants, engineers, astronomers, physicians, and poets—for the foundation of faith and the world is dependent and bound upon the virtuous efforts of their bold pens and their graceful knowledge."[146]

Classes 2 to 5 appear in descending order of intellectual sophistication. The second class in Davani's scheme stands intellectually below the first but is important for transmitting knowledge to the common folk. As in Tusi's formulation, this class represents the element of water, which he states can transmit light more luminous than the sun, an important metaphor of emanating wisdom and spirituality for Davani. They "are a group that invites the public toward human perfection and prohibits evils with words. Their work includes rhetoric, jurisprudence, oration, poetry, and such" and includes artisans and craftsmen.[147] Davani's third class is that of "measurers," the group that "watches over the laws of justice among the people of the city, and who are entrusted with assigning the measurements of things (wind). Their work includes mathematics, accounting, engineering, medicine, and astronomy."[148] Again, the notions of measurement and equity come together in this class. The fourth class are soldiers (fire), who "guard the city from enemy oppression and take-over. . . . Their work is bravery, pageantry, and awesomeness."[149] Fifth are the tradesmen, who "organize food and clothing for the above groups," (earth) whether privately or through the state.[150]

In addition to outlining these classes of men, Davani also outlines five classes of "weeds" of society who are basically types of unethical men.[151] These include hypocrites who act like philosophers and scholars, but who are really self-serving; inverted men who accommodate religion to their worldly and bodily desires instead of vice versa; rebels against the righteous state; distorters who lack enough intellect to correctly interpret religion; and impersonators who misrepresent themselves in order to gain financial and social capital.[152] These "weeds" are the lowliest of all men, even if they are situated in the uppermost classes, because they are unethical. At the same time, as I mention in chapter 2, the description of the imposter serves not just as someone to avoid, but also as a mirror for the reader to check his own sincerity in the acquisition of virtues. All of this seemingly individual-level ethics of people from various classes inevitably represents broader societal ethics and shows how a city shapes the *nafses* of men who may or may not be ethical.

Even though Davani includes a metaphor for the elements of nature corresponding to each class, just as Tusi does, more important to him are the distinctions among people based on their attentiveness to their souls' needs and ability to perceive the Unseen. Most importantly, this is a classification of ethical worth that corresponds to social class. Davani considers only men as having spiritual rank, and even that is rooted in a hierarchy of mental capacity and intelligence. The highest class are the saints and sages, who "are endowed with divine favor and are free from the filth of natural relations, who know the source of truth by the attributes of majesty and signs of beauty, who know that the quality of the chain of existing things came to be ordered from the beginning, and can picture the return of the *nafs* in a manner that is according to principles."[153]

These are the most superior intellects. Their mental abilities are untainted by intercourse with the female body, or any bodies. The class of men below this is also intelligent but cannot comprehend imaginative conceptions or purely intellectual realities. They do understand their own deficiencies and thus are called "men of faith."[154] Below these are the "men of resignation," who simply do not possess imaginative faculties but admit to their abilities.[155] They are resigned to their fate, knowing the rank of their intellects. Individuals in the class beneath this are known as the "weak ones" because they cannot conceive of anything beyond what they feel through the five senses. Nonetheless, "since everyone endures exertions according to the measure of his own abilities, and they arrive at the limits of their aptitude, they cannot be marked with blame. Rather, everyone has their face directed toward reality."[156] Middle- and lower-class men cannot perceive or imagine unobservable or immeasurable concepts and ideas, but their realities are relative, and their deserts are only according to their reality. For Davani, the mental ability to comprehend spiritual knowledge is an added component to his profession, which designates a man's social class in the grand scheme of society.

According to the ethicists' discussions on how to choose a career for one's son, an individual's role in society is ideally based upon his aptitude and skill set.[157] However, in reality, intellectual hierarchy maps onto the constellation of jobs that sustain human life. Similar to how gendered assumptions define spousal roles in the domestic realm, so too in the public realm, the notion of occupational aptitude is based on fixed assumptions about rational abilities possessed by people of various classes. Although theoretically in *akhlaq* all men have the potential to be naturalized to perfection, elites have more capacity than nonelites.

Ethics Among Men of Different Rationality/Class Levels

In addition to dividing homosocial society along professional class lines, the ethicists also consider individuals' intellectual abilities as a basis for classification. Capability of rational thought, which in ethics is the principal part of a man's *nafs*, determines his rank in the social hierarchy and determines how much power and influence he wields. In theory, more intelligent individuals are members of higher social classes (such as the class of philosophers or scholars); but in reality, less intelligent or corrupt people can still hold power by virtue of birth, such as in the case of a stupid king who nevertheless had the potential to demonstrate the highest order of virtue simply because he possessed great power that he could wield in exercising virtue.[158] This hierarchy of wealth and power thus maps onto a hierarchy of intellect.

In Tusi's and Davani's advice on interacting with people of various classes, they prescribe speaking to people according to their intellectual level and general capability. Although general rules govern men's interactions with kings, princes, superiors, equals, and subordinates, a specific interaction with a given person of any class is determined by the intellectual level of that person relative to oneself. Tusi presents an underlying principle for how to act with people in each category: "If he be above [one] in rank, this should impel his confidence in protection of that rank so that he does not decline toward loss; if he is of comparable [rank], he should impel ascension from that rank on the stairway to perfection; and if he is below in rank, he should struggle for reaching the degree of that rank."[159] In other words, one should always focus on one's own virtues, either improving them or, at the very least, maintaining them. More specifically, for interaction with those in superior classes, one generally should use the guidelines of how to treat rulers and superiors, as discussed in the preceding section, especially in situations in which one is employed by men ranked above oneself.

In dealing with subjects of lower rank, a man should be aware of the intellect as the ultimate determinant of social rank and behave accordingly:

> Watch over those who apply themselves to learn their goodness and natural disposition. If they are worthy of the branches of the sciences and characterized by good disposition, do not prevent them from learning or burden them with seeking their needs, but try removing their afflictions. For the masters of corrupt natures, who seek knowledge out of greed, teach them *tahzib-i akhlaq* and

punish their faults and perfect them according to their abilities. Hold back any knowledge that is the basis of reliance on decadent intent. For the less intelligent, stimulate them with the things that are closer to their understanding and more inclusive of benefits, so they avoid wasting their lives.[160]

This passage demonstrates how natural disposition and mental capacity (*khulq*) are themselves a hierarchal marker that affects social class. Thus, only in some cases may the *tahzib-i akhlaq* (discipline of ethics) prove to be an effective correction to people of lower mental capacities or corrupt *nafses*. In general, one must be congenial to all men, but the deeper principle that governs how one treats men of other classes is whether they can be corrected, uplifted, and taught. This advice suggests that character and intelligence are the most important criteria for assessing others. However, because intellectual hierarchy maps onto social class hierarchy, categories of intelligence become bases of exclusion of nonelites. An ethical man is supposed to be paternalistic toward the excluded, intellectually deficient. This suggestion follows the same principle as the advice that the ethicists give to husbands regarding charge over their wives: since women are in general considered to have lower mental capacity than men, wives are suitable to play an instrumental role in their husbands' lives. Likewise, less intelligent men are in service to elite men, who use them to ethically order society and distribute justice.

In a rare use of first-person plural, which shows he is speaking to his own elite class of fellow scholars, Davani advises on how to treat men of inferior classes. If the inferiors are one's students, he says, we should "hold them precious just as one's children," and observe their natures and dispositions carefully to steer them to achieve according to their own abilities.[161] Here Davani's use of familial ethics to prescribe how to conduct oneself socially shows how paternalism drives man's ethical behavior in both domestic and public spheres. Davani further instructs that one should be haughty with arrogant people and ignore the stupid. The key point here is that knowing the science of the *nafs* enables one to recognize the intellectual merits and deficiencies of others, no matter to which social class they belong. As I discuss in chapter 2, people of all social and intellectual classes have full *nafses* and possess all the associated faculties, but an individual can be deficient in one or all of the faculties.

Further, a man with power and privilege has an ethical responsibility to help the lowest members of society but in a discerning way that also uplifts them; however, only the truly needy should be given provisions and gifts.[162] In Tusi's and Davani's expositions, beggars belong to two classes, those who beg out of true need and those who beg out of greed and covetousness of what others possess. In the section on how to treat those of other social classes, Tusi makes a simple statement about the unfortunate: "Take the hands of the weak and show them mercy, and assist the oppressed."[163] The remainder of his exposition on helping people comes under the discussion of how to preserve justice. Davani adds that a man's every act should ultimately reflect upon the aspirant's charitable actions, "so that he may reach the rank of divine vicegerency."[164] Davani drives home the fact that how one treats others in the outside world—in addition to one's behavior on a personal and domestic level—amounts to the complete account of one's actions in life. Worldly ethics is ultimately connected to one's relationship with the Divine and is the cornerstone of the *akhlaq* cosmology in which an ethical man is a microcosm of the world.

The Unjust Justice of Khilafah *and Social Hierarchy*

In chapter 2, I noted an incompatibility between two of the ethicists' premises: the a priori metaphysical equality of all human *nafses* and the de facto inequality of the very faculty, rationality, that is supposed to raise humans as a class above animals. In chapter 3, I showed a dissonance between the assumed ontological equality between husband and wife and the actual inequality in their power relations. In a parallel way, the societal ethics highlighted in this chapter shows how the hierarchical structure of society as reflected and constructed in the *akhlaq* texts is in tension with the *akhlaq* goal of achieving justice, that is, becoming a just vicegerent (*khalifah*) who serves as an ethical mirror of the macrocosm. Tusi and Davani define the virtue of justice as the continuous struggle, on an individual and societal level, against evil and oppression and for the fair division of resources among people according to their individual deserts. Injustice, then, is denying people what they are owed. Tusi explains that treating "all [persons] as one" does not mean that one has to treat individuals equally, but rather that everyone deserves to be treated thoughtfully according to what he deserves.[165] The ethicists' definition of justice as fair treatment of others based on their deserts leaves the possibility of determining deserts based on grounds other than intellect—including class, gender, race, or other factors.

According to Tusi, class-based inequalities in society arise from differences in occupations and in the roles that each individual plays in society. To his way of thinking, inequality is actually just because it is necessary for survival:

> Diversity in states of wealth and poverty and smartness and stupidity is predetermined, for if everyone were wealthy they would not serve one another, or likewise if they were all poor—in the first case out of being independent from one another and in the second case out of lack of ability for pay in exchange for service to one another. Because crafts vary in their nobility or ignobility, if everyone were equal in their faculty of discernment, they would choose to be one class and the other classes would remain unfilled and their purpose would not be attained. This is why the philosophers have said, "if people were equal, they would all perish." Instead, because some [people] are excellent in management and others are blessed with strength, and some have great dignity, others have excessive capability, and there are people devoid of discernment who are tools and instruments with respect to the people of discernment.[166]

The skills and abilities that Tusi notes are determinative of social class are themselves determined by natural predilection. Thus, the hierarchy of society, in which some men are in service to others, is predetermined by nature or by God. Such a conception of society, in which individuals are rightfully unequal, recalls the explanation Tusi and Davani provide for why the "free city" is unvirtuous: in the free city, even though everyone's ideas, professions, and actions are considered equally valid and no one tries to defeat others, the notions of good and evil and right and wrong are eluded. In other words, they argue that not all ideas, or all people, carry equal moral value. Tusi and Davani reason that because human beings are selfish, if all people were equal, no one would help anyone; when people are given the chance, they are greedy and domineering, especially those who do not have their *nafses* in balance or who let their other faculties overrule rationality. Thus, humans require judicial management by those above them in the hierarchy. As Tusi puts it, "A kind of management is necessary to make each one content with the station that he deserves and bring him to his rights, and to cut off each one's hands from usurping and aggressing against the rights of others, and to busy with work that is entrusted with the matters of cooperation. And that management is called politics."[167]

The term for *management* here—and, by extension, for *politics*—is *siyasat*, a term with a coercive connotation that is also used elsewhere to refer to household order. By using this term, Tusi confirms that justice and other virtue ethics cosmologically link the domestic and societal planes of human behavior.

A fundamental problem with the societal hierarchy of the *akhlaq* texts is that it does not allow social mobility, no matter a person's level of intellect. This fact shows that the hierarchy itself is inconsistent with the tenet that the intellect has ethical value: no intelligent man, much less an intelligent woman, can change his social class, even though his refinement is more important than his rank at birth. Tusi and Davani both agree that people situated in the various social classes of a city cannot cross boundaries of their social station because such boundary-crossing would be unjust. Both their texts contain a variation of the following passage that explains why this is so:

> Justice requires that each one should stay in his rank and not transgress that rank. A person should not be employed in [many] different crafts. . . . Firstly, natures have peculiarities and not every nature can be employed in every work; secondly the master of a craft attains authority in the rules of that craft with scrutinizing vision and ascending ambition over a long lifetime. When that vision and ambition are divided and distributed over different crafts, all remain attenuated and fall short of perfection.[168]

In the ethicists' view, nature and professional aptitude automatically and naturally confer class rank, notwithstanding the obvious fact that not all professions are open to all persons. In the ethicists' ideal world, fathers carefully consider a boy's aptitude, disposition, and ability until he finds his rightful place in society, based on whichever profession is appropriate and suitable.[169]

While there may have been standard elements in education for elite boys, it is unclear whether the ethicists would ever advocate that a child learn a craft lower than his father's station. Taking the argument to its furthest conclusion, they would advocate for a child to take up whatever profession he has aptitude for, regardless of what social class that would land him in, but that would contradict the responsibility of his becoming a just vicegerent (*khalifah*), which only true members of the elite classes can fully realize, given their responsibilities for setting the ethical agenda of the city. The ethicists devote significant space to explaining the differing ranks of class/intellect both in discussion of inculcating virtues (as I discuss in chapter 2) and in discussion of practical societal ethics because they view the ultimate role of elite men as ethically ordering society as *khalifahs* or as forces for societal flourishing (*sa'adat*). The ethical guidelines the ethicists present for this aspect of life contain a tension because their definition of justice is premised on inequality, and thus is inherently unjust.

HOMOSOCIAL ETHICS AT COURT

The ethicists each devote an entire section of their texts to the central institution in the hierarchical society, the court. These sections indicate, perhaps more than the sections on other homosocial ethics, how power and masculinity together culminate in ethical selves. Much scholarship has been devoted to parsing out what responsibilities the *akhlaq* texts assign to the ruler, in efforts to extract Islamic political theory and political ethics.[170] In particular, Muzaffar Alam outlines how influential the *Akhlaq-i Nasiri* and *Akhlaq-i Jalali* were as political ethics texts during the Mughal period.[171] Scholars often reduce the comprehensive, wide-ranging ethics texts to their political ethics, treating them as akin to *fürstenspiegel* (the "mirrors for princes" genre from medieval and renaissance Europe), or to political works from similar contexts, such as Farabi's *Aphorisms of a Statesman* or the *Qabusnama* of Kay Kavus Ibn Iskander (d. 1082). Of all the sections in the *Akhlaq-i Nasiri* and *Akhlaq-i Jalali*, arguably the most famous are the relatively short discussions on ethics of rulership and maintaining justice.[172] However, my focus here is on unpacking the gendered ethics of the philosopher-king and the gendering of his subjects. I do so by asking what kind of man a king needs to be, how courtiers are supposed to behave, and what kinds of manhood are appropriate for subjects and kings. In so doing, I reflect upon how the structural power that underpins societal ethics is imagined as masculine.

A ruler, as a philosopher-king, serves as a model for all other men, and ethics at court demonstrates how power that is reinforced in state power is integral to ethical masculinity. The ethicists treat the ruler as the central figure of the macrocosm, the one who sets the ethical tone of justice for the land. His role resembles that of the Hellenic philosopher-king. In premodern Muslim society, the king is construed as the ultimate ethical man, the one with the greatest potential to enact God's justice. Although the ruler is exceptional in his macrocosmic responsibilities, the ethicists address the entire audience in mandating their common goal of becoming a *khalifah* (vicegerent). Therefore, they must all follow the same ethics with respect to their subordinates.

In the ethics texts, rulers and subjects have a symbiotic relationship that is focused on creating justice in the macrocosm amid rampant corruption, injustice, political posturing, and other unethical behaviors. At times, the ethicists use the concepts of love, affection, and paternal and filial responsibility in their descriptions of the ideal power relationship between rulers and subjects. At other times, they are more realistic, likely in acknowledgment of corruption and court conspiracies; they address how to manage the hierarchical power dynamics between rulers and their subjects, as well as between high-ranking officials and their subordinates. In addressing both rulers and subordinates, the ethicists use the specific guidelines from court ethics as a blueprint to generalize ethical behavior in all-male master-subordinate relationships.

Ethical Rules, Characteristics, and Knowledge for Rulers and Masters

All three ethicists held, with slight variations, that society was best managed by a virtuous government. Ghazali's rules for kings focus on prevention of the abuse of power and being mindful of responsibilities.[173] By contrast, Tusi's list of the ideal leadership traits figures kings as the potential embodiment of a virtuous government.[174] Davani's outline of the ideal leader's seven qualities is similar to Tusi's, although it deemphasizes the leader's genealogy because Davani does not share Tusi's sectarian allegiance. These rules and lists are important not only because they tell the king how to rule justly (as discussed in chapter 2, justice is one of the major virtues of the perfected *nafs*), but also because, in the king's role as a worldly lawgiver, he has the unparalleled potential to be a paragon of ethics.

The central concern of Ghazali's discussion on "governance and the running of the state" is to establish these normative rules for ethical governance, which combat corruption and maintain the goal of achieving "vicegerency of God, most high, on Earth if it is run in the way of justice." He adds that "If [governance] lacks compassion and justice, it is the vicegerency of Iblis."[175] Only a king has the far-reaching power to affect so many lives, set the agenda for public institutions, and institute laws that create a just society. As such, he is the ultimate ethical subject for *akhlaq* training. The actual audience of the ethics texts, nonroyal courtiers and educated elites, did also possess the power to affect change, but their power was limited to their jurisdictions or to the members of their own households. Still, relevant to all men is Ghazali's emphasis on using power responsibly and not abusing it. He prefaces his ten rules that a king must observe by reminding readers that the world is only a station on the journey of life, and that an ethical man must remember he will leave all the riches and power of this world behind when he dies. He admits that this is not an easy idea for kings to grasp, but affirms their power and potential to do good for the lands they rule.

Ghazali's first six rules for leaders deal with consideration for others and moderation of oneself. First, in general, a king should apply the same standards to himself as he does to others: "whatever events occur, he should assess as if he is the peasant and the other is the ruler: whatever he dislikes for himself, he should dislike for other Muslims."[176] Second, the king should attend to the needs of the people before engaging in his own supererogatory acts of worship, which implies that broader ethical care for society supersedes personal piety.[177] Third, he should not "make himself accustomed to being occupied with pleasures such as wearing fine clothes or eating good food; rather, he should be content in everything, for justice is not possible without contentment."[178] This is the same advice that Ghazali gives to the text's broader audience with respect to moderation in food, clothing, and other human needs; moderation frees one up to focus on sufficiency of the rational faculty over the indulgence that marks the other faculties of the *nafs*. Fourth, the "foundation of works should [be] benevolence as much as possible, not cruelty."[179] Fifth, one should strive for mutual amicability between oneself and one's subjects, and not take on a sense of superiority from hearing the praise that is customarily given to kings. Sixth, a king is not to violate the law merely to please anyone.[180]

The seventh rule for kings is the heart of Ghazali's advice for rulers: a king should know that "the danger of having power is that it is difficult, and to execute the work of God, most high, is a great undertaking. Whoever has obtained this favor achieves a happiness beyond which there is no happiness. If he fails, he will fall upon a misery beyond which there is no misery like it."[181] This seventh rule seals the idea that it is within a king's power, and perhaps only his, to achieve ultimate happiness of happiness, which Ghazali articulates is the goal of *akhlaq*. It also reminds kings of the responsibility that comes with power and emphasizes that all their deeds, good and bad, have high-stakes consequences. Holding power provides the unique opportunity for widespread exercise of ethical behaviors. The same is the case for a husband's ethical behavior with his wife, children, and servants. And thus the king's ethics are not just important as political ethics, but demonstrate how the hierarchy of power keeps the cosmological structure of ethics stable. Ghazali elaborates on this rule at great length with hadiths from the Prophet about the responsibilities of just rule that also extend to associates of the king. In the eighth rule, we see that a king should actively seek counsel from pious religious scholars and be wary of corrupt ones, showing an interplay between the ruler (the most potentially ethical man) and the *'ulama'* class, who might be more ethical.

The ninth rule is that a king should "discipline his own slaves, servants, and representatives and not be content with their injustices, for he will be accountable for their injustices."[182] The rule also encompasses the idea that being just or ethical by example transfers that justice to others. The transfer occurs through the bestowal of justice upon them or by inspiring them to be just themselves. In other words, for Ghazali, as well as Tusi and Davani, the king's ethics is meant to be contagious to those around him. Further, a king is not just if he is not just with his "own wife, children, and slaves."[183] Within all the discussion of ethics on a broader community or society level, this rule is the ethicists' only mention of judging a man's justice through how he treats his wife and children. Here it is meant as an evaluation of a king's fitness to mete out justice; however, this condition also suggests that marriage is a shared experience in the ethical manhood of kings and nonroyal readers. The average ethical man and the king both perform ethical behavior by acting ethically with members of their own households. The three levels of ethics—personal, domestic, and social—are connected through male refinement.

Finally, the tenth rule is for kings to pay attention to the treatments of the *nafs* for anger, for that is a common ailment among kings that stems from royal arrogance. This also suggests that the same rules of ethics apply to kings, but with the special condition that they hold power over the fate of others.[184] Overall, Ghazali's advice to kings is based on the metaphysical science of improving the *nafs*. That advice is derived from the importance of being just, which in turn comes from "perfection of the intellect, which is seeing affairs as they are, and understanding their hidden reality, and not being fooled by appearances."[185] Between the ninth and tenth rules, Ghazali gives specific examples of reasons for why a king might commit unjust acts, each of which corresponds to a distinct imperfection of the *nafs*:

> If his purpose is that he eats delicious food, he should know that he is a beast in the figure of a man, for eating greedily is the work of animals. If he does it to wear clothes of brocade, he is a woman in the figure of a man, for beautification is women's work. If he does it for waging his anger out on his own enemies, he is a predator in the figure of a man, for tearing apart and fighting are the work of predators. If he is doing it so that people serve him, he is an ignoramus in the figure of a wiseman, for if he had rationality he would know that all of them are servants of their own stomachs, in service to their own pleasures and sexual organs.[186]

In this passage, Ghazali identifies gluttony as a violation of the concupiscible faculty (*quwwat-i shahwat*). Being predatory is a violation of the irascible faculty (*quwwat-i ghazbi*). Acting like a woman is not a specific violation of a faculty of the *nafs* (because women have the same kind of *nafses* as men do), but paying attention to one's beauty is womanly, and therefore unmanly, and thus is a deficiency of the concupiscent faculty. Being crafty in subordinating people is a violation of the rational faculty (*quwwat-i 'ilm*). In the last sentence of the passage, Ghazali makes it clear that kings should also realize that those serving him have *nafses* too. The same virtue ethics of the *nafs* applies to kings, as it does to male heads of household and men at various other levels, although it is adjusted according to their skills, office, or place in the homosocial hierarchy. Unsurprisingly, he provides the same reminder to husbands—that ultimately their wives have *nafses* too that must be managed responsibly. Thus, the rules for kings in many ways resemble all master–subordinate ethics.

While Ghazali focuses on the rules kings should follow in order to govern justly, Tusi and Davani list qualities of the ideal leader. For Tusi, the leader's ideal traits are embodied in the virtuous government. Tusi explains that, first and foremost, a ruler must have good descent and genealogy that inspire men to respect and be in awe of him.[187] The term Tusi uses for the quality of being awe-inspiring is *haybat*, the very same term he uses to describe how a husband should appear to his wife. This choice of terminology underlines the ways in which the ethical levels of the home and the sovereignty are scale representations of each other in the broader ethics cosmology. The center of this cosmology is the ethical man, a powerful leader who actively "lords" over his subjects. On the domestic level, the leader's subjects are his wife, children, and servants, while on the sovereign level, the subjects are the inhabitants of the city or nation. He is responsible for the ethical behavior of his underlings, as well as for his own.

Tusi's and Davani's lists of ideal kingly qualities are similar, except for the placement of the king's genealogy, which appears first for Tusi, but for Davani it is a feature of kingship, not a prerequisite for ruling. In Davani's list, he mentions the king's family genealogy last and does not refer to it as a requirement for a king.[188] This variation could be accounted for by Tusi's and Davani's differences in sectarian leanings, since for Shi'is having a biological relationship to an imam legitimated his rulership, and in the case of Isma'ilis the imam himself was the rightful ruler. Instead of genealogy, Davani's first quality in a king is the possession of purpose and high concentration that comes from *tahzib-i akhlaq,* or the discipline of ethics.[189] The second quality for Tusi is the "lofty ambition" that comes about when the irascible and concupiscent faculties of the king's *nafs* are subdued.[190]

The third quality on Tusi's list (second for Davani) is firmness of opinion and right thinking. The fourth quality (third for Davani) is the "manly resolve and the royal resolve" (*'azm ar-rijal va 'azm al-muluk*). Resoluteness is a distinctly masculine characteristic, without which it is "not possible to acquire any virtue or reject any vice."[191] This characteristic is about being willing to change oneself according to a code of ethics. It is here that we see the most direct connection in Tusi's and Davani's works between maleness and the ability for ethical refinement; resoluteness is assumed to be purely gendered. As we saw in the last chapter, women were thought not to possess this resolve or discipline, and this was a very fundamental premise upon which the entire edifice of ethics in these texts was built. The story that Tusi and Davani tell of the need for manly resolve is that of the caliph Ma'mun, who had what modern physicians would call "pica," an uncontrollable urge to eat nonfood items to make up for a particular nutrient deficiency. In Tusi, Ma'mun was eating dirt, but Davani changes the dirt to roses, perhaps because he has greater respect for the caliphate than Tusi does. Ma'mun told the physicians that he did not have enough manly resolve to remedy his disease, so they should not bother with finding cures. The episode with Ma'mun exemplifies the ways in which gendered expectations of manliness meets the qualities of good rulership.

Tusi's fifth quality of an ideal leader (fourth in Davani) is "patience in enduring adversity, and persevering in one's quest without weariness or pain, for the key to all objects desired is patience."[192] This advice is important for a king or prince with his own aspirations, either personal or for his state. But also, since kings are seen as covetous by nature, the prescription of this virtue is an attempt to regulate the lengths to which kings would go to fulfill their desires. The sixth quality of an ideal leader (fifth in Davani) is affluence.[193] Tusi says that ordinary men should despise wealth and gold because of the many ills they cultivate, but that kings ought to be affluent in order to avoid covetousness. The seventh quality (sixth for Davani) is bringing in external counsel for good kingship, having "upstanding assistants" who need not be of noble descent but must have "ambition, opinions, greatness, and patience."[194] Davani describes this quality as having obedient soldiers.

For both Tusi and Davani, the king's true goal should be to seek faith and enable the sovereign realm to reach the goals of faith. Davani does not specify what these goals are.[195] In a cosmic metaphor, Tusi and Davani liken a king to a physician of the whole world, who is supposed to cure the evils of domination, chaos, and evil.[196] This metaphor recalls the microcosmic way in which, at the level of the individual, the *nafs* is healed by putting the irascible and concupiscent faculties behind the rational one. Davani concludes with a story about the pharaoh and Moses in order to illustrate that generosity is among the best qualities in a ruler, along with mercy and kindness to subjects.[197] Both ethicists' vision of leadership is one of ideal masculinity that has far-reaching potential for vice-gerency (*khilafah*).

After listing the qualities of an ideal leader, Tusi and Davani consider what knowledge of human nature is necessary to the leader. Both assert that a king should also be aware of people's different types of temperaments so that he can manage them. Tusi and Davani enumerate five temperaments of average people around the king:

> People who are good by nature and whose goodness is contagious. . . . Thus they should be the people closest to the king. . . . Second are people who are good by nature but their goodness is not contagious. This group should be held dear and their concerns should be taken seriously. Third are people who are by nature neither good nor evil. This party should be secured and encouraged to goodness, so that they reach perfection by measure of their aptitude. Fourth are people who are evil but their evil is not contagious; this group should be disposed of and disdained and should be warned, taught good by counsel, prohibition, encouragement, and deterrents. . . . Fifth are people that by nature are evil and their evil is contagious. This party is the lowliest of creation. . . . These people also have grades: a group whose correction is hopeful by way of discipline and prohibition must be corrected or else should be prevented from evil; and for a group whose correction is hopeless, if their evil is not all encompassing, one should pacify them; but if their evil is general and comprehensive, then it is compulsory to remove their evil.[198]

From this passage, we glimpse the normativity of Tusi's ethics of court life, as Tusi may have derived it from standard behavior he observed at court. Tusi expected kings and princes to find it challenging to determine who carries which temperament; the ethicists advised the rulers that before any man became involved in the court, he should first be carefully evaluated in his demonstration of merit, aptitude, and potential benefits to government. Along the same lines, Tusi advises kings to be cautious with sentencing, punishments, and dealing with aggressive petitioners.[199] Tactics of negotiation, using carrots and sticks, rewarding some people over others for their favors, advice, or seemingly kind gestures, were all matters of personal politics that were connected to ethical behavior.

The ethicists' brief mentions of women at court are telling of their frustration at women's participation in politics and make it clear that the ethicists view court as a male-only space where men practice and refine their ethics. On the subject of employing informers and spies, for example, Tusi advises that a king should only reveal royal plans to intelligent men, but never to women or children, who are "of weak mind."[200] On the other hand, the ethicists also advise kings to stay abreast of gossip from the women's quarters: "one can make deductions from watching and being informed from sources and places of friends and special people, such as people of the haram, and that which is heard from the mouths of children and slaves and their attendants, who are known for scarcity of intelligence and discernment."[201] Ghazali, too, shares this sentiment in response to women's historical involvement in conspiracies, politics, and court gossip, although not specifically in the *Kimiya*. Omid Safi argues that women in the Saljuq court, especially Tarkan Khatun, had a profound impact on "theological and political Muslim writings [against] the participation of women in society and politics."[202] As a result of conspiracies at court, "Nizam al-Mulk and al-Ghazali warned the sultan of the evils of listening to women's advice and the deficiencies of women's intellects."[203] Another historical example of women in court is more positive: Saray Khatun, Davani's patron and Aqquyunlu Sultan Uzun Hasan's mother, mediated several power disputes with Uzun Hasan and his brother and also played significant roles in negotiations with Ottomans.[204] In any case, as mentioned in the previous chapter, all the ethicists were concerned about the dangers of allowing women to participate in public. They said little about women or children at court, and they advised men to shield their wives even from the idle pastime of gossiping about goings-on outside the home. It is clear that the ethicists were managing the discrepancy between the reality of female behavior they observed and the ideal behaviors they wanted to prescribe. The ethicists wished the court to be a man's world in which women did not meddle. It is a public sphere in which men, including kings and nonroyal subjects, exercise their masculinity and ethical training.

Ethics of Subordinates: Interacting with Kings

While the ethics of the ruler reflects Ghazali's, Tusi's, and Davani's notions of ultimate masculinity, the ethics of his subjects is aimed at maintaining their own ethical masculinity in light of the king's more formidable masculinity, and in the face of the political posturing and corruption at court. According to the ethicists, even though court life is inherently corrupt, their audience of wealthy elites still ought to act ethically in interactions with kings and government officials at court. Ghazali is skeptical of kings, while Tusi and Davani are cautiously pragmatic in their ethics of court life for their average reader.

Ghazali's ethics of interacting with kings, or any superiors, reflects his own disenchanting experience working for the Saljuq vizier Nizam al-Mulk, who had been assassinated. Ghazali states that rulers are corrupt, insisting that all the wealth in state coffers is obtained from corrupt and unlawful means, save for the small percentage that comes from *jizya* (poll taxes) paid by non-Muslims and property that is inherited from persons with no heirs. The state's palaces and tents, together with their furnishings and carpets, "have been seized by force, so it is improper to go inside there."[205] Further, Ghazali proclaims that it is unlawful to accept money from the ruler, except for students and the poor, who can accept meager wages.[206] The disillusioned Ghazali also categorically rejects the need for religious scholars to initiate salutations to the ruler, bow before him, or kiss his hand unless the ruler is just. He quotes a hadith in which the Prophet allegedly stated, "the *'ulama'* are the trustees of the messengers as long as they do not associate with the kings. For when the trustees associate with the kings, they betray their trusteeship. Guard against them and stay away from them."[207] If one must offer prayers for the king, as is customary, then one should pray for him to engage in good deeds. Ghazali states, "Upon dispensing with this, it is customary that the tyrant say some lies, and one must nod his head and approve. All of this is sinful."[208] However, there is sin in silence too, so it is best to stay away in all circumstances except if one is interceding on behalf of another Muslim or protesting an injustice. Ghazali suggests subtle ways to confront their abuses without eliciting punishment, because, as Michael Cook has shown, Ghazali believed it virtuous to do so.[209] If a religious scholar is unfortunate enough to have a king call upon him, then the scholar must honor the king who has sought him for his knowledge, but the scholar must also speak the truth and counsel the king toward justice.[210]

In contrast to Ghazali, Tusi and Davani take a cautious but pragmatic approach to advising subordinates on dealing with rulers. Within their discussions on how to behave with others in the social arena, the most attention is dedicated to how one should attend upon the ruler. This fact speaks to the composition of the treatises' audiences. They are not only male, wealthy, upper-class, educated elites, but also often subjects of the court. It is likely that in the time period these texts were written, it was not possible to be elite or significantly wealthy without having contact with court or even the king himself. The gist of Tusi's and Davani's advice is that in general, men should be supportive of their kings, well wishing, obedient to their commands, and willing to put their life, property, house, and home at the disposal of protecting their faith, community, wife, children, and city.

Despite their political-sectarian differences, Tusi does agree with Ghazali on how corrupting court life can be. Along with Davani, Tusi warns that "people who are not in service to the king should not take steps to seek proximity to them."[211] In general, distance between the ruler and the people is healthy. Tusi later states that for men, a king is an "obstacle [to] the enjoyment of the world and work for the hereafter."[212] So not only does working for a king rob men of opportunities to perform good acts that earn rewards for judgment day; it also destroys the pleasures of this life. Here Tusi warns readers that the supposed wealth and prestige of court life may be illusory. Life in service to the king is not easy and is not to be coveted. It requires one to suppress one's own ego and ethical principles.

In order to serve the king, one has to "train the *nafs* in their duplicity and [agree] with them in contradiction to one's own opinions."[213] A man in this situation must do difficult things with the intent of benefiting the greater good, such as keeping secrets and manipulating others.[214] Many of these acts could be considered contradictory to ethical behaviors produced by a balanced *nafs*, although Tusi makes an exception for utilitarian acts that are performed for the greater good.

Tusi further explains that when serving a king, one must pay close attention to the responsibility to be available at his beck and call and to praise all his actions. In addition, one should prepare carefully when providing counsel to the king, should guard the royal secrets, and should not repeat the king's faults. (The king, in turn, should not be unduly suspicious of betrayal by competent and trustworthy advisors.) Another prescription for servants of the king is that they should recognize that kings are demanding of "service and devotion from all of creation, and consider themselves correct in that and everything they do"; servants should also recognize that kings are used to being praised by everyone around them.[215] Regarding money and other benefits, one should not make direct requests of the king, but rather ask for a free hand in matters that would result in the king accumulating some profit. A servant should be willing to expend the master's wealth readily so that the king's predilection for amassing wealth does not become stinginess. Indeed, as discussed elsewhere, because the ruler–subject relationship serves as a model for all homosocial male master–subordinate relationships, we can draw parallels between conduct at court and domestic ethics. For example, a master should not provide his subordinate with benefits, but rather should provide him with the means of benefit. As I have argued elsewhere, this principle is consistent with how a father is meant to raise a son, focusing on the process of training him and his *nafs* before giving him access to wealth.[216]

Tusi has specific advice for the vizier, who holds the most envied position at court. The situation of this man is tragic, for the ones who covet his position, who set traps and scrutinize his every move, are supposedly his friends and associates. Tusi recommends that the vizier rise above the plots and act as if he has no knowledge of them; he assures the reader that "victory is always for the patient one."[217] Relatedly, Tusi advises that men of any rank should avoid attracting others' jealousy. For example, when asked a question in a group, one should not be the first to answer. Also, one should not seek favor over those whom the ruler holds close, such as the ruler's friends and relatives, because such a behavior is known as a marker of "foolish" people, or the *sufahah*.[218]

In summary, courtly conduct requires a man to carefully manage his masculinity, his pride, and the position for which he is employed at court. He must do so in light of the king's authority and the political posturing of court officials and other opportunistic courtiers. As I argued in previous chapters, masculinity functions in ethical cosmology within a hierarchy defined by gender, intellect, and spirituality; based on these characteristics, the ruler in the male homosocial realm holds the highest status of power and moral responsibility over others. Put another way, the ethicists imagine the king as the ultimate man, and even though they recognize that many actual rulers are unjust, the theoretical ruler whose attributes they describe exemplifies the masculine ideal. The ethicists' advice to the king's subordinates complements this view of the king. The king's status requires the average court official or court-appointed scholar (*'alim*) to maintain a high level of ethical masculinity to fulfill his own ethical potential. According to the ethicists, a man must take extra care to be ethical at court, because he is supposed to be a microcosm of the world with enhanced virtues and curbed vices. However, when he speaks at court or offers counsel to the king, he must be aware of proper courtly behavior, particularly the mandate that he seek to elevate the king at all costs, without negating his own ethical standing and responsibilities. In this way, court politics tests an ethical man's *nafs*, as do the domestic and public homosocial realms; it is an arena of competition between ethical masculinities of men from different social classes. However, court ethics is also premised upon the utilization of subordinates. The fact that at court the subordinates are men also on the path to ethical refinement gives us a glimpse into how an *akhlaq*-based world in which refinement is open to everyone might look. The ethicists' principle is to always do what is best to safeguard one's own *nafs* and that of others. However, as it stands as an ethical tradition, *akhlaq* excludes women and nonelite men.

Elite men's practice of homosocial love and their exertion of power over nonelite men in the hierarchical society contribute to the exclusive nature of *akhlaq* in the Ghazali-Tusi-Davani tradition. Although the tradition's goal is for elite men to mirror God's cosmic laws in enacting justice, becoming a vicegerent (*khalifah*) or a source of society's flourishing (*sa'adat*), the very definition of justice is premised upon inequality: the ethicists hold that humans do not carry equal moral or metaphysical value. At all levels of the microcosm and macrocosm, the ethicists define ultimate masculinity in terms of power, hierarchy of intellect, and ethical comportment in homosocial structures of court, civic, and community life. The very definition of what it means to be a man and the nature of his responsibilities in *akhlaq* are dependent upon his place in society's hierarchical structure. The more rational/intellectual a man is, the higher his ethical station and social status in the eyes of the ethicists, as they viewed mental capacity as a simultaneous indicator of refinement and social class. The more powerful a man is, the more potential and responsibility he has to do good and bring God's justice to society.

Ghazali, Tusi, and Davani all describe the ethics of male association, pure love and friendship between men, and behavior among different social classes of men in order to explain to the reader his place in society, his responsibilities, and the ways in which society ought to work. In order to be an ethical man in society, one must follow the principles of a balanced *nafs* in all homosocial settings. The institutions of learning, worship, court, and commerce are all sites in which the ethicists are concerned about men's behavior with one another. In these locations, men have the opportunity to demonstrate their ethics while attempting to earn a living, obtain an education or training, move up in social or political rank, or simply do their jobs. A man who aspires to be ethical must attract benefits to himself and his friends, must repel harms inflicted by enemies, and must take care not to injure others' dignity or violate their rights. In so doing, the innate tendencies of human nature, including the desire for association and the notion of preserving justice, must be sorted out on both the individual and societal (cosmological) levels.

Overall, the picture of the ethical man that emerges from the Ghazali-Tusi-Davani tradition is of one who is tempered in public, chary of revealing his feelings or secrets, and discerning of others' characters. In relationships with his superiors, he knows how to play a supportive role in their enterprises while maintaining his own integrity and prestige. He is a good friend, attending to his friends in their times of need and thinking about how to share his good fortune with them. He is a kind and equitable employer and generous to the poor. The masculine characteristics he possesses in social settings are nobility, uprightness, self-respect, and awareness, which are an extension of the traits of the ethical *nafs*. In short, he is a microcosm—a mirror of God's cosmos—as he operates in society, all while striving to be a representative of God's intent for human beings.

In the ethicists' view, the entire cosmos is created for men, radiating from the king at the center to the various ranks of subordinates and social classes around him. The enslaved and other nonelite men have a place in the hierarchy based on their occupational skills, but only as instruments of elite men's refinement. And outside of society's hierarchical structure, women stand as a class of their own. The construction of masculinity in the societal level of *akhlaq* guidelines, which conflates professional class and rational/intellectual potential, is disruptive to the God-conscious and intellect-centered goals of *akhlaq* in three ways. First, because women are excluded as persons with superior intellects, only elite men can be the true lovers of other men, and thus only men can be vicegerents (*khalifahs*). Because the hierarchy prohibits social mobility for nonelite men, regardless of their intellectual capacities, they too are excluded from vicegerency (*khalifah*). Second, societal ethics is based on hierarchical power structures that are meant to uphold definitions of justice that are inherently unjust because they are premised on inequality. Finally, because social ethics upholds social hierarchy, it entrusts too much power to the sovereign or elites to create justice. In this system based on the subordination of others, the subordinates are at the mercy of the elite men with the most power to do good (or be corrupt). The ethics is based on the intellect as a primary standard for refined humanity; however, because the concept of the intellect maps onto the social hierarchy of occupation and gender, the intellect itself becomes a corrupt standard for moral worth. I take up this contradiction between social hierarchy and the exclusivity of the goals of *akhlaq* in the conclusion of this book.

Conclusion

Prolegomenon to Feminist Philosophy of Islam

The world and the work of this world are nothing upon nothing /
I have seen this truth a thousand times / Until now I didn't know
about lies and pain, but the Alchemy of Happiness is my friend.
—HAFEZ

Modern engagement with the Islamic ethics tradition almost entirely
ignores the gendered and hierarchical nature of the genre. We find evidence of the problem scattered across cultural sites as mundane as
reviews of the *akhlaq* texts on Amazon.com and Goodreads.com. In a
review of the Kindle edition of a translation of the *Kimiya-i Sa'adat* from
1909, a female reader named Georgiana T. laments, "I like everything in
this book except his views on women and the role of women. . . . I was
all in awe and admiration up until that page which showed that al-Ghazali
is still a man of his times. I felt slightly offended as a woman to learn that
the teachings were actually not addressed to me, but to a Male. Otherwise, great book."[1]

Likewise, S. Fadlamoula praises the book as being "inspiring and
meditative" but realizes that "It is not until you get to that chapter [on
marriage] that you realize he is really only talking to men, as if spiritual
duties were a gendered thing. He speaks of women as if they couldn't
mentally and intellectually develop enough to grasp, let alone realize his
message. If you can excuse this to a mere consequence of reading a book

that is at least a millennium old (despite which, its message remains relevant and novel), you will find great value in this book."[2]

A third reviewer, out of countless others, states unequivocally: "This book is not intended for women! While I enjoyed reading a lot from it, it stroke [sic] me at the end, when the author was advising on how to get a proper wife, who would cook and take care of all the mundane things, so that the religious affairs of the MAN would be much eased as he doesn't have to bother with those things. . . . Clearly I understood at that point, oops, this book was not for me, I am a woman, my role is in the kitchen."[3]

These twenty-first-century readers' ambivalence toward a foundational Islamic ethics text arises from the fact that, on the one hand, the text is distressingly male normative, implying women's exclusion from Ghazali's audience, while, on the other hand, it leaves them with the strong sense that the text still has something worthwhile to say to them. These reviews, and other reader responses like them, serve as prompts to critique the ways in which *akhlaq* texts, particularly those of Ghazali but also others in the tradition, are being reproduced in the present day without adequate reflection on their gender-biased metaphysical suppositions or the problematic hierarchies in their ideal structure of society—or reflection on the effects this unexamined reproduction may have on modern female or nonelite male readers. The texts' assumptions about gender and hierarchy are off-putting precisely because the texts still enjoy influence over ethical thought and practice in a world where some consider these assumptions exclusionary and problematic.

The ambivalent online reviews of Ghazali's ethics text signal a larger unresolved problem in Islamic ethics: contemporary attempts to describe Islamic ethics are beset by a lack of tools for critically engaging with the premodern genre of *akhlaq*. In the case of the biopic-documentary from 2004 I describe at the beginning of this book, Ovidio Salazar's film *The Alchemist of Happiness*, the film adulates Ghazali, and yet all but erases his wife, even fetishizing this erasure by depicting her waiting on Ghazali in pious submission to his needs. The film thus becomes an example of a modern engagement with the Islamic ethics tradition that entirely ignores the gendered and hierarchical nature of the genre. While Salazar fetishizes women's silence, the online reviewers of the *akhlaq* texts, lay readers, point it out and relate it to their own feelings of exclusion from the audience.

Hafez captures the fundamental problem in his poem that I excerpted in this conclusion's epigraph: namely, the premodern Islamic ethics treatises *Kimiya-i Sa'adat, Akhlaq-i Nasiri*, and *Akhlaq-i Jalali* have long been embedded in Muslim thought as truth. Read thousands if not millions of times over by Muslims around the world over the past eight centuries, these texts are so foundational as to be perceived as identical to Islamic normativity and even reality itself. Yet, troublingly, these texts also contain internal contradictions that raise rather difficult questions. For example, how do the *akhlaq* ethicists begin with a seemingly egalitarian metaphysics but use it to construct patriarchy and social hierarchy? How do the ethicists construe only elite men as possessing ethical potentiality? What is the place of women and nonelites in the Islamic philosophical ethics tradition? I have explored these questions throughout this work by reading the *akhlaq* texts through the lens of a gender analytic, uncovering the conceptions of gender and hierarchy embedded in these texts as they present ethics of the self, family, and society. I have argued that the ethicists' metaphysics and their virtue ethics are both hierarchical and contradict their own overarching goal of *akhlaq*, which is to create the vicegerency of God that in turn facilitates conditions of human happiness and fulfillment of humans' cosmic purpose.

What my readings reveal are the many ways in which the *akhlaq* texts are based upon concepts of being, ontology, and metaphysics that are actually not egalitarian at all, but rather starkly gendered and hierarchical in nature. That is, women of all classes, men of lower classes, and enslaved people are excluded from the discipline of ethics on the assumption that they are less rational or less human. Further, women as a class are construed as merely instrumental to elite men's ethical endeavors, which are to order the *nafs* and achieve vicegerency (*khilafah*). Despite these exclusions, though, *akhlaq* paradoxically remains compelling for a range of readers, perhaps because it is the genre that most provides a picture of how Muslim scholars have delineated adherence to faith commitments on a cosmic scale. *Akhlaq* focuses on the *nafs*, including its default propensities and emotions, as well as its ability to account for individuals' circumstances, upbringing, and socialization. Unique to this genre, the ethicists appeal to emotions involved in relationships with spouses, children, friends, and foes (albeit only through a male perspective). The genre is sensitive to individuals' needs, in that it is oriented around the pursuit of a *khilafah*-centered life: one that strives to fulfill divine purpose by cultivating the self and fulfilling ethical obligations to other humans. By contrast, other normative genres of Islamic thought, such as *fiqh* (jurisprudence) or *sufi* (mystical) discourses, orient their ideal subjects to a worship-centered (*ibadah*-centered) life or blessing-seeking (*thawab*-seeking) life.

Mindful of the status that *akhlaq* texts hold in the Islamic intellectual tradition, as well as in contemporary Muslim thought, this concluding chapter serves as a prolegomenon to a feminist philosophy of Islam. In this chapter, I identify the philosophical problems that arise as a result of my feminist reflections on the Ghazali-Tusi-Davani *akhlaq* tradition and that warrant continued philosophical engagement. It is not the intent of this study to pinpoint ways to apply the principles found in *akhlaq* texts to today; rather, my intent is to reflect on how we might engage with these texts philosophically and explore answers to the philosophical problems they pose. Such a philosophical engagement is fruitful and necessary because these texts address concerns that pertain far beyond the genre of *akhlaq* and beyond Muslim contexts. In short, they pursue perennial human questions about how to live. Toward this end, I review the findings of my study and discuss the need for philosophical approaches to the study of gender in Islam. Then, in the remainder of the chapter, I consider four central philosophical problems posed by the male-centered *akhlaq*: rationality as a standard for defining the human and human capacity, the contradiction of patriarchy and *khilafah*, essentialization in the representation of women that leads to new hierarchies, and individual ethical refinement at the cost of utilization of other individuals.

FINDINGS OF FEMINIST READING OF *AKHLAQ*

As my reading reveals, the texts frame the ethical man's ultimate goals, and the means by which he is to achieve them, as requiring the subordination of people who are thought to be deficient in rationality: namely, women of all classes and men of lower social classes. According to these texts, the ultimate goals for the ethical man are twofold: happiness/flourishing (*sa'adat*) and vicegerency (*khilafah*). The former is achieved by ordering one's *nafs* using *tahdhib-i akhlaq* and becoming an *'alam-i saghir* (microcosm of the world) unto oneself. Then, the latter is achieved by becoming a source of happiness/flourishing (*sa'adat*) or justice (*'adalat*) for people in one's household and city. The crux of the *akhlaq* texts is rationality, a faculty whose possession and use are explicitly associated with elite masculinity. In order for a man to reach either version (happiness/flourishing or justice) of the goal of *akhlaq*, he must subdue his irascible and concupiscent faculties to his rational faculty, promoting justice by placing things where they belong and ordering provisions for everyone around him according to their deserts. The ethical man practices moderation in all things, including eating, drinking, and relations with family, friends, and enemies. He works hard to train his *nafs*, learn his craft, and marry in such a way as to support God's creation. He ensures that the *nafses* of his wife and children are disciplined, and he continuously respects his father while financially supporting his mother. He has the ability to live a streamlined life, pragmatic and utilitarian. Yet, according to the ethicists, all of these ethical behaviors are achieved for the benefit of people who are thought to be deficient in rationality—that is, women in general, and men of lower social classes. Elite men achieve rationality so they do not have to.

The ethicists do have their share of justifications, however unsatisfactory, for elevating elite men over all women and over men of lower classes. First, they appeal to natural law, authenticating their patriarchal visions of society by ascribing their conception of ideal manhood to natural laws of God's creation and defining the metaphysics of the self using descriptions of human nature. Second, although the ethicists hail from differing sectarian perspectives and epistemologies, they refer to shared scriptural sources for support. Third and most significantly, the backbone of the *akhlaq* texts' patriarchal ethics are the authors' core assumptions about the nature of gender and intellectual hierarchies among people of differing classes. The gendered nature of their ethics supersedes any sectarian or epistemological allegiances they may have about the origin and authority of moral knowledge. In the *akhlaq* authors' view, women's *nafses* have intellectual defects, and they are thus limited to two roles. In their role as wives, women are charged with managing the home so that their husbands can occupy themselves with the lofty goals of transcendence and becoming microcosms of the world. In women's role as mothers, they are biological vessels for carrying and nourishing children in their early years. Similarly, the ethicists' view of men of lower social classes is that they are intellectually deficient, and therefore their role is likewise to provide ancillary support to men of higher social classes by fulfilling social and economic functions according to their skills. The ethicists' assumptions about gender and hierarchy, largely submerged in prior readings of these texts, are revealed and explicated by my close readings of the *akhlaq* texts.

Yet, even though my gendered reading of the *akhlaq* texts reveals their troubling exclusion of women, lower-class men, and enslaved persons, the tradition still remains deeply important to Muslim thought both historically and epistemologically. *Akhlaq* texts take on universal questions and themes as they offer guidance on how to live as an individual, in a family, and in society. And it seems clear that, for all their gendered elitism, the texts in some sense succeed in providing readers with answers to perennial questions on how to live the good, moral life in service of God's plan. Even as the *akhlaq* texts explicitly support elite male power, they simultaneously elevate a core constitution of humanity, the intellect, that may possibly be available to a much wider range of humanity. The value in these texts lies in the questions they ask about what makes us human and about the purpose of human life. Admittedly, the answers they develop to these questions entail an understanding of the self as male, the home as male-dominated, and society as a hierarchy headed by elite and natural male leadership. Still, it is possible for us to sort out how the views expressed in the texts are historically bound (concomitant to prevailing gender assumptions of the times), and how we might answer these same questions about the good life differently in the twenty-first century. At stake in engaging these texts is not just women's access to philosophical-ethical-religious thought about how to live the good life, but also the substance of that thought itself: the very definition of what it means to be human, the possibilities for women and subjugated others to exist in metaphysical understandings of the world, and the opportunities for virtue ethics to accommodate women, as well as men.

If we cannot dismiss the importance of these texts, then we must develop a set of tools for engaging with them philosophically in light of their implicitly gendered and hierarchical assumptions. The question is, how can highly celebrated *akhlaq* texts, which are even reproduced in convenient Kindle editions for popular consumption worldwide, still hold ethical validity and be read widely despite their problematic status as male normative? Can ethics texts that marginalize women and have a narrow vision of masculinity be recovered? Can an entire ethical tradition meant for men be in some ways useful to women? Can there be a virtue ethics, or account of transcendence and *khilafah*, that does not in some way depend on the utilization or immanence of others?

The problem runs deeper than the fact that the texts are rhetorically addressed only to men. Such a lexical issue could be solved with clever grammatical tricks and translation. The real problem is that the discipline of *akhlaq* itself—the path to happiness and fulfillment of God's intent for humanity—is, at its core, designed only for elite men and is reliant on the subordination of all others. It is an ethics of exclusion. What is the meaning of ethical refinement or good society, if only some people get to experience these particular ends? The issues underlying these questions are profound, raising still more questions about what constitutes knowledge, who has access to knowledge, and how we understand humanness. Considering such questions requires a philosophical framework, which as I show in the next sections, is the culmination of my argument.

TOWARD A FRAMEWORK OF FEMINIST PHILOSOPHY OF ISLAM

What I am advocating is a philosophical turn in the field of gender and Islam: a turn of our attention *away* from an exclusive focus on how Islamic texts have historically been read and what the authors appear to have meant to say about divine intent, and *toward* questions about the texts' philosophical underpinnings and the ongoing philosophical problems they pose. What philosophical assumptions about reality, the cosmos, and human nature are embedded in these texts? And once those assumptions are explicated, what alternative readings about ethical human behavior are possible? Such an expansion in approach will, I hope, produce feminist-philosophical theorizations of Islam in its various plural forms and practices, which can then accommodate diverse subjectivities, identities, and theoretical positions. The resulting framework might be one that blurs the lines between feminist philosophical approaches and Islamic philosophy. In order to achieve such a philosophical turn, though, we must first resolve the gap between the study of philosophy and the study of gender in Islam. I argue that this gap can most fruitfully be addressed by developing a feminist philosophy of Islam that draws on sources ranging from feminist philosophy of religion to Islamic texts and Muslim praxis.

Muslim feminist[4] scholarship on Islamic sources first emerged in the 1980s as a feminist-academic response to traditional forms of religious authority that exist both within and outside the academy.[5] Pioneers of that field, such as amina wadud and Asma Barlas, saw their work as developing feminist hermeneutics dedicated to unreading patriarchy in the Qur'an and critiquing male-centered exegesis. Recently, following the publication of Aysha Hidayatullah's important work that questions the effectiveness of feminist hermeneutics to override gender inequality in traditional exegesis of the Qur'an, Muslim feminist scholars of the Qur'an are beginning to debate feminist conceptions of theodicy and ontotheology, without necessarily using these terms. A philosophical framework could clarify feminist approaches to such concepts, either from within or outside faith perspectives or both.[6]

Assimilating feminist philosophy of religion to Islamic contexts is challenging because, to date, scholarship on Muslim philosophy has mostly ignored the category of gender, while feminist/prowomen's scholarship on Islam has mostly[7] taken historical, legal, or hermeneutical approaches. Several feminist scholars of Islam have indeed employed the category of Islamic ethics, especially Kecia Ali and amina wadud, although their understanding of ethics mostly rests on an Islamic ethos of justice. The desire to probe what Islamic ethics can mean first prompted me to undertake this textual-critical engagement with the genre of *akhlaq*.

However, despite the use of Islamic ethics in Muslim feminist discourses, there are several reasons why feminist philosophy of Islam has not developed. First, as Nancy Frankenberry has pointed out, philosophy of religion has been normatively Christian and Eurocentric, making it less hospitable to other traditions.[8] Second, up until a few decades ago, Islamic studies had almost exclusively been housed in Oriental studies programs that did not consider gender as a category of inquiry, although purporting objectivity in the study of Islam. As a response, feminist scholars of Islam have carved out a space in the discipline of religious studies in which they can critique male-centered concepts in Islamic texts or practices, whether from a historical perspective or from a constructive-theological one, with some overlaps between them. However, now that the study of Islam is included in the discipline of religious studies (and its scholars comprise six program units in the American Academy of Religion and deliver over one hundred papers annually),[9] arguments by scholars of Islam that can be construed as normative are seen as suspiciously departing from the so-called objective or scientific study of religion. This suspicion of Islam scholars' normativity, however, ignores the fact that nearly *all* feminist scholarship, across all disciplines, contains some implicit or explicit constructive claims about women, society, or patriarchy among their deconstructive or historical claims. In reference to her work on Muslim anti–domestic violence efforts in the United States, Juliane Hammer has reflected on the "inherently political project" that is gender studies of Islam.[10] We see a dichotomy in Islam and gender studies between historical and constructive faith-based claims imposed by male normative commitments to religious studies, a dichotomy that does not make sense for feminist scholarship in any field, including Islamic studies. However, even though as a Muslim woman I have a personal stake in discourses about Islam and gender, I am advocating for asking different questions than those of belief in order to have a more productive, philosophically driven conversation that addresses gender inequality and human hierarchies.

A major scholarly benefit in taking a philosophical turn in gender and Islam is that it enables us to shift away from the debate that dichotomizes history of religion versus theology, or that dichotomizes deconstructive versus constructive inquiry altogether, and turn toward feminist concerns in religion and ethics, such as gender hierarchy and oppression, in a way that neither discounts nor privileges either historical or faith concerns. In feminist philosophy, the link between philosophy and history of philosophy enables us to orient ourselves to our present, feminist concerns, thereby uncovering fissures in ethics texts, such as the metaphysical tension we are concerned with in this study. Michele LeDoeuff has argued that history of philosophy (including feminist history) *is* a philosophical activity, precisely because one must engage with what has been "thought" and "unthought," or left out. But she argues that we must think of philosophy and its history in a symbiotic relationship, "as a dynamic which can lead to and from each other."[11] For LeDoeuff, philosophy has neither "completion [n]or beginning" and is always alive and moving; philosophers are aware of the discipline's history, and of what might be missing from that history, and they are able to reflect on what might be needed in that discipline moving forward.[12]

Reflecting on LeDoeuff's proposal of the continuation of thought as a feminist philosophical approach, Genevieve Lloyd argues that in order to think of the relationship between philosophy and the history of philosophy as a continuation, we must make a radical shift to the present: "it is from the standpoint of the present that we see tensions that the author could not, between the explicit philosophical content and the imagery through which it is expressed—tensions which reveal the 'shameful face of philosophy.'"[13] This orientation point of the present moment enables us to see the shame of the metaphysical tension in *akhlaq* texts, which is the ethicists' a priori recognition of the *nafs* of all human individuals as the same, even as they consider all women and men of lower social class as having deficient rationality, and therefore lesser humanity. Orienting to the present allows us to recognize these tensions and also propose philosophical resolutions to them.

Some scholars recognize the hierarchy in Islamic philosophical thought but tend to sideline it. For example, attempting to resolve elitism in the Ibn Sinan tradition of Islamic ethics, Cyrus Zargar writes, "an ethical system that recognizes various types of virtuous conduct or even rankings of people will be open to the charge that it is elitist. . . . Because of the egalitarian impulse in modern thought, many of us will object to such ethical systems, or at least to what we perceive as elitist in them. . . . We say we can revive ancient virtue ethics . . . in a more classless, rankless, and thus 'modern' setting."[14] He goes on to sideline this concern by arguing that there are bigger concerns in the consideration of Ibn Sina's work: "Certainly, Avicenna pondered the wellbeing of all humans, including those who would not or could not achieve the completion of the intellect. . . . The major restriction seems to be that the most profound truths of philosophy would endanger the necessary, if incompletely true, beliefs of the masses."[15] But "the masses" are the excluded ones in the first place. Although Zargar acknowledges that a revival endeavor is difficult because Ibn Sinan ethics are "built upon the premise that some are inherently more qualified for perfection than others," the modern setting, in ideal or reality, is not as he states "class-less" or "rankless."[16] But the problem of the texts is not just the differences in Islamic ethicists' assumptions about individual capacity for refinement, which is a strategy that focuses on the agent. As I discuss later, the problem of Islamic philosophical ethics also lies in the supposedly virtuous behaviors and acts one is meant to carry out in accordance with the ethics tradition that depend on exclusion and utilization of others.

It is a familiar criticism of feminist readings of premodern Muslim texts that feminists are anachronistically concerned about things that the authors of the texts themselves were not concerned about doing. This criticism is not accurate. On the contrary, feminist philosophers are concerned with the same fundamental question as medieval philosophical ethicists: how to live. Lloyd writes in her precise account of why the shift to a present perspective may seem anachronistic and controversial, "We do not simply judge past meanings from a standpoint of perceptions available from the present; we appropriate insights drawn from the text to our own concerns."[17] The specific concerns of feminist philosophers within the philosophical ethics of how to live are inclusivity and justice. Shifting to the present "opens philosophy out to concerns not circumscribed by what authors think they are about. But the 'outside' of philosophy that intrudes on the text now goes beyond the author's cultural context. . . . The text is opened out not just to its own cultural context but to the independent concerns of the contemporary reader herself."[18] So then, feminist philosophy of Islam that contemplates the history of philosophy does not exist for the purpose of judging how sexist Muslim ethics traditions such as *akhlaq* may be; instead, it asks how the principles of *akhlaq* have pervaded Muslim thought and praxis, what can be appropriated, and what are the philosophical problems that the psychological and sociological program of the *akhlaq* texts poses for feminist visions of Islamic philosophy, whatever these visions might come to be.

Another payoff for developing the framework of feminist philosophy in gender and Islam is the ability to engage with the critiques of feminist scholars of Greek thought, since, as I discuss in chapter 1, Islamic ethics is a continuation of that tradition. In particular, this engagement allows us to ask the question of whether misogyny is intrinsic or extrinsic to the texts, which is significant to the question of how *akhlaq* texts can be read in the present. Feminist scholars of ancient Greek philosophy, which is the epistemological forerunner to the *akhlaq* tradition, have grappled with the question of whether misogyny is extrinsic or intrinsic to the ethical principles of those traditions. Christine Senack writes of Aristotle that "all one needs is general knowledge in areas such as biology, sociology, and psychology, to offer evidence against and successfully refute Aristotle's ideas about what sort of creatures women are."[19] To Senack, it has become self-evident that Aristotle is profoundly mistaken about the nature of women, as any number of feminist critics have observed. But his gender bias has lasting systematic effects that make them intrinsic in nature. Irigaray holds that it is impossible to redeem a philosophy that allows for the systematic erasure of women in its very language and structure. She argues that to have a philosophy that truly applies to women, a new ethics must be written with new, nonsubjugating language centering a "sensible transcendental" that recovers women's subjectivity.[20]

If we accept the possibility of intrinsic misogyny in *akhlaq*, then, because the very soul in question is imagined to be that of a man, an *akhlaq* in which women participate will require different concepts of the human soul itself. Following that, a virtue ethics inclusive of women could emerge from metaphysics that is inclusive of women. It is not sufficient to simply add women to an existing structure of virtue ethics, notwithstanding one anonymous response to Georgiana T.'s Amazon.com review that suggests such an appending is the solution to her problem of feeling excluded:

> At the time of Ghazali, mainly men were responsible for bringing money and food to their family. . . . What Ghazali means is that sharing [sic] the workload between wife and husband so that they both have enough time for additional prayers or other religious affairs. Although some parts of the book indeed seem to be addressing men directly, I do not think those parts are enough to validate the idea that the teachings in the book [are] only for males.[21]

The commenter acknowledges a historical gender disparity, but then makes the unfounded claim that Ghazali's principle of wives' instrumentality—that their role is to support their husbands' spiritual refinement—is in fact a principle of mutual responsibility between husband and wife. Following this, the commenter makes the general statement, perhaps based on wishful thinking, that the book is for women too. Such a sentiment ignores the historical fact that the ethicists imagined *akhlaq* to be enacted only by men, and therefore, their project not only reflects gender inequality but also requires a world and a cosmos in which men subjugate women and other nonelites to achieve the goals of *akhlaq*. The critique of intrinsic misogyny in *akhlaq* exposes several philosophical problems in the texts, especially the ways in which ethics has been constructed as an exclusively male tradition. However, as I discuss later, the greatest insight into the problems of misogyny posed by the *akhlaq* texts is found in works by feminist philosophers who argue that misogyny is extrinsic to Greek and Greek-inspired philosophies, and then ask what can be done with these traditions.

Feminist philosophers of religion have also theorized feminist concepts of the Divine. Probing the philosophical meanings of the Divine, and not just their metaphorical import, could help us to understand the historical connections between the origins of the social patriarchal order and male imaginations of the Divine as male. Irigaray and Mary Daly have both problematized the patriarchal concepts of God and theorized what feminist concepts of God would look like, as part of a larger effort to facilitate women's access to the Divine and reflect on women's full subjectivity. Frankenberry recounts the feminist critique of the social effects of traditional theism, the construct of a male god, with uncanny resemblance to the patriarchal effects of *akhlaq*:

[Theism] justif[ies] various social and political structures of patriarchy which exalt solitary human patriarchs at the head of pyramids of power. Drawn almost exclusively from the world of ruling class men, traditional theistic concepts and images legitimate social and intellectual structures that grant a theomorphic character to men who rule and relegate women, children, and other men to marginalized and subordinated areas.[22]

Unsurprisingly, the social effects of theism that Frankenberry articulates are analogous to the ideal effects of patriarchal cosmology from the *akhlaq* texts. While theism is mainly a Christian description of God, the critique holds true for the Muslim ethicists' imagining ideal men's virtues in their descriptions of God, which, in turn, solidifies their preeminent ethical standing in the household and society. The ethicists believed that patriarchy mirrors the cosmos; they looked at the state of male-dominated society, believed it to be beneficial, and imagined that God created the cosmic order on an analogous patriarchal structure. To be clear, God in Muslim thought is not male, at least not consciously. Although Muslims anthropomorphize God to some extent through constructs of the hand of God or the eyes of God, there is much discussion that resists thinking of God as a man, largely in response to pervasive Christian images of God as father or as Jesus. For example, scholars refer to the Qur'anic verse that states that God neither begets nor is begotten as evidence that God should not be thought of as a male parent.[23] However, one need only to look at *akhlaq* texts to see how Muslim ethicists historically saw themselves in their description of God. Men are the patriarchs of the home and of society, and therefore imagine themselves as miniatures of the Ultimate (patriarchal) ruler of the universe of which men are meant to become microcosms.

Reflecting on gendered understandings of the Divine, amina wadud has used the pronoun *She* for God, specifically to decenter the default use of the male pronoun that reinforces the idea that God is male and therefore inaccessible to her.[24] Although wadud's use of feminine pronouns for the Divine is meant to be a theological attempt to ungender God, it also serves as a first step to uncovering the deeper philosophical connection between the patriarchal ordering of the world and men's projections of themselves onto concepts of the Divine, despite the coexistence of so-called feminine features of God in Muslim thought. In other words, the philosophical turn in studies of gender in Islam can help us understand the ways in which Muslims conceptualize the Divine, particularly in relation to gendered human bodies and experience.

This framing leads us to consider how each approach—theological, hermeneutical, and philosophical—addresses the problem of gender inequality. The problem posed by gender inequality in religion is a *theological* question insofar as humans (men) have projected male attributes onto God and God's intent for humanity, which lead some to question the nature of such a god.[25] But the problem is not a theological problem at all if one posits God's conceptual gender neutrality without the projection of human gender onto the Divine, which admittedly may not transpire for Muslims, given the male-centered nature of religious authority, even if there is strong conceptual support for it in Islamic sources. The problem of gender inequality in Muslim discourses may or may not be *hermeneutical*, as some scholars claim it to be, if Muslims do not always appeal to the Qur'an directly for justification of gendered double standards for human goals. Indeed the problem may be a *philosophical* one that attempts to work out notions of how human beings understand themselves, the Divine, and who creates that knowledge and based on which standpoints. The philosophical approach to the problem of gender inequality in religion utilizes methods that shift away from the question of what Divine intent is for humanity, and toward gendered existential questions that contribute Muslim perspectives to perennial human problems. To build such a framework, we must first identify and explore the nature of the philosophical problems the texts raise.

PHILOSOPHICAL PROBLEMS POSED BY MALE-CENTERED *AKHLAQ*

Akhlaq has at least three important features to recommend it for contemporary philosophical engagement: the texts privilege rationality and the intellect as a means to understand the meaning of the good life and as an attempt to unify human existence; they promote human happiness, welfare, and justice over mere self-indulgence and self-interest; and they frame individual striving for virtue as a potential contribution to broad social justice for all members of society. Each of these features holds promise for ending oppression under the auspices of living a *khilafah*-centered life. However, each feature also has some caveats that pose philosophical problems requiring deeper reflection. The first feature to recommend *akhlaq*, that it privileges rationality and the intellect as central human faculties, means that it can promote an epistemology for humanistic ethics that is potentially egalitarian and stands in contrast to unquestioned religious authority. However, this epistemology is only compelling if rationality is tied to hierarchical social roles, reserved for the elite or those deemed to be morally deserving. To untangle rationality from exclusionary practices requires philosophically addressing what it means to prioritize rationality. The second promising feature of *akhlaq*, that the texts promote a form of human happiness/flourishing (*sa'adat*) and general social welfare via the concept of justice (*'adalat*)—is only compelling if it can be relocated from its basis in a hierarchical power structure and reconstructed on a foundation of equality. However, defining individuals in society as equals requires tackling the problem of exclusionary definitions of humanity, of which there are many manifestations in gender, class, and race hierarchies. Finally, the third feature of *akhlaq* that supports an enduring philosophical engagement with the genre is its emancipatory possibility that virtuous, empathetic individuals have the potential to cause positive social change on a macrocosmic level. However, in *akhlaq*, it is demonstrably not the case that all individuals are accorded this potential. To imagine each individual's potential to cause change requires rethinking what kind of change can occur in the context of hierarchy, and how an individual without power in that hierarchy might be able to cause change. Moreover, there is the question of at what point human responsibility for others turns into paternalism and exploitation. Can ethical refinement of any individual be achieved without the utilization of others? This third feature of *akhlaq*, in particular, requires addressing the social hierarchies built into *akhlaq* that may take the place of gender hierarchy. In other words, we must beware of the potential that addressing gender-based exclusion in *akhlaq* will lead to the emergence of new problematic hierarchies based on intersectional identities such as race and class.

In light of these compelling but vexing features of the Ghazali-Tusi-Davani tradition of *akhlaq*, I discuss in this prolegomenon four interrelated philosophical problems and potential avenues for their resolution via a framework of feminist philosophy of Islam: (1) the problem of having an exclusionary definition of humanity based on fixed hierarchy of rational capacity; (2) the problem of patriarchal, and therefore unjust, notions of *khilafah* (vicegerency); (3) the problem of the emergence of new hierarchies in addressing exclusion on the basis of gender in *akhlaq*; and (4) the problem of individual refinement through the utilization of women and nonelite others. Feminist philosophy does not have all the answers to these problems, but it is precisely through feminist philosophical reflection that we gain access to these core problems in *akhlaq*. These problems extend beyond this particular genre and are broader than specific gender concerns in Muslim traditions, and it is through feminist philosophy that we can begin to explore possible resolutions.

The Problem of Defining Humanity as Rationality: A Need for Liberating Reason from Exclusion

The *akhlaq* ethicists' elevation of rationality above the other virtues in their cosmology of humanity is promising in that it offers an organizing principle for human beings other than gender. Indeed, placing value in reason and rationality also often aligns with Muslim feminist strategies of scriptural interpretation because it breaks down the authoritarian approaches to religion.[26] And yet, the *akhlaq* authors' definition of rationality is exclusionary. As I discuss in chapter 1, even as the historiography of Islamic philosophical ethics shows that the human ability to reason has always been studied in contrast to religious authority, it has done so without problematizing the definitions of rationality and reasoning at play. Those definitions exclude women and nonelite others, who are believed to have deficient rational faculties. Considering that *akhlaq* has deployed rationality as a basis for excluding some humans from ethical refinement, we need a philosophical discussion of what a commitment to reason and rationality really means.

As I identified earlier, a major problem that the *akhlaq* texts pose is that they base the enterprise of ethics upon exclusionary definitions of humanity vis-à-vis individuals' different potentials to reason. They do this largely by prioritizing rationality as the primary faculty that defines ethical behavior, and assuming that only elite men possess enough rationality to fulfill human ethical potential. Ghazali, Tusi, and Davani all agree that rationality is the primary and best faculty of human beings. Even for Ghazali—who in principle disagrees according to his sectarian commitments that the source of moral knowledge is reason, arguing instead that it is religious authority—the moral life is only available to those who are capable of reasoned reflection on the moral life. The ethicists do believe that all human beings, including women and men of lower intelligence, are a priori in possession of all the faculties that comprise the *nafs*. Unfortunately, though, because the ethicists also use rationality as the element that defines human beings as distinct from other living creatures, they end up with definitions of humanity that are exclusionary. That is, elevating rationality above all other faculties dehumanizes those who are deemed as possessing less of it, namely, women, men of low social (and therefore intellectual) rank, all enslaved persons, and female children (male children grow into full rationality). While women can possess virtues that correspond to the concupiscent faculty, which they are thought to possess, they cannot display the virtue of wisdom, which originates in the rational faculty. The ethicists do not cite any specific reasons for why women or some men might possess less rationality, other than the circular reason that the jobs these people are required to do by virtue of their natural station obstruct the development of their rationality.

That females are always inferior to males is also not uniformly the case in the cosmology, even though the ethicists state that to be the case. The ethicists also believe all matter in the universe to be equal, with no atoms having higher intrinsic value over others. Thus, their hierarchy of humanity is at odds with this broader atomic equality as well as with assumptions that women have lower intellectual abilities, despite being in full possession of all the human faculties. This metaphysical tension between recognition of women's humanity and assertion of the inferiority of their human qualities, namely, their rationality, permeates the ethics of the domestic economy, in which husbands are meant to order their wives' *nafses* but are also meant to use their rational faculties for their own utility. Further, the overall hesitancy the ethicists express in the event of divorce is due partly to the cutting off of financial support that a husband provides for the wife; it is also due to the belief that the wife also has a *nafs*, and that treatment of her must take that into account.

In the elevation of rationality above the other faculties, it is not just that women are excluded; nonelite men also suffer. According to the *akhlaq* texts, these men are excluded from homosocial male structures and interactions, even though the texts' metaphysics and virtue ethics are male-centered. Ultimate masculinity is articulated in terms of elite men's lives, either making low-class or less intellectual men less masculine or simply denying their access to the science of *akhlaq* and therefore *khilafah*. How can a commitment to rationality avoid an exclusionary definition of humanity? Reflecting on Western philosophical traditions, feminist philosophers propose various ways of addressing exclusionary definitions of rationality, but these are limited in what they can contribute to feminist readings of *akhlaq* particularly due to the nuances of the vicegerency (*khilafah*) and justice (*'adl*) concepts, to which I will return later. Here I engage with five potential strategies for addressing women and nonelites' exclusion: constructing an ethics of care; reflecting on the concept of love for the rational soul embedded in the rational ideal; expanding the definition of rationality itself; decoupling rationality from its historio-cultural sexist context; and shifting away from valuing rationality as the basis of moral worth.

One strategy that feminist philosophers have previously used in grappling with the problem of women's exclusion from reason-based ethics is to devise an alternative model, the ethics of care, which promotes human flourishing by assigning moral value to care work and elevating individual and social well-being. Some argue that an ethics of care is necessary because the standard of rationality is always selective and bound up with the ontology of women. Carol Gilligan defines the ethics of care as centralizing the virtues of care and compassion that arise in the "psychological logic" in interpersonal relationships.[27] Proponents of this ethical paradigm often contrast it to the rational ideal's lack of female concerns, such as kindness or emphathy, as well as the rational ideal's exclusion of women from moral life. Further, Gilligan has critiqued the privileging of rationality for ignoring the role of emotion and situational concerns of human life.[28]

However, refocusing ethics on care does not necessarily address women's exclusion from rationality that serves as the basis of definitions of humanity. The ethics of care critiques of the rational model of ethics only partially apply to *akhlaq* since men are instructed in ethics on a situational basis largely premised upon the (patriarchal) care one must have for one's wards; sympathy, compassion, and emotional responsiveness are also elements of virtues that all tamed *nafses* have, specifically the irascible faculties, in both men and women. As I have shown earlier, the ethicists place great moral value in men's ability to care, not in spite of their rational faculties, but because of them. Yet, there is still a disregard of women's needs since the scenarios they imagine in which men are meant to provide care are obviously centered on elite male life. Other feminist philosophers continue to value rationality for various reasons, including the argument that the capacity to reason can be an equalizer, and instead strategize on how to reframe an ethics of rationality.

Marcia Homiak offers a second strategy to liberate reason from exclusion, and that is to shift focus onto Aristotelian love of the self that is embedded in his rational ideal. As in the *akhlaq* definition, love of the self entails knowing one's metaphysical self and being in service to its betterment. Homiak's reading of rationality is that it already encompasses the ethics of care. In line with a Hellenic move that Ghazali, Tusi, and Davani make in accounting for compassion and situational ethics, Homiak argues that because the ethics of rationality encompasses care, it must be, in turn, exercised within the rational ideal or else it may become exploitative. Aristotle, along with Ghazali, Tusi, and Davani in the Islamo-Hellenic philosophical tradition, does not deny passion, emotion, or feelings to bring about rationality in an individual; rather, it is the mediation of emotion that gives rise to rationality. Homiak points out that by itself, the ethics of care can backfire because one can suffer from becoming instrumentalized by another, or tricked into compassion by those who are hurting themselves. Further, it is a fallacy to essentialize emotion and care as feminine concerns. Homiak's solution to the exclusion problem is that rationality must be accompanied by love: "the proper operation of reason is limited and constrained by the specific feelings constitutive of true self-love and civic friendship."[29] Even self-love, she argues, is love of the human soul's rational abilities and the same of other humans and their execution of rationality: "Aristotle offers a way to explain how reason and emotion (passion and feeling) can operate together to produce psychologically strong and healthy individuals—individuals who take pleasure from their own lives and from the lives of others, who are caring and concerned but not in ways that are destructive of their own self-esteem, who are independent while retaining strong and enduring ties of friendship and relationship."[30]

For Homiak, far from a masculinist ethic, the rational ideal gives rise to love of all of humanity. More people can be the recipients of ethical treatment if love for rationality encompasses love for others' *nafses* and other persons. In the rational ideal, while loving others' selves is a tacit recognition of their ability to reason, it does not necessarily address the question of who is thought to possess more or less rationality, which can be addressed, as Helen Longino proposes, by further reflection on the definition of rationality.

Like Homiak, Longino holds that we need to keep valuing rationality primarily because abandoning it "collude[s] with [women's] cognitive subordination."[31] Women are rational too, and as LeDoeuff also points out, emphasizing care does not solve women's exclusion from ethics. Longino also points out that another line of argumentation that attempts to solve exclusion but fails is the acceptance of plural rationalities as an alternative to a singular standard of rationality. She argues that recognizing plurality in reasoning is not very different from creating multiple exclusive circles of people with fixed standards to measure others against—thereby multiplying the problem of exclusivity.[32]

As an alternative to adopting an ethics of care or emphasizing love for the rational self (or multiple selves), a third strategy for addressing women's exclusion from reason-based ethics is Longino's proposal to treat reason itself as *authoritative*, as opposed to authoritarian. She argues that what should anger us in philosophical history is not that women do not have capacity, but rather that what constitutes rationality and reason is so limited that it excludes women and other subordinates. Their actions have been deemed irrational. What is problematic is "confus[ing] the capacity [for reason] with the standards or criteria for evaluating exercises of that capacity."[33] The outcomes of people's actions are used to judge their ability to reason such that actions that seem irrational do not necessarily signify a lack of rationality of the individual undertaking them just because such acts may be defying common standards of behavior for any number of reasons. For Longino, people's actions should be judged separately from their ability to reason. However, Longino continues, not just any actions can be justified through reason, such as sexism or racism, because that would be an authoritarian (not authoritative) use of reason that regresses us back to authoritarian judgment of others' worth.

The question of how to define rationality in relation to religious authority and its authoritarian abuses is a familiar question in Islamic philosophy; yet this is still distinct from the question of whether or not rationality can be used as a tool for excluding women and others. Ghazali, Tusi, and Davani in the *akhlaq* tradition posit that rationality defines the human animal, but they exclude women from the category of rationality, and hence that of "human." Longino's proposal for avoiding authoritarian conceptions of rationality is to simplify its definition as the *ability to reason* and to demonstrate reason in order to convince authoritatively, but without authoritarian compulsion: "to be authoritative is to show the bearing, the relevance of one belief or bit of information to another belief or practice, in a way that can be appreciated, understood, by one's interlocutor, without supposing or claiming that it is decisive or determinative, unless in relation to rules agreed to by both. This would be to suggest that authoritative reasoning can be recognized as reasoning without commanding assent."[34]

According to Longino, we should be suspicious of definitions of rationality that (a) exclude people and (b) oscillate back and forth between denying that people have rational capacity and affirming when people do adhere to it, ostensibly creating an inaccessible standard of what rationality truly is. Longino holds that the definition of rationality should still be "flexible enough to accommodate pluralism."[35] It is through such a reflection on the definition of rationality and acts of reason as authoritative that we see another possible way to include nonelite others in rationality-based ethics, but it is one that requires us to philosophically question how knowledge and moral-religious authority are constructed, as I discuss in the next section.

A fourth strategy that feminist philosophers offer to liberate reason from exclusion is to wrestle rationality away from its culturally sexist history. It is important, moving forward, to revise the definition of rationality itself such that its standards include all people who reason, but who may reason differently. However, this move does not necessarily resolve the commitments of traditionalists who privilege classical discourses to historical exclusionary definitions of rationality as male that come in the guise of what is Islamic. Genevieve Lloyd's strategy for decoupling rationality from exclusion lies not in reasserting love in the definition of rationality or simplifying its understanding to the capacity and acts of reason so that it may become more inclusive, but rather in problematizing the cultural and historical context. LeDoeuff's calls for a shift to the present requires relegating the images philosophers use to their specific cultural context, and thinking collaboratively with them about the questions they ask. Lloyd argues that "past philosophers used the male–female distinction, consciously and creatively, to express ideals of reason. In consequence, features of the male–female distinction *as it operated in their cultural context* became part and parcel of understanding what it is to be rational."[36] The philosophers' declarations of women's intellectual deficiency then are incidental to their greater goal of defining rationality: what having it looks like, and what not having it looks like. Drawing on LeDoeuff, Lloyd argues that making women the foil for describing persons with rationality is an unthought (unconsidered) consequence of understandings of gender in philosophy; she holds that this "unthought" notion that women lack rationality can be rethought in a philosophical continuum.

Returning to Homiak, we see the possibility of retaining Aristotelian rationality if we eschew the historical-cultural sexist context. Homiak argues that just because the rational ideal has been "used to exclude particular groups from that ideal does not show that the rational ideal is defective."[37] Unlike for Longino, for Homiak, nothing is wrong with the definition of rationality; the problem lies in how it has been embodied (theoretically) in philosophy by elite men. She argues that "menial laborers, slaves, and women . . . fail to embody the rational ideal" in Aristotle, but studying closely how each of them fails to embody the rational ideal gives feminist philosophers a way to engender Aristotle's rational ideal.[38] She demonstrates that in Aristotle's rational ideal (which is similar in the Ghazali-Tusi-Davani tradition), everyone has the rational capacity, but not everyone has the awareness of that capacity, and so therefore everyone also has the capacity to become slavish to their own imbalanced faculties or to others in whose interests they act. Further, Aristotle believed in the existence of natural slaves, those who were actually enslaved, as well as women who were

> permanently stunted. Unlike free, male children, no amount of education and practice in decision-making, and no change in their economic or social circumstances, will enable women to deliberate properly about what is best. They may give too much weight to what is pleasant or to what appears to be good. In effect, a woman may give over the rule of her soul to its non-rational part and thereby endanger the proper functioning of the household. Hence decisions about what is best must be made for her by men. A free woman's

life will always then, be slavish, since her life is not controlled by her own decisions.[39]

Like Lloyd, but upholding Aristotelian rationality, Homiak believes that the exclusion of certain people on the basis of their natural irrationality is a cultural artifact, and one that can be decoupled from rationality when we consider that Aristotle believed that all human beings can lead slavish lives, including free elite men, when they give into concupiscent or irascible impulses, or act in favor of someone else's interest against their own. Homiak circumvents the important question of the natural defectiveness of nonelite others by arguing that, putting aside the historical-cultural exclusion, Aristotle's rational ideal applies to all those wishing to protect themselves from a slavish existence.

But is rationality really an equalizer in a society that is hierarchical, in which many people are born into situations in which they will in fact never have the opportunity to realize their potential? Instead, they are relegated to a slavish life without choice. Although Homiak's argument is successful in recuperating Aristotle's rational ideal, the question of women and nonelite men's reduced humanity remains. Her solution is that all individuals in society should share the menial instrumentalizing labor that obstructs the rational development of the nonelites. Because Aristotle's definition of menial labor allows for awareness, and therefore not slavish existence, if all citizens divide menial labor so as not to be mentally embrangled in it, then a rational life can, having accommodated some undevastating menial labor, not be exploitative.[40]

Still, recognizing women's full humanity is lacking in this formulation, so a fifth strategy that addresses exclusion is to problematize the very definition of humanity that rests on rationality. Such a feminist philosophical position surfaced in critiques of Peter Singer's argument that cognitive ability, which he holds can be objectively measured across the species, determines individuals' personhood and moral status. Singer's position, which insists that we can compare the cognitive functions of all species (and thus draw the line where rationality defines the human being), is consistent with the great chain of being that Arthur Lovejoy describes as fundamental to the Greek philosophical tradition—and that is also built into the Ghazali-Tusi-Davani *akhlaq* tradition. Drawing on feminist critiques of epistemology and moral theory, Rachel Tillman argues that moral subjects (those who know) and moral objects (moral knowledge) are determined by history, culture, and relational contexts and are also embodied by real persons, which means that they are not abstract or universal, but rather real, unobjective, and temporal. Tillman holds that

> Since each specific set of capacities emerges in a set of biological, species-determined living beings, these capacities do not necessarily retain their ability to function as criteria for evaluating worth when abstracted from their context and reapplied to other contexts and beings. . . . In complex living beings like human and non-human animals, capacity for [reason] is temporally determined, because capacity is *developmental*. Both innate and acquired capacities develop and may decline over time.[41]

In other words, since rationality is culturally specific and also embodied, it is both subjective and temporal. Even in cases in which there are permanent impairments to cognitive function (congenital, developmental, or accidental), Tillman holds that we cannot exclude human beings from personhood since our scientific knowledge about conditions of the brain are changing. So, in order to truly address exclusion of women or nonelites, we must abandon fallacious definitions of humanity that hinge on the ability to reason or on rationality.

I have argued that as it stands in the *akhlaq* tradition, rationality as the highest standard of human value is fraught with problems of the exclusion of nonelite human beings, especially women. Even as standards of reason are hurled about in attempts to discredit women, they are also used to define baseline definitions of humanity—and this move is a potentially equalizing one. As inspired by the philosophers cited earlier, there are five potential ways in which we can liberate reason from exclusion: by shifting toward an ethics of care; by emphasizing the concept of love for human potential within Aristotelian rationality and *akhlaq*; by rethinking the baseline definition of rationality as authoritative reason; by recognizing that rationality's exclusionary definition was a historio-cultural artifact; or by shifting away from rationality as the major criterion that defines humanity. Any strategy to address the problem of exclusionary definitions of humanity rooted in rationality requires further thought on the definition of humanity itself. An ethics of care does not really address hierarchy and exclusion, and perhaps concedes that women are less rational. Recasting rationality as love of all metaphysical selves or as individual authority and abandoning rationality itself as a unifying human definition are meritorious strategies but would require further philosophical discussions about what it means to be human and what human purpose is. Even the strategy of abandoning the historio-cultural definition of rationality would require abandoning the organizing principle of patriarchy, which is, I argue, built into the male-oriented concept of *khilafah*, the goal of *akhlaq* itself.

The Problem of Akhlaq's Selective Path: Deconstructing Patriarchal Khilafah

In *akhlaq*, individuals' capacity for reason, which determines their membership in the human race and their moral potential, also serves as the basis of their ethical relationships to other humans both at home and in society, to whom they have the responsibility to enact God's justice. This responsibility is captured in the concept of *khilafah* (vicegerency). The ethicists articulate ultimate goals of *akhlaq* in terms of achieving true happiness/flourishing (*sa'adat*), living an honorable life (*sharafat*), becoming a microcosm (*'alam-i saghir*) of the universe, or enacting the duty of a *khalifah* (a person who has achieved vicegerency). These four variations on the ultimate goal of *akhlaq* are connected through elite-male knowledge of the discipline of *akhlaq* and power over the collective on the basis of men's elite status and that knowledge. Although *khilafah* is an individual state, achieving it requires the interdependence of all individuals in society. Each person plays her own role, according to her aptitude, and receives according to her own moral deserts; meanwhile, the *khalifahs* of society self-actualize on the path of *akhlaq* and take care of everyone in society. This patriarchal arrangement reflects the order of the cosmos.

Because *khilafah* is tied to the moral potential of elite males, it is also exclusionary of women and nonelites. Thus, I argue that the key problem with the *akhlaq* concept of *khilafah* is that it rests on the assumption that some individuals know what is best for all of society by virtue of their male gender and elite status—that men know best, that there is knowledge to which only they have access, and that *khilafah* is really a goal exclusively for them. This is in a sense the very definition of patriarchy—society that is headed by (elite) men because they know what is best for everyone. That male ordering of society, in turn, benefits only men and others who uphold the patriarchy. Simply saying that becoming a *khalifah* can now be a goal for all Muslims (or all people) does not solve this problem with *akhlaq* because the *khalifah* has only ever been imagined by Muslim thinkers as a cosmic role that elite men play, one that is bounded and enabled by their privileged place in society.

Historically, the concept of *khilafah* has indeed been a patriarchal one, associated with male-only leadership in a variety of contexts, including Prophet Muhammad's companions' claims to succeed him after his death, as well as the later premodern period in which Muslim rulers proclaimed themselves *khalifahs*. In more recent memory, the concept of *khilafah* has been associated with the *Khilafat* Movement of South Asia, which sought to correct the loss of an imperial *khalifal* system with the fall of the Ottoman Empire at the onset of the colonial period. Through the *Khilafat* Movement, the concept of *khilafah* is associated with Muslim patriarchal order that, as any number of feminist historians have shown, many postcolonial Muslim states sought to restore through laws that regulate women's bodies. With such a strong historical association of the concept of *khilafah* with patriarchal order, philosophical interrogation of the concept must precede its feminist appropriation.

Given that we live in a world where not everyone has the opportunity to become a *khalifah*, how can we then reimagine the social responsibility of enacting justice—which is how vicegerency of God has been interpreted—as being the role of everyone in society? To explore the full extent of this philosophical problem, I discuss two related issues: first, the gendered nature of the concept of *khilafah*, which centers on specialized knowledge that constitutes the elite men's supposedly God-given or cosmic responsibility over nonelite others, and second, the unjust definition of justice embedded in the concept of patriarchal *khilafah*. I argue for the need to rethink definitions of justice and to decouple the concept of *khilafah* from patriarchy.

Although the concept of *khilafah* has been used to argue for human equality vis-à-vis equal human responsibility, it is philosophically bound up not with human stewardship of the world, but with male steward-ship and authority. This is, in part, because only men are viewed as full humans. With only men having the capacity for reason in *akhlaq* (as well as in other genres of Muslim thought), the knowledge and physical body required for achieving *khilafah* are also implicitly male. The way the eth-icists have imagined *khilafah* is that it comes about through the acquisi-tion of knowledge that is gendered male, specifically for inculcating male virtues and leadership. The knowledge that is worth knowing is male, and that is what makes men *khalifahs* over women and everyone else who is thought not to have the rational capacity for that knowledge. For this rea-son, gender-equal conceptions of knowledge require a deep philosophi-cal rethinking about what constitutes knowledge (what is worth know-ing), where it comes from, and who holds the authority to know. By knowledge here I do not just mean ultimate cosmic knowledge, but also the mundane knowledge about the known world and its inhabitants. These are central questions in feminist philosophy of religion that are based on standpoint epistemology/theory, which, although not without its own critiques for excluding intersectional gender-racial experi-ences,[42] is a position informed by the experience of oppressed persons in which there is no universal knowledge or impartial ways to acquire knowledge.[43]

Feminist scholars of Islam have long been critical of what texts and people compose religious authority, and critical of male-only religious authority and intellectual production; but few have considered the phil-osophical question of what is knowledge in Islamic thought. An excep-tion is Sa'diyya Shaikh, who has reflected on the role of experience in feminist epistemology for Islamic feminists,[44] and prior to this has argued that women's personal experiences are a valid form of exegetical/inter-pretive knowledge of the Qur'an,[45] though not specifically from a philo-sophical standpoint. We need more such reflections on what constitutes knowledge in Islamic thought in order for the concept of *khilafah*, which is the end goal of ethics, to be gender-egalitarian.

Khilafah as a goal of Islamic ethics is precisely a male-only enter-prise because the knowledge one must have to become a vicegerent (i.e., the science of *akhlaq*) is male-centered. So far, feminist scholars who have addressed *khilafah* in its cosmic relationship to human selves (*naf-ses*) created by God have used it as a Qur'anic argument for human equal-ity in terms of *nafs* and vicegerency. Asma Barlas writes, "God created men and women from the same self (*nafs*), made them vice-regents on earth (*khalifah*), charged them to be each other's guides (*awliya*), and will judge each *nafs* by the measure of *her* own endeavors in the end."[46] Amina wadud argues that the concept of *khilafah*, which she defines as trustee-ship or moral agency, enables a discourse of equality in which each per-son is responsible for enacting God's justice. Not unlike Ghazali's, Tusi's, and Davani's definition, wadud's *khilafah* resembles universal "citizen-ship" in the human race[47] and "is equivalent to fulfilling one's human destiny as a moral agent, whose responsibility is to participate in uphold-ing the harmony of the universe. With respect to society, harmony means justice."[48] She further argues that justice is served by belief in *tawhid* (belief in the unity and oneness of God), which requires the belief in equality of all human beings:

> *Tawhid* is the Arabic equivalent of monotheism, but because the word is an active participle, it has added dimension(s). I apply this to social justice by highlighting that a dual relationship with one God as essential to relationships among persons. This Islamic theo-logical principle mandates a direct and unmediated relationship between any person and God, which I use as an incentive for human-to-human relationships to be horizontal and reciprocal.[49]

Given these feminist allusions to Qur'anic egalitarianism, particularly on the ontological dimensions of concepts of *nafs* and *khilafah*, it would seem regressive to engage with *akhlaq* definitions of the same. However, it is not, as some have argued, that the *akhlaq* texts are antithetical to an egalitarian Qur'anic ideal and therefore should be ignored.[50] On the contrary, as Ayesha Chaudhry has argued, a comparison of the premod-ern patriarchal, idealized cosmology with an egalitarian ideal cosmology that shows they are "fundamentally irreconcilable" marks modern discussions of gender as having "serious theological and cosmological ramifications for modern Muslims' relationship to the "Islamic tradition."[51] Reflections on the *akhlaq* genre's conceptions of *khilafah* show us that premodern thinkers understood humans' roles in the cosmos differently than we do. The medieval Islamic ethicists see the goal of *khalifahs* as becoming *mirrors* of the cosmos—that is, they see men's responsibility to order the world as a patriarchy as following the divinely decreed nature of the cosmos—while feminist philosophers, in line with other moderns, view *khalifahs* as moral *agents* affecting some sort of change through which humans bring divinely decreed interventions to the cosmos. Since regarding men as mirrors of divine intent is still a common understanding of male roles in Muslim societies, the feminist project of shifting the concept of *khilafah* to moral agency requires philosophical reflection.

Ghazali, Tusi, and Davani were all aware of women's possession of *nafses*, their humanity. Yet, they only extend the enterprise of disciplining the *nafs* and the responsibility of *khilafah* toward men because they see the potentiality of disembodied, intellectual, and spiritual transcendence only in themselves, while they see only corporeal immanence in women, despite their humanity. For these ethicists, gender was, as it is now, arguably one of the fundamental ways of recognizing difference within humanity. Even if the premodern ethicists did not conceive of gender as a category of identity, they still were committed to gender roles, as evidenced by separate roles in virtue ethics and ideals of a gender-segregated society. Thus, whether or not egalitarian readings of human relations in the Qur'an are possible, the genre of Muslim thought that deals with metaphysics and philosophical ethics—and that is built upon male-centered definitions of the *nafs*, of its training, and of becoming a *khalifah* of God's justice—must be addressed on an equally philosophical level. Bringing ethical knowledge to bear only on regulating the particulars of human behavior is insufficient. In other words, to think that we can do without metaphysics is wrong. We always have an implicit metaphysics. If we are committed to egalitarianism, then we are committed to egalitarian metaphysics, and that project requires elaboration.

Tracing the epistemology of male superiority in the *akhlaq* texts to the inherited Hellenic notions of nature and human nature is a genre-specific form of patriarchy, but it still tells us about the embeddedness of gendered ideas concomitant to exegetical-legal concepts of men's *qiwama* or authority (which also appears by name in *akhlaq*)[52] and men's *wilayah* or guardianship. As wadud points out, *qiwamah* and *wilayah* are concepts originating from Qur'anic verses that demonstrate asymmetry in gender relations, but she emphasizes that there are only six or seven asymmetrical verses out of thousands that she argues follow an egalitarian ethos. Although reflection on the disproportionate emphasis on *qiwamah* and *wilayah* has exposed how these two concepts have caused the enactment of patriarchal laws, reading *akhlaq* shows us where that gender bias may originate on a deeper philosophical level. And those are core beliefs about gender differences among human beings that are simultaneously held by the *'ulama'* (ethicists who were also exegetes and jurists), not just prior knowledge, to ideas about *qiwamah* and *wilayah*. Wadud writes that *qiwamah* and *wilayah*

> are interpreted to deliver subservience of the female to the male in every kind of relationship between them: parent to child, brother to sister, and husband to wife. Once a means to overcome this asymmetry is proposed using the primary text to support it, then the path to transforming both the ethics and the politics of gender hegemony and all other forms of oppression is made transparent. Furthermore, this is built upon the faith-based location of accepting the Most Holy as partner in this liberation and even as its primary architect.[53]

In wadud's analysis, the concepts of *qiwamah* and *wilayah* are the cornerstones of how male superiority is justified in all male–female relationships from within a faith-based perspective, and thus a faith-based perspective is also needed to overcome the pervasive harm these concepts have done to women.

The historical gender inequality, however, is also a result of the deeply held philosophical position of the male as the natural *khalifah* of God, which manifests itself not necessarily through the Qur'anic or legal terminology *qiwamah* and *wilayah*, but through a perhaps even more implicit concept of direct vicegerency between God and man. Regardless of whether or not one believes in a divine origin of the concepts of *qiwamah* and *wilayah*, acknowledging that these concepts predate Qur'anic male superiority refocuses the question of how male superiority came to be Islamic away from questioning Divine intent altogether, toward human (male) endeavors to order society, the world, and the cosmos. Decoupling *khilafah* from gender inequality requires thinking not just about who is a *khalifah*, and what knowledge is required for *khilafah*, but also about what being a *khalifah* entails.

DECONSTRUCTING PATRIARCHAL *KHILAFAH*

The exclusivity of *khilafah* as imagined by Islamic ethicists is patriarchal and, indeed, contradictory to the goals of *akhlaq*. According to the *akhlaq* texts, in order for there to be justice in this world, humanity needs virtuous men to do their job of cultivating their [own] virtues, and everyone else needs to "stay in their own lane," by carrying out their respective purposes. The problem with that vision is that having elite men as the exclusive ones on the path of *akhlaq* leads to unjust conditions in the world. Enactment of the *akhlaq* notion of *khilafah* becomes the top-down meting out of justice. The perfect achievement of *khilafah* itself rests thus on unjust definitions of justice. The ethicists define justice as a virtue of fairness and equity that arises when an individual achieves other virtues, yet they gender the realm of justice as a male provenance by defining it as men's power to bestow upon friends and family according to their deserts. While enacting justice is meant to be one of the goals of *akhlaq* training, its definition is bound up in the male power of doling it out, determining recipients, and quantifying deserts.

In the scenario that not all people are meant to be on the path of *akhlaq*, with men alone thought to be in possession of rational powers and the ability to order society in a patriarchy, the nonelite others have no reason to engage in any virtue. In fact, according to the *akhlaq* texts, the virtues of the nonelite lie in supporting the male elite, not in participating in a collective ethical agenda, even one that is relative to each individual's own station. Ideally in the Ghazali-Tusi-Davani tradition, any evil generated by less rational persons who are not on the path of *akhlaq* is not enough to pervade the world or too much for the ideal patriarchy to control.

In effect, as Lisa Tessman argues is the case in Aristotle's ethics, it is only in the ideal patriarchal society in which one's own success on the path of *akhlaq* is equivalent to the success of the community—specifically, an elite man's ethical success is that of the cosmos.[54] The ethicists' view of the world is truly ideal, with ideal men as the only fully rational humans and an ideal world that can only be ordered by ideal men. Even in Tusi's and Davani's models of unvirtuous cities, the main cause of these cities' unvirtuousness is not that their forces of evil are too strong; rather, it is that the evil brought on by unvirtuous persons is not contained by strong enough leaders. It is not simply that virtue always wins over evil, but that male virtue (in patriarchy) is seen as the winning formula for a just cosmic order.

However, elite forms of *khilafah* do not bring about cosmic happiness. It is the patriarchal ordering of society itself, in conjunction with ideas about natural defectiveness of certain humans (women, the enslaved, men of lower class), that causes in those "lesser" humans the inability to reason or be virtuous, a harm that Claudia Card calls "moral damage" upon oppressed groups.[55] Although those who hold patriarchal views can claim that not all people are meant to achieve happiness/flourishing (*sa'adat*) or become a *khalifah* of God, I contend that in this nonideal, real world, patriarchy can ensure that eventually no one will, given that the path of *akhlaq* is not open to all and that this patriarchal exclusivity brings about a universality of unjust conditions. Those proclaiming that they are or have become *khalifahs* in the patriarchal context from which the concept emerges need only to look at the injustice to the persons they are ordering or utilizing to realize that patriarchal-*khilafah* does not bring about cosmic justice. Patriarchy as an ordering principle is contradictory to the goal of *akhlaq*—namely, the creation of a just, virtuous society in which all individuals are fulfilling their cosmic purpose. The next logical question—whether everyone's cosmic purpose is the same—leads us to another problem: that is, whether anyone's individual refinement can occur without the exclusion or utilization of some.

The Problem of Elite-Only Access to Ethics and the Re-Creation of Hierarchies: Incorporating Intersectional Concerns

The problem of elite-male-only access to ethics is dismantled not only by rethinking definitions of rationality and *khilafah*, but also by thinking through the interlocking hierarchies at play in the gender constructions found in *akhlaq* texts, which in turn influence reality. The question of how much access individuals have to ethical refinement is dependent upon the realities of their societal status. Feminist philosophers of race argue that dismantling hierarchies cannot involve a unified theory or be based on the fiction of unified experience of oppression, or else it risks the re-creation of new hierarchies. The reason for this risk is the now commonly accepted idea that gender is not a static category that can be essentialized, but rather a fluid one that intersects with multiple dimensions to human existence, including race, class, ability, variations in biology, sexuality, and so on. Each of these dimensions affects gendered identity and experience. What is less commonly accepted is that because many women, particularly women of color in predominantly white societies or transnational imperialistic contexts, face oppressions that are enmeshed with other extant hierarchies of race, class, sexuality, and so on, single-issue feminism that only advocates for gender justice inevitably does not break down gender hierarchies for individuals who rank low in other social hierarchies. In creating greater access to the path of *akhlaq*, it is therefore not enough to address issues of rationality or *khilafah* in the gender hierarchy. We must also consider other planes of personal identity.

My reflection on who the men and women are in the Ghazali-Tusi-Davani tradition has revealed problematic essentialized pictures of men and women as ethical subjects. While the texts easily lend themselves to a critique of a single dimension of hierarchy—particularly gender because the gender dynamics prescribed in the texts cross class, vocational, ethnic, and even racial stratifications that appealed to the massive expanse of the Persianate sphere from Anatolia to the far reaches of the Indian subcontinent—moving forward, I argue that feminist philosophy of Islam, and indeed the field of gender in Islam, must consider interlocking forms of oppression. This will both prevent the generation of new hierarchies in place of gendered ones, and also enable a more complete critique of gender hierarchy that accounts for the complexities of the category of woman.

Feminist philosophers of race, particularly black feminist philosophers, have argued for the need to consider multiple dimensions of difference, such as race and class, together with gender in breaking down hierarchies.[56] Two prominent contributions of black feminists to standpoint epistemology/theory are the concept of intersectionality (the idea that racial and gender identity and its oppression are concomitant),[57] and their continued advocacy of considering the experience of oppression in its various forms as a valid form of feminist epistemology. To be clear, intersectionality is not the use of "racial oppression as an analogy for gender oppression," a critique that Kathryn Gines makes of the works of Jean Paul Sartre and Simone de Beauvoir. Such work that treats "race as black man and gender as white woman . . . neglect[s] the situation of women of color" and ignores the intersectional nature of oppressions.[58] Critics of intersectionality such as Sonia Kruks argue that intersectional approaches bring about "debilitating subjectivism" and "deny more general visions and projects of emancipation."[59] However, as Anika Maaza Mann points out, "such general 'visions and projects' tend to replicate hierarchical power relations among women, for example, maintaining racism rather than challenging explicitly antiblack racism."[60] How can it be that standpoint theorists who argue that the experience of discrimination serves as a standpoint for emancipation also deny certain groups' experiences that necessitate more nuanced and careful moves toward emancipation? Mann explains that those who have experienced oppression based on a single identity marker, such as gender, are unable to imagine emancipation as richly as someone who has experienced the simultaneous oppressions of, say, race and gender together.[61] As Mann has shown using Sartre's theory of Us-object and We-subject, "there can be a blindness among the members of the We-subject and not simply a refusal to acknowledge the oppressive situation."[62] In other words, so normalized is the masculine as ethical that the ideal Muslim moral subject is invisible to men unless and until it is objectified by feminist terms in a "reversal of the gaze."[63] This act of reversing the gaze, in particular thinking through intersectional issues in gender justice work, has also been criticized as "intellectual slumming," to which Kristie Dotson has responded that a nuanced approach that incorporates race or class requires more, not fewer, intellectual resources than single-issue inquiry about race-only, class-only, or gender-only hierarchies.[64] Addressing a greater range of gender oppressions, those that are bound up with intersectional concerns, is what V. Denise James has argued "is a rejection of the supposed neutrality and universalist claims made by other philosophers."[65] We see this same supposed neutrality in the claims of those modern (mostly male) readers, scholars, and translators of Islamic ethics texts who argue that the texts are applicable to all Muslims regardless of gender, race, or class. They are not.

Indeed, in this book, I have tried to broaden gender-only critiques by reflecting on the ethicists' discussion of the class/vocation stratification of men, as well as mentioning race by itself or the discussions of race implicit in the *akhlaq* texts' few references to slavery and concubinage. Reflection on who are the elite Muslim men that the texts address, compared to their references to women and nonelites, necessitates consideration of the multiple dimensions of hierarchy. More specifically, the ethicists assume the elite men they address come from wealthy, moderately educated families, and social history shows that by and large the educated were also the wealthy, who held servants and slaves. The rank these men enjoyed above various women and men was also bound up with their wealth and professional status, if not their ethnic or racial advantages. Recall from chapter 3 that Tusi recommends that men not marry women who have more wealth than they do for fear of being dominated. In the Ghazali-Tusi-Davani rhetoric, men lord over women in terms of rationality, but also ideally and ethically do so in terms of their social or class dominance. Gender hierarchy takes on multiple forms in the texts, especially using the male/rational-female/instrumental trope, but the gender hierarchies also are bound up with class. Other premodern Muslim primary sources may reveal other dimensions of gender hierarchy that critiques of feminist philosophy of Islam could accommodate.

Reflecting on who are the women referenced in the texts also raises a related concern. Specifically, such reflections point to the need for attending to a philosophical concern about how the essentialization of women leads to the marginalization of some women and the consequent generation of new hierarchies. Aside from the few mentions of concubines, women appear as static, interchangeable accessories of men's ethical refinement. While the ethicists assume some variation in characteristics such as wealth or beauty, overall women are treated as a class of their own, wholly put aside from the nuanced profession-based stratification of men in society. Because women do not have a place in the social cosmology, they are ostensibly essentialized into a monolithic category, which, again, may be tempting us to only think of them in terms of gender hierarchies. Yet, we must remember that, by and large, the women who appear in the texts are the elite wives or mothers of the male audience. The ethicists' rhetoric pushes us only to think of them as all women, when we know that historically Muslim societies were diverse along many planes and enslaved women were either black or at least of different ethnic/racial makeup than the dominant Muslim society. Advocating for an ethic of gender equality could problematically become advocacy of the "kept women" of the elite, leading us to address only their particular brand of problems in gender hierarchy, thereby excluding nonelite women who experience gendered oppression because of their race, class, or sexuality, and creating new hierarchies along those dimensions. As an example of exclusion based on a narrow understanding of the category of women, Leila Ahmed references colonial feminism's adverse effects on "women of the popular classes and rural women."[66]

Given the dangers of essentialization, a feminist philosophy of Islam would greatly benefit from continuing work on social and intellectual histories about Muslim women of various classes and ethnicities, including premodern enslaved[67] women. To address the problem of elite-only access to the path of *akhlaq* and avoid the generation of new hierarchies, in addition to questioning definitions of rationality and *khilafah*, one of the goals of feminist philosophy of Islam would be to illuminate the broad range of gender oppression in the form of ethico-religious rhetoric that is intersectionally bound up with class, race, and sexuality.

The Problem of Utilizing Others for Elite Male Refinement: Rethinking the Goals of Akhlaq

The ethicists' male-centered ethics poses the problem that the concept of *khilafah*, as the foundation of the societal and cosmic order, is premised on the utilization of women and non-elite men for the gratification of elite men. There is a conflict between a man's ethics of ordering society as a patriarchy and the idealized notion that creating the patriarchal social order will create a universal moral state. In other words, patriarchy is inherently unjust, and the ethicists are evidently unaware of this. Upon first glance, the notion that an individual's actions can make a difference in all of society's moral state is a powerful one; but it loses its appeal when this moral agency, along with rationality, is held exclusively by elite male individuals who utilize others toward the ends of their own flourishing alone.

For an account of how to remove human utilization from the pursuit of human flourishing, we can turn to Martha Nussbaum's capabilities approach. Nussbaum defines human capabilities as "what people are actually able to do and to be, in a way [that is] informed by an intuitive idea of a life that is worthy of the dignity of the human being."[68] She considers the idea of human dignity to be "intuitive," meaning intuitively knowable by all people, and requires that "the capabilities in question should be pursued for each and every person, treating each as an end and none as a mere tool of the ends of others."[69] But in the case that human dignity is not necessarily intuitive or thought to apply universally, which is true in the *akhlaq* tradition, this basis in utilization must be undone more carefully.

In Lisa Tessman's argument that Aristotelian success in ethics can only be achieved in an ideal patriarchy, we find a possible solution to the problem of individual and societal flourishing at the cost of nonelite others: specifically, rethinking human perfectionism as the end goal of *akhlaq*. She argues that interdependence—the idea that an individual's flourishing leads to broad societal flourishing—is unduly optimistic. The reason is that "under actual conditions, interdependence can be destroyed and replaced by relationships of dominance and subordination, in which case it will not be true that exercising virtues that benefit others will create a flourishing community that one depends on for one's own well-being."[70] In other words, subordination of a group of people does not really lead to a virtuous society in which everyone is obeying God or living a virtuous and, therefore, happy life. Rather, it is naive to think that an individual's refinement automatically leads to the same for members of the individual's household or society, especially if those other persons are utilized for the individual's refinement in the first place. The "other-regarding virtues," as Tessman calls them,[71] of which there are many in the *akhlaq* texts, as I have shown throughout this book, are in fact self-serving. They are used primarily to discharge the elite individual's own perceived sense of his duties. As such, many of the *akhlaq* guidelines only facilitate the good of the community insofar as they assist elites toward flourishing.

In fact, far from utilization having any mutual benefits, the opposite is the case. Utilizing others for one's own ends, whatever the purported intent, diminishes both the utilizer and the utilized. Tessman argues that in order to achieve the goal of *eudemonia* (in the case of ancient Greek philosophy) or patriarchal *khilafah* (in the case of the *akhlaq* genre;

parallel to Ghazali's *sa'adat*, or cosmic happiness/flourishing), two ideal conditions need to be met. First, the ideal moral subject must be able to take pleasure in applying the rational faculty and subduing the other faculties as well as take pleasure in doing the "right thing."[72] Apart from the fact that only men are thought to possess rationality, what is deeply at play in success on the ethical path is whether or not people have the power and luxury to take pleasure in the right. But that condition is not universally realized. The second ideal condition for achieving eudemonia (and its *akhlaq* parallels) is that the world must be conducive to human flourishing, and its conditions must allow for at least some human flourishing. However, when the path of *akhlaq* is exclusive, neither of these ideal conditions exists, and thus achievement of human flourishing as suggested by the *akhlaq* model of patriarchal-*khilafah* is unattainable.

When the world's moral conditions are so imperfect, it is impossible to achieve perfect cosmic order, i.e., to become a *khalifah* or microcosm (*'alam-i saghir*). Tessman argues that in a nonideal situation, reaching one's own fullest potential should not be the central aim of moral thought.[73] This is because personal goals can conflict with societal goals; the idea that individuals' virtues could align perfectly with all of humanity's cosmic needs and goals is implausible. Although some have proposed that the answer is to abandon a singular definition of humanity's flourishing,[74] Tessman holds that we must keep *eudemonia* but add to it the idea that "oppressed people do still have a claim on flourishing."[75] Demolishing the idea that there are fixed roles for all human beings, in which only some people's job is to seek refinement while others' job is to support them in that endeavor, opens the enterprise of *akhlaq* to all. But this can happen only after doing the hard work of deconstructing the ethics that privilege some over others and require the utilization of others. The problem of the eudaemonist (patriarchal-*khilafah*) perspective that "'one should live so as to flourish in a fully human way, where the human way of flourishing is understood to be constituted, at least partially, by an exercise of the virtues,' leaves those who are barred every step of the way towards realizing the normative ideal . . . vulnerable to frustration and disappointment."[76] Tessman proposes that, instead, the relationship between virtues and human flourishing ought to be decoupled from the idealism of interdependence between elite individuals' virtuous achievements upon society's flourishing and society's service to those individuals. An individual's success in becoming a *khalifah* would thus be separated from the fixed structure of society that exists in the form of the hierarchy of professions and women's domestic subordination. Her answer to the question of how one should live is "one should live aiming at an unattainable ideal—flourishing in a fully human way and thus exercising the virtues—but with no expectation for 'success' given the unconducive conditions in which one must strive."[77]

In this formulation, the goals of virtue ethics are expressed as what it means to experience being fully human, and not the exploitative reverse arrangement in which only those who are thought to be fully rational can enact the science of ethics. Reading *akhlaq* through the lens of Tessman's proposal of nonidealized *eudaimonia* would not mean merely transforming the a priori recognition of women, the enslaved, and male others' *nafses* so that they were included in ethical refinement, but instead recognizing that it is the practice of *akhlaq* itself that allows for everyone to attempt to realize their full humanity, even if imperfectly. So, addressing the paradox of *akhlaq*—that individual refinement, which is supposedly for all of society's benefit, occurs at the cost of many individuals—entails rethinking the goals of *akhlaq* itself. The rationale for making *akhlaq* inclusive is not necessarily that everyone is human and thus should be included, since not everyone recognizes the full humanity of women and nonelites. Rather, the argument for rethinking *akhlaq* is that *no* humans can attain perfection, and so *all* humans should be allowed to refine themselves. The science of *akhlaq* then shifts from the perfection of some individuals who are utilizing others to an *akhlaq* that charts a perennial human struggle to live the good life even amid the impossibility of anyone ever attaining perfection.

POSSIBILITIES OF AN INCLUSIVE *AKHLAQ* TRADITION

The *akhlaq* tradition has proved powerful in the past, and we have reason to expect that it will continue to be so in the future. Over time, the Ghazali-Tusi-Davani *akhlaq* tradition has developed into a psychological and sociological program that is independent from the ethicists' own claims of providing the masses with insight into the path of living the virtuous life. The psychological program of *akhlaq* is the creation of elite male superiority through the diminution of the rational capacity of all other human beings. The sociological program is the naturalization of this hierarchy as the order of society. Historically, these texts provided a path to ordering a society that was suffering from chaos and wounds, specifically during what Hodgson calls the middle period of political turmoil and trauma (the tenth to fifteenth centuries and beyond). That the *akhlaq* texts may have served this uplifting purpose explains the revival of the category of the *tahdhib* (discipline) of *akhlaq* in the twentieth century as the desire to purify the system of the self, family, and society from the traumas caused by colonialism. Examples of this revival are Nusrat Amyn's translation in the 1930s of Ibn Miskawayh's Arabic treatise and Sir Syed Ahmed Khan's founding of an Urdu-language *akhlaq* journal of the same name. In Urdu, *tahzib* means civilization and cultivation of ethics. Khan's use of this term was his response to what he perceived to be a decay of Muslim thought in the colonial era. This recent revival of *akhlaq* points to a necessity for future ethnographic work investigating ethical beliefs and praxis in tandem with gendered beliefs and praxis in order to fully realize how ethical contradictions such as the metaphysical tension not only have shaped Muslim thought through the ages, but also continue to resonate today. Ethics has become an important category for Muslims following revival movements, as evidenced by several texts reviving the term *akhlaq* and attempting to distill Qur'an-only or Muhammad-only treatments of Islamic ethics as the truly Islamic ethics.

Yet, reading the ethics tradition as divorced from Muslim epistemology of ethics is tantamount to denying the very philosophical premises present in Muslim thought. It is to pretend that one can construct ethics from the sacred sources ex nihilo, uninformed by prior Muslim thought. As contemporary Muslims look for guidance on how to live, *akhlaq* texts are a powerful resource because they provide examples of individuals striving to find guidance on perennial problems such as how to live an individual life, how to live in a family, and how to live in society. Evolving answers to these and other questions have pervaded centuries of Muslim thought and praxis—a fact that points to the need for a continuation in philosophical thinking that keeps pace with our changing definitions of what it means to be human.

Glossary of Persian and Arabic Terms

'Adalat—justice, the ultimate or composite virtue
Akhlaq—Islamic philosophical ethics
'Alam-i saghir—microcosm of the universe
'Aql—rationality or intellection
Bimuruwwati—unmanliness
Fiqh—Islamic jurisprudence
Ghayrat—manly pride
Haybat—gravitas or maturity
Hikmat—virtue of wisdom or philosophy writ large
'Iffat— virtue of self-restraint
Karamat—benevolence
Khalifah—vicegerent of God
Khilafah—vicegerency of God and the goal of *akhlaq*
Muruwwah—manhood or manliness
Nafs—metaphysical soul or metaphysical self
Namardi—unmanliness; sexual impotence
Nikah—marriage contract
Qiwamah—male authority
Quwwat-i 'aqli—Rational Faculty
Quwwat-i ghazabi—Irascible Faculty
Quwwat-i shahwi—Concupiscent Faculty
Sa'adat—ultimate happiness/flourishing

Shahwat—carnal desire

Shuja'at—virtue of courage

Tahzib-i akhlaq—science of ethics or science/ordering of the *nafs*

Wilayah—male guardianship

Notes

INTRODUCTION

1. *Al-Ghazali: The Alchemist of Happiness*, directed by Ovidio Abdul Latif Salazar (2004; London: Matmedia Productions, 2007), DVD.
2. *Al-Ghazali: The Alchemist of Happiness*.
3. *Al-Ghazali: The Alchemist of Happiness*.
4. Zareena Grewal, *Islam Is a Foreign Country: American Muslims and the Global Crisis of Authority* (New York: New York University Press, 2014), 31–78. Grewal has shown in the context of nonsufi American Muslims that the quest for authentic Islamic knowledge is the result of a global crisis of Muslim religious authority.
5. Leila Ahmed, *Women and Gender in Islam* (New Haven: Yale University Press, 1992), 82, 91; and Fatima Mernissi, *The Veil and the Male Elite: A Feminist Interpretation of Women's Rights in Islam* (New York: Perseus Books Group, 1991), 43.
6. A good summary of feminist hermeneutics of the Qur'an developed by Riffat Hasan, amina wadud, Asma Barlas, and others can be found at Asma Barlas, "Women's Readings of the Qur'an," in *The Cambridge Companion to the Qur'an*, ed. Jane McAuliffe (Cambridge: Cambridge University Press, 2006), 255–71. Ziba Mir-Hosseini and Kecia Ali's work have been groundbreaking feminist engagements with *fiqh*. Ziba Mir-Hosseini, "Muslim Women's Quest for Equality: Between Islamic Law and Feminism," *Critical Inquiry* 32, no. 4 (Summer 2006): 629–45; Ziba Mir-Hosseini, "The Construction of Gender in Islamic

Legal Thought and Strategies for Reform," *Hawwa* 1, no. 1 (2003): 1–28; Kecia Ali, *Sexual Ethics and Islam: Feminist Reflections on Qur'an, Hadith, and Jurisprudence* (Oxford: Oneworld, 2006); and Kecia Ali, *Marriage and Slavery in Early Islam* (Cambridge, MA: Harvard University Press, 2010). Engagement with *fiqh* is also particularly fruitful because of its relevance to contemporary rights-based discourses for women in Muslim countries. The legislative adoption of marriage and divorce laws inspired in some measure by medieval Islamic jurisprudence and arguments for their continued legal relevance in many Muslim countries are well documented in scholarship. Entries in Abdullahi An-Na'im's volume *Islamic Family Law* reflect postcolonial movements in many Muslim countries that revived Islamic law only in matters of the family and regulation of women. Abdullahi An-Na'im, *Islamic Family Law in a Changing World: A Global Resource Book* (London: Zed, 2002).

7. Laury Silvers, "Early Pious, Mystic Sufi Women," in *Cambridge Companion to Sufism*, ed. Lloyd Ridgeon (New York: Cambridge University Press, 2015), 24–52; Sa'diyya Shaikh, *Sufi Narratives of Intimacy: Ibn Arabi, Gender, and Sexuality* (Chapel Hill: University of North Carolina Press, 2012); and Abu 'Abd ar-Raḥman as-Sulami, *Early Sufi Women: Dhikr an-niswa al-muta'abbidat as-sufiyyat*, trans. Rkia E. Cornell (Louisville: Fons Vitae, 1999).

8. amina wadud, *Qur'an and Woman: Rereading the Sacred Text from a Woman's Perspective* (London: Oxford University Press, 1999), 2, 35, 64.

9. Shaheen Sardar Ali, *Gender and Human Rights in Islam and International Law Equal Before Allah, Unequal Before Man?* (The Hague: Kluwer Law International, 2000), 3–4, 44–46.

10. Ahmed, *Women and Gender in Islam*, 65.

11. Ahmed, 66.

12. Kathryn Kueny, *Conceiving Identities: Maternity in Medieval Muslim Discourse and Practice* (Albany: State University of New York Press, 2013), 3.

13. Louise Marlowe, *Hierarchy and Egalitarianism in Islamic Thought* (Cambridge: Cambridge University Press, 1997), 59.

14. Aisha Geissinger, *Gender and Muslim Constructions of Exegetical Authority: A Rereading of the Classical Genre of Qur'an Commentary* (Leiden: Brill, 2015), 63–64.

15. Marlowe, *Hierarchy and Egalitarianism in Islamic Thought*, 9.

16. Marlowe, 7, 148.

17. Marlowe, 53.

18. Marlowe, 7; Ann K. S. Lambton, "Islamic Society in Persia," *International Affairs* 31, no. 3 (1954): 3–4; and Ann K. S. Lambton, "Justice in the Medieval Persian Theory of Kingship," *Studia Islamic* 17 (1962): 97.

19. Etin Anwar, *Gender and Self in Islam* (London: Routledge, 2006), 74.

20. Nasir-ad Din Muhammad ibn Muhammad Tusi, *Akhlaq-i Nasiri*, ed. Mojtaba Minvi and Alireza Haydari (Tehran: Zar, 1977), 115.

21. Sophia Vasalou, *Moral Agents and Their Deserts: The Character of Mu'tazilite Ethics* (Princeton: Princeton University Press, 2008), 67–70.

22. Abu Hamid al-Ghazali, *Kimiya-i Sa'adat*, ed. Hossein Khadivjam (Tehran: Ketabhaaye Jibi, 1975), 2:308; and Tusi, *Akhlaq-i Nasiri*, 218.

23. Ahmed, *Women and Gender in Islam*, 119–20; and Huda Lutfi, "Manners and Customs of Fourteenth-Century Cairene Women: Female Anarchy Versus Male Shar'i Order in Muslim Prescriptive Treatises," in *Women in Middle Eastern History: Shifting Boundaries in Sex and Gender*, ed. Nikki Keddie and Beth Baron (New Haven: Yale University Press, 1991), 101.

24. Nizam al-Mulk, *Book of Government or Rules for Kings*, trans. H. Darke (London: Routledge and Kegan Paul, 1978), 179–80; Omid Safi, *The Politics of Knowledge in Premodern Islam: Negotiating Ideology and Religious Inquiry* (Chapel Hill: University of North Carolina Press, 2006), 67–68; and Hamid Dabashi, *Truth and Narrative: The Untimely Thoughts of 'Ayn al-Qudat al Hamadani* (London: Curzon, 1999), 78–79.

25. Geissinger, *Gender and Muslim Constructions*, 63–65.

26. Jalal ad-Din Davani, *Akhlaq-i Jalali*, ed. Abdullah Masoudi Arani (Tehran: Intesharat-i Italat, 2013).

27. Marshall Hodgson, *The Venture of Islam* (Chicago: University of Chicago Press, 1977), 2. Hodgson demarcates the period in history of Islamdom that this book covers as the middle and late phases of the "middle periods," from 950 to 1500, which he divides into the early middle period, which saw the expansion of a cosmopolitan Muslim Persianate civilization, and the later middle period, marked by crisis caused by Mongol destruction and reconstruction. Muslim ethicists produced numerous *akhlaq* treatises throughout this period.

28. I use this term with feminist irony; the texts are "seminal" in that they are generated by men, foundational, and patriarchal.

29. Hodgson, *The Venture of Islam*, 2:57–59. *Islamicate* is a term coined by historian Marshall Hodgson to refer to the "social and cultural complex historically associated with Islam and Muslims," but is not necessarily directly related to the religion of Islam or the production of Muslims. *Persianate* is a similar term.

30. Throughout this work, I use the adjective *enslaved* to emphasize that a certain class of people were enslaved, rather using the word *slave* to describe them, as if slavery were a condition intrinsic to this class of people's nature. However, I maintain use of the word *slave* in my translations and discussions of passages from the primary texts in order to convey how the language of the time described this class of persons and how the classical ethicists indeed believed that slavery was an intrinsic condition of some people that were rationally deficient. In

their view, slaves suffered their enslavement because of their rational deficiencies, or else they would be higher in the hierarchy of rational beings, which corresponded to social hierarchy.

31. Hodgson, *The Venture of Islam*, 2:9; and Ross E. Dunn, *The Adventures of Ibn Battuta: A Muslim Traveler of the 14th Century* (Berkley: University of California Press, 2005), 7, 11–12, 312. Scholars, including Ghazali, Tusi, and Davani, benefited from the existence of this shared identity. As Hodgson writes, "representatives of the various arts and sciences moved freely, as a munificent ruler or an unkind one beckoned or pressed, from one Muslim land to another; and any man of great stature in one area was likely to be soon recognized everywhere else. . . . There continued to exist a single body of interrelated traditions, developed in mutual interaction throughout Islamdom." Governing courts demanded the knowledge of the *hakim*, learned doctor, or scholar of Islamic sciences. Dunn shows the fourteenth-century explorer Ibn Battuta seamlessly transitioned between royal courts and religious institutions during his twenty-four-year traveling career across the modern equivalent of forty-four countries in Islamdom—his qualifications as a specialist in Islamic law always earned him a welcome stay and income along the way.

32. Abu Hamid Al-Ghazali, *The Alchemy of Happiness*, trans. Claud Field (London: J. Murray, 1909); Nasir ad-Din Tusi, *The Nasirean Ethics*, trans. G. M. Wickens (London: George Allen and Unwin, 1964); and Jalal ad-Din Davani, *Practical Philosophy of the Muhammadan Peoples*, trans. W. F. Thompson (London: Oriental Translation Fund, 1839).

33. Abu Hamid Muhammad al-Ghazali, *The Alchemy of Happiness* (*Kimiya al-Sa'adat*) trans. Jay R. Crook (Chicago: Great Books of the Islamic World, 2008).

34. A few recent ones include Ebrahim Moosa, *Ghazali and the Poetics of Imagination* (Chapel Hill: University of North Carolina Press, 2005); Farouk Mitha, *Al-Ghazali and the Ismailis: A Debate on Reason and Authority in Medieval Islam* (London: I. B. Tauris, 2001); Frank Griffel, *Al-Ghazali's Philosophical Theology* (Oxford: Oxford University Press, 2009); and Eric Ormsby, *Makers of the Muslim World: Ghazali* (Oxford: Oneworld, 2007).

35. Safi, *The Politics of Knowledge in Premodern Islam*, 108.

36. Safi, 109.

37. Ghazali, *Kimiya-i Sa'adat*, 9.

38. Moosa, *Ghazali and the Poetics of Imagination*, 27.

39. Edward N. Zalta, "Al-Ghazali." *Stanford Encyclopedia of Philosophy*, Summer 2016 ed.

40. Ghazali, *Kimiya-i Sa'adat*, 5.

41. Nasir-ad Din Muhammad ibn Muhammad Tusi, *Sayr wa Suluk*, trans. Sayyad Badakhchani (London: I. B. Tauris, 1998), 26.

42. S. J. Badakhchani, "Introduction," in *Contemplation and Action: The Spiritual Autobiography of a Muslim Scholar*, ed. S. J. Badakhchani (London: I. B. Tauris, 1998), 7.

43. Badakhchani, 1.

44. Wilfred Madelung, "Nasir al-Din Tusi's Ethics Between Philosophy, Shi'ism, and Sufism," in *Ethics in Islam*, ed. R. G. Hovannisian (Malibu: Undena, 1985), 85–101.

45. Farhad Daftary, *The Isma'ilis: Their History and Doctrines* (Cambridge: Cambridge University Press, 2007), 173.

46. Badakhchani, "Introduction," 4.

47. Guy N. A. Attewell, *Refiguring Unani Tibb: Plural Healing in Late Colonial India* (Hyderabad: Orient Longman, 2007), 2–5. Appropriately, the term *hakim* is used as a title for the polymaths who were philosophers, physicians, and more. The title continues to be used in modern South Asia for those who practice traditional *yunani tibb* or "Greek" medicine because its origin came from practitioners who were trained in this natural science as part of the applied knowledge branch of philosophy.

48. Hamid Dabashi, "Khwajah Nasir al-Din al-Tusi: The Philosopher/Vizier and the Intellectual Climate of His Times," in *History of Islamic Philosophy*, ed. Seyyed Hossein Nasr and Oliver Leaman (London: Routledge, 1996), 527–84, 532. He was allegedly testing whether an astrologer's prediction of Hulegu's illness would come true following the caliph's execution.

49. Dabashi, "Khwajah Nasir al-Din al-Tusi," 559–61.

50. Ahmad ibn Muhammad Ibn Miskawayh, *The Refinement of Character: A Translation from the Arabic of Ahmad ibn-Muhammad Miskawayh's Tahdhib al-akhlaq*, trans. Constantine K. Zurayk (Beirut: American University of Beirut, 1968).

51. G. M. Wickens, "Aklaq-e Naseri," in *Encyclopaedia Iranica*, ed. Ehsan Yarshater (London: Routledge and Kegan Paul, 1984), 1:725. Badakhchani argues that the work remains largely Isma'ili since he only changed approximately ten lines. Badakhchani, "Introduction," 61.

52. Tusi, *Akhlaq-i Nasiri*, 34.

53. Andrew J. Newman, "Davani, Jalal-al-Din Mohammad b. As'ad Kazeruni Seddiqi," in *Encyclopaedia Iranica*, vol. 7 (London: Routledge and Kegan Paul, 1994), 132–33.

54. Newman, 132–33.

55. G. M. Wickens, "*Aklaq-i Jalali*: An 'Ethical' Treatise in Persian by Mohammad b. As'ad Jalal- al-din Davani," in *Encyclopaedia Iranica*, vol. 1, ed. Ehsan Yarshater (London: Routledge and Kegan Paul, 1984), 724; and John Cooper, "al-Dawani, Jalal al-Din (1426–1502)," in *Routledge Encyclopedia of Philosophy* (London: Routledge, 1998).

1. EPISTEMOLOGY AND GENDER ANALYTICS OF ISLAMIC ETHICS

1. Nasir-ad Din Muhammad ibn Muhammad Tusi, *Akhlaq-i Nasiri*, ed. Mojtaba Minvi and Alireza Haydari (Tehran: Zar, 1977), 37–41.

2. Tusi, 101. Making the word *nafs* (metaphysical soul) plural in English is a complicated matter. It is a broken plural in Arabic (*anfas*) and using the broken plural instead of pluralizing it in English unnecessarily alienates non-Arabic readers. So *nafses* is my preferred plural.

3. W. F. Thompson, *Practical Philosophy of the Mohammadan People* (London: Oriental Translation Fund of Great Britain and Ireland, 1839), xxi–xxii. For example, W. F. Thompson, one of the earliest English translators and commentators on the *Akhlaq-i Jalali*, stated in 1839 that rather than being Islamic, "it appears that Mohammedan philosophy is neither more nor less than Grecian philosophy in an Eastern garb; a twin offspring of that common parent from which the sciences of Europe are proud to acknowledge their derivation."

4. Oliver Leaman, "Orientalism and Islamic Philosophy," in *Routledge Encyclopedia of Philosophy* (London: Routledge, 1998), 159. Leaman discusses Richard Walzer's colonialist agenda.

5. George Fadlo Hourani, *Islamic Rationalism: The Ethics of 'Abd al-Jabbar* (Oxford: Clarendon, 1971), 2, 70; and Majid Fakhry, *History of Islamic Philosophy* (New York: Columbia University Press, 2005), 132–33.

6. Oliver Leaman, *Islamic Philosophy: An Introduction* (Cambridge: Polity, 2009), 23; and Mohammad Azadpur, *Reason Unbound: On Spiritual Practice in Islamic Peripatetic Philosophy* (Albany: State University of New York Press, 2011), 18. Nasr holds that Ibn Sina's later writing and Suhrawardi's establishment of the Ishraqi (Illuminationist) school of thought were a rejection of the Aristotelian separation between virtue and ethics. Azadpour disagrees with Nasr's characterization of Aristotle that it separates theory from practice.

7. Oliver Leaman and Seyyed Hossein Nasr, "Introduction," in *History of Islamic Philosophy*, ed. Seyyed Hossein Nasr and Oliver Leaman (London: Routledge, 1996), 3, 15.

8. Mohammad Azadpur, "Is 'Islamic Philosophy' Islamic?," in *Voices of Change*, ed. Omid Safi, vol. 5, *Voices of Islam*, ed. Vincent Cornell (Westport: Preager, 2007), 23.

9. Azadpur, 24.

10. Elizabeth Bucar, "Islamic Virtue Ethics," in *The Oxford Handbook of Virtue*, ed. Nancy Snow (Oxford: Oxford University Press, 2018), 209.

11. Charles E. Butterworth, "Ethics in Medieval Philosophy," *Journal of Religious Ethics* 11, no. 2 (Fall 1983): 224–39.

12. Butterworth, 228–29, 231, 233. Butterworth reads Farabi and Ibn Sina as philosophers who felt that religion and philosophy both are needed to explain the universe and the goal of human life. Farabi held that philosophy determines what happiness is but does not explain how to achieve it, while religion does the reverse. It explains what people should do to be happy but does not explain what happiness is. Human endeavor through philosophy is similar to the wisdom in religion in that philosophy can achieve understanding of the world from the bottom up, while in religion the human examines the wisdom given from religion (God) from the top down. On the other hand, Ibn Sina ties religion and philosophy together through the Prophet, who is the highest intellect we strive to know and is the perfect human being because he has direct communication with the ultimate wisdom of God, the ultimate goal of humans. A prophet is the best human being because he has developed his moral habits and establishes rules for people.

13. Shahab Ahmed, *What Is Islamic? The Importance of Being Islamic* (Princeton: Princeton University Press, 2016), 13–19, 26.

14. Tusi, *Akhlaq-i Nasiri*, 341.

15. Tusi, 341–44.

16. Jalal ad-Din Davani, *Akhlaq-i Jalali*, ed. Abdullah Masoudi Arani (Tehran: Intesharat-i Italat, 2013), 294–304.

17. Pierre Hadot, "Spiritual Exercises," in *Philosophy as a Way of Life*, trans. Michael Chase (Cambridge, MA: Harvard University Press, 2004), 107, quoted in Azadpur, *Reason Unbound*, 8.

18. Azadpur, *Reason Unbound*, 7, 18.

19. Fatima Seedat, "When Islam and Feminism Converge," *Muslim World* 103, no. 3 (2013): 406.

20. Abu Hamid al-Ghazali, *Kimiya-i Sa'adat*, ed. Hossein Khadivjam (Tehran: Ketabhaaye Jibi, 1975), 2:29; Tusi, 223; and Davani, 195.

21. Ghazali, 396.

22. Ghazali, 311, 318; Tusi, *Akhlaq-i Nasiri*, 215; and Davani, *Akhlaq-i Jalali*, 188.

23. Paul Heck, "Mysticism as Morality: The Case of Sufism," *Journal of Religious Ethics* 34, no. 2 (2006): 253–86, 258–59.

24. William Schweiker, *The Blackwell Companion to Religious Ethics* (Malden, MA: Blackwell, 2005). The articles in this volume by Kevin Reinhart, Abdulaziz Sachedina, and Ebrahim Moosa are indicative of the debate over how to define Islamic ethics. Additionally, scholars of *tafsir* and hadith collections also claim these modes of writing comprise Islamic ethics. There is also a long-standing claim that the poetry and prose of *adab* (Persianate poetic literature) are Muslim ethics discourses that are often at odds with theological works but reveal cultural approaches to how to present oneself with proper mannerisms

in Muslim ethics. D. J. Khaleghi-Motlagh, "Adab in Iran," in *Encyclopaedia Iranica*, ed. Ehsan Yarshater (London: Routledge and Kegan Paul, 1983), 1:432–39.

25. Abdulaziz Sachedina, "Islamic Ethics: Differentiations," in *The Blackwell Companion to Religious Ethics* (Malden, MA: Blackwell, 2005), 255–56.

26. Kevin Reinhart, "Islamic Law as Islamic Ethics," *Journal of Religious Ethics* 11, no. 2 (Fall 1983): 186–203, 195.

27. A prominent example is sufi poet Sa'adi Shirazi's thirteenth-century epic, *Bustan* (*The Fragrant Garden*), which contains allegories extolling virtues and an implicit political critique. Like other learned men of his time, Sa'adi was also trained in the Islamic sciences broadly from the Baghdad Nizamiya.

28. Andrew J. Newman, "Davani, Jalal-al-Din Mohammad b. As'ad Kazeruni Seddiqi," in *Encyclopaedia Iranica*, vol. 7 (London: Routledge and Kegan Paul, 1994), 132–33.

29. Davani does not include a theoretical discussion on the branches of knowledge and instead embarks directly on his exposition of *akhlaq* for the individual, the household, and the city with greater references to the sufi sages than Ghazali and Tusi.

30. Abu Hamid Muhammad al-Ghazali, *Ihya' 'Ulum ad-Din: Kitab al-'Ilm*, trans. Nabih Faris (New Dehli: Islamic Book Service, 1962), 33.

31. Ghazali, 34.

32. Ghazali, 23.

33. Ghazali, 26–27.

34. Pamela Sue Anderson, *A Feminist Philosophy of Religion* (Oxford: Blackwell, 1998), 16.

35. Lev Weitz, "Al-Ghazali, Bar Hebraeus, and the 'Good Wife,'" *Journal of the American Oriental Society* 134, no. 2 (2014): 203–23, 207.

36. Tusi, *Akhlaq-i Nasiri*, 41.

37. Tusi, 41.

38. Ghazali, *Kimiya-i Sa'adat*, 312.

39. Sa'diyya Shaikh, *Sufi Narratives of Intimacy: Ibn Arabi, Gender, and Sexuality* (Chapel Hill: University of North Carolina Press, 2012), 40.

40. Shaikh, 203.

41. Shaikh, 26.

42. Gordon Newby, "Ibn Khaldun and Fredrick Jackson Turner: Islam and the Frontier Experience," *Journal of Asian and African Studies* 18, nos. 3–4 (1983): 274–85, 276.

43. Ignaz Goldzihir, *Muslim Studies*, ed. S. M. Stern (New Brunswick, NJ: Allen and Unwin, 1966), 22, 43–44.

44. Newby, "Ibn Khaldun and Fredrick Jackson Turner," 276.

45. Lloyd Ridgeon, *Jawanmardi: A Sufi Code of Honor* (Edinburgh: Edinburgh University Press, 2011), 1.

46. Ridgeon, 2.

47. Ridgeon, 2.

48. Ridgeon, 2.

49. Ridgeon, 107.

50. Ridgeon, 8.

51. Ridgeon, 8. Anonymous sufi-*futuwwat* treatise.

52. 'Abd al-Haqq Muhaddith Dihlawi al-Bukhari, *Akhbar al-akhyar fi asrar al-abrar*, ed. 'Alim Ashraf Khan (Tehran: Anjuman-i Athar o Mafakhar-i Farhangi, 2004), 589. To which Nizamuddin Awliya responded, "when the lion comes out of the woods, does anyone ask if the lion is male or female? The children of Adam should have obedience and piety, be it man or woman."

53. Karen Bauer, *Gender Hierarchy in the Qur'an: Medieval Interpretations, Modern Responses* (Cambridge: Cambridge University Press, 2015), 64–65.

54. Ghazali, *Kimiya-i Sa'adat*, 308; and Tusi, *Akhlaq-i Nasiri*, 218.

55. Shaikh, *Sufi Narratives of Intimacy*, 37–38.

56. Ghazali and Tusi were employed by the Saljuqs and Nizari Isma'ilis, respectively, and produced works meant to lend legitimacy to the regimes' brand of sectarian rule. By the time Davani wrote the *Akhlaq-i Jalali*, political uncertainty and injustice had reached such heights that the ethicist argued for just leadership, regardless of which sect ruled.

57. Majid Fakhry, *Ethical Theories of Islam* (Leiden: Brill, 1991); George Hourani, *Reason and Tradition in Islamic Ethics* (Cambridge: Cambridge University Press, 1985); and Cyrus Zargar, *The Polished Mirror: Storytelling and the Pursuit of Virtue in Islamic Philosophy and Sufism* (Oxford: Oneworld Academic, 2017), 79–80. On the contrary, Cyrus Zargar argues that Ibn Miskawayh and Ghazali can be categorized together because they are both concerned with virtue ethics and build a shared tradition.

58. Bucar, "Islamic Virtue Ethics," 214. Bucar argues it does connect "individual and social dimensions of ethics."

59. Hourani, *Reason and Tradition in Islamic Ethics*, 19, 135.

60. Hodgson, *The Venture of Islam* (Chicago: University of Chicago Press, 1977), 2:9. Hodgson argues that despite differences, Islamdom "was held together in virtue of a common Islamicate social pattern which, by enabling members of any part of the society to be accepted as members of it anywhere else, assured [sic] the circulation of ideas and manners throughout its area. Muslims always felt themselves to be citizens of the whole Dar al-Islam."

61. Davani, *Akhlaq-i Jalali*, 77–78.

62. Mozaffar Alam, *The Languages of Political Islam: India 1200–1800* (Chicago: University of Chicago Press, 2004), 50.

63. Alam, 51–52.

64. Alam, 76–80.

65. Ulrike Stark, *An Empire of Books: The Naval Kishore Press and the Diffusion of the Printed Word in Colonial India* (Ranikhet Cantt: Permanent Black, 2008), 192.

66. Stark, 3.

67. Alam, *The Languages of Political Islam*, 51–53.

68. A Sindhi monograph by Hakim Fateh Muhammad Sewhani from 1916 is called *Akhlaq-i Muhammadi*. See also Sayyid Khurshid Husain, *Akhlaq-i Muhammadi* (Lucknow: Hindu Samat Press, 1920). More recent scholars have looked at hadith collections as comprehensive *akhlaq* works. A recent example of a hadith collection reproduced as ethics is Muhammad ibn Isma'il Bukhari, *Moral Teachings of Islam: Prophetic Traditions from Al-Adab Al-Mufrad*, trans. Abdul Ali Hamid (Walnut Creek, CA: Altamira Press, 2003).

69. Stark, *An Empire of Books*, 46–47, 307.

70. Jalal ad-Din Davani, *Akhlaq-i Jalali*, ed. Hafiz Shabir Ahmad Haidery (New Delhi: Urdu Book Review, 2007), 6, 18.

71. Brian Spooner and William Hannaway, "Persian as Koine: Written Persian in World-Historical Perspective," in *Literacy in the Persianate World: Writing and the Social Order*, ed. Brian Spooner and William Hannaway (Philadelphia: University of Pennsylvania Press, 2012), 2.

72. Spooner and Hanaway, 1.

73. Spooner and Hanaway, 3.

74. The word Ghazali uses for Arabic is *tazi*, the premodern Persian word for Arab persons and the Arabic language.

75. Ghazali, *Kimiya-i Sa'adat*, 9.

76. Travis Zadeh, *The Vernacular Qur'an: Translation and the Rise of Persian Exegesis* (Oxford: Oxford University Press, 2012), 62–68.

77. Zadeh, 265.

78. Zadeh, 427–29.

79. Hamid Dabashi, "Khwajah Nasir al-Din al-Tusi: The Philosopher/Vizier and the Intellectual Climate of His Times," in *History of Islamic Philosophy*, ed. Seyyed Hossein Nasr and Oliver Leaman (London: Routledge, 1996), 560.

80. Dabashi, 538–39; and Farhad Daftary, *The Isma'ilis: Their History and Doctrines* (Cambridge: Cambridge University Press, 2007), 41, 112.

81. Sarah Pessin, "Loss, Presence, and Gabirol's Desire: Medieval Jewish Philosophy and the Possibility of Feminist Ground," in *Women and Gender in Jewish Philosophy*, ed. Hava Tirosh-Samuelson (Bloomington: Indiana

University Press, 2004), 27–50; and Idit Dobbs-Weinstein, "Thinking Desire in Gersonides and Spinoza," in Tirosh-Samuelson, *Women and Gender in Jewish Philosophy*, 51–77. This question was articulated prominently by Martha Nussbaum and Marcia Homiak. Also, Jewish feminist philosophers Sarah Pessin and Idit Dobbs-Weinstein, who trace the phallocentric Aristotelian and Platonic influences on medieval Jewish philosophy, a shared epistemology with Islamic philosophy, likewise find feminist possibilities in their recovery.

82. Luce Irigaray, *This Sex Which Is Not One*, trans. Catherine Porter (Ithaca: Cornell University Press, 1985), 25–26; and Thomas Walter Laqueur, *Making Sex: Body and Gender from the Greeks to Freud* (Cambridge, MA: Harvard University Press, 1990). Thomas Laqueur has argued that ancient Greeks did not believe in sexual difference; rather they had a one-sex model in which women were imperfect iterations of males, which are still the primary form of the species.

83. Irigaray, *This Sex Which Is Not One*, 28–31.

84. Luce Irigaray, *An Ethics of Sexual Difference*, trans. Carolyn Burke and Gillian C. Gill (Ithaca: Cornell University Press, 1993), 10.

85. Irigaray, 10.

86. Kathryn Kueny, *Conceiving Identities: Maternity in Medieval Muslim Discourse and Practice* (Albany: State University of New York Press, 2013), 53–54, 117.

87. Ghazali, *Kimiya-i Sa'adat*, 430; Tusi, *Akhlaq-i Nasiri*, 238; and Davani, *Akhlaq-i Jalali*, 206.

88. Susan Shapiro, "A Matter of Discipline: Reading for Gender in Jewish Philosophy," in *Judaism Since Gender*, ed. Miriam Peskowitz and Laura Levitt (New York: Routledge, 1997).

89. Charlotte Witt, "Form, Normativity, and Gender in Aristotle: A Feminist Perspective," in *Feminist Interpretations of Aristotle*, ed. Cynthia Freeland (University Park: Pennsylvania State University Press: 1998), 119–37, 122–24.

90. Simone de Beauvoir, *The Second Sex*, trans. H. M. Parshley (London: Jonathan Cape, 2009), xxii.

91. de Beauvoir, xxxv.

92. Carolyn Krosmeyer, "Gendered Concepts and Hume's Standard of Taste," in *Feminism and Tradition in Aesthetics*, ed. Peggy Zeglin Brand and Carolyn Krosmeyer (University Park: Pennsylvania State University Press, 1995), 49.

93. Shapiro, "A Matter of Discipline," 165. She argues that Maimonides's metaphor that matter takes on physical form like a married harlot who is always with a man but never free is no "mere metaphor." It contributes to a real culture of gender hierarchy and even violence against women, as Maimonides elsewhere

in the legal work *Mishneh Torah* condones the "correction" of disobedient wives by striking them.

94. Judith Butler, *Gender Trouble: Feminism and the Subversion of Identity* (New York: Routledge, 1999), 9–11, 18.

95. Judith Butler, "Performative Acts and Gender Constitution: An Essay in Phenomenology and Feminist Theory," in *Performing Feminisms: Feminist Critical Theory and Theatre*, ed. Sue-Ellen Case (Baltimore: Johns Hopkins University Press, 1990), 272.

96. Butler, 272.

97. Ghazali, *Kimiya-i Sa'adat*, 308.

98. Gullvag Oystein Holter, "Social Theories for Researching Men and Masculinities: Direct Gender Hierarchy and Structural Inequality," in *Handbook of Studies on Men and Masculinities*, ed. Michael Kimmel, Jeff Hearn, and R. W. Connell (Thousand Oaks, CA: Sage, 2005), 16.

99. Amanullah De Sondy, *The Crisis of Islamic Masculinities* (London: Bloomsbury, 2013), 8.

100. de Beauvoir, *The Second Sex*, 301; and Lahoucine Ouzgane, *Islamic Masculinities* (London: Zed, 2006), 46.

101. R. W. Connell, *The Men and the Boys* (Berkley: University of California Press, 2001), 29.

102. Connell, 10, 11.

103. Connell, 31.

104. Abdullah Yusuf Ali, *The Meaning of the Holy Qur'an* (Brentwood, MD: Amana Corporation, 2001), 564. Ironically, traditional commentators on the Qur'an, most notably Ibn Kathir, note that this observation about the soul is part of a woman's speech, that of the Aziz's wife (Potiphar's wife) during her confession about seducing Prophet Yusuf (Joseph). The modern commentator Yusuf Ali notes that there is a significant contingent of commentators who believe that the observation of the soul's predilection for evil was part of Joseph's speech.

105. Silvia Walby, *Theorizing Patriarchy* (Oxford: Basil Blackwell, 1990), 178–79.

106. Connell, *The Men and the Boys*, 10.

107. Nancy F. Partner, *Studying Medieval Women: Sex, Gender, Feminism* (Cambridge: Medieval Academy of America, 1993).

108. Carole Hillenbrand, "Women in the Saljuq Period," in *Women in Iran from the Rise of Islam to 1800*, ed. Guity Nashat and Lois Beck (Champaign: University of Illinois Press, 2003), 116–17.

109. Leila Ahmed, *Women and Gender in Islam* (New Haven: Yale University Press, 1992), 118–21; Huda Lutfi, "Manners and Customs of Fourteenth-Century

Cairene Women: Female Anarchy Versus Male Shar'i Order in Muslim Prescriptive Treatises," in *Women in Middle Eastern History: Shifting Boundaries in Sex and Gender*, ed. Nikki Keddie and Beth Baron (New Haven: Yale University Press, 1991), 103–4; and James E. Lindsay, *Daily Life in the Medieval Islamic World* (Westport, CT: Greenwood, 2005), 182.

110. Holter, "Social Theories for Researching Men and Masculinities," 22.

2. GENDERED METAPHYSICS, PERFECTION, AND POWER OF THE (HU)MAN'S SOUL

1. Luce Irigaray, *An Ethics of Sexual Difference*, trans. Carolyn Burke and Gillian C. Gill (Ithaca: Cornell University Press, 1993), 6.

2. Abu Hamid al-Ghazali, *Kimiya-i Sa'adat*, ed. Hossein Khadivjam (Tehran: Ketabhaaye Jibi, 1975), 28; Nasir-ad Din Muhammad ibn Muhammad Tusi, *Akhlaq-i Nasiri*, ed. Mojtaba Minvi and Alireza Haydari (Tehran: Zar, 1977), 70–71; and Jalal ad-Din Davani, *Akhlaq-i Jalali*, ed. Abdullah Masoudi Arani (Tehran: Intesharat-i Italat, 2013), 124.

3. Even though the ethicists understood the existence of people who could not be strictly identified as only male or female, and also recognized that men can be sexually attracted to other men, by and large the ethicists think of male and female roles in society as binary. The concept of gender identity did not exist for them, much less awareness of gender binaries. Thus, I am aware of the gender binary and heteronormativity the texts pose. In fact, as I argue in chapter 4, the texts promote a particular kind of male heteronormative profile that insists on sexual intimacy with one's wife but spiritual, intellectual, and personal intimacy with close male friends.

4. Spelled alif, vav: او

5. Jay Crook, "Translator's Introduction," in *The Alchemy of Happiness (Kimiya al-Sa'adat)* (Chicago: Great Books of the Islamic World, 2008), xxii.

6. Tusi, *Akhlaq-i Nasiri*, 218; Ghazali, *Kimiya-i Sa'adat*, 316; and Davani, *Akhlaq-i Jalali*, 156, 189.

7. amina wadud, *Qur'an and Woman: Rereading the Sacred Text from a Woman's Perspective* (London: Oxford University Press, 1999), 4–5.

8. Tusi, *Akhlaq-i Nasiri*, 250.

9. Ghazali, *Kimiya-i Sa'adat*, 313; Tusi, *Akhlaq-i Nasiri*, 203; and Davani, *Akhlaq-i Jalali*, 178.

10. Tusi, *Akhlaq-i Nasiri*, 310–11.

11. Sohayl Muhsin Afnan, *Vazhah Namah-i Falsafi* (Lebanon: Dar El-Mashreq, 1969), 294.

12. Tusi explains that vegetables and animals have their own simplified *nafses* too.

13. Hanna Kassis, *A Concordance of the Quran* (Berkeley: University of California Press, 1983), 824–30.

14. Ghazali, *Kimiya-i Sa'adat*, 316. Ghazali mentions women's *nafses* explicitly by stating that "a woman's *nafs* is really like your own," but Tusi and Davani imply women have *nafses* because they discuss women's relatively weak resolve in correcting their vices in the context of various suggestions for men. For example Davani, *Akhlaq-i Jalali*, 156, in which he gives examples of the weak-minded, and Tusi, *Akhlaq-i Nasiri*, 215, in which he mentions virtues of a good wife that are partly the virtues of a tamed *nafs*.

15. Tanvir Anjum, "The Perpetually Wedded Wife of God: A Study of Muha Sada Suhag, as the Founder of Sada Suhagiyya Silsila," *Journal of Religious History* 39, no. 3 (2015): 420–30; and Sachiko Murata, *The Tao of Islam: A Sourcebook on Gender Relationships in Islamic Thought* (Albany: State University of New York Press, 1992), 266, 284. An unusually severe example of this sufi gender dynamic is the fifteenth-century Gujurati sufi Shaykh Musa Sada Suhag, who founded the Sada Suhagiyya *silsila*. His sobriquet and the name of the *silsila* meant perpetually wedded wife. Members of this *silsila* "conceptualized the relationship of human beings with God in gendered terms, and taking on androgynous appearance, identified themselves with the feminine while imagining God in masculine terms."

16. Annemarie Schimmel, *My Soul Is a Woman: The Feminine in Islam* (New York: Continuum, 1997), 69–70.

17. Ghazali, *Kimiya-i Sa'adat*, 47.

18. Ghazali, 316.

19. Tusi, *Akhlaq-i Nasiri*, 49.

20. Tusi, 48–54; Ghazali, *Kimiya-i Sa'adat*, 18; and Davani, *Akhlaq-i Jalali*, 77–78. Davani quotes both Tusi and Ghazali to explain the *nafs*, so he assumes its similar metaphysical properties of the *nafs*.

21. Ghazali, *Kimiya-i Sa'adat*, 18–28; and Tusi, *Akhlaq-i Nasiri*, 58–72.

22. Ghazali, *Kimiya-i Sa'adat*, 18–22.

23. Ghazali, 18–22.

24. Ghazali, 47.

25. Ghazali, 18–19. In this one instance, he uses the term *dil*, or heart, to refer to the soul, while the *nafs* is more related to a person's entire selfhood. The reason for this may be to keep the metaphor appropriate. The whole body and the *'aql* cannot both be the *nafs*, especially if there are parts of the *nafs* that undermine rationality, so he uses the *dil* as the soul here. Elsewhere in the treatise he reverts back to using only the term *nafs* as the soul and self.

26. Davani, *Akhlaq-i Jalali*, 74.

27. Susan Shapiro, "A Matter of Discipline: Reading for Gender in Jewish Philosophy," in *Judaism Since Gender*, ed. Miriam Peskowitz and Laura Levitt (New York: Routledge, 1997), 165.

28. Ghazali, *Kimiya-i Sa'adat*, 33, 314.

29. Tusi, *Akhlaq-i Nasiri*, 48–49.

30. Tusi, 58.

31. Tusi, 58. Tusi's terms for the components of the *nafs* are grammatical variations of the same terms Ghazali uses.

32. Tusi, 58.

33. Tusi, 69–70.

34. Davani, *Akhlaq-i Jalali*, 74.

35. Davani, 73.

36. Davani, 74.

37. Murata, *The Tao of Islam*, 314.

38. Kecia Ali, *Sexual Ethics and Islam: Feminist Reflections on Qur'an, Hadith, and Jurisprudence* (Oxford: Oneworld, 2006), 6–7.

39. Tusi, *Akhlaq-i Nasiri*, 86. See Aladdin Yaqub, *Al-Ghazali's "Moderation in Belief"* (Chicago: University of Chicago Press, 2013).

40. Tusi, *Akhlaq-i Nasiri*, 108–9; Ghazali, *Kimiya-i Sa'adat*, 7; and Davani, *Akhlaq-i Jalali*, 81.

41. Tusi, *Akhlaq-i Nasiri*, 109; Ghazali, *Kimiya-i Sa'adat*, 8; and Davani, *Akhlaq-i Jalali*, 81.

42. Tusi, *Akhlaq-i Nasiri*, 122–30; and Davani, *Akhlaq-i Jalali*, 94–100. Ghazali does not have a standalone section on pseudovirtues but does include the *nafs's* false good deeds throughout the *Kimiya*.

43. Annemarie Schimmel, *Mystical Dimensions of Islam* (Chapel Hill: University of North Carolina Press, 1975), 112.

44. Ghazali, *Kimiya-i Sa'adat*, 7.

45. Tusi, *Akhlaq-i Nasiri*, 112; and Davani, *Akhlaq-i Jalali*, 83.

46. Tusi, *Akhlaq-i Nasiri*, 112; and Davani, *Akhlaq-i Jalali*, 83.

47. Tusi, *Akhlaq-i Nasiri*, 112; and Davani, *Akhlaq-i Jalali*, 83.

48. Tusi, *Akhlaq-i Nasiri*, 112; and Davani, *Akhlaq-i Jalali*, 83.

49. Tusi, *Akhlaq-i Nasiri*, 112; and Davani, *Akhlaq-i Jalali*, 83.

50. Tusi, *Akhlaq-i Nasiri*, 112; and Davani, *Akhlaq-i Jalali*, 83.

51. Tusi, *Akhlaq-i Nasiri*, 112; and Davani, *Akhlaq-i Jalali*, 83.

52. Tusi, *Akhlaq-i Nasiri*, 112; and Davani, *Akhlaq-i Jalali*, 84.

53. Davani, *Akhlaq-i Jalali*, 94–95; Tusi, *Akhlaq-i Nasiri*, 122–25; and Ghazali, *Kimiya-i Sa'adat*, 25–27. It is important to note that Ghazali does not include vices of the rational faculty because he feels that one can never have too much rationality; it is an angelic faculty and can never do wrong.

54. Davani, *Akhlaq-i Jalali*, 94–95; and Tusi, *Akhlaq-i Nasiri*, 122–25.

55. Davani, *Akhlaq-i Jalali*, 95.

56. Davani does not elaborate much on the *quwwat-i ghazabi* beyond Tusi's explanation.

57. Tusi, *Akhlaq-i Nasiri*, 58.

58. Tusi, 58.

59. Ghazali, *Kimiya-i Sa'adat*, 7.

60. Tusi, *Akhlaq-i Nasiri*, 112–13; and Davani, *Akhlaq-i Jalali*, 84.

61. Tusi, *Akhlaq-i Nasiri*, 113; and Davani, *Akhlaq-i Jalali*, 84.

62. Tusi, *Akhlaq-i Nasiri*, 113; and Davani, *Akhlaq-i Jalali*, 84.

63. Tusi, *Akhlaq-i Nasiri*, 113; and Davani, *Akhlaq-i Jalali*, 84. Davani uses the term *'allav-i himmat*.

64. Davani, *Akhlaq-i Jalali*, 84.

65. Davani, 84.

66. Tusi, *Akhlaq-i Nasiri*, 113; and Davani, *Akhlaq-i Jalali*, 85.

67. Tusi, *Akhlaq-i Nasiri*, 113; and Davani, *Akhlaq-i Jalali*, 85.

68. Tusi, *Akhlaq-i Nasiri*, 113; and Davani, *Akhlaq-i Jalali*, 85.

69. Tusi, *Akhlaq-i Nasiri*, 113; and Davani, *Akhlaq-i Jalali*, 85.

70. Tusi, *Akhlaq-i Nasiri*, 113; and Davani, *Akhlaq-i Jalali*, 85.

71. Tusi, *Akhlaq-i Nasiri*, 113; and Davani, *Akhlaq-i Jalali*, 85.

72. Tusi, *Akhlaq-i Nasiri*, 113; and Davani, *Akhlaq-i Jalali*, 85.

73. Tusi, *Akhlaq-i Nasiri*, 113; and Davani, *Akhlaq-i Jalali*, 85.

74. Davani, *Akhlaq-i Jalali*, 85. This is my translation of the hadith as it is quoted in Arabic.

75. Muhammad ibn Isma'il Bukhari, *Sahih al-Bukhari: The Translation of the Meanings of Sahih Bukhari*, trans. Muhammad Muhsin Khan (Chicago: Kazi, 1976–79), 9:512.

76. Bukhari, 9:512.

77. See Sohail Akbar Warraich, "'Honor Killings' and the Law in Pakistan," in *"Honor": Crimes, Paradigms and Violence Against Women*, ed. Sara Hossain and Lynn Welchman (London: Zed, 2005), 90. For example, in contemporary Pakistan, the context of the hadith is taken quite literally. Murders involving *ghayrat* are seen as less punishable than *qatl-i amd*, or deliberate murder, because it is seen as a crime of passion protecting a man's honor from another man's sexual enjoyment of his wife.

78. Toshihiko Izutsu, *Sufism and Taoism: A Comparative Study of Key Philosophical Concepts* (Berkley: University of California Press, 1983), 249. Toshihiko Izutsu explains that Ibn Arabi read the hadith as "God is jealous . . . because He does not like the secret between Him and His servants be disclosed to others." Attributing jealousy to God in effect discourages confession of sins.

79. Davani, *Akhlaq-i Jalali*, 85.

80. Tusi, *Akhlaq-i Nasiri*, 113; and Davani, *Akhlaq-i Jalali*, 85.

81. Ghazali, *Kimiya-i Sa'adat*, 7; Tusi, *Akhlaq-i Nasiri*, 112–13; and Davani, *Akhlaq-i Jalali*, 84–85.

82. Ghazali, *Kimiya-i Sa'adat*, 7; and Tusi, *Akhlaq-i Nasiri*, 119.

83. Ghazali, *Kimiya-i Sa'adat*, 7.

84. Ghazali, 7–8.

85. Tusi, *Akhlaq-i Nasiri*, 119.

86. Tusi, 126.

87. Tusi, 58.

88. Tusi, 215; and Davani, *Akhlaq-i Jalali*, 188.

89. Francis Joseph Steingass, *A Comprehensive Persian-English Dictionary: Including the Arabic Words and Phrases to Be Met with in Persian Literature*, 5th ed. (London: Rutledge and Kegan Paul, 1892), 856. It is also a fairly common given name for girls in many Muslim societies.

90. Tusi, *Akhlaq-i Nasiri*, 58.

91. Steingass, *A Comprehensive Persian-English Dictionary*, 1319.

92. Edward William Lane, *Arabic-English Lexicon* (London: Williams and Norgate, 1863), 2848.

93. Ghazali, *Kimiya-i Sa'adat*, 8.

94. Tusi, *Akhlaq-i Nasiri*, 112–14; and Davani, *Akhlaq-i Jalali*, 86–88. Davani's discussion is identical to Tusi's here; however, he has additional sayings or examples explaining the qualities of *'iffat* that I indicate throughout.

95. Tusi, *Akhlaq-i Nasiri*, 114; and Davani, *Akhlaq-i Jalali*, 86.

96. Tusi, *Akhlaq-i Nasiri*, 114; and Davani, *Akhlaq-i Jalali*, 86.

97. Tusi, *Akhlaq-i Nasiri*, 114; and Davani, *Akhlaq-i Jalali*, 86.

98. Tusi, *Akhlaq-i Nasiri*, 114; and Davani, *Akhlaq-i Jalali*, 86.

99. Tusi, *Akhlaq-i Nasiri*, 114; and Davani, *Akhlaq-i Jalali*, 86.

100. Ali, *Sexual Ethics and Islam*, 9.

101. Tusi, *Akhlaq-i Nasiri*, 114; and Davani, *Akhlaq-i Jalali*, 86.

102. Tusi, *Akhlaq-i Nasiri*, 114; and Davani, *Akhlaq-i Jalali*, 87.

103. Tusi, *Akhlaq-i Nasiri*, 114; and Davani, *Akhlaq-i Jalali*, 86.

104. Davani, *Akhlaq-i Jalali*, 86.

105. Tusi, *Akhlaq-i Nasiri*, 215–16; and Davani, *Akhlaq-i Jalali*, 188–89.

106. Tusi, *Akhlaq-i Nasiri*, 114; and Davani, *Akhlaq-i Jalali*, 87.

107. Davani, *Akhlaq-i Jalali*, 87.

108. Davani, 190.

109. Tusi, *Akhlaq-i Nasiri*, 114; and Davani, *Akhlaq-i Jalali*, 87.

110. Tusi, *Akhlaq-i Nasiri*, 114; and Davani, *Akhlaq-i Jalali*, 87.

111. Tusi, *Akhlaq-i Nasiri*, 114; and Davani, *Akhlaq-i Jalali*, 87.

112. Tusi, *Akhlaq-i Nasiri*, 114–15; and Davani, *Akhlaq-i Jalali*, 87.

113. Ghazali, *Kimiya-i Sa'adat*, 307; Tusi, *Akhlaq-i Nasiri*, 206; Davani, *Akhlaq-i Jalali*, 179–81; and Yossef Rapoport, *Marriage, Money and Divorce in Medieval Society* (Cambridge: Cambridge University Press, 2005), 31–32.

114. Tusi, *Akhlaq-i Nasiri*, 115; and Davani, *Akhlaq-i Jalali*, 88.

115. Tusi, *Akhlaq-i Nasiri*, 115.

116. Davani, *Akhlaq-i Jalali*, 88–89.

117. Minlib Dallh, "Path to the Divine: Ansari's Sad Madyan and Manzi al-Sa'irin," *Muslim World* 103, no. 4 (2014): 467.

118. Dallh, 467.

119. Scott Kugle, *Sufis and Saints' Bodies: Mysticism, Corporeality, and Sacred Power in Islam* (Chapel Hill: University of North Carolina Press, 2007), 84, 108. Unlike sufism, *akhlaq* does not have any record of female practitioners; it was a school of thought, but not necessarily a school of practice, as in sufism. Even in sufi circles, Scott Kugle notes that although sufi women "broke through the stereotypes that surround [them] as holy people in women's bodies, . . . it could be said to not really be women at all but rather to have become 'men' through their spiritual aspiration and fortitude."

120. Gordon Newby, "Ibn Khaldun and Fredrick Jackson Turner: Islam and the Frontier Experience," *Journal of Asian and African Studies* 18, nos. 3–4 (1983): 274–85, 276.

121. Tusi, *Akhlaq-i Nasiri*, 115.

122. Ghazali, *Kimiya-i Sa'adat*, 8.

123. Ghazali, 8.

124. Ghazali, 302–3.

125. Tusi, *Akhlaq-i Nasiri*, 120; and Davani, *Akhlaq-i Jalali*, 104–5.

126. Davani, *Akhlaq-i Jalali*, 95.

127. Tusi, *Akhlaq-i Nasiri*, 109.

128. Tusi, 131.

129. George Fadlo Hourani, *Islamic Rationalism: The Ethics of 'Abd al-Jabbar* (Oxford: Clarendon, 1971), 10. The notion of justice as one of the key virtues of philosophical ethics is an extension of Shi'i and *Mu'tazilite* theology. As a Sunni, *ash'ari*, or determinist, school thinker who polemicized against philosophers earlier in his career, Ghazali does not state *'adl* as a fourth virtue of the soul as Tusi and Davani do, even though the latter two differ on how the virtue of *'adl* actually comes forth from the *nafs*.

130. Ghazali, *Kimiya-i Sa'adat*, 6–7.

131. Ghazali, 390–433.

132. Ghazali, 390–433.

133. John Woods, *The Aqquyunlu: Clan, Confederation, Empire* (Salt Lake City: University of Utah Press, 1999), 145. Justice is an important theological issue for Tusi, who was a Shi'i thinker. *'Adl* is an integral attribute of God, but also an important part of man's potential legacy and duty as vicegerent. Davani follows Tusi's approach to *tahdhib-i akhlaq* and so he retains Tusi's emphasis on justice, even though his broader theological views are *ishraqi* sufi. John Woods argues that Davani's political discourse is distinguished by an emphasis on just leadership, as opposed to favoring the "right" sect of Islam, as Ghazali and Tusi argue in some of their works.

134. amina wadud, *Inside the Gender Jihad* (Oxford: Oneworld, 2006), 32–35. Amina wadud reads that Qur'anic text as emphasizing human responsibility, not just male responsibility, to be *khalifahs* of God.

135. Tusi, *Akhlaq-i Nasiri*, 111, 115. Note that Ghazali does not discuss specific qualities of *'adl*, as discussed earlier.

136. Tusi, 115; and Davani, *Akhlaq-i Jalali*, 88–89.

137. Davani, *Akhlaq-i Jalali*, 89.

138. Tusi, *Akhlaq-i Nasiri*, 115–16; and Davani, *Akhlaq-i Jalali*, 89.

139. Tusi, *Akhlaq-i Nasiri*, 116; and Davani, *Akhlaq-i Jalali*, 89.

140. Tusi, *Akhlaq-i Nasiri*, 116; and Davani, *Akhlaq-i Jalali*, 89.

141. Davani, *Akhlaq-i Jalali*, 89.

142. Davani, 90. Davani is most likely referring to Shaykh Abu Bakr Shibli (d. 946).

143. Davani, 90.

144. This ethics of compassion allows one to use one's imagination and accounts for emotions such as sympathy in determining how one treats others.

145. Tusi, *Akhlaq-i Nasiri*, 116; and Davani, *Akhlaq-i Jalali*, 90–91.

146. Davani, *Akhlaq-i Jalali*, 91.

147. Tusi, *Akhlaq-i Nasiri*, 116; and Davani, *Akhlaq-i Jalali*, 91.

148. Tusi, *Akhlaq-i Nasiri*, 116; and Davani, *Akhlaq-i Jalali*, 91.

149. Tusi, *Akhlaq-i Nasiri*, 116; and Davani, *Akhlaq-i Jalali*, 91.

150. Tusi, *Akhlaq-i Nasiri*, 116; and Davani, *Akhlaq-i Jalali*, 91.

151. Tusi, *Akhlaq-i Nasiri*, 116; and Davani, *Akhlaq-i Jalali*, 91.

152. Tusi, *Akhlaq-i Nasiri*, 116.

153. Tusi, 315.

154. Tusi, 114; and Davani, *Akhlaq-i Jalali*, 86.

155. Davani, *Akhlaq-i Jalali*, 91.

156. Tusi, *Akhlaq-i Nasiri*, 114.

157. Tusi, 109.

158. Tusi, 110.

159. Tusi, 70–71.

160. Tusi, 71.

161. Ghazali quoted in Davani, *Akhlaq-i Jalali*, 78–79. The quotation is in Arabic. In its footnote on the same page, Arani notes that there are several words in this quotation that are different across various manuscripts of *Akhalq-i Jalali*.

162. Davani, 57.

163. Davani, 223.

164. Tusi, *Akhlaq-i Nasiri*, 134, 136.

165. Tusi, 135.

166. Tusi, 206–7, 307–8; and Davani, *Akhlaq-i Jalali*, 184–85, 263–66.

167. Khaliq Ahmad and Arif Hassan, "Distributive Justice: The Islamic Perspective," *Intellectual Discourse* 8, no. 2 (2000): 159–72, 163.

168. Tusi, *Akhlaq-i Nasiri*, 120.

169. Tusi, 124; and Davani, *Akhlaq-i Jalali*, 95–96.

170. Tusi, *Akhlaq-i Nasiri*, 110.

171. Tusi, 59.

172. Louise Marlowe, *Hierarchy and Egalitarianism in Islamic Thought* (Cambridge: Cambridge University Press, 1997), 54. In line with Ibn Sinan philosophy, humans have less intelligence than angels, who are more proximate to God.

173. Ghazali and Davani hold this view as well, even though they do not discuss the *nafs* in the context of nonhuman life.

174. Arthur Lovejoy, *The Great Chain of Being: The Study of the History of an Idea* (Cambridge, MA: Harvard University Press, 1966).

175. Lovejoy, 58.

176. Lovejoy, 58.

177. Lovejoy, 59.

178. Tusi, *Akhlaq-i Nasiri*, 60; and Nancy Tuana, "Aristotle and the Politics of Reproduction," in *Engendering Origins: Critical Feminist Readings in Plato and Aristotle*, ed. Bat-Ami Bar On (Albany: State University of New York Press, 1994), 195–200. Tuana shows the parallel ways in which Aristotle also considered the male form as primary and refuted the strength of the female seed.

179. Tusi, *Akhlaq-i Nasiri*, 60.

180. Tusi, 60.

181. Tusi, 60. He quotes the hadith in Arabic.

182. Tusi, 60.

183. Ghazali, *Kimiya-i Sa'adat*, 22.

184. Ghazali, 22.

185. Ghazali, 22.

186. Ghazali, 24.

187. Ghazali, 24.

188. Ghazali, 24.

189. Ghazali, 24.

190. Ghazali, 24.

191. Ghazali, 28.

192. Tusi, *Akhlaq-i Nasiri*, 72.

193. Tusi, 61.

194. Tusi, 61–62.

195. Tusi, 62.

196. Davani, *Akhlaq-i Jalali*, 94–95; and Tusi, *Akhlaq-i Nasiri*, 122–25.

197. Sarra Tlili, *Animals in the Qur'an* (Cambridge: Cambridge University Press, 2012), 219–20.

198. Tusi, *Akhlaq-i Nasiri*, 62.

199. Tusi, 216; Ghazali, *Kimiya-i Sa'adat*, 305–6, 311; and Davani, *Akhlaq-i Jalali*, 188.

200. Tusi, *Akhlaq-i Nasiri*, 218; Ghazali, *Kimiya-i Sa'adat*, 316; and Davani, *Akhlaq-i Jalali*, 156, 189.

201. Tusi, *Akhlaq-i Nasiri*, 63–64.

202. Ann K. S. Lambton, *Continuity and Change in Medieval Persia: Aspects of Administrative, Economic and Social History, 11th–14th Century* (Albany: Bibliotheca Persica, 1988), 145.

203. Tusi, *Akhlaq-i Nasiri*, 62.

204. Ibn Khaldun, *The Muqaddimah: An Introduction to History*, ed. N. J. Dawood and trans. Franz Rosenthal (Princeton: Princeton University Press, 1969), 63. In his *Muqaddimah*, a prolegomenon to an encyclopedia of world history, Ibn Khaldun (d. 1406) describes how climate and heat affect human character. He reasons that because Negroes live in hot climates, "heat dominates their temperament and formation," their "animal spirit" (probably the *quwwat-i shahwi*) is more prominent than their other faculties. For Ibn Khaldun, this explains why "Negroes are in general characterized by levity, excitability, and great emotionalism. They are found eager to dance whenever they hear a melody. They are everywhere described as stupid." Ibn Khaldun lived between the lifetimes of Tusi and Davani. As a premodern Muslim polymath, Tusi would have held similar ideas about racialized sociologies and behaviors based on climate and geography.

205. Luce Irigaray, *Speculum of the Other Woman*, trans. Gillian C. Gill (Ithaca: Cornell University Press, 1985), 18–20.

206. Irigaray, *An Ethics of Sexual Difference*, 6. Irigaray arrives at this point by arguing that because men are normative, women do not exist in Western philosophy except as maternal vessels. She moves into the direction of establishing sex differences by recovering the male body and reimagining the female body, and as such has been critiqued by Judith Butler as being a sex-difference essentialist. Butler argues instead that both sex and gender are constructed through embodied acts, not biologically predetermined.

207. L. Goodman, "Razi's Myth of the Fall of the Soul: Its Function in His Philosophy," in *Essays in Islamic Philosophy and Science*, ed. G. Hourani (Albany: State
University of New York Press, 1975), 198–215, 202.

208. L. Goodman, "Muhammad ibn Zakariyya' al-Razi," in *History of Islamic Philosophy*, ed. S. H. Nasr and O. Leaman (London: Routledge, 1996), 25–40, 25,
32. Interestingly, even though the soul is always embodied and material, and
therefore its refinement is embodied, the soul itself is feminine for Razi because
it is unruly and in need of order.

3. ETHICS OF MARRIAGE AND THE DOMESTIC ECONOMY

1. Judith Butler, "Performative Acts and Gender Constitution: An Essay in Phe-
nomenology and Feminist Theory," in *Performing Feminisms: Feminist Critical
Theory and Theatre*, ed. Sue-Ellen Case (Baltimore: Johns Hopkins University
Press, 1990), 272.

2. Abu Hamid al-Ghazali, *Kimiya-i Sa'adat*, ed. Hossein Khadivjam (Tehran: Ketabhaaye Jibi, 1975), 308; and Tusi, Nasir-ad Din Muhammad ibn Muhammad
Tusi, *Akhlaq-i Nasiri*, ed. Mojtaba Minvi and Alireza Haydari (Tehran: Zar,
1977), 218.

3. Lev Weitz, "Al-Ghazali, Bar Hebraeus, and the 'Good Wife,'" *Journal of the
American Oriental Society* 134, no. 2 (2014): 203–23, 210.

4. Weitz, 222.

5. Weitz, 221.

6. Elizabeth Clark, "Thinking with Women: the Uses of the Appeal to 'Woman' in
Pre-Nicene Christian Propaganda Literature," in *The Spread of Christianity in
the First Four Centuries: Essays in Explanation*, ed. W. V. Harris (Leiden: Brill,
2005), 45.

7. Weitz, "Al-Ghazali, Bar Hebraeus, and the 'Good Wife,'" 222.

8. Carole Hillenbrand, "Women in the Saljuq Period," in *Women in Iran from the
Rise of Islam to 1800*, ed. Guity Nashat and Lois Beck (Champaign: University
of Illinois Press, 2003), 107.

9. Marion Katz, *Women in the Mosque: A History of Legal Thought and Social Practice* (New York: Columbia University Press, 2014), 7.

10. Roxanne Euben, *Journeys to the Other Shore: Muslim and Western Travelers in
Search of Knowledge* (Princeton: Princeton University Press, 2006), 81. Examples of real women do not exist in the *akhlaq* texts. Roxanne Euben explains
that Ibn Battuta did not mention specific women in his *rihla* because he "conforms to [the] convention" that women belong in the private sphere, and thus

are not noteworthy. This common attitude from the middle periods is responsible for the scarcity of rich narrative sources about women's lives.

11. Nadia El Cheikh, *Women, Islam, and Abbasid Identity* (Cambridge, MA: Harvard University Press, 2015), 15.

12. Euben, 81.

13. Euben, 80.

14. Euben, 81.

15. Euben, 81. Carl Ernst and I, along with my colleagues Mathew Hotham and Mathew Lynch, have counted Ibn Battuta as having contracted ten marriages throughout his journeys as published in Ross Dunn's volume. Euben states that he married four women from Maldives at the same time and "swears that he lived only on coconuts known as aphrodisiacs for his entire year and a half stay there."

16. Huda Lutfi, "Manners and Customs of Fourteenth-Century Cairene Women: Female Anarchy Versus Male Shar'i Order in Muslim Prescriptive Treatises," in *Women in Middle Eastern History: Shifting Boundaries in Sex and Gender,* ed. Nikki Keddie and Beth Baron (New Haven: Yale University Press, 1991), 102.

17. Lutfi, 101.

18. Lutfi, 106.

19. Tusi, *Akhlaq-i Nasiri,* 217; Ghazali, *Kimiya-i Sa'adat,* 317; and Jalal ad-Din Davani, *Akhlaq-i Jalali,* ed. Abdullah Masoudi Arani (Tehran: Intesharat-i Italat, 2013), 189–90.

20. Ghazali, *Kimiya-i Sa'adat,* 308; and Tusi, *Akhlaq-i Nasiri,* 218.

21. Ghazali, *Kimiya-i Sa'adat,* 308, 316; Tusi, *Akhlaq-i Nasiri,* 218, 310; and Davani, *Akhlaq-i Jalali,* 156, 189.

22. Karen Bauer, *Gender Hierarchy in the Qur'an: Medieval Interpretations, Modern Responses* (Cambridge: Cambridge University Press, 2015), 165; and Kecia Ali, *Marriage and Slavery in Early Islam* (Cambridge, MA: Harvard University Press, 2010), 6.

23. Tusi, *Akhlaq-i Nasiri,* 215.

24. Davani, *Akhlaq-i Jalali,* 178.

25. Christian Lange, "Crime and Punishment in Islamic History (Early to Middle Period): A Framework for Analysis," *Religion Compass* 4, no. 11 (2010): 694–706, 699–700.

26. Sharon Y. Nickols, *Remaking Home Economics: Resourcefulness and Innovation in Changing Times* (Athens: University of Georgia Press, 2015). By an unexpected but appropriate coincidence, use of the term *economics* to describe the household order harkens back to nineteenth- and twentieth-century home economics curricula. Home economics courses, taught mostly to girls in US middle schools and high schools, covered interior design, cooking, cleaning, sewing,

nutrition, child development, and family planning. The notion that these are areas of economics shows how intimately connected the home and therefore marriage are to the management and deputyship of the husband.

27. Davani, *Akhlaq-i Jalali*, 188.

28. Tusi, *Akhlaq-i Nasiri*, 215.

29. Tusi, 215.

30. Ghazali, *Kimiya-i Sa'adat*, 302.

31. Ghazali, 303.

32. Ghazali, 305.

33. Ghazali, 305–6. Ghazali himself benefited from this feature of marriage.

34. Ghazali, 306.

35. Ghazali, 307.

36. Ghazali, 308.

37. Ghazali, 308.

38. Ghazali, 308.

39. Ghazali, 318.

40. Weitz, "Al-Ghazali, Bar Hebraeus, and the 'Good Wife,'" 210.

41. Ghazali, *Kimiya-i Sa'adat*, 308.

42. Tusi, *Akhlaq-i Nasiri*, 221–22; and Davani, *Akhlaq-i Jalali*, 193.

43. Ghazali, *Kimiya-i Sa'adat*, 302.

44. Ghazali, 305–306; Tusi, *Akhlaq-i Nasiri*, 215; and Davani, *Akhlaq-i Jalali*, 180–81.

45. Katz, *Women in the Mosque*, 4.

46. Ghazali, *Kimiya-i Sa'adat*, 311.

47. Tusi, *Akhlaq-i Nasiri*, 215.

48. Ghazali, *Kimiya-i Sa'adat*, 311.

49. Ghazali, 311.

50. Ghazali, 311.

51. Ghazali, 312.

52. Ghazali, 311.

53. Ghazali, 312.

54. Ghazali, 312.

55. Ghazali, 312. Perhaps this was an implicit comment on greed or on the social practice of heavy dowers.

56. Ghazali, 312.

57. Kathryn Kueny, *Conceiving Identities: Maternity in Medieval Muslim Discourse and Practice* (Albany: State University of New York Press, 2013), 13.

58. Ghazali, *Kimiya-i Sa'adat*, 312.

59. Carolyn Baugh, *Minor Marriage in Early Islamic Law* (Leiden: Brill, 2017), 10.

60. Ali, *Marriage and Slavery*, 33.

61. Baugh, *Minor Marriage in Early Islamic Law*, 150.

62. Ali, *Marriage and Slavery*, 33.

63. Ali, 113.

64. Ghazali, *Kimiya-i Sa'adat*, 312.

65. Asma Sayeed, *Women and the Transmission of Religious Knowledge in Islam* (Cambridge: Cambridge University Press, 2013), 114; Richard Bulliet, "Women and the Urban Religious Elite in the Pre-Mongol Period," in *Women in Iran from the Rise of Islam to 1800*, ed. Guity Nashat and Lois Beck (Champaign: University of Illinois Press, 2003), 71, 78; and Richard Bulliet, *The Patricians of Nishapur: A Study in Medieval Islamic Social History* (Cambridge, MA: Harvard University Press, 1972), 47–60. Sayeed argues that among other reasons for the revival of women's participation in hadith scholarship from the tenth to fifteenth century was that kinship networks of *'ulama'* families benefited from women's participation in knowledge transmission, which became part of their cultural and social capital and even led the *'ulama'* to relax the "legal and normative aversion to contact between non-mahram men and women." Often, these were women of the scholars' own households.

    Bulliet writes that in eleventh-century Nishapur, Baghdad, and Gorgan, biographical dictionaries of *'ulama'* show minimal presence of women in the context of praising their educational accomplishments. Since education was hereditary, the women in the household of *'ulama'* families acquired the same education as their male siblings or relations. They had the same Qur'an and hadith lessons, excelled in writing and Arabic, and also gave instruction to their children. Bulliet concludes that among the Nishapur patricians, women were equal to men in the realm of education.

66. Ghazali, *Kimiya-i Sa'adat*, 312–13.

67. Tusi, *Akhlaq-i Nasiri*, 215–16; and Davani, *Akhlaq-i Jalali*, 188. Quoted here is my translation of Tusi's passage. Davani has an identical list.

68. Mir-Hosseini, "Construction of Gender in Islamic Thought and Strategies for Reform," 1–28. *Akhlaq* frames motherhood not as a primary role of a wife, but as a primary instrumental role of a wife that she performs for her husband. Ziba Mir-Hosseini has written that neotraditionalists of *fiqh* who believe in the complementarity of the sexes uphold unequal models of gender relations, which originate in the notion of a wife's instrumentality. She writes that they "take issue with the assumption that 'women are created of or for men,' contending instead that in the Islamic view women are equal to men in creation, and do not depend on men for attaining perfection, but can attain their perfection independently. Yet they uphold the *fiqh* model of gender relations, reject gender equality and instead put forward the notion of complementarity of gender rights and duties."

69. Davani, *Akhlaq-i Jalali*, 188.

70. Ghazali, *Kimiya-i Sa'adat*, 311; and Tusi, *Akhlaq-i Nasiri*, 215.

71. Ghazali, *Kimiya-i Sa'adat*, 311.

72. Tusi, *Akhlaq-i Nasiri*, 215.

73. Ghazali, *Kimiya-i Sa'adat*, 305–6.

74. Ali, *Marriage and Slavery*, 66.

75. Tusi, *Akhlaq-i Nasiri*, 216; and Davani, *Akhlaq-i Jalali*, 188.

76. Ghazali quotes this saying in the *Ihya' 'Ulum ad-Din*, not the *Kimiya*.

77. Tusi, *Akhlaq-i Nasiri*, 221; and Davani, *Akhlaq-i Jalali*, 193.

78. Tusi, *Akhlaq-i Nasiri*, 221; and Davani, *Akhlaq-i Jalali*, 193.

79. Tusi, *Akhlaq-i Nasiri*, 219; and Davani, *Akhlaq-i Jalali*, 192.

80. Tusi, *Akhlaq-i Nasiri*, 220. This is very similar to the description of the love a mother has for a child in later sections.

81. Tusi, *Akhlaq-i Nasiri*, 220.

82. Tusi, *Akhlaq-i Nasiri*, 220.

83. Ali, *Marriage and Slavery*, 30.

84. The term *haybat* also implies being impressive or having gravity and sternness.

85. Tusi, *Akhlaq-i Nasiri*, 216; and Davani, *Akhlaq-i Jalali*, 189. The passage I quote here is from Tusi; Davani's passage is identical.

86. Ghazali, *Kimiya-i Sa'adat*, 315.

87. Ghazali, 315.

88. Hanna Kassis, *A Concordance of the Quran* (Berkeley: University of California Press, 1983), 955; and Ziba Mir-Hosseini, Mulki Al-Sharmani, and Jana Rumminger, *Men in Charge? Rethinking Authority in Muslim Legal Tradition* (London: Oneworld, 2015). The other two appearances of *qawwam* are about being securers of justice. Mir-Hosseini's volume problematizes the widespread reliance on this term/concept to describe gender relations in Islam.

89. Tusi, *Akhlaq-i Nasiri*, 216; and Davani, *Akhlaq-i Jalali*, 189.

90. Ghazali, *Kimiya-i Sa'adat*, 314.

91. Tusi, *Akhlaq-i Nasiri*, 217; and Davani, *Akhlaq-i Jalali*, 190.

92. Davani, *Akhlaq-i Jalali*, 189–90.

93. Davani, 190–91.

94. Davani, 191.

95. Ghazali, *Kimiya-i Sa'adat*, 302–3; Tusi, *Akhlaq-i Nasiri*, 120; and Davani, *Akhlaq-i Jalali*, 189–90.

96. Judith Tucker, *Women, Family, and Gender in Islamic Law* (Cambridge: Cambridge University Press, 2008), 53.

97. Ghazali, *Kimiya-i Sa'adat*, 317.

98. Tusi, *Akhlaq-i Nasiri*, 218.

99. Tusi, 215, 219; and Davani, *Akhlaq-i Jalali*, 192.

100. Tusi, *Akhlaq-i Nasiri*, 218.

101. Kecia Ali, *Sexual Ethics and Islam: Feminist Reflections on Qur'an, Hadith, and Jurisprudence* (Oxford: Oneworld, 2006), 6–9.

102. Ali, 13.

103. Ghazali, *Kimiya-i Sa'adat*, 319.

104. Ghazali, 314.

105. Ghazali, 320.

106. Ghazali, 320.

107. Sa'diyya Shaikh, "Family Planning, Contraception, and Abortion in Islam: Undertaking *Khilafa*," in *Sacred Rights: The Case for Contraception and Abortion in World Religions*, ed. Daniel C. Maguire (Oxford: Oxford University Press 2003), 105–28.

108. Ali, *Sexual Ethics and Islam*, 8.

109. Tusi, *Akhlaq-i Nasiri*, 155.

110. Tusi, 220; and Davani, *Akhlaq-i Jalali*, 192.

111. Ghazali, *Kimiya-i Sa'adat*, 401; Tusi, *Akhlaq-i Nasiri*, 220; Davani, *Akhlaq-i Jalali*, 193; and Ali, *Marriage and Slavery*, 22.

112. Tusi, *Akhlaq-i Nasiri*, 120, 215; and Davani, *Akhlaq-i Jalali*, 188–90.

113. Ghazali, *Kimiya-i Sa'adat*, 302–3; Tusi, *Akhlaq-i Nasiri*, 120; and Davani, *Akhlaq-i Jalali*, 190.

114. Davani, *Akhlaq-i Jalali*, 190; Ghazali, *Kimiya-i Sa'adat*, 302–3; and Tusi, *Akhlaq-i Nasiri*, 120. I quote Davani here, but Ghazali and Tusi express identical sentiments.

115. Tusi, *Akhlaq-i Nasiri*, 217; and Davani, *Akhlaq-i Jalali*, 189.

116. Ghazali, *Kimiya-i Sa'adat*, 316.

117. Katz, *Women in the Mosque*, 100, 102.

118. Ghazali, *Kimiya-i Sa'adat*, 316–17.

119. Ghazali, 316.

120. Ghazali, 317.

121. Tusi, *Akhlaq-i Nasiri*, 149. Tusi also says that if one's *shahwat* is too sluggish, then one is not motivated to have any children.

122. Tusi, 215; and Ghazali, *Kimiya-i Sa'adat*, 311.

123. Ali, *Marriage and Slavery*, 65.

124. Yossef Rapoport, *Marriage, Money and Divorce in Medieval Society* (Cambridge: Cambridge University Press, 2005), 13–15.

125. Ghazali, *Kimiya-i Sa'adat*, 311; Tusi, *Akhlaq-i Nasiri*, 216–17; and Davani, *Akhlaq-i Jalali*, 188–89.

126. Tusi, *Akhlaq-i Nasiri*, 231; and Davani, *Akhlaq-i Jalali*, 193.

127. Tusi, *Akhlaq-i Nasiri*, 216–17.

128. Davani, *Akhlaq-i Jalali*, 188–89.

129. Tusi, *Akhlaq-i Nasiri*, 215.

130. Tusi, 216; and Davani, *Akhlaq-i Jalali*, 190.

131. Tusi, *Akhlaq-i Nasiri*, 225.

132. Tusi, 218; and Davani, *Akhlaq-i Jalali*, 190.

133. Ghazali, *Kimiya-i Sa'adat*, 318.

134. Rapoport, *Marriage, Money and Divorce in Medieval Society*, 32.

135. Rapoport, 33.

136. Rapoport, 52.

137. Rapoport, 52.

138. Tusi, *Akhlaq-i Nasiri*, 225.

139. Tusi, 216–17.

140. Ghazali, *Kimiya-i Sa'adat*, 430; Tusi, *Akhlaq-i Nasiri*, 238; and Davani, *Akhlaq-i Jalali*, 206.

141. Kueny, *Conceiving Identities*, 3, 53.

142. G. M. Wickens, "Nasir ad-Din Tusi on the Fall of Baghdad: A Further Study," *Journal of Semitic Studies* 7, no. 1 (1962): 27. Tusi explains that the emperor of the world, 'Abd al-'Aziz al-Nishapuri (Hulegu), commissioned an addendum about virtues and avoiding vices in the treatment of parents. Tusi defends the first version of his work as mentioning the rights of parents in several places, but he admits that there was a serious lacuna that warrants the addition of the section on parents' rights. G. M. Wickens hypothesizes it is possible that the addendum was suggested by Hulegu's son after he succeeded his father, since Tusi dates the addendum to 663, about ten years before he died.

143. Ghazali does not discuss medical ideas about reproduction.

144. Tusi, *Akhlaq-i Nasiri*, 237–38.

145. Kueny, *Conceiving Identities*, 54.

146. Kueny, 52–55.

147. Kueny, 9.

148. Tusi, *Akhlaq-i Nasiri*, 238; and Davani, *Akhlaq-i Jalali*, 206.

149. Davani, *Akhlaq-i Jalali*, 181.

150. Judith Tucker, *In the House of the Law* (Berkley: University of California Press, 1998), 113, 118.

151. Zahra Ayubi, "Rearing Gendered Souls: Childhood and the Making of Muslim Manhood in Pre-Modern Islamic Ethics," *Journal of the American Academy of Religion*, forthcoming.

152. Tusi, *Akhlaq-i Nasiri*, 238.

153. Ghazali, *Kimiya-i Sa'adat*, 2:29; and Tusi, *Akhlaq-i Nasiri*, 223.

154. Tusi, *Akhlaq-i Nasiri*, 224.

155. Ghazali, *Kimiya-i Sa'adat*, 2:28; and Tusi, *Akhlaq-i Nasiri*, 225.

156. Tusi, *Akhlaq-i Nasiri*, 228.

157. Ghazali, *Kimiya-i Sa'adat*, 2:469; and Tusi, *Akhlaq-i Nasiri*, 226–27.

158. Davani, *Akhlaq-i Jalali*, 189, 193.

159. Tusi, *Akhlaq-i Nasiri*, 227.

160. I have not been able to verify this in Giladi's or Kueny's works. With regard to girls' education, Asma Sayeed and Richard Bulliet argue that in elite and *'ulama'* families, girls would have instruction in reading, writing, and reciting the Qur'an, but it is not clear who is in charge of their lessons.

161. Tusi, *Akhlaq-i Nasiri*, 229–30; and Davani, *Akhlaq-i Jalali*, 200.

162. Ghazali, *Kimiya-i Sa'adat*, 321–22.

163. Kueny, *Conceiving Identities*, 6.

164. Tusi, *Akhlaq-i Nasiri*, 339; and Davani, *Akhlaq-i Jalali*, 207.

165. Tusi, *Akhlaq-i Nasiri*, 238.

166. Tusi, *Akhlaq-i Nasiri*, 237–38; and Davani, *Akhlaq-i Jalali*, 206.

167. Tusi, *Akhlaq-i Nasiri*, 236–37.

168. Tusi, 238.

169. Ghazali, *Kimiya-i Sa'adat*, 430.

170. Ghazali, 430. Ghazali's quotation is not a Qur'anic quotation but Khadivjam, the editor of the manuscript, has still set it off in the text with italics.

171. Ghazali, 430. Ghazali uses the term *ghaza* for war instead of *jihad* because he specifically means that doing good deeds for parents is better than the lesser *jihad* for the sake of Islam.

172. Ghazali, 430.

173. Ghazali, 430.

174. Tusi, *Akhlaq-i Nasiri*, 238–39.

175. Tusi, 239.

176. Tusi, 239.

177. Tusi, 238.

178. Since these texts are addressed to men, it is unknown exactly what reasons the ethicists would suggest to daughters for their indebtedness to parents. But likely it is also that they are the biological causes of their existence (perhaps the father more so than the mother, but we do not know for sure), as well as the financial resources fathers pour into their daughters' upbringing.

179. Kueny, *Conceiving Identities*, 8.

180. Tusi, *Akhlaq-i Nasiri*, 239; and Davani, *Akhlaq-i Jalali*, 208.

181. Tusi, *Akhlaq-i Nasiri*, 239; and Davani, *Akhlaq-i Jalali*, 208.

182. Ghazali, *Kimiya-i Sa'adat*, 432.

183. Ghazali, 430.

184. Ghazali, 468; and Ghazali, *Ihya' 'Ulum ad-Din* (Cairo: Mu'assasat al-Halabi, 1968), 3:92.

185. Avner Giladi, *Infants, Parents, and Wet-Nurses: Medieval Islamic Views on Breastfeeding and Their Social Implications* (Leiden: Brill, 1999), 49, 54. Nonetheless, physicians and jurisconsults preferred maternal nursing because it was thought to mutually benefit mother and child.

186. Ghazali, *Kimiya-i Sa'adat*, 430–32. Tusi's and Davani's sections on children's upbringing are also three times as long as the sections on the rights of parents.

187. Ghazali, 430.

188. Ghazali, 432.

189. Weitz, "Al-Ghazali, Bar Hebraeus, and the 'Good Wife,'" 219–20.

190. Tucker, *Women, Family, and Gender*, 85; and Rapoport, *Marriage, Money and Divorce in Medieval Society*, 3, 70.

191. Rapoport, *Marriage, Money and Divorce in Medieval Society*, 69.

192. Rapoport 69, 113; and Tucker, *Women, Family, and Gender*, 104–11. Tucker outlines the ways in which courts provided women with recourse but also how the divorce jurisprudence itself favors men.

193. Ghazali, *Kimiya-i Sa'adat*, 311.

194. Ghazali, 311; Tusi, 215–16; and Davani, *Akhlaq-i Jalali*, 189.

195. Tusi, *Akhlaq-i Nasiri*, 220.

196. Ali, *Marriage and Slavery*, 138.

197. Ghazali, *Kimiya-i Sa'adat*, 313.

198. Ghazali, 322.

199. Tusi, *Akhlaq-i Nasiri*, 220; and Davani, *Akhlaq-i Jalali*, 192.

200. Ali, *Marriage and Slavery*, 12.

201. Tusi, *Akhlaq-i Nasiri*, 220; and Davani, *Akhlaq-i Jalali*, 193. Davani paraphrases from Tusi's list.

202. Ghazali, *Kimiya-i Sa'adat*, 319.

203. Kecia Ali, "Religious Practices: Obedience and Disobedience in Islamic Discourses," in *The Encyclopedia of Women in Islamic Cultures*, ed. Suad Joseph (Leiden: Brill, 2007), 5:310.

204. Ghazali, *Kimiya-i Sa'adat*, 319.

205. Ali, "Religious Practices," 310.

206. Ayesha Chaudhry, *Domestic Violence and the Islamic Tradition* (Oxford: Oxford University Press, 2013), 119. She is drawing his opinion from his text *Al-Wasit fi al-Madhhab*.

207. Behnam Sadeghi, *The Logic of Law Making in Islam: Women and Prayer in the Legal Tradition* (Cambridge: Cambridge University Press, 2013), 165–71. Behnam Sadeghi calls such assumptions "legal reasons" that change over long periods of time as a result of cumulative and incremental changes in jurists' attitudes toward a given topic. However, he argues, changes in legal reasons do not always change the laws themselves, but rather the justifications for them.

208. Tucker, *Women, Family, and Gender in Islamic Law*, 86.
209. Tucker, 86.
210. Tusi, *Akhlaq-i Nasiri*, 220.
211. Ali, "Religious Practices," 311.
212. Ghazali, *Kimiya-i Sa'adat*, 322.
213. Adrien Leites, "Ghazali's Alteration of Hadiths: Process and Meaning," *Oriens* 40, no. 1 (2012): 133–48. Leites argues that Ghazali was not a very good scholar of hadith and strategically altered them.
214. Zahra Ayubi, "Negotiating Justice: American Muslim Women Navigating Islamic Divorce and Civil Law," *Journal for Islamic Studies* 30, no. 1 (2010): 78–102. However, in contemporary Muslim societies, the hadith is commonly used to discourage women from seeking divorce.
215. Ghazali, *Kimiya-i Sa'adat*, 322.
216. Ghazali, 322.
217. Davani, *Akhlaq-i Jalali*, 193.
218. Tucker, *In the House of the Law*, 113, 118. Tucker discusses mothers being awarded custody by courts in Ottoman Syria and Palestine.
219. Davani, *Akhlaq-i Jalali*, 193.
220. Ghazali, *Kimiya-i Sa'adat*, 322.
221. Tusi, *Akhlaq-i Nasiri*, 217.

4. HOMOSOCIAL MASCULINITY AND SOCIETAL ETHICS

1. Nasir-ad Din Muhammad ibn Muhammad Tusi, *Akhlaq-i Nasiri*, ed. Mojtaba Minvi and Alireza Haydari (Tehran: Zar, 1977), 254.
2. R. W. Connell, *The Men and the Boys* (Berkley: University of California Press, 2001), 11.
3. Connell, 11, 43–44.
4. For example, Marion Katz, *Women in the Mosque: A History of Legal Thought and Social Practice* (New York: Columbia University Press, 2014), 102; Carole Hillenbrand, "Women in the Saljuq Period," in *Women in Iran from the Rise of Islam to 1800*, ed. Guity Nashat and Lois Beck (Champaign: University of Illinois Press, 2003), 107, 115; Julie Scott Meisami, "Eleventh-Century Women: Evidence from Bayhaqi's History," in *Women in Iran from the Rise of Islam to 1800*, ed. Guity Nashat and Lois Beck (Champaign: University of Illinois Press, 2003), 81–83; and several essays about archival and legal records about women, in Amira El-Azhary Sonbol, *Beyond the Exotic: Women's Histories in Islamic Societies* (Syracuse: Syracuse University Press, 2005).
5. Susan Ossman, "Cities: Islamic Cities," in *Encyclopedia of Women in Islamic Cultures*, ed. Suad Josef (Leiden: Brill, 2005), 3:23–26. Susan Ossman reviews

the substantial work of scholars such as Janet Abu-Lughod and Leslie Pierce who refute the Orientalist view of the "Islamic city," in which women were "powerless and homebound."

6. Ultimately Irigaray calls for reinterpretation of "everything concerning the relations between the subject and discourse, the subject and the world, the subject and the cosmic, the microcosmic and the macrocosmic," precisely because all of these have been articulated with males as the universal humans. Irigaray, *An Ethics of Sexual Difference*, 6.

7. Tusi, *Akhlaq-i Nasiri*, 258.

8. Tusi, 322; and Jalal ad-Din Davani, *Akhlaq-i Jalali*, ed. Abdullah Masoudi Arani (Tehran: Intesharat-i Italat, 2013), 281–82.

9. Tusi, *Akhlaq-i Nasiri*, 322.

10. Louise Marlowe, *Hierarchy and Egalitarianism in Islamic Thought* (Cambridge: Cambridge University Press, 1997), 159.

11. Davani, *Akhlaq-i Jalali*, 228.

12. Davani, 230–31.

13. Tusi, *Akhlaq-i Nasiri*, 260.

14. Tusi, 260.

15. Abu Hamid al-Ghazali, *Kimiya-i Sa'adat*, ed. Hossein Khadivjam (Tehran: Ketabhaaye Jibi, 1975), 394.

16. Ghazali, 394.

17. Ghazali, 403.

18. Tusi, *Akhlaq-i Nasiri*, 270.

19. Tusi, 270–71, 238; and Davani, *Akhlaq-i Jalali*, 206. They mention the love and respect mothers are due elsewhere.

20. Davani, *Akhlaq-i Jalali*, 235–36.

21. Davani, 237.

22. Davani, 237.

23. Davani, 207–8.

24. Davani, 233.

25. Davani, 234.

26. Roy Mottahedeh, "Friendship in Islamic Ethical Philosophy," in *Essays in Islamic Philology, History, and Philosophy*, ed. Alireza Korangy et al. (Berlin: De Gruyter, 2016), 236.

27. Davani, *Akhlaq-i Jalali*, 229.

28. Davani, 229–30.

29. Davani, 238.

30. Tusi, *Akhlaq-i Nasiri*, 321.

31. Ghazali, *Kimiya-i Sa'adat*, 390.

32. Brenna Moore, "Friendship and the Cultivation of Religious Sensibilities," *Journal of the American Academy of Religion* 83, no. 2 (2015): 439.

33. Moore, 441.

34. Moore, 440.

35. Fedwa Malti-Douglas, *Women's Body, Women's Word: Gender and Discourse in Arabo-Islamic Writing* (Princeton: Princeton University Press, 1991), 5.

36. Mottahedeh, "Friendship in Islamic Ethical Philosophy," 237.

37. Ghazali, *Kimiya-i Sa'adat*, 401.

38. Ghazali, 401.

39. Ghazali, 403.

40. Ghazali, 403.

41. Ghazali, 406.

42. Ghazali, 407.

43. Ghazali, 408.

44. Ghazali, 410.

45. Ghazali, 410.

46. Ghazali, 412.

47. Ghazali, 411.

48. Ghazali, 413.

49. Tusi, *Akhlaq-i Nasiri*, 261.

50. Davani, *Akhlaq-i Jalali*, 230–31.

51. Davani, 232; and Tusi, *Akhlaq-i Nasiri*, 340.

52. Ghazali, *Kimiya-i Sa'adat*, 322.

53. Davani, *Akhlaq-i Jalali*, 283.

54. Tusi, *Akhlaq-i Nasiri*, 330.

55. Mottahedeh, "Friendship in Islamic Ethical Philosophy," 236.

56. Tusi, *Akhlaq-i Nasiri*, 328.

57. Davani, *Akhlaq-i Jalali*, 285.

58. Davani, 234.

59. Tusi, *Akhlaq-i Nasiri*, 329; and Davani, *Akhlaq-i Jalali*, 286.

60. Davani, *Akhlaq-i Jalali*, 286.

61. Tusi, *Akhlaq-i Nasiri*, 330.

62. Tusi, 335.

63. Tusi, 335.

64. The term here is *khulq*, which could also be translated as temperament in this context.

65. Tusi, *Akhlaq-i Nasiri*, 335.

66. Tusi, 339.

67. Davani, *Akhlaq-i Jalali*, 284.

68. Tusi, *Akhlaq-i Nasiri*, 332.

69. Tusi, 333.

70. Jonathan Katz, "The Invention of Heterosexuality," in *Race, Class, and Gender in the United States*, ed. Paula Rothenburg (New York: Worth, 2007), 69.

71. Khalid El-Rouayheb, *Before Homosexuality in the Arab-Islamic World, 1500–1800* (Chicago: University of Chicago Press, 2005), 3.

72. Susanne Kurz, "Never Just for Fun? Sexual Intercourse in Persophone Medicine, Erotology and Ethics," in *Muslim Bodies: Body, Sexuality and Medicine in Muslim Societies*, ed. Susanne Kurz, Claudia Preckel Eadem, and Stefan Reichmuth (Berlin: Lit, 2016), 14:97–130, 106.

73. Kurz, 124.

74. Scott Siraj al-Haqq Kugle, *Homosexuality in Islam: Critical Reflection on Gay, Lesbian, and Transgender Muslims* (Oxford: Oneworld, 2010), 49.

75. Ghazali, *Kimiya-i Sa'adat*, 523; Roziya Mukminova, "Central Asia: 15th to Mid-18th Century," in *Encyclopedia of Women and Islamic Cultures*, ed. Suad Joseph (Leiden: Brill, 2003), 1:82–85; Fatma Muge Gocek, "Ottoman Empire: 15th to Mid-18th Century," in Joseph, *Encyclopedia of Women and Islamic Cultures*, 1:72–81; and Elizabeth Thompson, "Civil Society: Overview," in Joseph, *Encyclopedia of Women and Islamic Cultures*, 1:34–40. Women frequented their own bathhouses too.

76. Ghazali, *Kimiya-i Sa'adat*, 523.

77. Davani, *Akhlaq-i Jalali*, 284.

78. Ghazali, *Kimiya-i Sa'adat*, 507.

79. Ghazali, 507.

80. Kecia Ali, *Sexual Ethics and Islam: Feminist Reflections on Qur'an, Hadith, and Jurisprudence* (Oxford: Oneworld, 2006), 85.

81. Kurz, "Never Just for Fun?," 104.

82. Kurz, 106.

83. Ghazali, *Kimiya-i Sa'adat*, 206; and Davani, *Akhlaq-i Jalali*, 190–91.

84. Hodgson, *The Venture of Islam* (Chicago: University of Chicago Press, 1977), 2:146; and Tusi, *Akhlaq-i Nasiri*, 223–24.

85. Tusi, *Akhlaq-i Nasiri*, 149.

86. Ghazali, *Kimiya-i Sa'adat*, 396. Note also, this is a rare place in the texts that equates the ethical with the Islamic/being Muslim. The context for the text is unquestionably Muslim and taken for granted.

87. Ghazali, 396.

88. Ghazali, 397.

89. Ghazali, 397.

90. Ghazali, 397.

91. Tusi, *Akhlaq-i Nasiri*, 336. The term for womenfolk here is *haram*, which, as we saw earlier, refers to the private or women's quarters of the home. In the plural, *harim*, the term also means those under a man's protection, which would be more than just his womenfolk. However here it is likely to mean womenfolk. Dishonor could be of the sanctity of the haram itself or the actual women who live there, since Tusi is referring to acting upon one's desire or *shahwat*, which includes inappropriate kinds or amounts of lust.

92. Tusi, 338.

93. Tusi, 338.

94. Tusi, 336–37.

95. Tusi, 337.

96. Tusi, 338.

97. Ghazali, *Kimiya-i Sa'adat*, 391.

98. Ghazali, 395.

99. Ahmed Karamustafa, "The Ghazali Brothers and Their Institutions," in *Ötekilerin Peşinde: Ahmet Yaşar Ocak'a Armağan (Festschrift in Honor of Ahmet Yaşar Ocak)*, ed. Mehmet Öz and Fatih Yeşil (Istanbul: Timaş Yayınları, 2015), 265–75. Ahmet Karamustafa argues how Ghazali's internalization of Ibn Sina's philosophy, as well as sufi thought, brought him closer to (or perhaps was inspired by) his sufi brother, Ahmad Ghazali.

100. Ghazali, *Kimiya-i Sa'adat*, 395.

101. Tusi, *Akhlaq-i Nasiri*, 143–45.

102. Tusi, 248.

103. Tusi, 303.

104. Tusi, 250.

105. Davani, *Akhlaq-i Jalali*, 221.

106. Davani, 225.

107. Davani, 225.

108. Davani, 239.

109. Davani, 242.

110. David Morgan, "Class and Masculinity," in *Handbook of Studies on Men and Masculinities*, ed. Michael Kimmel, Jeff Hearn, and R. W. Connell (Thousand Oaks, CA: Sage, 2005), 168.

111. Morgan, 169–70.

112. Roxanne Euben, *Journeys to the Other Shore: Muslim and Western Travelers in Search of Knowledge* (Princeton: Princeton University Press, 2006), 66. Euben makes this case using Ibn Battuta's strong self-identification as a Tanji (from Tangier).

113. Davani, *Akhlaq-i Jalali*, 221.

114. Muhsin Mahdi, "Farabi vi. Political Philosophy," in *Encylopaedia Iranica*, online ed. (New York: Columbia University, 2002).

115. Muhsin Mahdi, "Avicenna vii. Practical Sciences," in *Encylopaedia Iranica*, online ed. (New York: Columbia University, 2011).

116. Charles E. Butterworth, "Ethics in Medieval Philosophy," *Journal of Religious Ethics* 11, no. 2 (Fall 1983): 224–39, 236.

117. Amira Bennison, *The Great Caliphs: The Golden Age of the 'Abbasid Empire* (New Haven: Yale University Press, 2009), 70.

118. Bennison, 71. The Umayyads in Spain and Fatimids in Egypt were inspired by Baghdad to build cities that made similar regal statements of power residing at the city centers. Although Baghdad was the preeminent city of its region and time, multiple cities in Persianate lands developed along similar plans, but to lesser scales.

119. Amira K. Bennison and Alison Gascoigne, *Cities in the Pre-Modern Islamic World: The Urban Impact of Religion, State and Society* (London: Routledge, 2007), 2.

120. Ghazali, *Kimiya-i Sa'adat*, 520–24.

121. Tusi, *Akhlaq-i Nasiri*, 299. Davani omits this discussion but retains discussion of the profession-based classes of mankind.

122. Nadia El Cheikh, *Women, Islam, and Abbasid Identity* (Cambridge, MA: Harvard University Press, 2015), 15.

123. Tusi, *Akhlaq-i Nasiri*, 280–81.

124. Tusi, 289–96.

125. Tusi, 296.

126. Tusi, 299.

127. Tusi, 299.

128. Tusi, 299.

129. Ghazali implicitly uses the same social structure as Tusi and Davani do, but he does not contain lengthy explanations of social classes or interactions between them.

130. Ann K. S. Lambton, *Continuity and Change in Medieval Persia: Aspects of Administrative, Economic and Social History, 11th–14th Century* (Albany: Bibliotheca Persica, 1988), 221–23; Ann K. S. Lambton, *Theory and Practice in Medieval Persian Government* (London: Variorum Reprints, 1980), section 7, 4; and Marlowe, *Hierarchy and Egalitarianism in Islamic Thought*, 8. Although she recognizes that Tusi and Davani are speaking of ideal societies, Lambton argues that Tusi and Davani are important sources of social history as well since very little writing was done by nonelites in medieval Persia. Marlowe explains the widespread influence that Tusi's discussion on society had in Turkish, Arabic, and Indian Muslim contexts.

131. Oliver Leaman, *Islamic Philosophy: An Introduction* (Cambridge: Polity, 2009), 101–2.

132. Tusi, *Akhlaq-i Nasiri*, 286.

133. Tusi, 286.

134. Quote from Tusi, 286. On women's presence in mosques, see Katz, *Women in the Mosque*, 6–7. Katz explains that "scholars seeking evidence of women's presence in mosques have often taken male duties and activities as representative of mosque usage in general and simply examined the extent to which women did or did not partake in these same religious pursuits." However, "women's mosque-based activities were not simply more limited or constrained versions of men's." Like men, women used the mosque for a range of social, leisure, and legal purposes, much to the chagrin of 'ulan_____ious periods in history who attempted to curb their attendance legally

135. Tusi, *Akhlaq-i Nasiri*, 286.

136. Tusi, 305.

137. Tusi, 286. The term I have translated as "dignity" is actually *baizat*, which literally means egg, testicle, or the center of anything, especially a city, which suggests that the center or essence of a city is sexualized in the context of needing protection against pillage from another city.

138. Heidi Hartmann, "The Unhappy Marriage of Marxism and Feminism: Toward a More Progressive Union," in *Women and Revolution: The Unhappy Marriage of Marxism and Feminism*, ed. Lydia Sargent (Boston: South End, 1981), 14.

139. Tusi, *Akhlaq-i Nasiri*, 286.

140. Tusi, 305.

141. Bennison, *The Great Caliphs*, 85; and Togan Isenbike, "Turkic Dynasties: 9th to 15th Century," in *Encyclopedia of Women in Islamic Cultures*, ed. Suad Josef (Leiden: Brill, 2003), 1:24. Many of the local rural producers of textiles and fabrics were women. Women's groups in Turkic dynasties from the ninth to the fifteenth centuries were located in the market, where they weaved textiles. According to Yosef Rapoport, in late medieval Damascus, the textile industry largely relied upon women's ability to spin fabrics at home due to their need for private income apart from their husbands' provisions or if they were divorced, as was common. Apart from this participation, the market was primarily where men dealt with one another as they exchanged both money and ideas. Customers were also mostly male, but it was common for women to venture into the marketplace to purchase goods and services for the home. Rich women would often stay at home and send male or female servants to the market.

142. Tusi, *Akhlaq-i Nasiri*, 305.

143. Tusi, 305; and Davani, *Akhlaq-i Jalali*, 247.

144. Tusi, *Akhlaq-i Nasiri*, 284.

145. Davani, *Akhlaq-i Jalali*, 247.

146. Davani, 257.

147. Davani, 257.

148. Davani, 247.

149. Davani, 247–48, 257. Note that the term for "awesomeness" here is *haybat*, the same adjective used in the domestic management chapters to describe how a husband should appear to a wife. *Haybat* means to have awe, gravity, or dignity, or to command respect out of sternness. Here it would be the kind of fear and awe that a uniform would command.

150. Davani, 248, 258.

151. Davani, 248.

152. Davani, 249.

153. Davani, 244.

154. Davani, 245.

155. Davani, 245.

156. Davani, 245.

157. Marlowe, *Hierarchy and Egalitarianism in Islamic Thought*, 58; and Tusi, *Akhlaq-i Nasiri*, 228.

158. Ghazali, *Kimiya-i Sa'adat*, 379–80; Tusi, *Akhlaq-i Nasiri*, 301; and Davani, *Akhlaq-i Jalali*, 222–23.

159. Tusi, *Akhlaq-i Nasiri*, 334.

160. Tusi, 340.

161. Davani, *Akhlaq-i Jalali*, 292.

162. Davani, 292.

163. Tusi, *Akhlaq-i Nasiri*, 341.

164. Davani, *Akhlaq-i Jalali*, 293.

165. Tusi, *Akhlaq-i Nasiri*, 132–33.

166. Tusi, 251.

167. Tusi, 252.

168. Tusi, 288; and Davani, *Akhlaq-i Jalali*, 248.

169. Marlowe, *Hierarchy and Egalitarianism in Islamic Thought*, 58; and Tusi, *Akhlaq-i Nasiri*, 228.

170. Mehrzad Boroujerdi, *Mirror for the Muslim Prince: Islam and the Theory of Statecraft* (Syracuse: Syracuse University Press, 2013). Most recently, a volume edited by Mehrzad Boroujerdi performs the salubrious task of updating arguments against Orientalist understandings of political ethics in *falsafa* and *akhlaq*.

171. Mozaffar Alam, *The Languages of Political Islam: India, 1200–1800* (Chicago: University of Chicago Press, 2004), ix–x.

172. Alam, 12–13.

173. Ghazali's main treatise on this topic is the *Kitab Nasihat al-Muluk* (*Book of Advice for Kings*).

174. Badakhchani, 11–13. In *Sayr wa Suluk*, Tusi describes the Isma'ili imamate as the only legitimate form of government since he was most impressed with Isma'ili knowledge and was attempting to join their court at the time that he wrote the work.

175. Ghazali, *Kimiya-i Sa'adat*, 525.

176. Ghazali, 527.

177. Ghazali, 528.

178. Ghazali, 528.

179. Ghazali, 528.

180. Ghazali, 529.

181. Ghazali, 530.

182. Ghazali, 537.

183. Ghazali, 538.

184. Ghazali, 539.

185. Ghazali, 539.

186. Ghazali, 539.

187. Tusi, *Akhlaq-i Nasiri*, 301.

188. Davani, *Akhlaq-i Jalali*, 254.

189. Davani, 254.

190. Tusi, *Akhlaq-i Nasiri*, 301; and Davani, *Akhlaq-i Jalali*, 254.

191. Tusi, *Akhlaq-i Nasiri*, 301; and Davani, *Akhlaq-i Jalali*, 254.

192. Tusi, *Akhlaq-i Nasiri*, 302; and Davani, *Akhlaq-i Jalali*, 254.

193. Tusi, *Akhlaq-i Nasiri*, 302; and Davani, *Akhlaq-i Jalali*, 254.

194. Tusi, *Akhlaq-i Nasiri*, 302; and Davani, *Akhlaq-i Jalali*, 254.

195. John Woods, *The Aqquyunlu: Clan, Confederation, Empire* (Salt Lake City: University of Utah Press, 1999), 6, 89. Built upon the notion of divine favor for the just ruler that emerged with the Mongol upset, the idea that God would install and favor only a just sovereign dominates Davani's political discourse in *Akhlaq-i Jalali*, as opposed to notions of the "right" sectarian persuasion, as argued in the time of Ghazali or Tusi. Instead, the fall of a sultanate would signal the sultan's corruption and injustice. Further, the title *ghazi* "had a distinct ideological significance exploited throughout the Later Middle Period of Islamic history by those Muslim rulers who sought to endow their regimes with a semblance of religio-political legitimacy." Thus Davani's use of the term "Ghazi in the path of God" and description of his patron's just rulership in *Akhlaq-i Jalali* was an important show of his support.

196. Davani, *Akhlaq-i Jalali*, 223; and Tusi, *Akhlaq-i Nasiri*, 302.

197. Davani, *Akhlaq-i Jalali*, 264–65.

198. Tusi, *Akhlaq-i Nasiri*, 306; and Davani, *Akhlaq-i Jalali*, 258–60.

199. Tusi, *Akhlaq-i Nasiri*, 308–9.

200. Tusi, 310.

201. Tusi, 311.

202. Omid Safi, *The Politics of Knowledge in Premodern Islam: Negotiating Ideology and Religious Inquiry* (Chapel Hill: University of North Carolina Press, 2006), 71.

203. Safi, 71.

204. Woods, *The Aqquyunlu*, 82, 235.

205. Ghazali, *Kimiya-i Sa'adat*, 382.

206. Ghazali, 380.

207. Ghazali, 381. The authenticity of this and similar hadiths is dubious; it is not clear what religious scholars the Prophet would be speaking of, since he was the religious and political authority of his age, unless he was referring to scholars "belonging" to past prophets such as rabbis or Zoroastrian priests.

208. Ghazali, 383.

209. Michael Cook, *Forbidding Wrong in Islam* (New York: Cambridge University Press, 2003), 75–76.

210. Ghazali, *Kimiya-i Sa'adat*, 384.

211. Tusi, *Akhlaq-i Nasiri*, 314; and Davani, *Akhlaq-i Jalali*, 275–76.

212. Tusi, *Akhlaq-i Nasiri*, 319.

213. Tusi, 319.

214. Tusi, 319.

215. Tusi, 316.

216. Zahra Ayubi, "Rearing Gendered Souls: Childhood and the Making of Muslim Manhood in Pre-Modern Islamic Ethics," *Journal of the American Academy of Religion*, forthcoming.

217. Tusi, *Akhlaq-i Nasiri*, 319.

218. Tusi, 320; and Karen Bauer, *Gender Hierarchy in the Qur'an: Medieval Interpretations, Modern Responses* (Cambridge: Cambridge University Press, 2015), 35–36. Although Tusi is speaking of men here, Karen Bauer has shown that the term *sufahah* is a Qur'anic term that sometimes is interpreted as referring to women or weak-minded people such as orphans.

CONCLUSION: PROLEGOMENON TO FEMINIST PHILOSOPHY OF ISLAM

Epigraph: Hafiz, Ghazal Number 298, Ganjoor, https://ganjoor.net/hafez/ghazal/sh298/.

1. Georgiana T., "I Like Everything in This Book Except His Views on Women," March 10, 2016, *Amazon*, www.amazon.com/gp/customer-reviews/R100BXZ4Q55FIS/ref=cm_cr_getr_d_rvw_ttl?ie=UTF8&ASIN=1557427143.

2. Shahd Fadlamoula, "Shahd Fadlamoula's Review," May 21, 2018, *Goodreads*, www.goodreads.com/review/show/2398116277?book_show_action=true& from_review_page=1.

3. Voulpit, "Voulpit's Review," January 31, 2016, *Goodreads*, www.goodreads.com /review/show/1532912966?book_show_action=true&from_review_page=1.

4. Fatima Seedat, "When Islam and Feminism Converge," *Muslim World* 103, no. 3 (2013): 406. Fatima Seedat explains that not all of the scholars who have been characterized as Islamic/Muslim feminists are comfortable with the term *feminism* because of its colonial past.

5. Juliane Hammer, *More Than a Prayer: American Muslim Women, Religious Authority, and Activism* (Austin: University of Texas Press, 2012), 116.

6. See the exchange between Aysha Hidayatullah, Asma Barlas, and amina wadud in the *Journal of Feminist Studies in Religion* 32, no. 2 (2016).

7. The notable exception is Etin Anwar, *Gender and Self in Islam* (London: Routledge, 2006).

8. Nancy Frankenberry, "Feminist Philosophy of Religion," in *Stanford Encyclopedia of Philosophy Online*, ed. Edward N. Zalta (Summer 2018) (Stanford: Stanford University, 2018).

9. Charles Kurzman and Carl Ernst, "Islamic Studies in US Universities," in *Middle East Studies for the New Millennium: Infrastructures of Knowledge*, ed. Seteney Shami and Cynthia Miller-Idriss (New York: New York University Press, 2016), 333.

10. Juliane Hammer, "Gender Matters: Normativity, Positionality, and the Politics of Islamic Studies," *Muslim World* 106, no. 4 (2016): 655–70, 656.

11. Michele LeDoeuff, *Hipparchia's Choice: An Essay Concerning Women, Philosophy, Etc.* (New York: Columbia University Press, 1989), 168.

12. LeDoeuff, 168.

13. Genevieve Lloyd, "LeDoeuff and History of Philosophy," in *Feminism and History of Philosophy* (Oxford: Oxford University Press, 2002), 28.

14. Cyrus Zargar, *The Polished Mirror: Storytelling and the Pursuit of Virtue in Islamic Philosophy and Sufism* (Oxford: Oneworld Academic, 2017), 61.

15. Zargar, 61–62.

16. Zargar, 61.

17. Lloyd, "LeDoeuff and History of Philosophy," 29.

18. Lloyd, 31.

19. Christine Senack, "Aristotle on the Woman's Soul," in *Engendering Origins: Critical Feminist Readings in Plato and Aristotle*, ed. Bat-Ami Bar On (Albany: State University of New York Press, 1994), 223.

20. Luce Irigaray, *An Ethics of Sexual Difference*, trans. Carolyn Burke and Gillian C. Gill (Ithaca: Cornell University Press, 1993), 32.

21. Georgiana T., "I Like Everything."

22. Frankenberry, "Feminist Philosophy of Religion."

23. Zain Ali, "Concepts of God in Islam," *Philosophy Compass* 11, no. 12 (2016): 892–904, 893.

24. amina wadud, *Inside the Gender Jihad* (Oxford: Oneworld, 2006), 29–30.

25. Aysha A. Hidayatullah, *Feminist Edges of the Qur'an* (New York: Oxford University Press, 2014), 194. Hidayatullah poses two mutually exclusive conditions for feminist approaches to the Qur'an: either we must question the just nature of God or we must question the Qur'an's divinity since God may be just. But in her view, the Qur'an is not, and feminist hermeneutical strategies to unread gender inequality are insufficient.

26. For an example, see wadud, *Inside the Gender Jihad*, 37–38.

27. Carol Gilligan, *In a Different Voice: Psychological Theory and Women's Development* (Cambridge: Harvard University Press, 1982), 73.

28. Marcia L. Homiak, "Feminism and Aristotle's Rational Ideal," in *Feminism and History of Philosophy*, ed. Genevieve Lloyd (Oxford: Oxford University Press, 2002), 81. Homiak critiques this position of Gilligan as does Claudia Card in "Women's Voices and Ethical Ideals: Must We Mean What We Say?," *Ethics* 99, no. 1 (1988): 125–35.

29. Homiak, 94.

30. Homiak, 99.

31. Helen Longino, "Circles of Reason: Some Feminist Reflections on Reason and Rationality," *Episteme* 2, no. 1 (June 2005): 80.

32. Longino, 80.

33. Longino, 83.

34. Longino, 86.

35. Longino, 84.

36. Lloyd, "LeDoeuff and History of Philosophy," 36.

37. Homiak, "Feminism and Aristotle's Rational Ideal," 81.

38. Homiak, 82.

39. Homiak, 87.

40. Homiak, 89.

41. Rachel Tillman, "Ethical Embodiment and Moral Reasoning: A Challenge to Peter Singer," *Hypatia* 28, no. 1 (2013): 18–31, 24–25.

42. Anika Maaza Mann, "Race and Feminist Standpoint Theory," in *Convergences: Black Feminism and Continental Philosophy*, ed. Maria del Guadalupe Davidson, Kathryn Gines, and Donna-Dale Marcano (Albany: State University of New York Press, 2010), 112.

43. Tillman, "Ethical Embodiment and Moral Reasoning," 22; and Pamela Sue Anderson, *A Feminist Philosophy of Religion* (Oxford: Blackwell, 1998), 33.

Anderson's concept of feminist standpoint epistemology is the knowledge gained from women's experiences of oppression by certain religious beliefs, which challenges sources of knowledge that are purported to be objective truths or neutral.

44. Sa'diyya Shaikh, "Feminism, Epistemology and Experience: Critically (En)gendering the Study of Islam," *Journal for Islamic Studies* 33, no. 1 (2013): 14–47.

45. Sa'diyya Shaikh, "A Tafsir of Praxis: Gender, Martial Violence, Resistance, in a South African Muslim Community," in *Violence Against Women in Contemporary World Religions: Roots and Cures*, ed. Daniel Maguire and Sa'diyya Shaikh (Cleveland: Pilgrim Press, 2007), 66–89, 69.

46. Asma Barlas, "Secular and Feminist Critiques of the Qur'an: Anti-Hermeneutics as Liberation?," *Journal of Feminist Studies in Religion* 32, no. 2 (2016): 118.

47. wadud, *Inside the Gender Jihad*, 33.

48. wadud, 34.

49. amina wadud, "Can One Critique Cancel All Previous Efforts?," *Journal of Feminist Studies in Religion* 32, no. 2 (2016): 132–33.

50. Anwar, *Gender and Self in Islam*, 74.

51. Ayesha Chaudhry, *Domestic Violence and the Islamic Tradition* (Oxford: Oxford University Press, 2013), 13.

52. Abu Hamid al-Ghazali, *Kimiya-i Sa'adat*, ed. Hossein Khadivjam (Tehran: Ketabhaaye Jibi, 1975), 315.

53. wadud, "Can One Critique Cancel All Previous Efforts?," 134.

54. Lisa Tessman, "Feminist Eudaimonism: Eudaimonism as Non-Ideal Theory," in *Feminist Ethics and Social and Political Philosophy: Theorizing the Non-Ideal*, ed. Lisa Tessman (Dordrecht: Springer, 2009), 47–58, 49–50.

55. Claudia Card, *The Unnatural Lottery: Character and Moral Luck* (Philadelphia: Temple University Press, 1996), 53–54.

56. Kathryn Gines, "Sartre, Beauvoir, and the Race/Gender Analogy: A Case for Black Feminist Philosophy," in *Convergences: Black Feminism and Continental Philosophy*, ed. Maria del Guadalupe Davidson, Kathryn Gines, and Donna-Dale Marcano (Albany: Sate University of New York Press, 2010), 35.

57. See Mann, "Race and Feminist Standpoint Theory," 117n5. Although the concept of intersectionality is first cited in Kimberle Crenshaw, "Mapping the Margins: Intersectionality, Identity, Politics, and Violence Against Women of Color," *Stanford Law Review* 43, no. 6 (1991): 1241–99, several other black feminist thinkers have written on similar ideas.

58. Gines, "Sartre, Beauvoir, and the Race/Gender Analogy," 36.

59. Sonia Kruks, *Retrieving Experience: Subjectivity and Recognition in Feminist Politics* (Ithaca: Cornell University Press, 2001), 109, 111, quoted in Mann, "Race and Feminist Standpoint Theory," 112.

60. Mann, "Race and Feminist Standpoint Theory," 112.

61. Mann, 112.

62. Mann, 110.

63. Mann, 110.

64. Kristie Dotson, "Word to the Wise: Notes on a Black Feminist Metaphilosophy of Race," *Philosophy Compass* 11, no. 2 (2016): 69–74, 72.

65. V. Denise James, "Musing: A Black Feminist Philosopher: Is That Possible?," *Hypatia* 29, no. 1 (2014): 189.

66. Leila Ahmed, *Women and Gender in Islam* (New Haven: Yale University Press, 1992), 133.

67. Matthew Gordon and Kathryn Hain, *Concubines and Courtesans: Women and Slavery in Islamic History* (Oxford: Oxford University Press, 2016). This recent volume investigates social mobility and the variations in status of enslaved women.

68. Martha Nussbaum, *Frontiers of Justice: Disability, Nationality, Species Membership* (Cambridge, MA: Belknap Press of Harvard University Press, 2007), 70.

69. Nussbaum, 70.

70. Tessman, "Feminist Eudaimonism: Eudaimonism as Non-Ideal Theory," 49.

71. Tessman, 49.

72. Tessman, 49.

73. Tessman, 48.

74. Christine Swanton, *Virtue Ethics: A Pluralistic View* (New York: Oxford University Press, 2003), 3.

75. Tessman, "Feminist Eudaimonism: Eudaimonism as Non-Ideal Theory," 54.

76. Tessman, 55.

77. Tessman, 56.

Bibliography

Afnan, Sohayl Muhsin. *Vazhah namah-i falsafi*. Lebanon: Dar El-Mashreq, 1969.

Ahmad, Khaliq, and Arif Hassan. "Distributive Justice: The Islamic Perspective." *Intellectual Discourse* 8, no. 2 (2000): 159–72.

Ahmed, Leila. *Women and Gender in Islam*. New Haven: Yale University Press, 1992.

Ahmed, Shahab. *What Is Islamic? The Importance of Being Islamic*. Princeton: Princeton University Press, 2016.

Alam, Mozaffar. *The Languages of Political Islam: India, 1200–1800*. Chicago: University of Chicago Press, 2004.

Ali, Abdullah Yusuf. *The Meaning of the Holy Qur'an*. Brentwood, MD: Amana, 2001.

Ali, Kecia. *Marriage and Slavery in Early Islam*. Cambridge, MA: Harvard University Press, 2010.

——. "Religious Practices: Obedience and Disobedience in Islamic Discourses." In *The Encyclopedia of Women in Islamic Cultures*, edited by Suad Joseph, vol. 1, 309–13. Leiden: Brill, 2007.

——. *Sexual Ethics and Islam: Feminist Reflections on Qur'an, Hadith and Jurisprudence*. Oxford: Oneworld, 2006.

Ali, Shaheen Sardar. *Gender and Human Rights in Islam and International Law Equal Before Allah, Unequal Before Man?* The Hague: Kluwer Law International, 2000.

Ali, Zain. "Concepts of God in Islam." *Philosophy Compass* 11, no. 12 (2016): 892–904.

Anderson, Pamela Sue. *A Feminist Philosophy of Religion*. Oxford: Blackwell, 1998.

Anjum, Tanvir. "The Perpetually Wedded Wife of God: A Study of Muha Sada Suhag, as the Founder of Sada Suhagiyya Silsila." *Journal of Religious History* 39, no. 3 (2015): 420–30.

Anwar, Etin. *Gender and Self in Islam*. London: Routledge, 2006.

Attewell, Guy N. A. *Refiguring Unani Tibb: Plural Healing in Late Colonial India*. Hyderabad: Orient Longman, 2007.

Ayubi, Zahra. "Negotiating Justice: American Muslim Women Navigating Islamic Divorce and Civil Law." *Journal for Islamic Studies* 30 (2010): 78–102.

——. "Rearing the Gendered Soul: Childhood and the Making of Muslim Manhood in Pre-Modern Islamic Ethics." *Journal of the American Academy of Religion*, forthcoming.

Azadpur, Mohammad. "Is 'Islamic Philosophy' Islamic?" Edited by Omid Safi. Vol. 5 of *Voices of Change*, edited by Vincent Cornell. Westport, CT: Praeger, 2007.

——. *Reason Unbound: On Spiritual Practice in Islamic Peripatetic Philosophy*. Albany: State University of New York Press, 2011.

Badakhchani, S. J. "Introduction." In *Contemplation and Action: The Spiritual Autobiography of a Muslim Scholar*, edited by S. J. Badakhchani. London: I. B. Tauris, 1998.

Barlas, Asma. "Secular and Feminist Critiques of the Qur'an: Anti-Hermeneutics as Liberation?" *Journal of Feminist Studies in Religion* 32, no. 2 (2016): 118.

——. "Women's Readings of the Qur'an." In *The Cambridge Companion to the Qur'an*, edited by Jane McAuliffe, 255–71. New York: Cambridge University Press, 2006.

Bauer, Karen. *Gender Hierarchy in the Qur'an: Medieval Interpretations, Modern Responses*. Cambridge: Cambridge University Press, 2015.

Baugh, Carolyn. *Minor Marriage in Early Islamic Law*. Leiden: Brill, 2017.

Bennison, Amira K. *The Great Caliphs: The Golden Age of the 'Abbasid Empire*. New Haven: Yale University Press, 2009.

Bennison, Amira K., and Alison Gascoigne. *Cities in the Pre-Modern Islamic World: The Urban Impact of Religions, State and Society*. London: Routledge, 2007.

Boroujerdi, Mehrzad. *Mirror for the Muslim Prince: Islam and the Theory of Statecraft*. Syracuse: Syracuse University Press, 2013.

Bucar, Elizabeth. "Islamic Virtue Ethics." In *The Oxford Handbook of Virtue*, edited by Nancy Snow, 206–23. Oxford: Oxford University Press, 2018.

al-Bukhari, 'Abd al-Haqq Muhaddith Dihlawi. *Akhbar al-akhyar fi asrar al-abrar*. Edited by 'Alim Ashraf Khan. Tehran: Anjuman-i Athar o Mafakhar-i Farhangi, 2004.

Bukhari, Muhammad ibn Isma'il. *Moral Teachings of Islam: Prophetic Traditions from Al-Adab Al-Mufrad*. Translated by 'Abd al-'Ali 'Abd al-Hamid. Walnut Creek, CA: Altamira, 2003.

——. *Sahih al-Bukhari: The Translation of the Meanings of Sahih Bukhari*. Translated by Muhammad Muhsin Khan. Vol. 9, bk. 93. Chicago: Kazi, 1976–79.

Bulliet, Richard W. *The Patricians of Nishapur: A Study in Medieval Islamic Social History*. Cambridge, MA: Harvard University Press, 1972.

——. "Women and the Urban Religious Elite in the Pre-Mongol Period." In *Women in Iran from the Rise of Islam to 1800*, edited by Guity Nashat and Lois Beck, 103–20. Champaign: University of Illinois Press, 2003.

Butler, Judith. *Gender Trouble: Feminism and the Subversion of Identity*. New York: Routledge, 1999.

——. "Performative Acts and Gender Constitution: An Essay in Phenomenology and Feminist Theory." In *Performing Feminisms: Feminist Critical Theory and Theatre*, edited by Sue-Ellen Case, 270–82. Baltimore: Johns Hopkins University Press, 1990.

Butterworth, Charles E. "Ethics in Medieval Philosophy," *Journal of Religious Ethics* 11, no. 2 (Fall 1983): 224–49.

Card, Claudia. *The Unnatural Lottery: Character and Moral Luck*. Philadelphia: Temple University Press, 1996.

——. "Women's Voices and Ethical Ideals: Must We Mean What We Say?" *Ethics* 99, no. 1 (1988): 125–35.

Chaudhry, Ayesha. *Domestic Violence and the Islamic Tradition*. Oxford: Oxford University Press, 2013.

El Cheikh, Nadia. *Women, Islam, and Abbasid Identity*. Cambridge, MA: Harvard University Press, 2015.

Clark, Elizabeth. "Thinking with Women: The Uses of the Appeal to 'Woman' in Pre-Nicene Christian Propaganda Literature." In *The Spread of Christianity in the First Four Centuries: Essays in Explanation*, edited by W. V. Harris, 43–52. Leiden: Brill, 2005.

Connell, R. W. *The Men and the Boys*. Berkeley: University of California Press, 2001.

Cook, Michael. *Forbidding Wrong in Islam*. New York: Cambridge University Press, 2003.

Cooper, John. "al-Dawani, Jalal al-Din (1426–1502)." In *Routledge Encyclopedia of Philosophy*, vol. 2, 806–7. London: Routledge, 1998.

Cornell, Rkia E. "Introduction: As-Sulami and his Sufi Women." In *Early Sufi Women: Dhikr an-Niswa al-Muta'abbidat as-Sufiyyat*, edited by Abu 'Abd ar-Rahman as-Sulami, translated by Rkia Cornell. Louisville: Fons Vitae, 1999.

Crenshaw, Kimberle. "Mapping the Margins: Intersectionality, Identity, Politics, and Violence Against Women of Color." *Stanford Law Review* 43, no. 6 (1991): 1241–99.

Crook, Jay. "Translator's Introduction." In *The Alchemy of Happiness (Kimiya al-Sa'adat)*, by Abu Hamid Muhammad Ghazali Tusi, translated by Jay Crook, xxii. Chicago: Great Books of the Islamic World, 2008.

Dabashi, Hamid. "Khwajah Nasir al-Din al-Tusi: The Philosopher/Vizier and the Intellectual Climate of His Times." In *History of Islamic Philosophy*, edited by Seyyed Hossein Nasr and Oliver Leaman, 527–84. London: Routledge, 1996.

——. *Truth and Narrative: The Untimely Thoughts of 'Ayn al-Qudat al Hamadani*. London: Curzon, 1999.

Daftary, Farhad. *The Isma'ilis: Their History and Doctrines*. Cambridge: Cambridge University Press, 2007.

Dallh, Minlib. "Path to the Divine: Ansari's Sad Madyan and Manzi al-Sa'irin." *Muslim World* 103, no. 4 (2014): 467.

Davani, Jalal ad-Din. *Akhlaq-i Jalali*. Edited by Abdullah Masoudi Arani. Tehran: Intesharat-i Italat, 2013.

——. *Akhlaq-i Jalali*. Edited by Hafiz Shabir Ahmad Haidery. New Delhi: Urdu Book Review, 2007.

——. *Akhlaq-i Jalali*. Lucknow: Tej Kumar Press, 1957.

——. *Practical Philosophy of the Muhammadan Peoples*. Translated by W. F. Thompson. London: Oriental Translation Fund, 1839.

de Beauvoir, Simone. *The Second Sex*. Translated by H. M. Parshley. London: Jonathan Cape, 2009.

De Sondy, Amanullah. *The Crisis of Islamic Masculinities*. London: Bloomsbury Academic, 2013.

Dobbs-Weinstein, Idit. "Thinking Desire in Gersonides and Spinoza." In *Women and Gender in Jewish Philosophy*, edited by Hava Tirosh-Samuelson, 51–77. Bloomington: Indiana University Press, 2004.

Dotson, Kristie. "Word to the Wise: Notes on a Black Feminist Metaphilosophy of Race." *Philosophy Compass* 11, no. 2 (2016): 69–74.

Dunn, Ross E. *The Adventures of Ibn Battuta: A Muslim Traveler of the 14th Century*. Berkeley: University of California Press, 2005.

Euben, Roxanne. *Journeys to the Other Shore: Muslim and Western Travelers in Search of Knowledge*. Princeton: Princeton University Press, 2006.

Fakhry, Majid. *Ethical Theories in Islam*. Leiden: Brill, 1991.

——. *History of Islamic Philosophy*. New York: Columbia University Press, 2005.

Frank, Richard. *Al-Ghazali and the Ash'arite School*. Durham: Duke University Press, 1994.

——. "al-Ghazali's Use of Avicenna's Philosophy." *Revue des Etudes Islamiques* 55–57 (1987–89): 271–85.

Frankenberry, Nancy. "Feminist Philosophy of Religion." In *Stanford Encyclopedia of Philosophy Online*, edited by Edward N. Zalta. Summer 2018 ed. Stanford: Stanford University, 2018.

Geissinger, Aisha. *Gender and Muslim Constructions of Exegetical Authority: A Rereading of the Classical Genre of Qur'an Commentary*. Leiden: Brill, 2015.

al-Ghazali, Abu Hamid Muhammad. *The Alchemy of Happiness*. Translated by Claud Field. London: J. Murray, 1909.

——. *The Alchemy of Happiness (Kimiya al-Sa'adat)*. Translated by Jay R. Crook. Chicago: Great Books of the Islamic World, 2008.

——. *Edition of Kitab Nasihat al-Muluk*. Edited by Haskell D. Isaacs. Manchester: University of Manchester, 1956.

——. *Ihya' 'Ulum ad-Din*. Vol. 3. Cairo: Mu'assasat al-Halabi, 1968.

——. *Ihya' 'Ulum ad-Din: Kitab al-Ilm*. Translated by Nabih Faris. New Delhi: Islamic Book Service, 1962.

——. *Kimiya-i Sa'adat*. Edited by Hossein Khadivjam. Vol. 2. Tehran: Ketabhaaye Jibi, 1975.

Giladi, Avner. *Infants, Parents and Wet Nurses: Medieval Islamic Views on Breast-feeding and Their Social Implications*. Leiden: Brill, 1999.

Gilligan, Carol. *In a Different Voice: Psychological Theory and Women's Development*. Cambridge, MA: Harvard University Press, 1982.

Gines, Kathryn. "Sartre, Beauvoir, and the Race/Gender Analogy: A Case for Black Feminist Philosophy." In *Convergences: Black Feminism and Continental Philosophy*, edited by Maria del Guadalupe Davidson, Kathryn Gines, and Donna-Dale Marcano, 35–52. Albany: State University of New York Press, 2010.

Gocek, Fatma Muge. "Ottoman Empire: 15th to Mid-18th Century." In *Encyclopedia of Women and Islamic Cultures*, edited by Suad Joseph, vol. 1, 72–81. Leiden: Brill, 2003.

Goldzihir, Ignaz. *Muslim Studies*. Edited by S. M. Stern. New Brunswick, NJ: Allen and Unwin, 1966.

Goodman, L. "Muhammad ibn Zakariyya' al-Razi." In *History of Islamic Philosophy*, edited by S. H. Nasr and O. Leaman, 25–40. London: Routledge, 1996.

——. "Razi's Myth of the Fall of the Soul: Its Function in His Philosophy." In *Essays in Islamic Philosophy and Science*, edited by G. Hourani, 198–215. Albany: State University of New York Press, 1975.

Gordon, Matthew, and Kathryn Hain. *Concubines and Courtesans: Women and Slavery in Islamic History*. Oxford: Oxford University Press, 2016.

Grewal, Zareena. *Islam Is a Foreign Country: American Muslims and the Global Crisis of Authority*. New York: New York University Press, 2014.

Griffel, Frank. *Al-Ghazali's Philosophical Theology*. Oxford: Oxford University Press, 2009.

Hadot, Pierre. "Spiritual Exercises." In *Philosophy as a Way of Life*, translated by Michael Chase, 81–125. Cambridge, MA: Harvard University Press, 2004. Quoted in Mohammad Azadpur, *Reason Unbound: On Spiritual Practice in Islamic Peripatetic Philosophy*. Albany: State University of New York Press, 2011.

Hamid, Abdul Ali. *Moral Teachings of Islam: Prophetic Traditions from al-Adab al-Mufrad by Imam al-Bukhari*. Walnut Creek, CA: Alta Mira, 2002.

Hammer, Juliane. "Gender Matters: Normativity, Positionality, and the Politics of Islamic Studies." *Muslim World* 106, no. 4 (2016): 655–70.

——. *More Than a Prayer: American Muslim Women, Religious Authority, and Activism*. Austin: University of Texas Press, 2012.

Hartmann, Heidi. "The Unhappy Marriage of Marxism and Feminism: Toward a More Progressive Union." In *Women and Revolution: The Unhappy Marriage of Marxism and Feminism*, edited by Lydia Sargent, 1–42. Boston: South End, 1981.

Heck, Paul. "Mysticism as Morality: The Case of Sufism." *Journal of Religious Ethics* 34, no. 2 (2006): 253–86.

Hidayatullah, Aysha A. *Feminist Edges of the Qur'an*. New York: Oxford University Press, 2014.

Hillenbrand, Carole. "Women in the Saljuq Period." In *Women in Iran from the Rise of Islam to 1800*, edited by Guity Nashat and Lois Beck, 103–20. Champaign: University of Illinois Press, 2003.

Hodgson, Marshall. *The Venture of Islam: Conscience and History in a World Civilization*. Vol. 2. Chicago: University of Chicago Press, 1974.

Holter, Oystein Gullvag. "Social Theories for Researching Men and Masculinities: Direct Gender Hierarchy and Structural Inequality." In *Handbook of Studies on Men and Masculinities*, edited by Michael Kimmel, Jeff Hearn, and R. W. Connell, 15–34. Thousand Oaks, CA: Sage, 2005.

Homiak, Marcia L. "Feminism and Aristotle's Rational Ideal." In *Feminism and History of Philosophy*, edited by Genevieve Lloyd, 79–102. Oxford: Oxford University Press, 2002.

Hourani, George Fadlo. *Islamic Rationalism: The Ethics of 'Abd al-Jabbar*. Oxford: Clarendon, 1971.

——. *Reason and Tradition in Islamic Ethics*. Cambridge: Cambridge University Press, 1985.

Hovannisian, Richard. *Ethics in Islam*. Malibu: Undena, 1985.

Husain, Sayyid Khurshid. *Akhlaq-i Muhammadi*. Lucknow: Hindu Samat, 1920.

Irigaray, Luce. *An Ethics of Sexual Difference*. Translated by Carolyn Burke and Gillian C. Gill. Ithaca: Cornell University Press, 1993.

——. *Speculum of the Other Woman*. Translated by Gillian C. Gill. Ithaca: Cornell University Press, 1985.

——. *This Sex Which Is Not One*. Ithaca: Cornell University Press, 1985.

Izutsu, Toshihiko. *Sufism and Taoism: A Comparative Study of Key Philosophical Concepts*. Berkeley: University of California Press, 1983.

James, V. Denise. "Musing: A Black Feminist Philosopher: Is That Possible?" *Hypatia* 29, no. 1 (2014): 189.

Karamustafa, Ahmed. "The Ghazali Brothers and Their Institutions." In *Ötekilerin Peşinde: Ahmet Yaşar Ocak'a Armağan (Festschrift in Honor of Ahmet Yaşar Ocak)*, edited by Mehmet Öz and Fatih Yeşil, 265–75. Istanbul: Timaş Yayınları, 2015.

Kassis, Hanna. *A Concordance of the Quran*. Berkeley: University of California Press, 1983.

Katz, Jonathan. "The Invention of Heterosexuality." In *Race, Class, and Gender in the United States*, edited by Paula Rothenburg, 68–79. New York: Worth, 2007.

Katz, Marion. *Women in the Mosque: A History of Legal Thought and Social Practice*. New York: Columbia University Press, 2014.

Kazemi, Reza Shah. *Justice and Remembrance: Introducing the Spirituality of Imam Ali*. London: I. B. Tauris. 2006.

Ibn Khaldun. *The Muqaddimah: An Introduction to History*. Edited by N. J. Dawood. Translated by Franz Rosenthal. Princeton: Princeton University Press, 1969.

Khaleghi-Motlagh, D. J. "Adab in Iran." In *Encyclopaedia Iranica*, edited by Ehsan Yarshater, 432–39. London: Routledge and Kegan Paul, 1983.

Korsmeyer, Carolyn. "Gendered Concepts and Hume's Standard of Taste." In *Feminism and Tradition in Aesthetics*, edited by Peggy Zeglin Brand and Carolyn Korsmeyer, 49–65. University Park: Pennsylvania State University Press, 1995.

Kruks, Sonia. *Retrieving Experience: Subjectivity and Recognition in Feminist Politics*. Ithaca: Cornell University Press, 2001. Quoted in Mann, Anika Maaza. "Race and Feminist Standpoint Theory." In *Convergences: Black Feminism and Continental Philosophy*, edited by Maria del Guadalupe Davidson, Kathryn Gines, and Donna-Dale Marcano, 105–20. Albany: State University of New York Press, 2010.

Kueny, Kathryn. *Conceiving Identities: Maternity in Medieval Muslim Discourse and Practice*. Albany: State University of New York, 2013.

Kugle, Scott. *Sufis and Saints' Bodies: Mysticism, Corporeality, and Sacred Power in Islam*. Chapel Hill: University of North Carolina Press, 2007.

Kugle, Scott Siraj al-Haqq. *Homosexuality in Islam: Critical Reflection on Gay, Lesbian, and Transgender Muslims*. Oxford: Oneworld, 2010.

Kurz, Susanne "Never Just for Fun? Sexual Intercourse in Persophone Medicine, Erotology and Ethics." In *Muslim Bodies: Body, Sexuality and Medicine in Muslim Societies*, edited by Susanne Kurz, Claudia Preckel Eadem, and Stefan Reichmuth, vol. 14, 97–130. Berlin: Lit, 2016.

Kurzman, Charles, and Carl Ernst. "Islamic Studies in US Universities." In *Middle East Studies for the New Millennium: Infrastructures of Knowledge*, edited by Seteney Shami and Cynthia Miller-Idriss, 320–48. New York: New York University Press, 2016.

Lambton, Ann K. S. *Continuity and Change in Medieval Persia: Aspects of Administrative, Economic and Social History, 11th–14th Century*. Albany: Bibliotheca Persica, 1988.

———. "Islamic Society in Persia." *International Affairs* 31, no. 3 (1954): 3–4.

———. "Justice in the Medieval Persian Theory of Kingship." *Studia Islamic* 17 (1962): 97.

———. *Theory and Practice in Medieval Persian Government*. London: Variorum Reprints, 1980.

Lane, Edward William. *Arabic-English Lexicon*. London: Williams and Norgate, 1863.

Lange, Christian Lange. "Crime and Punishment in Islamic History (Early to Middle Period): A Framework for Analysis." *Religion Compass* 4, no. 11 (2010): 694–706.

Laqueur, Thomas Walter. *Making Sex: Body and Gender from the Greeks to Freud*. Cambridge, MA: Harvard University Press, 1990.

Leaman, Oliver. *Islamic Philosophy: An Introduction*. Cambridge, MA: Polity, 2009.

———. "Orientalism and Islamic Philosophy." In *Routledge Encyclopedia of Philosophy*, 159. London: Routledge, 1998.

Leaman, Oliver, and Seyyed Hossein Nasr. "Introduction." In *History of Islamic Philosophy*, edited by Seyyed Hossein Nasr and Oliver Leaman. London: Routledge, 1996.

LeDoeuff, Michele. *Hipparchia's Choice: An Essay Concerning Women, Philosophy, Etc.* New York: Columbia University Press, 1989.

Leites, Adrien. "Ghazali's Alteration of Hadiths: Process and Meaning." *Oriens* 40, no. 1 (2012): 133–48.

Linday, James E. *Daily Life in the Medieval Islamic World*. Westport, CT: Greenwood, 2005.

Lloyd, Genevieve. "LeDoeuff and History of Philosophy." In *Feminism and History of Philosophy*, edited by Genevieve Lloyd, 27–39. Oxford: Oxford University Press, 2002.

Longino, Helen. "Circles of Reason: Some Feminist Reflections on Reason and Rationality." *Episteme* 2, no. 1 (June 2005): 80.

Lovejoy, Arthur. *The Great Chain of Being: The Study of the History of an Idea*. Cambridge, MA: Harvard University Press, 1966.

Lutfi, Huda. "Manners and Customs of Fourteenth-Century Cairene Women: Female Anarchy Versus Male Shari Order in Muslim Prescriptive Treatises." In *Women in Middle Eastern History: Shifting Boundaries in Sex and Gender*, edited by Nikki Keddie and Beth Baron, 99–121. New Haven: Yale University Press, 1991.

Madelung, Wilfred. "Nasir al-Din Tusi's Ethics Between Philosophy, Shi'ism, and Sufism." In *Ethics in Islam*, edited by R. G. Hovannisian, 85–101. Malibu: Undena, 1985.

Mahdi, Muhsin. "Avicenna vii. Practical Sciences." In *Encylopaedia Iranica*. Online ed. New York: Columbia University, 2011.

———. "Farabi vi. Political Philosophy." In *Encylopaedia Iranica*. Online ed. New York: Columbia University, 2002.

Malti-Douglas, Fedwa. *Women's Body, Women's Word: Gender and Discourse in Arabo-Islamic Writing*. Princeton: Princeton University Press, 1991.

Mann, Anika Maaza. "Race and Feminist Standpoint Theory." In *Convergences: Black Feminism and Continental Philosophy*, edited by Maria del Guadalupe Davidson, Kathryn Gines, and Donna-Dale Marcano, 105–20. Albany: State University of New York Press, 2010.

Marlow, Louise. *Hierarchy and Egalitarianism in Islamic Thought*. Cambridge: Cambridge University Press, 1997.

Meisami, Julie Scott. "Eleventh-Century Women: Evidence from Bayhaqi's History." In *Women in Iran from the Rise of Islam to 1800*, edited by Guity Nashat and Lois Beck, 80–102. Champaign: University of Illinois Press, 2003.

Mernissi, Fatima. *The Veil and the Male Elite: A Feminist Interpretation of Women's Rights in Islam*. New York: Perseus, 1991.

Mir-Hosseini, Ziba. "The Construction of Gender in Islamic Legal Thought and Strategies for Reform." *Hawwa* 1, no. 1 (2003): 1–28.

———. "Muslim Women's Quest for Equality: Between Islamic Law and Feminism." *Critical Inquiry* 32, no. 4 (Summer 2006): 629–45.

Mir-Hosseini, Ziba, Mulki Al-Sharmani, and Jana Rumminger. *Men in Charge? Rethinking Authority in Muslim Legal Tradition*. London: Oneworld, 2015.

Ibn Miskawayh, Ahmad ibn Muhammad. *The Refinement of Character: A Translation from the Arabic of Ahmad ibn-Muhammad Miskawayh's Tahdhib al-akhlaq*. Translated by Constantine K. Zurayk. Beirut: American University of Beirut, 1968.

Mitha, Farouk. *Al-Ghazali and the Ismailis: A Debate on Reason and Authority in Medieval Islam*. London: I. B. Tauris, 2001.

Moore, Brenna. "Friendship and the Cultivation of Religious Sensibilities." *Journal of the American Academy of Religion* 83, no. 2 (2015): 437–63.

Moosa, Ebrahim. *Ghazali and the Poetics of Imagination*. Chapel Hill: University of North Carolina Press, 2005.

———. "Islamic Ethics: Muslim Ethics?" In *The Blackwell Companion to Religious Ethics*, edited by William Schweiker. Malden, MA: Blackwell, 2005.

Morgan, David. "Class and Masculinity." In *Handbook of Studies on Men and Masculinities*, edited by Michael Kimmel, Jeff Hearn, and R. W. Connell. Thousand Oaks, CA: Sage, 2005.

Mottahedeh, Roy. "Friendship in Islamic Ethical Philosophy." In *Essays in Islamic Philology, History, and Philosophy*, edited by Alireza Korangy et al., 229–39. Berlin: De Gruyter, 2016.

Mukminova, Roziya. "Central Asia: 15th to Mid-18th Century." In *Encyclopedia of Women and Islamic Cultures*, edited by Suad Joseph, vol. 1, 82–85. Leiden: Brill, 2003.

al-Mulk, Nizam. *Book of Government or Rules for Kings*. Translated by H. Darke. London: Routledge and Kegan Paul, 1978.

Murata, Sachiko. *The Tao of Islam: A Sourcebook on Gender Relationships in Islamic Thought*. Albany: State University of New York Press, 1992.

an-Na'im, Abdullahi. *Islamic Family Law in a Changing World: A Global Resource Book*. London: Zed, 2002.

Nasr, Seyyed Hossein, and Oliver Leaman. *History of Islamic Philosophy*. London: Routledge, 1996.

Newby, Gordon. "Ibn Khaldun and Fredrick Jackson Turner: Islam and the Frontier Experience." *Journal of Asian and African Studies* 18, nos. 3–4 (July 1983): 274–85.

Newman, Andrew J. "Davani, Jalal-al-Din Mohammad b. As'ad Kazeruni Seddiqi." In *Encyclopaedia Iranica*, vol. 7, 132–33. London: Routledge and Kegan Paul, 1994.

Nickols, Sharon Y. *Remaking Home Economics: Resourcefulness and Innovation in Changing Times*. Athens: University of Georgia Press, 2015.

Nussbaum, Martha. *Frontiers of Justice: Disability, Nationality, Species Membership*. Cambridge, MA: Belknap Press of Harvard University Press, 2007.

Ormsby, Eric. *Makers of the Muslim World: Ghazali*. Oxford: Oneworld, 2007.

Ossman, Susan. "Cities: Islamic Cities." In *Encyclopedia of Women in Islamic Cultures*, edited by Suad Joseph, vol. 3, 23–26. Leiden: Brill, 2005.

Ouzgane, Lahoucine. *Islamic Masculinities*. London: Zed, 2006.

Partner, Nancy F. *Studying Medieval Women: Sex, Gender, Feminism*. Cambridge: Medieval Academy of America, 1993.

Pessin, Sarah. "Loss, Presence, and Gabirol's Desire: Medieval Jewish Philosophy and the Possibility of Feminist Ground." In *Women and Gender in Jewish Philosophy*, edited by Hava Tirosh-Samuelson, 27–50. Bloomington: Indiana University Press, 2004.

Pierce, Leslie P. *The Imperial Harem: Women and Sovereignty in the Ottoman Empire*. New York: Oxford University Press, 1993.

Rapoport, Yossef. *Marriage, Money and Divorce in Medieval Society*. Cambridge: Cambridge University Press, 2005.

Reinhart, Kevin. "Islamic Law as Islamic Ethics." *Journal of Religious Ethics* 11, no. 2 (Fall 1983): 186–203.

——. "The Origin of Islamic Ethics." In *The Blackwell Companion to Religious Ethics*, edited by William Schweicker, 244–53. London: Blackwell, 2005.

Ridgeon, Lloyd. *Jawanmardi: A Sufi Code of Honor*. Edinburgh: Edinburgh University Press, 2011.

el-Rouayheb, Khaled. *Before Homosexuality in the Arab-Islamic World, 1500–1800.* Chicago: University of Chicago Press, 2005.

Sachedina, Abdulaziz. "Islamic Ethics: Differentiations." In *The Blackwell Companion to Religious Ethics*, edited by William Schweiker, 254–55. London: Blackwell, 2005.

Sadeghi, Behnam. *The Logic of Law Making in Islam: Women and Prayer in the Legal Tradition.* Cambridge: Cambridge University Press, 2013.

Safi, Omid. *The Politics of Knowledge in Premodern Islam: Negotiating Ideology and Religious Inquiry.* Chapel Hill: University of North Carolina Press, 2006.

Sajoo, Amyn B. *A Companion to Muslim Ethics.* London: I. B. Tauris, 2010.

——. *Muslim Ethics: Emerging Vistas.* London: Institute of Isma'ili Studies, 2004.

Salazar, Ovidio Abdul Latif, dir. *Al-Ghazali: The Alchemist of Happiness.* 2004; London: Matmedia Productions, 2007. DVD.

Sayeed, Asma. *Women and the Transmission of Religious Knowledge in Islam.* Cambridge: Cambridge University Press, 2013.

Schimmel, Annemarie. *My Soul Is a Woman: The Feminine in Islam.* New York: Continuum, 1997.

——. *Mystical Dimensions of Islam.* Chapel Hill: University of North Carolina Press, 1975.

Schweiker, William. *The Blackwell Companion to Religious Ethics.* Malden, MA: Blackwell, 2005.

Seedat, Fatima. "When Islam and Feminism Converge." *Muslim World* 103, no. 3 (2013): 404–20.

Senack, Christine. "Aristotle on the Woman's Soul." In *Engendering Origins: Critical Feminist Readings in Plato and Aristotle*, edited by Bat-Ami Bar On, 223–36. Albany: State University of New York Press, 1994.

Sewhani, Hakim Fateh Muhammad. *Akhlaq-i Muhammadi.* Jamshoro: Sindhi Adabi Board, 1916.

Shah-Kazemi, Reza. *Justice and Remembrance: Introducing the Spirituality of Imam Ali.* London: I. B. Tauris, 2007.

Shaikh, Sa'diyya. "Family Planning, Contraception, and Abortion in Islam: Undertaking Khilafah." In *Sacred Rights: The Case for Contraception and Abortion in World Religions*, edited by Daniel C. Maguire, 105–28. Oxford: Oxford University Press, 2003.

——. "Feminism, Epistemology and Experience: Critically (En)gendering the Study of Islam." *Journal for Islamic Studies* 33, no. 1 (2013): 14–47.

——. *Sufi Narratives of Intimacy: Ibn Arabi, Gender, and Sexuality.* Chapel Hill: University of North Carolina Press, 2012.

——. "A Tafsir of Praxis: Gender, Martial Violence, Resistance, in a South African Muslim Community." In *Violence Against Women in Contemporary World*

Religions: Roots and Cures, edited by Daniel Maguire and Sa'diyya Shaikh, 66–89. Cleveland: Pilgrim Press, 2007.

Shapiro, Susan. "A Matter of Discipline: Reading for Gender in Jewish Philosophy." In *Judaism Since Gender*, edited by Miriam Peskowitz and Laura Levitt, 158–73. New York: Routledge, 1997.

Silvers, Laury. "Early Pious, Mystic Sufi Women." In *Cambridge Companion to Sufism*, edited by Lloyd Ridgeon, 24–52. New York: Cambridge University Press, 2015.

Sonbol Amira El-Azhary. *Beyond the Exotic: Women's Histories in Islamic Societies*. Syracuse: Syracuse University Press, 2005.

——. *Women, the Family, and Divorce Laws in Islamic History*. Syracuse: Syracuse University Press, 1996.

Spooner, Brian, and William Hannaway. "Persian as Koine: Written Persian in World-Historical Perspective." In *Literacy in the Persianate World: Writing and the Social Order*, edited by Brian Spooner and William L. Hanaway, 1–68. Philadelphia: University of Pennsylvania Press, 2012.

Stark, Ulrike. *An Empire of Books: The Naval Kishore Press and the Diffusion of the Printed Word in Colonial India*. Ranikhet Cantt: Permanent Black, 2008.

Steingass, Francis Joseph. *A Comprehensive Persian-English Dictionary: Including the Arabic Words and Phrases to Be Met with in Persian Literature*. 5th ed. London: Routledge and Kegan Paul, 1892.

Swanton, Christine. *Virtue Ethics: A Pluralistic View*. New York: Oxford University Press, 2003.

Tessman, Lisa. "Feminist Eudaimonism: Eudaimonism as Non-Ideal Theory." In *Feminist Ethics and Social and Political Philosophy: Theorizing the Non-Ideal*, edited by Lisa Tessman, 47–58. Dordrecht: Springer, 2009.

Thompson, Elizabeth. "Civil Society: Overview." In *Encyclopedia of Women and Islamic Cultures*, edited by Suad Joseph, vol. 1, 34–40. Leiden: Brill, 2003.

Thompson, W. F. *Practical Philosophy of the Mohammadan People*. London: Oriental Translation Fund of Great Britain and Ireland, 1839.

Tillman, Rachel. "Ethical Embodiment and Moral Reasoning: A Challenge to Peter Singer." *Hypatia* 28, no. 1 (2013): 18–31.

Tlili, Sarra. *Animals in the Qur'an*. Cambridge: Cambridge University Press, 2012.

Togan, Isenbike. "Turkic Dynasties: 9th to 15th Century." In *Encyclopedia of Women in Islamic Cultures*, edited by Suad Joseph, vol. 1, 22–28. Leiden: Brill, 2003.

Tuana, Nancy. "Aristotle and the Politics of Reproduction." In *Engendering Origins: Critical Feminist Readings in Plato and Aristotle*, edited by Bat-Ami Bar On, 195–200. Albany: State University of New York Press, 1994.

Tucker, Judith. *In the House of the Law*. Berkeley: University of California Press, 1998.

——. *Women, Family, and Gender in Islamic Law*. Cambridge: Cambridge University Press, 2008.

Tusi, Nasir-ad Din Muhammad ibn Muhammad. *Akhlaq-i Nasiri*. Edited by Mojtaba Minvi and Alireza Haydari. Tehran: Zar, 1977.

——. *The Nasirean Ethics*. Translated by G. M. Wickens. London: George Allen and Unwin, 1964.

——. *Sayr wa Suluk*. Translated by Sayyad Badakhchani. London: I. B. Tauris, 1998.

Vasalou, Sophia. *Moral Agents and Their Deserts: The Character of Mutazilite Ethics*. Princeton: Princeton University Press, 2008.

wadud, amina. "Can One Critique Cancel All Previous Efforts?" *Journal of Feminist Studies in Religion* 32, no. 2 (2016): 132–33.

——. *Inside the Gender Jihad*. Oxford: Oneworld, 2006.

——. *Qur'an and Woman: Reading the Sacred Text from a Woman's Perspective*. Oxford: Oxford University Press, 1999.

Walby, Silvia. *Theorizing Patriarchy*. Oxford: Basil Blackwell, 1990.

Warraich, Sohail Akbar. "'Honor Killings' and the Law in Pakistan." In *"Honor": Crimes, Paradigms and Violence Against Women*, edited by Sara Hossain and Lynn Welchman, 78–110. London: Zed, 2005.

Weitz, Lev. "Al-Ghazali, Bar Hebraeus, and the 'Good Wife.'" *Journal of the American Oriental Society* 134, no. 2 (2014): 203–23.

Wickens, G. M. "Aklaq-e Naseri." In *Encyclopaedia Iranica*, edited by Ehsan Yarshater, vol. 1, 725. London: Routledge and Kegan Paul, 1984.

——. "*Aklaq-i Jalali*: An 'Ethical' Treatise in Persian by Mohammad b. As'ad Jalal-al-din Davani." In *Encyclopaedia Iranica*, edited by Ehsan Yarshater, vol. 1, 724. London: Routledge and Kegan Paul, 1984.

——. "Nasir ad-Din Tusi on the Fall of Baghdad: A Further Study." *Journal of Semitic Studies* 7, no. 1 (1962): 27.

Witt, Charlotte. "Form, Normativity, and Gender in Aristotle: a Feminist Perspective." In *Feminist Interpretations of Aristotle*, edited by Cynthia Freeland, 119–37. University Park: Pennsylvania State University Press, 1998.

Woods, John. *The Aqquyunlu: Clan, Confederation, Empire*. Salt Lake City: University of Utah Press, 1999.

Yaqub, Aladdin. *Al-Ghazali's "Moderation in Belief."* Chicago: University of Chicago Press, 2013.

Zadeh, Travis. *The Vernacular Qur'an: Translation and the Rise of Persian Exegesis*. Oxford: Oxford University Press, 2012.

Zargar, Cyrus. *The Polished Mirror: Storytelling and the Pursuit of Virtue in Islamic Philosophy and Sufism*. Oxford: Oneworld Academic, 2017.

Index

Page numbers in *italics* refer to tables and illustrations

Hillenbrand, Carole, 66
Hodgson, Marshall, 199, 278, 283n27, 284n31, 289n60
Holter, Oystein, 63, 67
home economics, 303n26
Homiak, Marcia, 63, 257–58, 260–61, 290–91n81
homoeroticism, 196–200
homosexuality, 65, 196–200. *See also* sexuality
homosocial society: Aristotle on friendship in, 180; enmity in, 200–202; ethics in, 186–202, 237; friendship in, 177–81, 183, 186–95, 200–202; and hierarchy, 177–78, 192, 199–200, 211, 213–14, 216–23, 235–37; *khalifah* in, 152, 179, 203–7, 220–24, 236–37; *khilafah* in, 172–74, 177, 186–87, 193, 220–23, 237; and patriarchy, 12, 65–67, 207, 214, 240–44; and social class, 177–78, 199–200, 209–19, 235–37; and women, 178–79, 182, 188–90, 192, 199, 213–14, 231–32
Hotham, Mathew, 303n15
Hourani, George, 31
Hulegu, 18–19
Husain Wa'iz al-Kashifi, 49
husbands' rulership, 132–38
hylomorphism, 60

Ibn al-Hajj, 119
Ibn 'Arabi, 43
Ibn Battuta, 118–19, 302n10
Ibn Hanbal, Ahmad, 126, 130, 200
Ibn Hanbal's one-eyed wife, 126, 130, 200
Ibn Kathir, 292n104
Ibn Khaldun, 43, 95, 111, 301n204
Ibn Miskawayh, Ahmad ibn Muhammad, 19–20, 47, 278

Ibn Qayyim al-Jawziyya, 148
Ibn Rushd, 143, 208–9
Ibn Sina, 21, 32, 110, 204, 208, 247–48, 300n172
Ihya' 'Ulum ad-Din (*The Revival of Religious Sciences*) (Ghazali), 16, 38, 101, 116–17, 159–60, 165
Ilkhanids, 177
Illuminationist School, 21, 43, 48, 286n6. *See also* mysticism
integrity (*hurriyat*), 89, 93, 135, 236
International Journal of Middle Eastern Studies, 15
intersectionality, 271–74, 323n57
irascible faculty (*quwwat-i ghazabi*): as male, 86–90; in *nafs*, 77, 84; nature of, 84, 86–90, 107, 133; restraint of, 83, 112–13, 133, 144, 153, 230, 242; in Tusi's concept of knowledge, 40; of women, 133
Irigaray, Luce, 59–60, 71, 112, 149, 179, 249–50
Islamicate, 283n29
Islamic ethics: as academic construct, 35–36; scholarship on, 22–23, 30–31, 238–40, 247–48, 278, 287n24; traditions of, 35–57, 278; use of terms of, 3, 245. See also *akhlaq*
Islamic philosophy: epistemology and genealogy, 30–34; feminist approaches to, 26, 244–52; and gender, 3–6, 245, 258, 278; and Greek philosophy, 30–34; and hierarchy, 8
Isma'ilism, 18–19, 39, 48, 228, 319n174
Izutsu, Toshihiko, 296n78

James, V. Denise, 272
javanmardi, 43–46. *See also* masculinity

Lovejoy, Arthur, 105, 261
loyalty (*wafa'*), 97–98, 148, 190, 202
Lutfi, Huda, 11, 119
Lynch, Mathew, 303n15

Madelung, Wilfred, 18
Maimonides, 60–62
Ma'in, Yahya, 200
male normativity, 7, 43–44, 59–63, 82,
    239, 244, 246. *See also* masculinity
Malti-Douglas, Fedwa, 187
Ma'mun, 229
Mann, Anika Maaza, 272
Marlowe, Louise, 5, 8–9, 316n130
marriage: and children, 140, 148–61;
    and concubines, 132, 136, 138, 142,
    163–64; divorce, 116–17, 152, 161–74,
    192, 255, 281–82n6, 310n192,
    317n141; dower (*mahr* or *kabin*), 126,
    166–67, 169; financial implications,
    131–32, 145–48, 158–59, 161, 164,
    168, 170, 249; *fiqh* on, 120, 127, 131,
    145, 163–64, 167, 171–72; hierarchy
    in, 115–24, 130–31, 163–64; *nikah*
    (marriage contract), 91, 99, 125, 163;
    polygyny, 135–36, 142–43; rationale
    for, 120–24; seclusion of women, 11,
    119–20, 125, 136–37, 143–44, 154;
    sexual ethics in, 138–45; as slavery,
    163–64; subordinate status of
    women in, 130, 132–38; virginity,
    125, 127, 131–32
masculinity: construction of, 11–12,
    63–67, 115–20, 177–79, 207–8, 237;
    ghayrat (manly pride), 88–89, 93,
    144, 171–72, 194; hegemonic
    masculinity, 44, 64–67, 200;
    javanmardi (young manliness),
    43–46; male normativity, 7, 43–44,
    59–64, 82, 115–20, 179, 239, 244, 246;

masculinity studies, 28, 58, 64;
    muruwah (manhood), 43–45, 65, 76,
    94–96, 124, 194, 202; in mysticism,
    42–46; and rationality, 10–11, 60–61,
    75; unmanliness, 22, *84*, 95–96, 113
medicine: childbirth and primacy of
    fathers, 60, 149–51; Greek influence,
    112, 150–51, 160, 285n47; in knowledge
    classifications, *40*, 213, 216
Mernissi, Fatima, 3
microcosm of the world, 71, 77–78, 87,
    96, 100–104, 113
Minvi, Mojtaba, 14, 55
Mir-Hosseini, Ziba, 305n68
misogyny, 5, 7, 63, 248–50
monotheism, 266
Moore, Brenna, 186–87
Moosa, Ebrahim, 16, 287n24
Morgan, David, 207
motherhood, 59–62, 98, 128, 149–61,
    243, 273, 305n68
Mottahedeh, Roy, 187, 193
Muhammad (Prophet): and *akhlaq*
    texts and tradition, 13, 34, 36, 39, 52,
    68, 287n24, 290n68; egalitarian
    message of, 4, 8; on family, 147, 149,
    157, 159–60; on friendship, 98, 188;
    on governance, 226, 232; on
    marriage, 125–27, 131–32, 163, 170;
    on masculinity, 43, 88–89, 106–7,
    278; as the perfect human, 287n12;
    on self-restraint, 92; on women, 44,
    125–27, 136, 140, 144, 165
Mulk, Nizam al-, 11, 15–16, 231–32
muruwah (manhood), 43–45, 65, 76,
    94–96, 124, 194, 202. *See also*
    masculinity
Musa Sada Suhag, 294n15
Mu'tazilite ideas, 9, 16, 32, 39,
    298n129

164–65, 169–70, 267–68;
vernacularization of, 56
Qur'an and Woman (wadud), 73–74

race and national origin, 110–11,
271–74. *See also* hierarchy
rah-i din (path of faith), 38, 78, 108, 201.
See also happiness/flourishing
(*sa'adat*)
Rapoport, Yossef, 145, 147–48, 162,
317n141
rational faculty (*quwwat-i 'aqli*):
characteristics of, 84, 85–86, 107,
113, 130, 255, 276; and contradictions
in *akhlaq* texts, 254–63; and
hierarchy, 26, 211–12, 217–20; as
male, 8, 77–80, 85–86, 242–43; and
nafs, 77, 77–80, 84; of nonelite men,
26, 217, 219; rule of over other
faculties, 8, 45, 79–81, 83–85, 91,
242; in Tusi's concept of knowledge,
40; of women, 143
Razi, Abu Bakr ar-, 112
Razi, Fakhr ad-Din ar-, 32
Reinhart, Kevin, 287n24
religious studies, 245–47
Ridgeon, Lloyd, 43–44

Sa'adi Shirazi, 288n27
Sachedina, Abdulaziz, 287n24
Sadeghi, Behnam, 310n207
Safavids, 20–21
Safi, Omid, 11, 15–16, 231
Sajoo, Amyn, 3
Salazar, Ovidio Abdul Latif, 1–3, 239
Saljuqs, 11, 13, 15, 66, 177, 231–32,
289n56
Saray Khatun, 231
Sartre, Jean Paul, 272
Sassanian Empire, 8–9

Sayeed, Asma, 128, 309n160
Sayr wa Suluk (Tusi), 17–18, 319n174
Schimmel, Annemarie, 5, 75
Second Sex, The (Beauvoir), 60–61
Seedat, Fatima, 34, 321n4
self-restraint (*'iffat*): and concupiscent
faculty, 81–83, 84, 90–96, 107, 113;
and masculinity, 82–83, 92, 129, 141;
of women, 62, 81, 90, 92, 128, 154
Senack, Christine, 249
sexuality: concubines, 132, 136, 138, 142,
163–64, 273; control of sexual
appetite, 78–79, 95–96, 101, 107, 121,
141–45, 198–99; erotology, 197;
ethics in marriage, 138–45;
heteronormativity, 181, 190,
196–200, 293n3; homosexuality, 65,
196–200; pederasty, 198–99;
sodomy, 196; and women, 75, 82
Shah-Kazemi, Reza, 3
Shaikh, Sa'diyya, 42–43, 140, 265
Shapiro, Susan, 60–62, 66, 78
Shi'ism, 13, 18–19, 21, 48, 228, 298n129,
299n133
Singer, Peter, 261
slavery, 110–11, 134–35, 142, 199,
260–61, 274, 283n30, 324n67
social class: basis of, 209–17;
contradictions of, 103–14, 235–37,
247; and gender, 177–78, 199–200,
211, 213–14; and rationality, 211,
216–19, 236–37, 241–43, 247. *See also*
hierarchy
Socratic ideas, 32. *See also* Greek
philosophy
sodomy, 196. *See also* sexuality
soul. See *nafs*
speculative intellect, 80–81
Spooner, Brian, 55–56
Steingass, Francis Joseph, 90–91

Stoic philosophy, 32. *See also* Greek philosophy
sufism, 35–37, 42–46, 58, 75–76, 298n119. *See also* mysticism
Suhrawardi, 21, 43, 286n6
Sunnism, 13, 21, 48, 102, 298n129
Syed Ahmed Khan, 50, 52, 278

Tahdhib al-Akhlaq (Ibn Miskawayh), 19–20, 47, 278
tahdhib-i akhlaq, 29, 242, 278, 299n133. See also *akhlaq*
Tahzib-i Ahklaq (Discipline of Ethics) (Syed Ahmed Khan), 50, 52, 278
tahzib-i akhlaq, 11, 110, 218–19, 228. See also *nafs*
Tarkan Khatun, 11, 231
tasawwuf, 32, 35–37, 42–46, 58. *See also* mysticism
tawhid, 266
Tessman, Lisa, 269, 275–77
theism, 250–51
theodicy, 245
This Sex Which Is Not One (Irigaray), 59
Thompson, W. F., 286n3
Tillman, Rachel, 262
Tlili, Sarra, 109–10
Tuana, Nancy, 300n178
Tucker, Judith, 152, 155, 310n192
Tusi, Nasir-ad Din, 17–20, 47, 289n56

Umar ibn al-Khattab, 136
urban/societal ethics, *40*. *See also* cities
Uzun Hasan, 231

Vasalou, Sophia, 5, 9
vices: controlling of, 20, 22, 38, 41, 103, 294n14; and masculine nature of the *nafs*, 82, 85, 103; origin and nature

of, 32, *40*, 83–86, *84*, 90, 92, 102, 144, 295n53
virginity, 125, 127, 131–32. *See also* marriage
virtues: benevolence (*karamat*), 133–35, 152, 226; courage (*shuja'at*), 82, *84*, 86–90, 113, 138, 144; dignity (*vaqar*), *84*, 92–93, 128–29, 154, 195, 317n137, 318n149; emergence of, 38–41, *40*, 48, 70–71, 81–101, *84*; friendship (*sadaqat*), *40*, 97–99, 177–81, 183, 186–95, 200–202; and future egalitarianism, 252, 254–56, 269–70, 275–77; and hierarchy, 109–11, 240, 247; Ibn Sina on, 32; integrity (*hurriyat*), 89, 93, 135, 236; judgment (*husn-i qada*), 97, 99; loyalty (*wafa'*), 97–98, 148, 190, 202; as masculine, 81–83, 85–101, 103, 113–14; pseudovirtues, 83–85, *84*; of women, 113, 124–25, 128–30, 138, 143, 243, 249. *See also* justice ('*adalat*); self-restraint ('*iffat*); wisdom (*hikmat*)

wadud, amina, 3–4, 73–74, 245, 251, 266, 268, 299n134
Walby, Sylvia, 65–66
Walzer, Richard, 286n4
Weitz, Lev, 38, 116–17, 123, 160–61
Wickens, G. M., 22, 121, 308n142
wilayah, 268–69
wisdom (*hikmat*): and justice, 100–102, 113; as masculine virtue, 82, 84–87; and rational faculty, 79, 83–87, *84*, 113; and speculative intellect, 80; of women, 130, 138, 255
Witt, Charlotte, 60
women: Aristotle on, 260–61; carnal appetite of, 75, 82, 139; and

concupiscent faculty, 62, 81–82, 90–92, 113, 128–29, 139–41, 143–44, 154, 255; contradictions regarding, 124, 127–30, 156, 160–61, 173–74, 255; enslaved, 134–35, 142, 199, 274, 324n67; essentialization of, 24–26, 149, 273–74; as ideal wives, 117, 124–32; instrumental role of, 24, 61, 67, 116–32, 137–38, 172–74, 240, 249–50; medieval scholars on, 125; *nafs* of, 62–63, 90–92, 110–14, 124, 130; and rationality, 75, 110–14, 143, 182, 192, 242–43; seclusion of, 11, 119–20, 125, 136–37, 143–44, 154; sexual rights of, 139–41; social role, 11, 118–19, 147–48, 155, 178–79, 213–14, 231–32, 317n141; subordinate status of, 103–14, 130, 134, 156, 190, 267–68; as unworthy/bad, 163–64; and virginity, 125, 127, 131–32

Woods, John, 299n119

Zadeh, Travis, 56
Zargar, Cyrus, 247–48, 289n57